Charles Laughton

Charles Laughton
A Filmography, 1928–1962

DAVID A. REDFERN

McFarland & Company, Inc., Publishers
Jefferson, North Carolina

LIBRARY OF CONGRESS CATALOGUING-IN-PUBLICATION DATA

Names: Redfern, David A., 1960– author.
Title: Charles Laughton : a filmography, 1928-1962 / David A. Redfern.
Description: Jefferson, North Carolina : McFarland & Company, Inc., Publishers, 2021 | Includes bibliographical references and index.
Identifiers: LCCN 2021030885 | ISBN 9781476670898 (paperback : acid free paper) ∞
ISBN 9781476642635 (ebook)
Subjects: LCSH: Laughton, Charles, 1899-1962—Criticism and interpretation. | Motion picture actors and actresses—Great Britain—Biography. | Motion picture producers and directors—Great Britain—Biography. | Motion pictures—History—20th century. | BISAC: PERFORMING ARTS / Film / History & Criticism
Classification: LCC PN2598.L27 R43 2021 | DDC 792.02/8092—dc23
LC record available at https://lccn.loc.gov/2021030885

BRITISH LIBRARY CATALOGUING DATA ARE AVAILABLE

ISBN (print) 978-1-4766-7089-8
ISBN (ebook) 978-1-4766-4263-5

© 2021 David A. Redfern. All rights reserved

No part of this book may be reproduced or transmitted in any form or by any means, electronic or mechanical, including photocopying or recording, or by any information storage and retrieval system, without permission in writing from the publisher.

Front cover: *left to right, top to bottom*
Laughton in *Devil and the Deep* (1932); in *The Suspect* (1945); in *Witness for the Prosecution* (1957); in *Advise & Consent* (1962)

Printed in the United States of America

McFarland & Company, Inc., Publishers
Box 611, Jefferson, North Carolina 28640
www.mcfarlandpub.com

To Commander Sturm,
Philip Marshall,
Sir Wilfrid Robarts, QC,
and Senator Seabright Cooley.
May their sparkle never dim.

Table of Contents

Acknowledgments ix

A Note on Citations xi

Preface 1

Biography 4

The Films (1928–1962) 9

Blue Bottles (1928) 9
Day-Dreams (1928) 10
The Tonic (1928) 11
Piccadilly (1929) 12
Comets (1930) 13
Wolves (1930) 14
Down River (1931) 15
Devil and the Deep (1932) 16
The Old Dark House (1932) 19
Payment Deferred (1932) 22
If I Had a Million (1932) 24
The Sign of the Cross (1932) 26
Island of Lost Souls (1932) 30
White Woman (1933) 34
The Private Life of Henry VIII (1933) 37
The Barretts of Wimpole Street (1934) 40
Ruggles of Red Gap (1935) 42
Mutiny on the Bounty (1935) 46
Les Misérables (1935) 49
Rembrandt (1936) 53
Vessel of Wrath (1938) 57
St. Martin's Lane (1938) 59
Jamaica Inn (1939) 62
The Hunchback of Notre Dame (1939) 65
They Knew What They Wanted (1940) 69
It Started with Eve (1941) 72
The Tuttles of Tahiti (1942) 75
Tales of Manhattan (1942) 77

Stand By for Action (1942) 79
Forever and a Day (1943) 82
This Land Is Mine (1943) 84
The Man from Down Under (1943) 89
The Canterville Ghost (1944) 92
The Suspect (1945) 94
Captain Kidd (1945) 96
Because of Him (1946) 99
The Paradine Case (1947) 102
Arch of Triumph (1948) 106
The Big Clock (1948) 109
The Girl from Manhattan (1948) 113
The Bribe (1949) 114
The Man on the Eiffel Tower (1949) 118
The Blue Veil (1951) 121
The Strange Door (1951) 123
O. Henry's Full House (1952) 125
Abbott and Costello Meet Captain Kidd (1952) 128
Salome (1953) 130
Young Bess (1953) 133
Hobson's Choice (1954) 135
The Night of the Hunter (1955) 138
Witness for the Prosecution (1957) 142
Under Ten Flags (1960) 145
Spartacus (1960) 146
Advise & Consent (1962) 150

Shorts and Miscellaneous Films (1930–1952) 154
Unreleased and Re-Edited Films (1937–1959) 157
Film Projects Announced but Abandoned or Rejected (1932–1962) 159
Amateur Stage Appearances (1913–1926) 162
Professional Stage Appearances (1926–1959) 164
Select British and American Radio Broadcasts (1928–1955) 173
Television Broadcasts (1949–1962) 182
Select Audio Recordings (1934–1962) 188

Appendix I: The Films Listed By Studios 189
Appendix II: The Films Listed By Performers 190
Appendix III: The Films Listed By Cinematographers 192
Chapter Notes 195
Bibliography 203
Index 207

Acknowledgments

It is with much gratitude and pleasure that I acknowledge the following individuals for their invaluable assistance in my researches: Malcolm Arthur; Patricia Arthur; Brian Beard; Chris Bryan; Graham Fisher for finding a Laughton memento; Dr. Sheldon Hall; the late Laurie Ringrow; Tony Shrimpton; John Urmson; and Tony Walker for allowing me the opportunity to inspect his complete run of issues of *Film Weekly* (1928–1939). I am especially grateful to Richard Chatten, Geoff Medland, Dr. Peter Stephenson and Keith Withall for casting their eagle eyes over the manuscript and offering helpful suggestions. Additional thanks to Richard for reacquainting me with the wealth of film material readily available in the Westminister Reference Library: a gem for serious film scholars. A final word of gratitude for his illuminating commentary while viewing a collection of early Laughton films at the British Film Institute in May 2018.

The following institutions and people have also been most helpful: British Film Institute Mediatheque at Manchester Central Library; Eddie Dunne and David Govier at the Local History Archives at Manchester Central Library; David Knight, genial archivist at Stonyhurst College, for his helpful expertise in locating unique primary source material relating to Laughton's formative years as a pupil at the school. David's affability made for an immensely informative and enjoyable day. John Oliver former curator at the British Film Institute; Kathleen Dickson, access officer, and Stephen Tollervey at the British Film Institute, National Film and Television Archive for their efficient organizing of several rare Laughton film prints for research viewings; Sarah Sweet and Angela Kale, service development officers at Scarborough Library and Customer Services Center; the late Eileen Bowser, former curator at the Museum of Modern Art, New York City; Helen Gush at the Sir Michael Redgrave Archives in the V&A Theatre and Performance Collections at Blythe House, London; Bob Geoghegan for his generosity in sourcing rare archival film material; David Pierce, founder and director of the Media History Digital Library website which gives rare access to contemporary film publications containing much invaluable research material. Thanks also to: former UCLA Preservation Officer Robert Gitt for his splendid presentation "Charles Laughton Directs *The Night of the Hunter*," screened at the seventeenth edition of *Il Cinema Ritrovato* in Bologna on July 2, 2003; friends at *Il Cinema Ritrovato* and *Le Giornate del Cinema Muto*, two annual archive festivals essential to a greater understanding of the origins and historical development of world cinema; executive director Jared Case, technical director Deborah Stoiber, and the team behind the third annual *Nitrate Picture Show*, held May 2017 at the George Eastman Museum, Rochester, New York. George Eastman Museum operates not only an important and expanding archival source of film preservation and conservation, but also provides rare public showings of original 35mm nitrate prints. This event grows from strength to strength every year; students on the weekend film history study course devoted to Charles Laughton I was privileged to lead during June 2013 at the former residential adult college Alston Hall, Longridge, Lancashire; the group of aficionados who gather annually for segments of film history at Chester University; Renown Films who, under their broadcasting arm, Talking Pictures TV, and through their annual film festivals, cater for vintage film enthusiasts and film historians; Jane Blain for access to her late mother's diaries; special friends Barbara and Brian Milner for their kindness; a big thank you to my late beloved mother and my sister for their steadfast belief in my efforts on this project. Also not forgetting Matilda, the best of mascots who, although she is yet to discover, has distant antecedents in the British and Hollywood cinema of yesteryear. Finally, a special thank you to Charlie Perdue and the McFarland team who steered the manuscript through the editorial process in a friendly and supportive fashion. The photographic illustrations are taken from the author's archives.

A Note on Citations

I have aimed to keep the system of referencing as simple as possible without sacrificing scholarly accuracy. When introducing a film, I have cited the production company, the director and the date of production. Newspaper, periodical and trade press quotations are dated within the main text rather than in endnotes. Citations from books are also referenced, but in abbreviated form with full publication details in the bibliography. In the case of website content, rather than give the full URL, which can extend to a full line or more, I have opted to cite the website and access date. In my experience, search engines can provide more direct access to a citation rather than transcribing a cumbersome link which, over a period of time, risks becoming broken and unusable.

Preface

The private and public life of Charles Laughton has caught the attention of various biographers but there has been, until now, no systematic attempt to gather the full range of his film work and present a detailed consideration of each film. Though the cycle of fashion is certainly a factor in this neglect, there is also the practical issue of the inaccessibility of the films for viewing. However, times change and advances in contemporary digital media provide the opportunity to acquire most of Laughton's extant films, either on disc or through online streaming. It is therefore both appropriate and timely to offer a comprehensive examination of his filmography of 54 films. Whether the reader is an aficionado of Laughton's screen canon, or a casual viewer seeking more information on a given Laughton film, this monograph attempts to offer an analysis and appreciation of Laughton's work in the cinema. In addition, listings of his amateur and professional stage appearances, radio and television work and various recordings are provided. For additional reference, itemized listings of Hollywood studios Laughton worked for, star names he appeared with and names of cinematographers who worked on his films are also given.

What of the man behind the acting persona? Two formidable Hollywood actresses provide some perspective. In her acceptance speech on the occasion of the American Film Institute Lifetime Achievement Award on March 1, 1977, actress Bette Davis recalled Charles Laughton's advice to her while on the set of *The Private Lives of Elizabeth and Essex* (Warner Bros., Michael Curtiz, 1939) playing Queen Elizabeth I. Davis told Laughton she was taking on a role in which the character was 60 and she was only 30. Laughton in reply counseled, "Never not dare to hang yourself. One must always attempt the impossible if one is to grow as an artist."[1] In her memoirs, Maureen O'Hara recalled,

> No one brought characters to life like Laughton. As an actor, Laughton painted a physical portrait. He was very focused on the physical and oratory aspects of [acting]. Laughton used his body in his performance much as a dancer would [and] he could also make a character completely unforgettable by the mere gleam in his eyes. This combination gave him a superior screen presence..." [O'Hara: 26].

Laughton, unlike contemporaries on the legitimate English stage who viewed films with some condescension as subsidiary to the art of the theater, was serious in his intentions towards the medium of cinema and approached it with insight and passion.[2] As biographer Simon Callow noted, Laughton was captivated by two filmic devices: the close-up and the retake. These two procedures allowed him to have the artistic control and aesthetic perfectionism that were hallmarks throughout his career. They contributed to him apparently effortlessly "becoming" the character on the screen.

Laughton's stature as a theater and screen actor has suffered a precipitous decline since his death, almost in proportion to his meteoric rise during his lifetime. From the beginning of his career, Laughton's name alone commanded box office attention, and yet acting for him came with contradictions and paradoxes. His physiognomy relegated him to character roles rather than straight leads and yet he excelled as that rarest of hybrids: the star character actor.

While he successfully achieved fluency in the French language, giving acclaimed performances of Molière for the Comédie Francaise, numerous attempts to present a satisfactory rendition of Shakespearean verse eluded him. On film Laughton's performances alternate between larger-than-life villains such as cuckold Commander Sturm, sybarite Emperor Nero, and monomaniac Dr. Moreau and, on the other hand, roles offering nuance, inconspicuousness and discretion. The mild-mannered suburbanite Philip Marshall and the wily Senator Seabright Cooley are apt demonstrations of his capacities for variation and versatility. Yet behind his public acting style of effortlessness and transparency lay private self-doubt, personal loathing and vindictive behavior. His dazzling parade of monsters, villains, misfits and kings tended to obscure the fact that he himself was insecure, self-critical, demanding and overbearing. He told a young Peter Bogdanovich, "I've looked like the hind end of an elephant since I was 21" (Bogdanovich: 8). His extraordinary physique was a boon, of course, to various impersonators such as radio and television personality Hughie Green, vaudevillians the Ritz Brothers, English comedian Max Wall, American impressionist Arthur Blake and actor and chat-show mimic Peter Ustinov.[3]

Unsurprisingly, the madcap universe of film animation also provided fertile ground for Laughton caricatures. At Disney, for instance, artists drew a recognizable Laughton in an animated parody of Captain Bligh in their Silly Symphony *Mother Goose Goes Hollywood* (Walt Disney, Wilfred Jackson, 1938). In this amusing one-reel short, a selection of Mother Goose's nursery rhymes are retold using parodies of Hollywood personalities. In the "Rub-a-Dub Dub" nursery rhyme, Laughton's Captain Bligh is joined by Spencer Tracy's Portuguese fisherman Manuel and Freddie Bartholomew's spoiled rich boy as they appear in *Captains Courageous*. When these three men in a tub try to hitch a ride on a small powerboat navigated by Katharine Hepburn's Little Bo Peep, the tub overturns and all three characters fall into the ocean. At Warner Bros., the animation department produced fast-moving storylines full of topical gags combined with a subversive streak. The artists who worked on these cartoons referred to their workplace as Termite Terrace. A piratical yarn, *Buccaneer Bunny* (Warner Bros./Looney Tunes, I. Freleng, 1948) finds the streetwise Bugs Bunny confronting his nemesis, Yosemite Sam, in a battle of wits on a desert island. On board an otherwise deserted galleon, Sam encounters Bugs in the guise of Captain Bligh. To make the impersonation good, Bugs begins issuing a flurry of zany orders delivered at pace, and while Sam is busy with these many chores, Bugs turns to camera and exclaims, "What a maroon!" Naturally his disguise is soon uncovered and this gives way to several hilarious minutes of sparring confrontations with each character determined to outdo the other and emerge triumphant.

Laughton's constant striving to tackle new areas of professional development led him to undertake what is regarded today as his outstanding legacy: his one shot at directing, *The Night of the Hunter* (United Artists, 1955), a unique film that captures both the innocence and trauma of childhood. Speaking of his admiration for director D.W. Griffith when preparing to direct *The Night of the Hunter*, Laughton observed, "Griffith's pictures made you sit up straight in your chair in anticipation of what was coming" (Gish: 364). He went on to lament, "All the surprise has gone out of modern films" (Gish: 364).

As I hope the book demonstrates, Laughton's film performances, at their very best, still have the capacity to make an audience sit up straight. They also continue to present many surprises beyond their commercial box office value, and they frequently have groundbreaking artistic qualities. If this book assists in a rediscovery and newfound appreciation of this remarkable body of films, I will be well satisfied. Needless to say, I aim to be thorough and any oversights are my responsibility alone.

Biography

Several excellent Laughton biographies have been published, but it is appropriate here to at least summarize his remarkable life and acting career. For a fuller account, I refer the reader to those volumes given in the bibliography.

Charles Laughton was born on July 1, 1899, in the English seaside town of Scarborough in the North Riding of Yorkshire.[1] His parents, Robert Laughton (1869–1924) and Eliza *née* Conlon Laughton (1869–1953), were in the hotel trade. Charles was born in the Victoria Hotel opposite Scarborough railway station, as were his two younger brothers Robert Thomas, "Tom" (1903–1984), and Francis, "Frank" (1907–1964).[2] Laughton began his education at a Scarborough school within walking distance of his home and this was supplemented by private tuition in the French language from a Sister Matilda at a school in Filey run by French nuns.

His mother was a staunch Catholic with ambitions for her eldest child. She ensured that his education took place at two prestigious Catholic boarding schools. Laughton studied for one term at St. John's Beaumont, Windsor in Berkshire, where he sat a naval examination to gain a commission in the Royal Navy. However, the thought of spending long periods of his life at sea was not something he relished and he failed the exam. He was then transferred to another Catholic boarding school run by Jesuit priests, Stonyhurst College in Lancashire.[3] There he gave his first stage performance in a 1913 production of Charles Hawtrey's *The Private Secretary*.[4] His acting debut received a positive review in the school magazine: "We were greatly taken by the acting of Charles Laughton as the solicitous old lodging-house keeper. His part was far too short; we wanted more of him for it seemed to suit him excellently" (*Stonyhurst Magazine*, No. 191, December 1913).

After leaving Stonyhurst in the summer of 1915 he was sent to Claridges in London as training for running the family hotel business. But this was interrupted by war service. Though he had served in the Officer Training Corps at Stonyhurst College, he joined the army as a private during the summer of 1917, despite attempts by his ambitious mother to have him receive an army commission. Laughton served first in the Bedfordshire Regiment (service #48603) and later in the Northamptonshire Regiment, 7th Battalion (service #42063) Huntington Bicycle Regiment.[5] His war service was a subject he never publicly discussed. An examination of Laughton's naturalization papers, taken out in California in 1942 and 1950, appear to suggest he may have had a permanent reminder of the war, as he carried a visible scar on the left side of his neck.[6]

After his demobilization on February 14, 1919, Laughton resumed managing the family hotel as a career, but he spent most of his spare time acting and stage-managing in a local amateur group in Scarborough. Following the death of his father Robert in 1924, and despite opposition from his mother, he decided to try his luck in the acting profession.[7] He enrolled at the Royal Academy of Dramatic Art and won the Bancroft Medal for acting. His first professional performance was in *The Government Inspector* in April 1926, and thus began a stage career of over 40 plays stretching over 30 years.

It was in 1927 on stage at the first rehearsal of the Arnold Bennett play *Mr. Prohack* that the 5'10", 200-pound, brown-haired, blue-eyed Laughton met the 5'4", 118-pound, auburn-haired, brown-eyed Elsa Sullivan Lanchester.[8] Physically they were an incongruous couple, though in temperament they shared a liking for the natural world and a disdain for figures of authority. Elsa was born on October 28, 1902, to non-conformist and bohemian parents James "Shamus" Sullivan (1867–1945) and Edith "Biddy" Lanchester (1871–1966).[9] She was the youngest of two children. Her elder sibling, Waldo Sullivan Lanchester (1897–1978), was a renowned puppeteer. With his wife Muriel Bell, he was instrumental in leading the revival of marionette performances in Britain. The Lanchesters were the first to present marionettes on British television in 1933. From 1936 to 1952, the couple ran the Lanchester Marionette Theatre at their home, Foley House in Malvern. George Bernard Shaw, a devotee of the Lanchesters' work, wrote a short puppet play featuring the characters of Shakespeare and Shaw. *Shakes versus Shav* was performed by the Lanchester Marionette Theatre in 1949. This was Shaw's last completed dramatic work. As a child, Elsa had trained as a dancer in Paris under the celebrated dance instructor Isadora Duncan (1877–1927), whom she disliked. She made her displeasure very plain many years later when interviewed on Dick Cavett's talk show on August 11, 1970. Elsa described Duncan as "an untalented bag of beans."

Because of the outbreak of the First World War, Elsa did not complete her dancing training. She opened her own school of acting and dance training and later joined a troupe of cabaret artists in a London club known as the Cave of Harmony, situated on Gower Street. On February 10, 1929, Elsa and Charles were married in a London registry office.[10]

If Laughton never discussed his participation in the First World War in public, then his homosexuality was equally concealed. For his generation, the prurient pillorying of playwright Oscar Wilde, under the laws of "gross indecency" (he had fallen foul of the Criminal Law Amendment Act 1885, and a sensational trial in 1895 resulted in a sentence of imprisonment) was seared into the public consciousness. Though Laughton confessed his gay orientation to Elsa, the couple nevertheless remained married until his death. In keeping with her unconventional upbringing, she accepted, though did not approve of, Laughton's infidelities, and the couple maintained what would be called an "open" marriage. Speaking in 1978 of the deceit and subterfuge such a relationship entailed, his widow said, "I know that I've become a more live, completer person since he died. But if I'd died first I would say that Charles would be a more tortured man because we all think of what we might have done, but didn't and I know he would suffer deeply because of what he might have done" (Norman: 197).

Elsa inherited her parents' flagrant disregard for social convention, and as a consequence, many of her memorable screen performances are of social misfits and uncanny eccentrics. From the monster's mate in *Bride of Frankenstein* (Universal, James Whale, 1935) to the cantankerous elderly mother in the cult horror film *Willard* (Bing Crosby Productions, Daniel Mann, 1971), the family trait of deviance is apparent. Elsa had previous experience of acting in silent films and it was she who introduced Laughton to the movies in 1928 when they both appeared in a series of silent comic shorts produced by, among others, H.G. Wells and his family. It was the beginning of Laughton's film career, which spanned 30-plus years and consisted of more than 50 films. Initially, Laughton concentrated on his stage career with film appearances confined to cameos and second-feature material. The huge success of his London and New York stage performances as murderer William Marble in *Payment Deferred* brought international stardom and offers from Hollywood. Though he remained committed to the English theater, he accepted a contract from Paramount in 1932. And so began an eight-year period of unparalleled creativity as the name Laughton became synonymous with such historical figures as Emperor Nero and King Henry VIII; for his portrayal of the latter, he received an Oscar for Best Actor. Tyrannical figures of authority such as Captain Bligh, for which he was Oscar nominated for Best Actor, and Javert were also memorable and distinctive. When questioned about how he achieved these performances Laughton declared, "You can't censor a leer" (*Film Daily*, January 26, 1940). In fact, his preparation for any role was meticulous, as he set out to probe the character and agonized trying to capture the essence of a role. This quest for perfection led him to be self-critical, hyper-sensitive and often temperamental. His critics, on the other hand, accused him of "playing to the gallery" and taking roles beneath his competence. There is some truth in the charge, for if Laughton became bored with playing a part, he lapsed into what writer Graham Greene described as a "ham actor" (Parkinson: 158). By the late 1930s, Laughton's name was to be found in the trade papers being used to promote such merchandise as Alexander Smith Carpets, a commodity of fitted carpet found in American film theater chains. The brash copy asserts, "[Y]ou can *always* (my italics) depend on *both* (my italics) to give superb performances" (*Film Daily*, February 24, 1939).

During his early Hollywood career, Laughton found a creative soulmate in MGM producer Irving Thalberg. Thalberg's premature death at 37 (September 14, 1936) robbed Laughton of a staunch ally. George Sanders, musing on the motives for acting in his acerbic autobiography, suggested, "Perhaps the greatest fulfillment in acting is not just the satisfaction involved in the opportunity for the extrovert to exhibit himself but more the opportunity to act out that part of himself for which he has the imagination and the capacity, but not the heart or the courage" (Sanders: 72). He goes on to describe the divergence between actors displaying assurance and talent in their performances, against their compromised and difficult private lives. "Charles Laughton, an unprincipled sadist on the screen and stage, in life is interested in the gentle arts, paintings, porcelain, people and poetry" (Sanders: 72).

In spite of their heavy work schedules, Laughton and Elsa Lanchester reacted with humanity and commitment to the rise of international conflict across Europe by acting as host and hostess of a charity ball for Jewish refugees on March 16, 1939, at Grosvenor House, London (London *Times*, January 21, 1939). Laughton gave £1,200 to the Lord Mayor's Red Cross and St. John Fund for the Sick and Wounded in London during the war (London *Times*, September 13, 1940). Such generosity was a rebuff to those critics in Britain who excoriated the British colony in Hollywood for their apparent unpatriotic attitude and half-hearted support of the British war effort, following the September 1939 outbreak of war. In fact, the 1940s saw Laughton spread his artistic wings, taking on much radio broadcasting, often in partnership with the remarkable radio producer Norman Corwin (1910–2011). Following America's entry into World War II in December 1941, Laughton undertook a series of nationwide tours giving readings to U.S. troops. He again began performing and directing on the stage and enjoyed teaching a select group of aspiring drama students. He also developed an expensive taste in art works and *objets d'art*. As a consequence, his film roles during the 1940s appeared to diminish into inconsequential star vehicles such as *The Tuttles of Tahiti* (RKO, Charles Vidor, 1942) and expensive misconceptions as in *Arch of Triumph* (United Artists, Lewis Milestone, 1948). He was happy to appear in these types of productions for the lucrative income they generated. By far his most significant professional challenge during the decade was meeting Marxist playwright Bertolt Brecht (1898–1956), a Finnish émigré who had arrived in the U.S. on July 21, 1941. When the two met in March 1944, Brecht asked Laughton why he wished to act. Laughton is reported to have given two replies: "Because I like to imitate great men" (Callow: 168) and "Because people don't know what they're like and I think I can show them" (Callow: 169). Brecht was intrigued enough to ask Laughton if he would like to appear in, and collaborate on, the translation of his 1938 German play *Life of Galileo*. Though Laughton was initially flattered and happy to take on the project, he soon began to exhibit all his old insecurities of fear and petulance during the long gestation of the play's production (1945–1947). The painstaking process by which Laughton came to fashion his Galileo through translation, editing and performance is contained in Brecht's detailed essay "Building Up a Part: Charles Laughton's *Galileo*." The play opened at the small Coronet Theater in Los Angeles on July 30, 1947, and then transferred to New York for a limited run. Though Laughton received praise for his performance, the anticipated widespread acclaim did not materialize. The public was unenthusiastic and stayed away, while the critics were mixed and perplexed in their responses to such a radical piece of theater.

By the early 1950s, Charles' film career appeared to be in freefall with *The Strange Door* (Universal-International, Joseph Pevney, 1951) and *Abbott and Costello Meet Captain Kidd* (Warner Bros., Charles Lamont, 1952) viewed as the nadir. Yet his fortunes were about to take a favorable turn when he met producer Paul Gregory (1920–2015), who persuaded him to revive his nationwide speaking tours, and produce what is today seen by many critics as the highpoint of Laughton's film career: his incomparable direction of 1955's *The Night of the Hunter*. At the time, the film flopped financially, and Laughton was consequently thwarted in his ambition to direct further film projects.

Despite this setback, his acting career began to flourish once more, with a succession of performances that saw him regain his creative energy on the screen. These included the crusty advocate Sir Wilfrid Robarts in *Witness for the Prosecution* (United Artists, Billy Wilder, 1957), for which he was Oscar-nominated, the wily senator in the ancient Roman epic *Spartacus* (Universal-International, Stanley Kubrick, 1960), and another schemer, Senator Seabright "Seab" Cooley, in *Advise & Consent* (United Artists, Otto Preminger, 1962), a contemporary story of Washington political skullduggery.

During the last decade of his career, Laughton participated in the medium of television with verve and passion. Whether as guest or host on TV shows, he occupied a special niche in providing gravitas to the commercial schedules. In the event, TV provided another platform to perform to a new and diverse audience in exchange for regular and substantial financial rewards.[11]

At the beginning of 1962, Laughton's health was in steep decline. When director Billy Wilder offered him the role of Moustache in *Irma La Douce* (1963), he clung to the notion that he would recover and play the part. He even invited Wilder to his house and gave a masterly performance designed to convince the director, and him*self*, of his impending recovery and fitness to take on the role. Although in excruciating pain, he rose from his chair and walked nonchalantly around the garden pool on the grounds of his home. By September 1962, he was fading fast and his two brothers flew to Los Angeles to offer their elder sibling, should he choose, a return to the Roman Catholic Church and to die in a state of grace.[12] On November 30, 1962, he checked out of Cedars of Lebanon Hospital (where he had undergone treatment for his metastatic renal cancer) to return his 1825 North Curson Avenue home. Laughton, 63, died there just three weeks later, in what was known as "the school room" where he gave acting lessons to aspiring actors. His remains are buried in Forest Lawn Memorial Park, Hollywood Hills, Los Angeles.[13]

His widow lived on for another 24 years. Following a series of strokes, Elsa Lanchester died of pneumonia at age 84 on December 26, 1986. In accordance with her instructions, her remains were scattered in the Pacific Ocean and no memorial service was held. The couple had no children.

The Films
(1928–1962)

Charles Laughton's 54 films are all included here, and apart from those few that are believed lost, all have been viewed by the author, and the opinions expressed are based on these viewings. Entries are arranged in release order. Where a specific date of general release is unavailable, the earliest available date, whether that be the registration date given on the film credits, trade show, premiere date or censor records, is given instead. Where obtainable, publicity taglines have been appended near the beginning of each entry. These have been compiled from a variety of sources and aim to give a contemporary flavor of how the film was sold through the "hard sell" of mass marketing campaigns. Wherever possible, all technical credits and cast lists are taken from surviving film prints. Working title or titles are also given. Also included: details of select archival holdings of 35mm film prints, and commercial DVD and Blu-ray releases of the films in both the U.S. (DVD Region 1 and Blu-ray Region A) and U.K. (DVD Region 2 and Blu-ray Region B). In the spirit of diversity, I have indicated whether discs include subtitle captions for the deaf and hard of hearing. Many of the film synopses are detailed and therefore contain plot spoilers. If applicable, Academy Awards nominations and wins are also mentioned. Laughton's film performances provided no end of celebrated and inimitable dialogue and a selection of his more memorable lines are, where applicable, included for reader interest.

Blue Bottles (1928)

United Kingdom (Ideal Films/Angle Pictures)

Credits: From a story invented by H.G. Wells; Screen Version and Art Direction: Frank Wells; Production Manager: Lionel Rich; Photography: F.A. Young; Directed by Ivor Montagu; Assistants: Roy Kellino, E. Hellstern ("Helle" Montagu, Ivor Montagu), Serge Nolbandov, M. Handkisson, W. Wichelow, H. Haslander; U.K. release: May 1928; Silent; Black and White; Genre: Comedy; Running Time: 1940 feet, 24 minutes (24 frames per second); 35mm print held at the British Film Institute, National Film and Television Archive; Not commercially available on digital media.

Cast: Elsa Lanchester (*Miss Lanchester*); Joe Beckett (*Police Constable Spiffkins*); Dorice Fordred (*Maggie*); Marie Wright (*Landlady*); **Charles Laughton** (*Burglar at the top of the stairs*); Norman Haire (*Crook*).

Synopsis: A Cockney girl picks up a police whistle outside the house of a gang of crooks and innocently blows it. A hundred whistles blow in response. The call is taken up by bugles and sirens until the civil and military authorities are called to action to restore order. Eventually the girl is thanked by the police force for inadvertently helping to capture a gang of crooks and she is given an umbrella from the Lost Property Office as a reward.

Production Commentary: This silent short was conceived as part of a series of two-reel comedies produced and directed by Ivor Montagu. Erudite, politically active and well-connected, Montagu was a founding member of the famed Film Society (dedicated to giving private screenings of films ignored by the commercial cinema of the day, such as Sergei Eisenstein's *The Battleship Potemkin*). The influence of slapstick and Charlie Chaplin, and European and international avant-garde film movements such as French Impressionism, German Expressionism and Russian formalism, is evident both in the form and content of these films.

Elsa Lanchester is very much the central star of *Blue Bottles* with Laughton's appearance being confined to a fleeting cameo in the guise of a masked member of a burglary gang. Lanchester had already appeared in several silent films before embarking on this series of comedy shorts. Her first film, *The Scarlet Woman: An Ecclesiastical Melodrama* (Terence Greenidge, 1924), a ribald satire of the Roman Catholic Church, was an amateur film performed and written by Evelyn Waugh. Waugh played the Dean of Balliol College, Oxford, who holds sinister influence over the Prince of Wales, but this is countered by the influence of Beatrice de Carolle, played by the sinuous Lanchester. Her formal film debut was in *One of the Best* (Gainsborough, T. Hayes Hunter, 1927), followed by a small part in *The Constant Nymph* (Gainsborough, Adrian Brunel, 1928). In her 1983 memoir, Elsa recalled that Laughton was paid six pounds and six shillings for working in these films.

Day-Dreams (1928)

U.K. (Ideal Films/Angle Pictures)

Credits: From a story invented by H.G. Wells; Screen Version and Art Direction: Frank Wells; Production Manager: Lionel Rich; Photography: F.A. Young; **Uncredited Technical Credits**: Assistants: Roy Kellino, E. Hellster ("Helle" Montagu, Ivor Montagu), Sergei Nolbandov, M. Handkisson, W. Wichelow, H. Haslander; Directed by Ivor Montagu; U.K. release: May 1928; Silent; Black and White; Genre: Comedy; Running Time: 2071 feet; 25 minutes (22 fps); 35mm print held at the British Film Institute, National Film and Television Archive; Not commercially available on digital media.

Cast: Elsa Lanchester (*Elsa*); Harold Warrender (*Count Pornay*); Dorice Fordred (*Maggie*); **Charles Laughton** (*Lodger/Rajah*); Marie Wright (*Landlady*).

Synopsis: Elsa, a slatternly spinster maid, listens attentively to the story of a person of her circumstances who marries a rich man and is later kidnapped by an Indian potentate. During the telling of the story, she dreams that she is a French countess, wears magnificent clothes and jewelry, and is eventually captured by a rajah, who dangles ropes of pearls before her eyes. The film ends with an airplane (piloted by her husband, Count Pornay) crashing into the rajah's yacht. The three survivors (Elsa, Count Pornay and the rajah) cling to pieces of wreckage and while awaiting rescue the two men fight for the affections of Elsa. Eventually drown. When rescued, Elsa is hailed as the most popular widow in Europe. Waking to reality, she cannot wait to pack her bags and follow her "day-dreams."

Production Commentary: Scenarist and art director Frank (Richard) Wells (1903–1982) had previously adapted one of his father H.G. Wells' short stories, "Through a Window" (1894), for the screen while studying film in New York in 1926. The *Manchester Guardian* (October 3, 1926) described it as "a rather amateurish affair."

Filming of *Day-Dreams* began on August 20, 1927, and took some three weeks for location filming near Rye for ocean shots. When *Day-Dreams* was shown at New York's Film Guild Cinema, it received praise. "It has quite a Baroque touch, and in a way is reminiscent of *A Kiss for Cinderella*. [Ivor Montagu] carries out Mr. Wells' ideas in a pleasing fashion, especially in those scenes presumed to be a servant's girl impression of Paris and other Continental cities. Its simplicity adds to its charm" (*Times* [New York], February 4, 1930). As well as allusions to the J.M. Barrie story (filmed by Paramount's Herbert Brenon in 1925), the scenario's flight of fancy is aided and abetted by not being hamstrung to the conventions and methods of mainstream commercial filmmaking. In this regard, admirers of Elsa Lanchester will have a field day. A fusion of costume and art direction produces a *mise en scène* that serves her comic talent to best advantage. Her alternating wardrobe as she transforms into something evermore chic and translucent (including a swimming costume) is indicative of the outlandish and madcap scenario, rather than any real attempt to bring to the screen a stream of consciousness rooted in the theory and practice of Freudian psychoanalysis.

Laughton appears in the dual role of a boarding house lodger and an Arabian/

Indian rajah. The former obliges him to stick his head from behind a door for just a few seconds. The latter role is altogether meatier. Laughton's rendition of a sybaritic rajah, wearing enormous hoop earrings and displaying nefarious intentions to ensnare Elsa in his harem, is pure spectacle and fun to watch. In comparison to the previous short, Laughton gets the chance to act in a dual role, but Elsa remains very much the mainstay of the story.

The Tonic (1928)

U.K. (Ideal Films/Angle Pictures)

Credits: Director: Ivor Montagu; Producer: Simon Rowson; Story: H.G. Wells; First Camera Assistant: Roy Kellino; Makeup: Walter Wichelow; Production Manager: Lionel Rich; Continuity: Eileen Hellstern; Assistants: Sergei Nolbandov, Michael Hankinson, H. Haslander; U.K. release: May 1928; Silent; Black and White; Genre: Comedy; Running Time: 508 feet, 22 minutes (20 fps); 35mm print (blown up from 16mm German release copy) held at Deutsche Kinemathek, Berlin; Not commercially available on digital media.

Cast: Elsa Lanchester (*Elsa*); Renee de Vaux (*Aunt Louisa*); **Charles Laughton** (*The Father*); Marie Wright (*The Mother*); Lionel Rich (*Elder Brother*); Roy Kellino (*Younger Son*); Walter Wichelow (*Brother-in-Law*).

Synopsis: Members of a down-at-heel English family dream of an inheritance from their rich elderly and hypochondriac Aunt Louisa. When a vacancy arises for the position of a personal maid, the hapless Elsa is involved in devising a method of shortening the old lady's life. However, she becomes hopelessly confused with the old lady's medicine bottles. Only a great shock can effect a cure, so Elsa wheels her patient in a bath chair on to a railway line and after a good toss by an approaching rail engine, the old lady recovers her feet in perfect health.

Production Commentary: *The Tonic* was the third and last of what originally was to have been six silent comedy shorts. The advent of sound rendered these short films uncommercial and so further entries were cancelled. As in the previous two films, Laughton's role is a small, tangential part. As the father, he appears in just one scene, sitting, as head of the family, at the breakfast table. According to a *Manchester Guardian* review of these three short films (September 12, 1929), they lacked deftness of direction, and had a slowness of tempo in bringing the visual jokes to life on screen. The article concluded, "[I]t would be unfair to imagine that the films represent any realizations of the screen aspirations of either author or director." A later *Manchester Guardian* review (September 15, 1929) was even more scathing, suggesting that they were out of date by up to ten years: "Centered around a single comic character, they suggest more of the refined comedy of Sidney Drew rather than the rough-and-tumble of Mack Sennett pantomime."

As a result of the advent of talkies, Angle Pictures went into liquidation in March 1930. Despite the poor reception these films received in Britain, they proved very popular in Germany, where they were distributed by Carl Koch's company Deutscher Werkfilm. *The Tonic* was long thought lost, but a German 16mm print turned up among reels of an amateur home movie collection at the Deutsche Kinemathek Archives in Berlin. Digitally restored, it was transferred to 35mm and shown at the 29th *Le Giornate del Cinema Muto*—Pordenone Silent Film Festival—on October 2, 2010.

There was a private showing of all three comedies at the Shaftesbury Avenue Pavilion, London, on September 11, 1929. *The Times* congratulated H.G. Wells on providing film plots that lent themselves "admirably to cinema fantasy, and at the same time burlesques with great good humour the cruder manners of the cinema" (September 12, 1929). *The Tonic* found itself as a supporting short in a program of French films shown at the Pavilion during November 1929. These included *En Rade* (Alberto Cavalcanti, 1927), *Salome* (Charles Bryant, Nazimova, 1923) and the documentary short *La Tour* (Rene Clair, 1928). Elsa Lanchester's work in these short films resurfaced in the sound period when she appeared in a two-reel sound short, *Miss Bracegirdle Does Her Duty* (London Film, Lee Garmes, 1936).

Though Laughton is not the main focus of these short films, his cameo appearances were an indispensable induction to the film medium. These early appearances provided the foundation for later vignettes in such feature films as *Piccadilly* and *If I Had a Million*. Laughton was able to test his physical stamina and mental aptitude in blocking and character motivation, taking note of the capabilities and attributes of the camera. Even though he was not fully acquainted with the processes and procedures of filmmaking, these small-scale productions with their freedoms of creative improvisation, ensemble playing, and character motivation opened up creative possibilities which was something he came to relish.

Piccadilly (1929)

Tagline: "A World Beating Film"[1]

U.K. (British International Pictures)

Credits: An E.A. Dupont Production; Original Screenplay: Arnold Bennett; Photography: Werner Brandes; Art Director: Alfred Junge; U.K. release: Passed by the British Board of Film Censors on January 29, 1929; Silent; Black and White with Color Tints; Genre: Crime Melodrama; Running Time: 9756 feet, 108 minutes; 35mm print held at the British Film Institute, National Film and Television Archive; DVD Region 1, Milestone Films, released March 2005; DVD Region 2, British Film Institute, released June 2004.

Cast: Gilda Gray (*Mabel Greenfield*); Anna May Wong (*Shosho*); Jameson Thomas (*Valentine Wilmot*); **Charles Laughton** (***A Greedy Nightclub Diner***); Cyril Ritchard (*Victor Smiles*); King Ho Chang (*Jim*); Hannah Jones (*Bessie*); Debroy Somers Band (*Themselves*); **Uncredited Cast:** Gordon Begg (*Coroner*); Ellen Pollock (*Vamp*); Harry Terry (*Publican*); Charles Paton (*Doorman*); Ray Milland, Jack Raine (*Men in Night Club*).

Synopsis: At London's fashionable Piccadilly nightclub, patrons are treated to spectacular cabaret dancing to the accompaniment of syncopated jazz, alcohol and gourmet food. When an empty plate is placed in front of a disgruntled customer, he examines it and in high dudgeon exclaims, "Dirty plate!" The waiter brings the *maître d'hôtel*, who calls the general manager to calm the customer. Not placated, the customer thumps the table twice and demands immediate service, distracting dancer Mabel and other patrons. Eventually the plate is removed and he returns to his former comatose state. When the nightclub owner asks the meaning of the commotion, he is told, "A complaint about a plate, sir—perhaps too much champagne." The disturbance causes a chain reaction in the plotline and leads to the discovery of Shosho, a scullery maid, whose preoccupation with dancing distracts her from her job of cleaning dishes. Manager Valentine, having decided to sack his dancer, sees potential in Shosho and decides to promote her as a star attraction. Shosho's new Chinese dancing act becomes a sensation and receives kudos from the press. Valentine is attracted to Shosho and they become lovers, but this provokes the jealousy of former flame Mabel. Shosho is found murdered in her Limehouse apartment, under circumstances that implicate both Valentine and Mabel. An investigation reveals that Shosho's Chinese lover is the murderer.

Production Commentary: Appearing at the beginning of the second reel, Laughton has in a small cameo role as a disgruntled customer in his first feature-length film appearance. Both the character on screen and Laughton the actor had voracious appetites and also a reputation for being "awkward customers." The framing of Laughton in the picture reminds one of the famed works of noted Weimar artist George Grosz (1893–1959). It's a piece of social caricature brought effectively to the screen with connotations of middle-class corruption and greed. Laughton in a display of egomania dispenses with any pretense to manners, and as he devours his food he pays little mind to anyone around him except, of course, to the object of consuming his food with gluttonous passion. It is fascinating to watch these few minutes of a youthful Laughton on film. Filmed in medium close-up, his screen character is seated at a table in the background at the edge of a cabaret stage. Dancers in the foreground try to continue their act despite the atmosphere of self-centered distraction created by Laughton's character. This panjandrum is only satisfied when he acquires what he deems as his due. He then regains his sybaritic poise. His alteration of mood swings, from furious bombast to placid tranquility, is achieved with consummate ease and demonstrates his facility with honing gestures to the screen.

In embryonic form, this vignette looks forward to his later, justly celebrated banquet scene in *The Private Life of Henry VIII*. *Piccadilly*, an Anglo-German co-production, is part an exercise in stylistic Weimar continental glamor interspersed with condescending British morality in its depiction of miscegenation and warnings of impending cultural decadence. The production has much to commend it, but unfortunately its release coincided with the industry converting over to sound technology. In an attempt to cater to those theaters wired for sound, a music track with effects was hastily added. E.A. Dupont directs with fluid assurance using long tracking shots and also extensive cutting. All of this, alas, deserted him when he came to film the English sound version of *Atlantic* (British International Films, 1929), a scenario based on the sinking of the RMS *Titanic*. Dupont was used to directing actors with ample weight, gravitas and a penchant for adopting disguise and playing tragic roles. He had already given German actor Emil Jannings (1884–1950) a popular success with *Varieté* (UFA, 1925).

Welsh-born actor Ray Milland worked as an extra along with Jack Raine in *Piccadilly*'s cabaret sequences. It was their introduction to the world of the film studio just as much as it was for Laughton.

Comets (1930)

Tagline: "With the greatest cast ever assembled for one film...."[2]

U.K. (Alpha Film Corporation/Jury-Metro-Goldwyn)

Credits: Producer: Morris J. Wilson; Director: Sasha Geneen; U.K. release: premiere: January 31, 1930; Board of Trade Registration: September 20, 1930; Genre: Musical Revue; Black and White; Running Time: 4459 feet; 68 minutes; the film is believed lost.

Cast: Heather Thatcher; Billy Merson; **Charles Laughton**; Elsa Lanchester; Albert Sandler; Noni and Horace; Gladys Cruickshank; Gus McNaughton; Flora Le Breton; Randle Ayrton; Jack Raine; Rex Evans; Marie Monighetti; The Tiller Girls; Melton Club Orchestra; Golden Serenaders; Strelsky's Cossack Singers.

Synopsis: A film revue featuring musical and theatrical artists in songs, dances and dramatic and sketches.

Production Commentary: Produced at Twickenham Studios, *Comets* is the most anonymous and obscure of all Laughton's 54 films, as it is believed to be lost. The film's production was precarious, and traces of its reception are also difficult to come by.

Journalist Nerina Shute, writing in *Film Weekly* (January 11, 1930), gives an indication of the precipitous nature of the film's production. The shoot on *Comets* was completed back-to-back with a dramatic short starring Jeanne de Casalis under the working title of *The Call*, but later released as *Infatuation* (Alpha Film Corporation, 1930). Director Sasha Geneen worked on a tight schedule of just three and a half weeks for the completion of both films, but by putting in long hours was able to complete the task ahead of schedule. Shute describes Laughton's singing voice as husky and the actor unsuited to musical comedy. Laughton informed Shute that despite using words in a song which necessitated re-taking his scenes, he believed that talkies were the art of the future. Stage actor Jack Raine (1897–1979) had appeared as an extra in *Piccadilly*, and for a brief period he graduated to playing leads before taking on character roles, often unbilled. In the early 1950s, he relocated to Hollywood and there he appeared unbilled in two Laughton films, *Young Bess* as Governor of Tower and *Witness for the Prosecution* as a doctor. Revue and cabaret artist Rex Evans' (1903–1969) appearance in *Comets* marked his film debut. He later turned his hand to legitimate acting and appeared in a minor role in *Rembrandt*. In Hollywood, he befriended George Cukor and appeared in eight of the director's films. The well-built Evans played his share of butlers, majordomos, innkeepers and other domestic staff members. During the 1940s, he appeared in *The Man from Down Under* in the small uncredited role of Doyle.

According to a May 1930 review in the trade paper *Kine Weekly*, *Comets* had been drastically cut and reshaped from its first London trade show in January. It was shown some years later in the U.S. The *Motion Picture Daily* (October 22, 1934) describes further processes of re-cutting. Laughton and Lanchester's interpretation of "Frankie and Johnny," condensed to a single reel, is discussed and advertised under "Shorts." When it was given an American reissue in 1936, the distributers sought to edit all footage save Laughton and Lanchester's "Frankie and Johnny" Apache-style dance and produced a short of just two reels. *Variety* declared (April 25, 1933), "Among the flock of antiquated shorts preceding the stage performance was one in which a man and woman do a vocal satire on 'Frankie and Johnnie.' The man is Charles Laughton." Should *Comets* ever turn up, it would be of historic interest to view a record of Laughton and Lanchester's stage act of the 1920s.

Wolves (1930), reissued as *Wanted Men*

Tagline: "With the talking screen's Popular Artiste—DOROTHY GISH, who was brought over from America to play in this outstanding BRITISH ALL TALKING PRODUCTION."[3]

U.K. (British and Dominions Film Corporation)

Credits: Directed by Albert de Courville; Produced by Herbert Wilcox; Photography: David Kesson and Roy F. Overbaugh; Art Director: Lawrence P. Williams; Adapted by Captain R. Berkeley; Based on the play *Parmi les Loupes* by Georges Toudouze; Editor: Byron Haskin; U.K. release: May 19, 1930; U.S. release: July 7, 1936; Genre: Drama; Black and White; Running Time: 5041 feet; 57 minutes; U.S. Version cut to 35 minutes; Film is believed lost.

Cast: Dorothy Gish (*Leila McDonald*); **Charles Laughton** (*Captain Job*); Malcolm Keen (*Pierre*); Jack Osterman (*Hank*); Arthur Margetson (*Mark*); Betty Bolton (*Naroutcha*); Franklyn Bellamy (*Pablo*); Griffith Humphreys (*Semyon*); Andrews Engelmann (*Pfeiffer*).

Synopsis: In Greenland, a half-frozen girl, Leila McDonald, is discovered in a boat adrift in the Labrador Sea, and a young doctor nurses her back to health. In a whaling camp, the men, and in particular a Canadian, Pierre, fight among themselves for possession of the girl. They draw lots and Captain Job fakes the draw, planning to enable her escape. Mark learns of Job's intentions and sides with him and escapes with Leila while Job holds the gang of desperadoes at bay until he dies and the men are blown up by an explosion.

Production Commentary: This tale of the frozen north started production during August 1929. It was based on a play by John Protheroe, from a French original by Georges Toudouze, and produced on the West End stage at the New Theatre from September to October 1927. Malcolm Keen appeared as Pierre alongside Sam Livesey as Captain Job, Lawrence Andrew and Olga Lindo as Kitty MacDonald. It was announced that the film would feature the following stars: Oscar Asche, Franklyn Dyall and Abraham Sofaer. In the event, these three actors do not appear. Arthur Margetson (leading man in the West End stage show at the Palace Theatre), Betty Bolton, Jack Osterman and Laughton were later announced, and all used in the film. Herbert Wilcox had secured the services of Dorothy Gish for the title role of his period drama *Nell Gwyn* produced in 1926. *Nell Gwyn* did good business both in the domestic market and internationally, earning positive reviews in the U.S. *Wolves* did not emulate this earlier success. When Gish saw the finished picture, she was anything but impressed. In *Exhibitors Herald-World* (January 11, 1930), she is quoted as stating, "I made a talker in England. And it's awful, gosh-awful! It's one of those grimly serious things and it's a scream too. When I saw it, I laughed so hard they had to kick me out of the projection room."[4]

A young David Lean was on the film set and he was most impressed by the approach of Laughton's thorough preparation during rehearsals and the intensity of his performance during filming. This suggests that even at this early stage of his film career, Laughton devoted considerable energies to film work, even though his commitment to the stage was absolute. When *Wolves* was distributed in the United States by J.H. Hoffberg in September 1936, it was re-titled *Wanted Men*. The running time of eight reels was cut to just 36 minutes, but reportedly this did not improve the film. A scathing *Film Daily* review (July 8, 1936) called it "very weak entertainment.... Poor direction, shoddy photography and faulty sound conspire with crude editing to throttle the abilities of Charles Laughton and Dorothy Gish except for fleeting moments. Supporting players are badly cast." *Variety* (July 15, 1936) was equally blunt: "Everyone makes mistakes when young. This one was made by Charles Laughton in his native land ... and it's still hanging over his head." Noting that the film had been cut drastically, the reviewer suggested that the remaining film, "if cut up further, would make excellent celluloid collar and cuff sets."

Wolves was produced during a period of intense and often febrile technological transition. The film industry was under extreme pressure to convert over to sound as soon as possible. Consequently, producers such as Wilcox, who readily understood changes in market demand and popular taste, often sacrificed quality in preference to the commercial imperative of being in the vanguard of sound adaptation. How deserved its egregious reputation remains an open question, as all extant prints seem to have fallen into the limbo of "believed lost."[5]

Down River (1931)

Tagline: "A Gripping Melodrama of a girl's thrilling adventure among riverside smugglers"[6]

U.K. (The Gaumont Company Ltd.)

Credits: Director: Peter Godfrey; Production Manager: L'Estrange Fawcett; Assistant Director: G. Boothby; Scenario: R.G. Bettinson; Based on the novel by "Seamark" (Austin James Small); Photography: Percy Strong; Art Director: Andrew L. Mazzei; "Down River" Lyrics and Music: Roger Eckersley; Sound: S.A. Jolly; Sound System: British Acoustics Recording; Makeup: Philip Vallentine; Passed by the British Board of Film Censors on April 29, 1931; U.K. release: May 5, 1931; Genre: Underworld Melodrama; Black and White; Running Time: 6610 feet, 75 minutes; 35mm print held at the British Film Institute, National Film and Television Archive; Not commercially available on digital media.

Cast: Jane Baxter (*Hillary Gordon*); Harold Huth (*John Durham*); Kenneth Kove (*Ronnie Gordon*); Hartley Power (*Lingard*); Arthur Goullet (*Maxick*); Norman Shelley (*Blind Rudley*); Frederick Leister (*Superintendent Manning*); Cyril McLaglen (*Sergeant Proctor*); Humberstone Wright (*Sir Michael Gordon*); Hugh E. Wright (*Charley Wong*); Helen Howell (*Dancer*); **Charles Laughton** (*Grossman*).

Synopsis: Speeding down the river in her motorboat, accompanied by customs investigator John Durham, ambitious journalist Hillary Gordon pulls up beside a police boat which has just recovered a man from the river. Durham's friend, Superintendent Manning, tells him that the victim has been stabbed in the back with a knife bearing a Chinese inscription, and they suspect drug traffickers. That evening, Hillary goes with her brother Ronnie to the High Sea Night Club and discovers that the proprietor, Lingard, is on friendly terms with Captain Grossman, the half–Dutch, half–Oriental skipper of a tramp boat, who is suspected of drug smuggling. Hillary gets in touch with Durham and Manning and they raid the club. Seeing Lingard make his escape, Hillary follows him until she reaches Grossman's boat, where she indulges in a little investigation on her own. She is discovered and held by Grossman, but Durham continues his investigations and, after many exciting happenings, gets the incriminating evidence on Grossman and his gang, and rescues Hillary in the nick of time.

Production Commentary: This film has the reputation of being a low-budget affair, but on close inspection, there appears to have been some money expended on it. The surviving print shows a decently photographed scenario; the camera is mobile and there are copious open-air locations shot along the Thames River at the East End Docklands. Many of the action sequences are shot at silent speed and Percy Strong's camera uses day-for-night in an attempt to create an aura of mystery and suspense. Andrew L. Mazzei's sets are efficient and in particular the set of the High Sea Night Club is quite impressive in scale and ambiance.

Where the film falls down is in the amount of redundancy in the narrative. For instance, the use of close-ups is restricted for explicit on-screen clues to cue the viewer's attention (cryptic messages scrawled on secreted pieces of paper, etc.). When it comes to using the camera to highlight a suspect's face in close-up, the camera is conspicuous by its reticence.

Within a short space of time, the film depicts London's Docklands Chinese community as crime-ridden, fiendish and sinister. In this vein, Laughton first appears on camera looking through a ship's porthole with a distinct hint of the "otherness" that recalls Sax Rohmer's Dr. Fu Manchu. Laughton's accent (Dutch East Indies?) comes and goes, but he captures the eye of the camera by sheer charismatic presence. This is just as well, as his dialogue is both minimal and unmemorable. His name appears distinct and separate at the bottom of the cast list. Though the character of Englebert is referred to in the story, in the copy of the film held at the British Film Institute he does not appear on screen. Neither does Donald Wolfit, who is listed in some sources as playing the part, appear in the film credits. This situation seems to suggest that Wolfit was announced as being cast in the film, but later proved unavailable.

The film is based on a story by adventure and thriller writer Seamark a pseudonym used by British author Austin James Small

(1894–1929). Actor Peter Godrey (1899–1970) took up the directional reins on this feature film. Like Laughton, he would go across the pond to Hollywood, where he played minor film roles (including a monk in *The Hunchback of Notre Dame*). He also worked as a writer on *Forever and a Day*. However, he forged a career behind the camera and became a Warner Bros. contract director, helming such thrillers as *The Two Mrs. Carrolls* (1947), *Cry Wolf* (1947) and *The Woman in White* (1948).

Down River, a budget pot-boiler, is technically competent enough, if little else. For Laughton, it was a useful stepping stone before his launch in Hollywood.

Devil and the Deep (1932)

Tagline: "Box-Office in Every Frame!"[7]

United States (Paramount Publix Corporation)

Credits: Directed by Marion Gering; Screenplay: Benn W. Levy; Story: Harry Hervey; Photography: Charles Lang; **Uncredited Technical Credits**: Art Direction: Bernard Herzbrun; Editor: Otho Lovering; Music: Herman Hand, Rudolph G. Kopp, John Leipold; Camera Operator: Robert Pittack; Assistant Camera: Clifford Shirpser; Sound: Jack Goodrich; Still Photographer: Earl Crowley; Costumes: Travis Banton; U.S. release: August 12, 1932; U.K. release: Passed by the British Board of Film Censors on August 26, 1932; Genre: Submarine Drama; Black and White; Running Time: 78 minutes; DVD-R, TCM, released October 2010; DVD Region 1, *Cary Grant: The Early Years* box set, Turner Classic Movies, released May 2012; DVD Region 1, *Cary Grant: The Vault Collection* box set, Universal, released April 2016; no English subtitle captions for the deaf and hard of hearing.

Cast: Tallulah Bankhead (*Diana Sturm*); Gary Cooper (*Lieutenant Sempter*); **Charles Laughton (*Commander Sturm*)**; Cary Grant (*Lieutenant Jaeckel*); Paul Porcasi (*Hassan*); Juliette Compton (*Mrs. Planet*); Henry Kolker (*Commander Hutton*); Dorothy Christy (*Mrs. Crimp*); Arthur Hoyt (*Mr. Planet*); Gordon Westcott (*Lieutenant Toll*); Jimmie Dugan (*Condover*); **Uncredited Cast**: Peter Brocco (*Wireless*

Cary Grant (left) as Lieutenant Jaeckel with Charles Laughton as Commander Sturm in *Devil and the Deep* (1932).

A tempestuous triangle of disaffection. Left to right: Gary Cooper as Lieutenant Sempter, Tallulah Bankhead as Diana Sturm, and Laughton as naval supremo Commander Sturm in *Devil and the Deep* (1932).

Operator); John George (*Man in Crowd*); Jack Gardner, Henry Guttman, Fred Kohler Jr., Dave O'Brien, George Magrill (*Submarine Crewmen*); Anderson Lawler (*Sailor*); Lucien Littlefield (*Shopkeeper*); Wilfred Lucas (*Court Martial Judge*); Kent Taylor (*Friend at Party*).

Synopsis: At a submarine base somewhere in North Africa, Commander Charles Sturm appears to be a genial man, prone to telling tall stories and hackneyed jokes among fellow officers and wives. Behind his assumed bonhomie is an insanely jealous individual. He suspects his wife Diana of conducting several affairs and arranges for her latest conquest, Lieutenant Jaeckel, to be transferred from the naval base on grounds of gross inefficiency. Diana pleads for the young officer to remain at the base. Sturm agrees, *if* she will invite Jaeckel to their house, so he can observe the couple together on the veranda to see if his suspicions are justified. Though their meeting appears innocuous, Sturm is convinced that Diana warned Jaeckel that he, Sturm, was on the veranda. Following a confrontation with her husband, Diana leaves the house and encounters the handsome Lieutenant Sempter, who rescues her from a throng of natives. This time she realizes this is no mere flirtation and falls in love with him. On her return to the house, she is told that Sempter is Jaeckel's replacement. Sturm soon comes to realize an affair is developing between the two and he begins the cuckold's act of revenge. Failing to deliberately destroy his submarine by colliding with a vessel on the ocean surface, Sturm then decides to flood the sunken sub so that he, his wife and lover and crew will drown. Sempter has other plans and manages to save Diana and most of the crew, leaving Sturm to indulge himself in an orgy of destruction aboard the vessel. A later naval inquiry absolves Sempter of all blame for the loss of the submarine and declares Sturm's conduct grossly negligent due to insanity. With this verdict, the lovers are reunited.

Selected Dialogue:

STURM: "This is your first dive, too, isn't it, Carlson? ... Bad luck. Still, cheer up. We're not dead yet!"

STURM: "You didn't know there was a woman aboard, did you? Nor did I when we sailed. If it weren't for that, maybe we now shouldn't be at the bottom of the sea."

STURM: "She couldn't restrain herself. She's that kind of woman. She couldn't restrain herself! I say, she couldn't restrain herself!"

Production Commentary: When Laughton arrived in Hollywood with his wife Elsa Lanchester, they were taken for a meal at the Brown Derby by director James Whale. While there, they met Tallulah Bankhead, star of *Devil and the Deep*. She took an instant dislike to Laughton and this feeling was mutual. Cast as the romantic lead in the film was Gary Cooper, then currently riding high in the box office stakes, and also a young Cary Grant as a second lead who, like Laughton, was starting out on his film career. A casting director's dream apparently; yet there is little chemistry between Bankhead and Laughton, or anyone else for that matter. Bankhead simply walks through the picture, blasé in her lack of care or concern for either the script or the picture in general. Bankhead and Cooper receive joint credits above the main title with newcomer Cary Grant beneath the main title. Laughton's credit appears separately on screen: "And introducing CHARLES LAUGHTON—The eminent English character actor in the role of THE COMMANDER." When the end castlist appears, Grant is demoted to fourth place, Laughton promoted to third.

This was the second occasion where Laughton was called upon to portray a maritime officer on screen and this set something of a precedent. He went on to play other notable seafarers, including an incongruous collection of shoreline drunkards, during his illustrious film career. His playing of a "heavy" authoritarian role gave audiences an impression of Laughton as portraying a certain brand of villainy that was distinctive and done with relish. This practice of typecasting was something he was ambivalent about, but it also provided a challenge to infuse his best performances with a fine display of inimitable and indispensable acting skill. Laughton's striving to attain and perfect his performing abilities and acting techniques on screen often appeared a pointless and arduous process, not only for himself, but for those around him. *Photoplay* (February 1933) carried a story of Laughton hearing the studio was planning to use an extra's hands instead of his own for close-up shots. He protested. He was told the film had finished shooting and salary complications would arise if they used his hands in the close-up retakes. They would only need to pay $10 to the extra. After an altercation, he managed to persuade the management that monetary concerns were a minor issue, and he was allowed to perform the retakes using his own hands—gratis.

Casting and filming took place over eight weeks through May and June 1932. By the beginning of July, the film was in the cutting room and on August 5, 1932, it received a midnight preview screening at the Paramount in New York.

For location shoots involving a flotilla of small boats six miles away, a short-wave radio transmitter and receiver was installed by the studio. Communication took place using a microphone at the side of the director. Censorship of the day dictated that uniforms worn on screen should not readily identify any specific nationality. The opening title is suitably restrained in evading any national affiliation: "At a submarine base on the North African shore." There is an implicit assumption, never spelled out, that this is a British naval base. Major Frederick ("Ted") Herron of the Motion Picture Producers and Distributors of America (MPPDA) was in charge of the Hollywood Production Code and head of the foreign department charged with maintaining communications between the film industry and the U.S. State Department. He wrote in an internal memo to another MPPDA member, John V. Wilson, that *Devil and the Deep* would not generate objections from foreign governments in this regard:

> The actors speak with a decided British accent, their names are Germanic and their uniforms are nondescript. It is going to be difficult for any country to try to claim the story is that of its own navy. Even if that is done, I doubt very much if there will be any objection because what really happens is due to the insanity of the commander of the submarine [Vasey: 117-18].

Despite this, the New York State Censors saw fit to trim a fade-out embrace in reel four in which Diana and a man are in the desert.[8]

On release, the film received mixed reviews. Harold Weight of *Hollywood Filmograph* (July 23, 1932) described the Paramount production as "pretty much a mess." Marion Gering was certainly a competent studio house director, but nothing beyond that. He was unable to handle the material at his disposal with anything approaching a sufficient depth or subtlety. As it is, the film falls between sophisticated drama and melodrama. As in screenwriter Harry Hervey's previous hit, *Shanghai Express* (Paramount, Josef von Sternberg, 1932), he concocted a highly artificial story (the film was based on "Sirènes et tritons," a 1927 story by French author Maurice Larrouy). However, unlike von Sternberg, Gering fails to transform the unbelievable plot into something substantial and interesting in its appeal.

As the insanely jealous submarine commander, Laughton scores sensationally. Harold Weight in *Hollywood Filmograph* (July 23, 1932) called Laughton's performance "the most perfectly sustained characterization of the screen year." The critic for *Film Daily* (August 4, 1932) noted, "His acting carries an uncanny fascination. He makes everything count—his voice, his laugh, his remarkable facial expressions. He easily steals the picture." Other members in this starry cast are not seen to their best advantage. *Hollywood Filmograph* (July 23, 1932) noted that Laughton's screen presence made Tallulah Bankhead appear "a pallid dishrag" and Gary Cooper little more than "a frightened school boy." At this early stage in his Paramount contract, there is little on screen which hints of Cary Grant's later illustrious film career.

Motion Picture Herald (January 7, 1933) provided reaction to the film from various film exhibitors. The State Theatre, Portland, Oregon, reported that Laughton "took honors for acting from the billed stars. Not for children, but they came. Just average business." *Motion Picture Herald* (January 28, 1933) reported that at the Beacon Theatre in Omaha, Nebraska, audiences were none too impressed: "[M]ediocre picture.... Too heavy for our patrons." The *National Board of Review Magazine* (November 1932) remarked, "[W]ithin the limits imposed upon him by an all too preposterous plot, Mr. Laughton did create a character, through sheer acting."

The highlight of the film occurs when Sturm attempts to sink everybody, including himself, by opening the submarine bulkheads. Shuttered alone in his cabin, with flood doors open, he is submerged by the rising water. Just as he disappears, he lets out a piercing, shrieking, insane laugh. This scene manages to combine absurdity with a chill effect and remains one of those legendary moments of popular Hollywood cinema. Laughton was required to shoot this scene of demented frenzy up to ten times and was fortified with slugs of whiskey to keep the cold at bay. Long after the final credits have faded, Laughton's performance as Commander Sturm remains compelling and memorable. Put simply, whenever Laughton is off screen, the interest lags.

The Old Dark House (1932)

Tagline: "Beware the Night!"[9]

U.S. (Universal Pictures)

Credits: Producer: Carl Laemmle Jr.; From the novel by J.B. Priestley; Screenplay: Benn W. Levy; Directed by James Whale; **Uncredited Technical Credits**: First Cameraman: Arthur Edeson; Operative Cameraman: King Gray; Assistant Cameraman: Jack Eagan: Still Cameraman: Roman Freulich; Assistant Director: Joseph A. McDonough; Additional Dialogue: R.C. Sherriff; Set Decorator: Russell Gausman; Art Director: Charles D. Hall; Editor: Clarence Kolster; Supervising Editor: Maurice Pivar; Makeup: Otto Lederer, Jack P. Pierce; Special Effects: John P. Fulton; Music: David Broekman; Sound: William Hedgcock; U.S. release: October 20, 1932; Genre: Horror; Black and White; Running Time: 71 minutes; 35mm print held at the George Eastman Museum Motion Picture Collection, Rochester, New York, and the Library of Congress; 4K digital restoration carried out by Sony Columbia in 2016; DVD Region 1, Kino International, released September 2003; no English subtitle captions for the deaf and hard of hearing; Blu-ray Region A, Cohen Media, released October 2017; Dual format edition: DVD Region 2 and Blu-ray Region B, Masters of Cinema, Eureka Entertainment, released May 2018; English subtitle captions for the deaf and hard of hearing are available on these discs.

Cast: Boris Karloff (*Morgan*); Melvyn Douglas (*Penderel*); **Charles Laughton** (*Sir William Porterhouse*); Lillian Bond (*Gladys*); Ernest Thesiger (*Horace Femm*); Eva Moore (*Rebecca Femm*); Raymond Massey (*Philip Waverton*); Gloria Stuart (*Margaret Waverton*); John Dudgeon [Elspeth Dudgeon] (*Sir Roderick Femm*); Brember Wills (*Saul Femm*).

Synopsis: On a stormy night in the Welsh countryside, stranded travelers Philip Waverton, his wife Margaret and friend Roger Penderel seek refuge in an old dark house. It is the home of the eccentric Femm family: Horace Femm, a cadaverous host; his sister, Rebecca Femm, a religious fanatic who indulges in admonition of "sins of the flesh"; a younger brother, Saul Femm, a pyromaniac who is under lock and key lest he come to grief in his lethal fascination with fire; and, upstairs, the 102-year-old Sir Roderick Femm. Their mute butler is Morgan. During the night, this group is joined by two other travelers, businessman Sir William Porterhouse and chorus girl Gladys DuCane. In a drunken state, Morgan attacks Margaret but he is knocked unconscious by Philip. Gladys and Penderel find themselves falling in love. When Morgan recovers, he is devoured with hate and frees the insane Saul, who knocks Penderel to the floor and tries to set fire to the house. Penderel recovers and again battles with Saul, who is accidentally killed. The following

Among the sepulchral cobwebs and chiaroscuro shadows of director James Whale's wry delight, *The Old Dark House* (1932), are Melvyn Douglas (left) as shell-shocked war veteran Penderel and Laughton as self-made industrialist Sir William Porterhouse.

morning with the storm and rain having ceased, the five travelers leave the old dark house, never to return.

Selected Dialogue:

PORTERHOUSE: "Once you start making money, it's hard to stop. Especially if you're like me, there isn't much else you're good at."

Production Commentary: Laughton went across to Hollywood from England to appear in a Paramount picture, *Devil and the Deep*, but a prolonged illness on the part of the film's star, Tallulah Bankhead, held up the proceedings.[10] At the suggestion of director James Whale, Paramount decided to loan him to Universal for the supporting role of Sir William Porterhouse in Whale's *The Old Dark House* on condition that Universal would not show their film until *Devil and the Deep* had been finished and released. Having worked with Laughton on the London stage four years previously in *A Man with Red Hair*, Whale was well aware of Laughton's methodical approach in working his way through a part. True to form, in order to ensure that the arrival of his character from a violent storm was suitably authentic, Laughton ran up and down the sound stage continuously to imitate being out of breath. Though the film is already well underway when Laughton makes his entrance, his strength of characterization soon fills the screen. His Sir William is memorable for being ebullient and down to earth. Laughton delivers his lines in a broad Lancashire accent, indicative of the self-made millionaire who came from "nowt" and rose by "gumption" to become a man of property and substance. His façade of gusto is later belied by a smack of vulnerability which surfaces after a hearty meal. In reflective anger, Porterhouse, a widower, speaks of his late wife as someone who didn't fit in with high society and was snubbed by the middle classes for being common and unsophisticated. He infers that her death was hastened by this crushing experience. Laughton handles the scene with quiet authority and delivers this important speech with a suggestion of both bitterness and compassion. This episode has a psychological dimension to it and goes some way in refuting the charge of incessant overacting on Laughton's part. It should also be pointed out he was still finding his way around the filmmaking process. As Elsa Lanchester recalled, he was certainly glad "to get the camera experience for the larger part(s) to come" (Lanchester: 1938, 107).

Lanchester went on to note the differentiation between acting for the stage and on the screen. Laughton was quick to grasp the difference. Speaking about the making of the film over 60 years later, in 1995, actress Gloria Stuart recalled how the predominantly English cast were most respectful to Whale's firm and meticulous direction.[11] Stuart, playing Margaret, was a newcomer from the Pasadena Playhouse. Fellow American actor Melvyn Douglas was also a relative newcomer to the medium; it was his sixth film. He was loaned to Universal by Samuel Goldwyn. The two Americans soon bonded and spent their time together talking about the work of the actors' union. Raymond Massey, who played Philip, was Canadian by birth and *The Old Dark House* marked his Hollywood debut. Tea was served on the set daily at eleven and four for the cast's six English cast members. The other players included Ernest Thesiger, looking like an elder version of British comic actor Kenneth Williams, with flaring nostrils and camp demeanor. Eva Moore, at 62 the elder of the group, had an actress daughter Jill Esmond who was then married to young Laurence Olivier. At the time, both Esmond and Olivier were working at RKO Studios. Lillian Bond, at the beginning of a long film career, played a lively chorus girl, by far her best role. The same uniqueness of casting applies to Brember Wills' playing of the pyromaniac Saul Femm. At the time of his first (and only) trip to Hollywood, there was much talk in the British press about the brevity of his film contract. He told a reporter from *The Citizen* (April 7, 1932), "I believe it is the shortest contract ever signed by a film actor. Only a week's acting is required of me, but the journey to Hollywood and back will take 22 days. The company will pay all expenses. My wife will go with me and enjoy a holiday while I work." Whale had requested him specifically. Although this involved great expense for Universal, the studio was agreeable given Whale's track record in directing *Frankenstein*. Wills, accompanied by his wife, boarded the SS *Albert Ballin* at Southampton on April 8, 1932, and arrived in New York on April 16, 1932 (New York Passenger Lists

[1820–1957] 1932, Micro Serial, T715, Microfilm Roll, 5141, Line 1, P. 130). They then set off for Hollywood by train. Wills arrived in Hollywood in time for the start of filming.[12] The role of the centenarian Sir Roderick Femm proved difficult to cast, so Whale, in sardonic fashion, gave it to English actress Elspeth Dudgeon. To confuse matters, Whale ensured Dudgeon's gender was disguised in the credits as John Dudgeon!

Finally, there was Boris Karloff. Though Karloff had become an overnight star sensation at Universal, Whale and, it is claimed, Laughton tended to look down on his long road in gaining success as a named star. There was disparagement of Karloff's lack of legitimate West End stage experience and reminders of the many menial part-time jobs he had undertaken to finance his ambitions of becoming a professional actor. In consequence, Karloff and Laughton never struck up any real friendship or held each other in particular esteem.

The casting of the film went through several permutations. *Film Filmograph* (February 20, 1932) announced that Karloff and Colin Clive would appear in *The Old Dark House*. Both *Variety* (April 12, 1932) and *Film Daily* (April 13, 1932) announced another English actor, Walter Byron, as being part of the cast lineup. The film began shooting on April 18, 1932 and wrapped at the end of May. The *Motion Picture Herald* (May 14, 1932) reported that during their annual sales convention in May 1932, Universal announced the lineup for their 1932–1933 program: two roadshow attractions, 26 "special" features and 12 westerns, besides 88 one- and two-reel short subjects and the twice-weekly Universal newsreel. At the head of 26 feature "specials" was *The Old Dark House*. The film was produced on the back of the enormous success of the studio's investment in the horror genre. Beginning in the silent era with the Lon Chaney star vehicles and then with such prestige specials as *The Cat and the Canary* (Paul Leni, 1927) and continuing in the early sound period with *Dracula* (Tod Browning, 1931) and *Frankenstein* (James Whale, 1931), Universal went from strength to strength in its horror franchise. Whale's direction of small part character actor Boris Karloff in the role of the Monster in *Frankenstein* had catapulted Karloff to the zenith of Hollywood stardom. *The Old Dark House* was therefore conceived and sold on the strength of Karloff's star name. On surviving prints prior to the appearance of the studio logo (a small monoplane flying around the Universal globe), there appears a PRODUCER'S NOTE that states, "Karloff, the mad butler in this production, is the same Karloff who created the part of the mechanical monster in *Frankenstein*. We explain this to settle all disputes in advance…."

Universal, like the other studios, was undergoing financial turmoil during the great economic depression of the early 1930s. The signs of cost-cutting are apparent in the opening minutes of the film. The credits are sparse, and poor J.B. Priestley's name erroneously appears on screen as *Priestly*.[13] After this *faux pas*, there are some perfunctory studio exteriors of an open tourer motor car valiantly ploughing through a wild storm in the Welsh countryside, followed by an unconvincing model shot of a landslide. However, once the travelers take shelter in the Old Dark House, the humor and fun begin in earnest.

In an informative article, "Over Hollywood" in *Silver Screen* (July 1932), Donovan Pedelty gave an insight into the production details of the film. To simplify the filming process, the entire *Old Dark House* set was built on Stage 1, Universal's largest. In the film, Laughton and Lillian Bond, playing stranded motorists, make a dramatic entrance. They hammer on the front door in the dark while drenched by rain and are nearly blown sideways off their feet by a storm. In an age before computer-generated special effects, simulating the conditions of bedraggled travelers in a violent storm was an arduous and low-tech operation. Preparing to appear at the front door, both actors stood up to their ankles in a wooden box containing mud. Then a Japanese gardener perched high on a ladder with a garden hose aimed at the actors and began spraying. The force of the spray immediately saturated all their clothing. Next the director ordered airstream to replicate a storm. A giant airplane propeller, positioned in front of the door, went into action. Pelted with both water and air, the actors were very relieved when the take was finished successfully.

Contemporary reviews were often less than enthusiastic, and many Karloff fans were disappointed that the star appeared only intermittently. In *Hollywood Filmograph* (July 9, 1932), critic Arthur Forde conjectured, "We don't predict box-office returns for this [film] as the subject is passé and is not 'entertainment,' at the present day." In a similar vein, the *Manchester Guardian* (February 14, 1933) considered *The Old Dark House* as deficient and requiring "more skill than some film directors seem able to command, and the cooking of *The Old Dark House* … is beyond belief stodgy…. [I]t is high time that both the makers and exhibitors of films realized that this manufacture of horrors is beneath criticism." However, it found Laughton's role a redeemable attraction, as it would "amuse and please many." It went on to note that his performance "helps to throw into relief the unreality of the picture." *Variety* (November 1, 1932) struggled to see the potential of another Universal horror picture:

> A somewhat inane picture, its eeriness and general spooky character, further fortified by Boris (Frankenstein) Karloff's presence in the cast, should make *The Old Dark House* worthwhile at the box-offices of the lesser stands. As the title suggests, *The Old Dark House* lends itself to almost everything previously pulled by *Dracula*, *Frankenstein*, *White Zombie* and the rest of that ilk. The Priestley material must have been a bit more plausible in its literary form than as evidenced in the cinematic translation. But regardless, it has all the elements for horror and thriller exploitation.

Like the previous critic, the *Variety* reviewer found merit in Laughton's supporting performance: "Charles Laughton turned in one of his usually tophole performances as the Lancashire Knight." In *Motion Picture Herald* (February 25, 1933), exhibitor Edward L. Ornstein of the small-town Vernon Theatre, Mount Vernon, Kentucky, spoke highly of the film: "Played this one New Year's Eve and 75% of the audience of the regular performance came back to see it at the midnight show. Great little picture." In *Hollywood Filmograph* (July 16, 1932), it was stated, "James Whale has directed what looks like one of the worst pictures he has made for Universal."

The paying public knew better. For many years, Whale's gothic masterpiece was consigned to oblivion, having been withdrawn from circulation. Curtis Harrington, a friend of the late James Whale, instituted a search of the Universal vaults and it was due to his persistence that a print was discovered there in 1968. The recent 4k digital restoration of the surviving film elements enables audiences to once again appreciate all its eccentricities, delights, foibles and inconsistencies. Historian William K. Everson summed up the film accurately when he noted, "*The Old Dark House* is a film which on first viewing appears rather disappointing, but one ends up wishing to view it again. In so doing, the film gains enormously from such repeated viewings" (Theodore Huff Memorial Film Society, Program Notes, September 8, 1970).

Laughton's acting in the film is certainly all of a piece and stays in the memory. The film with only a small cast is meticulous in its form, and all ten performances are definitive. As suggested, *The Old Dark House* does accommodate numerous rescreenings.

Payment Deferred (1932)

Tagline: "The Supreme Acting of this Generation is provided by CHARLES LAUGHTON…."[14]

U.S. (Metro-Goldwyn-Mayer)

Credits: Directed by Lothar Mendes; Screenplay: Ernest Vajda and Claudine West; Based on the Play by Jeffrey F. Dell; Recording Director: Douglas Shearer; Art Director: Cedric Gibbons; Photography: Merritt B. Gerstad; Editor: Frank Sullivan; **Uncredited Technical Credits**: Assistant Director: Richard Rosson; Music: William Axt; Orchestrator: Charles Maxwell; Sound: Paul Neal; Costumes: Adrian; U.S. release: November 7, 1932; Genre: Thriller; Black and White; Running Time: 81 minutes; 35mm print held at the George Eastman Museum; Not commercially available on disc. Film excerpts are available to download on the Turner Classic Movies Website.

Cast: Charles Laughton (*William "Willie" Marble*); Maureen O'Sullivan (*Winnie Marble*); Verree Teasdale (*Mme. Collins*); Dorothy Peterson (*Annie Marble*); Ray Milland (*James Medland*); Billy Bevan (*Hammond*); Halliwell Hobbes (*A Prospective Tenant*); William Stack (*A Doctor*); **Uncredited Cast**: Ethel Griffies (*Customer in Collins' Dress Shop*); Crauford Kent (*Broker*); Doris Lloyd (*Woman Exchanging Foreign Currency in Bank*); C. Montague Shaw (*Mr. Edwards*); Carl Stockdale (*Jailer*); Harry Stubbs (*Mr. Evans*).

Synopsis: Winnie Marble is seen walking through her old neighborhood and looking at the deserted suburban South London home

Payment Deferred (1932)

where she grew up. Inside, an estate agent, Hammond, and a prospective client discuss the lurid history of its previous owner, notorious murderer William Marble. The story proper unfolds in a flashback of a tale of domestic debt as bank clerk Marble, due to his wife's pretensions and demands, becomes indebted to numerous creditors. On his way to the bank, local shopkeepers remind him of the money they are owed. Even at work, he is harangued by a colleague for the money he borrowed. The assistant bank manager calls him into his office to talk about £125 13/-6 d he is being sued for. On his return home, he confronts his wife about her incessant spending. All seems lost when a distant relative, James Medland, pays a visit. Attracted by Medland's apparent wealth, Marble invites him to invest in a lucrative speculation on the French franc. Medland is interested neither in financial investments or loaning capital with which Marble can use to speculate.

Driven to despair by this news, Marble decides to kill Medland by spiking his drink with cyanide. When he dies, Marble steals the money from his wallet and buries the body in the backyard. His sudden acquisition of money arouses the suspicion of his wife, who assumes he has embezzled from the bank. Marble begins to fret and makes the acquaintance of a French woman, Rita Collins, who blackmails him. He is arrested by the police on a charge of murdering his wife, who had in fact committed suicide when she heard of Marble's affair with Rita. As Marble languishes in prison preparing to be hanged, he is visited by his remorseful daughter Winnie, who blames herself for her mother's death. Marble comforts her by saying he is only paying back a delayed payment for his deeds in the past.

Selected Dialogue:

MARBLE: "You've got the capital and I've got the knowledge. It seems to me we ought to make a pretty strong combination."

MARBLE: "But, dash it all! You don't object to making money, do you? If the franc goes to 60 and you'd bought tonight you'd make a hundred percent on your money. But if you bought it on margin, you'd make a thousand!"

Production Commentary: *Payment Deferred* is of historical importance as it is a record of a stage performance Laughton had performed and honed on both the London and Broadway stages. Along with *On the Spot*, it marked public awareness of Laughton as a sensational young stage actor on both sides of the Atlantic. The play and film are taken from the 1926 crime novel of the same name by English novelist Cecil Louis Troughton Smith (1899–1966), who wrote under the pen name of Cecil Scott Forester.[15]

Laughton undertook a character role in an unsensational story of a timid and petulant man who murders someone to get out of debt and then lives undetected and unhappy in sordid luxury. He

A candid photo of Dorothy Peterson and Laughton sitting in reflective mood on the soundstage of MGM's murder thriller *Payment Deferred* (1932).

is later convicted of another crime he did not commit. Elsa Lanchester had appeared on stage in the part of Winnie his daughter. Because Laughton was not, as yet, an identified Hollywood star, MGM took the decision to surround him with named studio contract actors. The part of Winnie Marble therefore went to Maureen O'Sullivan. Although Lanchester had tried to lobby Irving Thalberg for the role, it was to no avail and she decided to return to England. During the opening film credits, Laughton's name appears beneath the main title. Beneath his name sits a joint billing of Maureen O'Sullivan and Verree Teasdale. Beneath their names is that of Dorothy Peterson. Another relative unknown in the cast was a callow, youthful British actor, Ray Milland. He had made his Hollywood debut just a year before in a minor role in *The Bachelor Father* (MGM, Robert Z. Leonard, 1931) and was already on his tenth picture. In his autobiography, Milland remembered catching Laughton on the London stage in a performance as a Chicago gangster in *On the Spot*. Milland was anything but impressed, finding Laughton's makeup and physique on stage bizarre and the widespread critical acclaim showered on the actor equally puzzling. Now he found himself acting opposite him. In his book, he gave a hostile account of the experience. He found Laughton was prone to performing outrageous grotesqueries. In a crucial scene, Laughton's character had to walk up into the camera lens for a huge close-up so the audience would read into his face the beginning of his decision to commit homicide. Milland recalled Laughton's eyes rolled, his upper lip twitched and quivered and then he salivated. Resuming his composure, he went on to finish the scene. The director yelled cut and while waiting for the next camera set-up, Milland asked the director his opinion of the scene they had just shot. Mendes said, "It's self-indulgence, theatrical masturbation" (Milland: 142). Because Mendes was a good editor, none or very little of these aberrations found their way in the final cut. He warned Milland not to feel superior about this as it was an occupational disease with many actors. If he was not careful, he would be doing the same thing if he should last that long. After the picture was finished, MGM opted not to renew Milland's contract.

Critical opinion was mainly respectful and mindful of Laughton's efforts. The *National Board of Review Magazine* (November 1932) wrote, "His performance, so carefully planned and expertly executed. So consistent, so seldom marred by extravagance or monotony, puts him a class with the German Kortner, Jannings and Krauss, at their frequent best, and with the American Barrymores at their best not so frequent. He is an actor, in the deliberately creative sense, and not merely a personality." *The New York State Exhibitor* (September 25, 1932) was more sanguine: "Granted that Charles Laughton is a fine actor, but that won't help him much. *Payment Deferred* just won't make the grade."

A pre–Code film, *Payment on Demand* encountered censorial disapproval. *What Shocked the Censor: Complete Record of Cuts in Motion Picture Films Ordered by New York* (October 1932) reveals that the censor insisted on three deletions and a dialogue cut. In reel three, a shot of Marble pouring poison into a glass was ordered eliminated. In reel five, a shot of Rita coming down the stairway in the Marble home was ordered eliminated as it explicitly demonstrated intimacy between them. Also in reel five, a dialogue cut was demanded: "It is I who give you everything, and you..."

Although the film was not popular at the box office, its subject matter being viewed as too downbeat and squalid, Laughton's performance as the milquetoast bank clerk garnered a measure of critical acclaim. The role is there for Laughton to shape with meticulous thoroughness. As was his wont, Laughton insisted on playing scenes over and over again using a low-pitched voice and sparing gestures. If the play is sordid and has little dignity, Laughton brings care and consideration to the role.

If I Had a Million (1932)

Tagline: "You've Dreamed It! Now See It Come True!"[16]

U.S. (Paramount Publix Corporation)

Credits: Directors: Ernst Lubitsch ("The Clerk"); Norman Taurog ("Prologue and Epilogue"); Stephen Roberts ("Violet" and "Grandma"); Norman McLeod ("China Shop" and "Road Hogs"); James Cruze ("Death Cell"); William A. Seiter ("The Three Marines"); H. Bruce Humberstone ("The Forger"); Writers: Claude Binyon, Whitney Bolton, Malcolm Stuart Boylan,

If I Had a Million (1932)

John Bright, Sidney Buchman, Lester Cole, Isabel Dawn, Boyce DeGaw, Oliver H.P. Garrett, Harvey Gates, Grover Jones, Ernst Lubtisch, Lawton Mackall, Joseph L. Mankiewicz, William Slavens McNutt, Robert Sparks; Based on the Novel *Windfall* by Robert D. Andrews (New York, 1931); **Uncredited Technical Credits**: Producer: Louis D. Lighton; Photographers: Gilbert Warrenton ("China Shop"), Harry Fischbeck ("The Clerk"); Alvin Wyckoff, Frank Titus (Second Camera) ("Road Hogs"), Charles Schoenbaum, George Clemens (Second Camera) ("Death Cell"), C. Edgar Schoenbaum ("The Three Marines"); U.S. release: November 30, 1932; Genre: Comedy Drama; Black and White; Running Time: 88 minutes; DVD Region 1, *W.C. Fields Comedy Essentials Collection* box set, released October 2015; DVD Region 2, *The W.C. Fields Collection* box set, released December 2007; English subtitle captions for the deaf and hard of hearing are available on these discs.

Cast: Gary Cooper (*Steven Gallagher*); **Charles Laughton (*Phineas Lambert*)**; George Raft (*Edward Jackson*); Jack Oakie (*Private Mulligan*); Richard Bennett (*John Glidden*); Charlie Ruggles (*Henry Peabody*); Alison Skipworth (*Emily La Rue*); W.C. Fields (*Rollo La Rue*); Mary Boland (*Mrs. Peabody*); Roscoe Karns (*Private O'Brien*); May Robson (*Mrs. Mary Walker*); **Uncredited Cast**: Willard Robertson (*Fred*); Reginald Barlow (*Otto K. Bullwinkle*); Larry Steers, John St. Polis, Herbert Moulton (*Glidden Associates*); Fred Santley (*Glidden's Assistant*); Bess Flowers (*Customer*); Fred Holmes (*China Shop Clerk*); Irving Bacon (*Charlie Smithers*); Russ Powell (*Bartender*); Wynne Gibson (*Violet Smith*); Jack Pennick (*Sailor*); Hooper Atchley (*Hotel Desk Clerk*); Kent Taylor (*Bank Teller*); Wallis Clark (*Mr. Monroe—Bank Manager*); Harry C. Bradley (*Bank Watchman*); Charles McMurphy (*Mike—Bank Plainclothesman*); Robert E. Homans (*Detective*); James Bush (*Bowen—Teller at Second Bank*); Edwin Stanley (*Mr. Galloway—Bank Manager*); William V. Mong (*Harry—Edward Jackson's Fence*); Morgan Wallace (*Mike—Edward Jackson's Gangster Associate*); Billy Butts (*Newsboy in Bank*); Jerry Tucker (*Crying Boy with Balloon*); Morgan Wallace (*Mike—Associate of Edward Jackson*); Cecil Cunningham (*Agnes Dupont*); Gene Raymond (*John Wallace*); Grant Mitchell (*Priest*); Fred Kelsey (*Prison Officer*); Frances Dee (*Mary Wallace*); Berton Churchill (*Prison Warden*); Clarence Muse (*Death Row Convict*); Lew Kelly (*Prison Barber*); Edward LeSaint (*Mr. Brown*); James P. Burtis (*Marine Jailer*); Joyce Compton (*Marie—Waitress*); Lucien Littlefield (*Zeb—Hamburger Stand Owner*); Walter Percival (*Carnival Worker*); Tom Kennedy (*Joe—Carnival Bouncer*); Frank Hagney (*Mike—Carnival Bouncer*); Gertrude Norman, Emma Tansey, Margaret Mann, Joy Winthrop, Lydia Knott, Clair T. Bracy, Vangie Beilby, Joy Winthrop, Mai Wells (*Idylwood Residents*); Edith Yorke (*Idylwood Resident with Parkinson's Disease*); Blanche Friderici (*Mrs. Garvey*); Dewey Robinson (*Mr. Popadopoulos*); Margaret Seddon (*Mrs. Small*); Samuel S. Hinds (*Lawyer*); Gail Patrick (*Secretary*); Eddie Baker (*Second Desk Clerk*); Marc Lawrence (*Mike's Henchman*); Thomas Ricketts (*Dancing Partner at Idylwood*); Syd Saylor (*Driver*); Lester Dorr (*Pedestrian at Accident*); Effie Ellsler (*Mrs. Scott*); Ida Lewis (*Mrs. Davis*); Lilian Harmer (*Attendant*); Shirley Grey (*Mae*).

Synopsis: Suffering from a terminal illness, eccentric multi-millionaire John Glidden decides to turn his financial back on his relatives and employees. Instead, he gives away $8,000,000 of his personal fortune to strangers chosen at random from the city phone directory. This is the pretext for Glidden to present a check for a million dollars to each recipient in person.

"China Shop": The first recipient is a henpecked husband, Henry Peabody. Because his wife docks his meager pay for breakage of china, he decides to smash all the china in the shop he works in.

"Violet": Prostitute Violet Smith receives her check and decides to rent a luxurious room in a top hotel, and sleep alone in a spacious double-bed without her "trade" stockings on.

"The Forger": Forger Edward Jackson is unable to convince either his underworld contacts or legitimate members of the banking community that his check is real and no forgery. Unable to cash it, he ends up in a flop house, deranged with laughter at his own misfortune. Jackson's check arouses the suspicions of the house manager. He phones the police authorities and then proceeds to burn the million-dollar check.

"Road Hogs": Ex-vaudevillians Emily and Rollo La Rue hate road hogs. They hire a fleet of old jalopies and deliberately drive road hogs off the road. When their vengeance spree is finished, they decide to buy a new motor car outright. As they drive their car from the showroom, another road hog irreparably damages it.

"Death Cell": When John Wallace, a man on Death Row, gets the news about the check, he is initially distressed, but then regains his composure when he realizes his widow Mary will be financially secure on his death.

"The Clerk": Phineas V. Lambert, a mild-mannered clerk, is at his desk at work when he receives his check. Lambert calmly confronts the company boss in his office and proceeds to give him a tongue-blowing "razzy." He then retires in quiet satisfaction.

"The Three Marines": The seventh check goes to a group of three boisterous Marines: Steven Gallagher and his pals Mulligan and O'Brien. They all suspect the check is a hoax and decide to head to Coney Island with their girlfriends. As they have little money, Gallagher decides to sign the check over to Zeb, the illiterate owner of a fair stand. He gets Zeb to cash the check, telling him it is worth just $10. Gallagher and his girlfriend Marie go to the carnival, but he cannot lose his buddies. Mulligan becomes embroiled in a fight and the three pals end up behind bars. Imagine their surprise when they see Zeb step from a limousine escorted by a well-dressed Marie.

"Grandma": Mary Walker is an oppressed inmate in a rest home for old ladies. The matron of the home insists the residents sit idly in their rocking chairs and they are barred from engaging in any activity or chores. When her check is presented to her, the old lady changes the regime. The inmates are given tasks around the home. The former matron and her staff are forced to sit in rocking chairs and helplessly watch the hive of activity around them. Observing Mary's can-do attitude, Glidden feels himself cured of his terminal illness and decides he must spend more time with Mary Walker in the former rest home. In time, he hopes, matrimony may result.

Production Commentary: "The Clerk," sixth vignette in *If I Had a Million*, remains a model of brevity and succinctness. Lasting just over two minutes, the scene is performed mainly in silence and contains just three words of dialogue. It stars Laughton as yet another downtrodden clerk who gives his boss a comeuppance: a Bronx cheer. The adroit direction was by that shrewd purveyor of sophisticated comedy Ernst Lubitsch.

At its best, this pre–Code portmanteau film uses social satire to observe the aftermath of the financial shock waves of the Great Depression as they work their way through the stratas of the social classes. This particular episode certainly enhanced the already considerable reputations of both an up-and-coming star and a celebrated director.

Along with the W.C. Fields "Road Hogs" episode, it has gone down in the folklore of Hollywood film comedy. *Film Daily* (October 5, 1932) reported that Mary Boland had been cast in the film in support of Richard Bennett and Charlie Ruggles. Fredric March, Sylvia Sidney, Gail Patrick and Blanche Friderici were also mentioned as being brought into the film's cast. Nearly two weeks later, *Film Daily* (October 18, 1932) stated that Laughton was cast under the direction of Lubitsch. Preparation on the film had begun by early September 1932. Filming began late October 1932 on Stage 10 at the Paramount studios. The film opened at New York's Rivoli Theatre on November 30, 1932. It was deemed to be only partially successful. In *A Pictorial History of the Movies*, it was given a backhanded compliment: "It was something of a hodgepodge, and ushered in no new era in picture-making, but it was undeniably entertaining" (Taylor: 258). *Hollywood Filmograph* (November 12, 1932) found the film exceptional in its ability to disregard the old adage of "too many cooks spoil the broth," and called it "a history-making talkie."

In retrospect, the greatest accolade the film received was from one master filmmaker to another. The international influence of Lubitsch's approach to comedy was recognized in the Japanese film *Tokyo no Onna* (*Woman of Tokyo*) (Schochiku, 1933), directed by the celebrated Yasujirô Ozu (1903–1963). In the story, a young couple goes to the cinema and on the screen they see the scene of the clerk finding his million dollar check and then proceeding upstairs and through many doors to the office of the company president. The confrontational climax between the clerk and his boss is, in typical Ozu style, omitted. (Toward the end of his life, Laughton was able to fulfill an ambition to travel to Japan and study the various flowers and plants in the countryside.)

Laughton and Lubitsch proved a formidable team and their creative endeavors are an imperishable highlight of this pre–Code talkie.

The Sign of the Cross (1932)

Tagline: "A picture which will proudly lead all the entertainments the world has ever seen"[17]

U.S. (Paramount Publix Corporation)

The Sign of the Cross (1932)

Credits: Directed by Cecil B. DeMille; Screenplay: Waldemar Young and Sidney Buchman; From the Play by Wilson Barrett; Photography: Karl Struss; Costumes: Mitchell Leisen; **Uncredited Technical Credits**: Art Director: Mitchell Leisen; Assistant Directors: Mitchell Leisen, Edward Salven; Editor: Anne Bauchens; Music: Rudolph Kopp, Nathaniel Finston; Sound: Harry Lindgren. U.S. release: February 10, 1933; U.S. reissue: December 1, 1944; Genre: Religious Epic; Black and White; Running Time: 124 minutes; 1944 reissue: 118 minutes; DVD Region 1, *Cecil B. DeMille Collection*, Universal, released May 2006; DVD Region 1, Universal Cinema Classics series, released May 2011; English subtitle captions for the deaf and hard of hearing are available on these discs.

Cast: Fredric March (*Marcus*); Elissa Landi (*Mercia*); Claudette Colbert (*Poppaea*); **Charles Laughton** (*Nero*); Ian Keith (*Tigellinus*); Arthur Hoyl (*Titus*); Harry Beresford (*Favius*); Tommy Conlon (*Stephan*); Ferdinand Gottschalk (*Glabrio*); Vivian Tobin (*Dacia*); William V. Mong (*Licinius*); Joyzelle (*Ancaria*); Richard Alexander (*Viturius*); Nat Pendleton (*Strabo*); Clarence Burton (*Servillius*); Harold Healy (*Tybul*); Robert Manning (*Philodemus*); Charles Middleton (*Tyros*); **Uncredited Cast**: Mischa Auer (*Christian in Dungeon*); Lionel Belmore (*Bettor of 300 Silver*); True Boardman (*Nero's Slave*); Marjorie Bonner (*Roman Woman*); Joe Bonomo (*Mute Torturer*); Henry Brandon (*Colosseum Spectator*); George Bruggeman (*Nero's Slave*); John Carradine (*Christian Martyr/Voice in Coliseum*); Lane Chandler (*Chained Christian*); Ruth Clifford (*Christian Mother at Meeting*); Wynne Gibson (*Orgy Guest*); Lillian Leighton (*Woman Getting Gold for Cup*); Edward LeSaint (*Enthusiastic Spectator*); Gertrude Norman, Florence Turner (*Christians*); Wedgwood Nowell (*Man Accepting 300 Silver Bet*); Dave O'Brien (*Christian on Stairway*); William H.

A pre–Code extravaganza. *The Sign of the Cross* (1932) showcased sumptuous art direction, opulent costumes and multitudes of extras. This biblical tale of Roman power versus Christian faith also provided memorable roles for an array of acting talent. Left to right: Unidentified player, Laughton as the decadent Emperor Nero, Claudette Colbert as the shrewd Empress Poppaea and Fredric March as Marcus Superbus, the fiery Prefect of Rome. All are marshaled to cinematic grandeur under the directorial baton of the legendary Cecil B. De Mille.

O'Brien (*Man Who Heard Lions*); Hal Price (*Spectator*); Sally Rand (*Crocodiles' Victim*); Tom Ricketts (*Sleeping Spectator*); Angelo Rossitto (*Impaled Pygmy*); Ynez Seabury (*Little Girl*); Kent Taylor (*Roman Spectator*); Ethel Wales (*Complaining Wife*).

Awards: Academy Award Nomination: Best Cinematography: Karl Struss.

Synopsis: In Rome 64 AD, a great fire is destroying the city. Emperor Nero is rumored to have been responsible for the start of the fire. He blames the Christians, who he feels are a potential threat to his rule as emperor and master of the civilized world. A stranger from Jerusalem, Titus, arrives in Rome. An apostle of Jesus, he has come to deliver the message of St. Paul. He identifies himself by drawing a half sign of the Christian cross with his stick on the ground. A native of Rome, Flavius, responds by drawing the other half sign of the cross. They are both caught and arrested. Marcus, Prefect of Rome, arrives and intervenes. Following appeals from Mercia, a young Christian girl, he sets the two men free. Dacia, a courtier to Empress Poppaea, is infatuated with Marcus, and she takes the news of his meeting with the Christian girl. Tigellinus, a rival of Marcus who is competing for Nero's attention, decides to arrest the two Christians released by Marcus. When Mercia sends young Stephan on an errand, Tigellinus has him abducted and tortured to reveal the site of a secret Christian meeting place. He reveals the meeting place but before he can name the Christian Mercia, he faints. Marcus, learning of Stephan's imprisonment, is able to tend his wounds and obtain from him the location of the meeting. Then with his legions he pursues Tigellinus. En route he is detained by the Empress Poppaea. By the time Marcus arrives, Tigellinus' men have broken up the meeting and Flavius and Titus have both been killed. Marcus rescues Mercia and orders the remaining Christians to be sent to prison. Marcus takes Mercia to his palace and there he meets Poppaea, who in an effort to crush Marcus's affection for Mercia professes her love for him. Tigellinus denounces Marcus' loyalty to the emperor and suggests Nero should execute him for treason. Poppaea intercedes, claiming that Marcus's disloyalty is based not on religious convictions, but on sexual attraction for the young Christian girl. She proposes that Mercia be taken away from Marcus. At that moment, Marcus expresses his love to Mercia, but she suggests he is only interested in her body. He rejects this and curses her devotion to Christianity. During a palace orgy, Marcus mocks Mercia and has an erotic dance performed to humiliate Mercia. Outside, Christians sing a hymn which drowns out both music and dance inside the palace. Marcus is therefore forced to curtail the orgy. Mercia explains the power of Christian faith and Marcus responds by forcing himself upon her. He is interrupted by Tigellinus, who orders Mercia's arrest. Marcus appeals to Nero to release Mercia, but Poppaea insists she should die. The following day at the Roman arena, thousands pack inside to witness the spectacle of Christians being fed to lions. Nero lays on other forms of bloodthirsty sport for the amusement of the crowds. In the dungeon where the Christians await their fate, Stephan tells Mercia he is afraid. She tells him they will both be reunited in Heaven. Marcus arrives and pleads with her to renounce her faith so she may live. She is not persuaded. Marcus decides he must join Mercia in eternal love and accompanies her to their final destiny in the arena. As they climb the steps of the dungeon arm in arm, doors leading to the arena are closed. As they shut, light from above shines and the sign of the cross appears on the doors.

Selected Dialogue:

NERO: "Burn, Rome! Burn!"
NERO: "My head is splitting. The wine last night, the music, the delicious debauchery."
NERO: "Have a little consideration. Would you have me late for the games?"

Production Commentary: *The Sign of the Cross* was produced during the period between 1927 and 1934, which film historians now refer to as the era of the pre–Code film. In 1922, a year after the Roscoe "Fatty" Arbuckle scandal in which Hollywood was cast in an unflattering light, the industry formed a trade association, the Motion Pictures Producers and Distributors of America (MPPDA). To "maintain a clean moral tone," the MPPDA instituted a code of conduct for film content. In 1930, the MPPDA (with the involvement of Catholic Church representatives) drew up a Production Code designed to assuage anxieties expressed by religious groups and educationalists that children would acquire antisocial tendencies from watching films. Much of this fear was intensified by the introduction of sound.

The Code therefore had a strong moral content in terms of dealing with the representation of sex and violence on the screen. The industry was eager to take up the opportunity afforded by self-regulation, given its challenging remit of satisfying worldwide audiences of diverse cultural, religious and political persuasions. Self-regulation rather than direct state control was the preferred option in that it afforded a better strategy to shape the content of films so they would be salable to as many markets as possible. The code was administered by the Studio Relations Committee (SRC) and its successor, the Production Code Administration (PCA). The precipitous slump of the world economy during the early 1930s encouraged the Hollywood studios to adopt a cynical and reckless tone in the content and depiction of violence, racy dialogue and suggestive situations. The Code appeared to be plainly contravened. In July 1934, the Catholic Legion of Decency, headed by Joseph Ignatius Breen (1888–1965), began strict enforcement of the Motion Picture Production Code (MPPC). All films had to have a PCA seal of approval to be exhibited in theaters. Failure to get a seal invited heavy fines and boycotts. Films produced before the enforcement of the MPPC in 1934 also had to comply with the new regime and be awarded a seal. Failure to resubmit a film for a seal of approval resulted in the film being kept indefinitely on the shelves of film vaults.

Cecil B. DeMille was no stranger to the controversy of film censorship. Titles such as *Old Wives for New* (1918), *Don't Change Your Husband* (1919), *Male and Female* (1919) and *Why Change Your Wife* set the tone of a new modernity based on consumerism, female sexuality and divorce which overturned the old domesticity based on Victorian morality. DeMille's *The Sign of the Cross* is an ingenious example of expedient commercial smoke and mirrors. It is a tribute to its director's ability to extract the maximum ingredients of an ancient world epic (grandiose spectacle, proportionate action, salacious sex and the barbarity of slavery), all successfully achieved in the face of budgetary constraints.

The film was based on the celebrated Wilson Barrett stage play first performed in 1895. This four-act historical tragedy became an overnight success on both sides of the Atlantic and spawned two silent film adaptations. The first, a 700-foot production by British film pioneer William Haggar (1851–1925), was distributed in 1904 by Gaumont.[18] The second was a five-reel 1914 feature produced by Frederick Thomson for Famous Players Film Company (the forerunner of Paramount Pictures).

By the early 1930s, DeMille had hit a run of bad luck in his choice of film material and there followed a series of box office flops. The deepening economic depression saw Paramount in corporate turmoil. Eventually the old studio, Paramount Publix, collapsed and a new corporate studio, Paramount Pictures, took its place. DeMille told studio bosses he would keep costs down and bring the picture in on schedule and proceeded to produce the film using various cost-cutting measures. The film performed extremely well at the box office both domestically and abroad, proving that DeMille's moneymaking skills had not deserted him. DeMille economized by reusing old costumes, building partial sets and employing back projection and model miniatures.

Within this spectacle, Laughton as Nero sits both literally and figuratively as a frivolous, capricious despot who holds his subjects' destinies by a thread. It is a testament to his acting abilities that he manages to create a memorable impression given that his character occupies so little of the two hours of screen time. However, his three appearances are concise and well-drawn by virtue of their strategic positioning within the narrative. Following the opening credits, he appears as megalomaniac Nero, strumming on his lyre surveying the conflagration of Rome. Next the sybaritic Nero is seen on his throne nursing his head, swollen from a night devoted to "delicious debauchery." And in the finale, both the extravagant and the tyrannical are on display as Nero is glimpsed surveying and controlling the spectacle of parades, crowds, games and sacrificial contests in the arena.

DeMille and Laughton disagreed on the portrayal of the character of Emperor Nero.

DeMille viewed Nero as a menace while Laughton saw him as risible. After some considerable argument, Laughton was allowed to interpret the role his way. At the preview, the audience did indeed laugh, but when DeMille confronted Laughton about their reaction, Laughton explained that if you were to meet such a person, you would find their egocentric foibles funny. Only the power they wielded made them sinister. Laughton portrays Nero as a spoiled child, by turns narcissistic, petulant and capricious. In a *Picture Play* interview (May 1935), Laughton mused, "Why is it, do you suppose, that I have gone as far as I have? [...] Is it because I suggest 'fleur de mal,' a dash of the decadent, a bit of the bestial, do you think?"

In his playing of a voluptuous Emperor Nero, Laughton creates just the appropriate amount of scandalous innuendo that pre–Code film and Cecil B. DeMille would tolerate. There are occasional moments in the script when the dialogue lapses into the risible humor found in Sondheim's "toga musical" *A Funny Thing Happened on the Way to the Forum* or its British spin-off, the television "toga comedy" series *Up Pompeii!* For instance, a cod remark spoken by Dacia, "I was famished for a chat." Or Poppaea's wry observation to Dacia, "Why, you're perspiring with news." The binary opposition of good vs. evil common to all historical epics permeates the narrative: stoical Christians being fed to lions, and the equally horrifying sights of bestial slayings of animals in the Roman arena, as braying and voracious crowds look on agog; a titillating lesbian dance scene at a Roman orgy; and Claudette Colbert's Poppaea naked bathing in asses' milk, as she schemes to hold Nero's favor, influence and power. All are played out against a background of Christian piety and faith.

Yet, despite DeMille's strategy of playing religion off with sex and violence and using a shrewd sense of what can be implied by means of proportionate and suitable good taste, the film subsequently underwent various alterations and cuts upon reissue. For a 1944 wartime reissue, a nine-minute prologue was added, in which American fliers are seen soaring over the eternal city of Rome in a bombardment of propaganda leaflets. Aboard are a Catholic and a Protestant chaplain as observers. The original release print was rediscovered in 1994 and the film today is restored to its original integrity. The luscious photography on display throughout was supplied by the inventive Karl Struss, who shot the black and white picture through bright red gauze to "give a feeling of a world remembered" (Higham: 128). He was Oscar-nominated for Best Cinematography.

Critics of the day were pretty unanimous in declaring the film a very sound commercial attraction. *Film Daily* (December 2, 1932) exclaimed, "[I]t fairly bristles with action, feminine pulchritude, royal dissipation, and orgies of mortal combat in the arena." *Variety* (December 6, 1932) noted that there was only one exceptional performance: Laughton's: "With upmost subtlety and a minimum effort, he manages to get over his queer character before his first appearance is a minute old. The few laughs in a picture that's very weak in the comedy department are all Laughton's." *The New York State Exhibitor* (December 10, 1932) didn't pull its punches when it estimated the film would be "Knockout." It went on to state, "*Sign of the Cross* will make money anywhere. It is worth all the attention every house can give it. In short, it is a phenomenal attraction."

The hyperbole was justified as the film was produced on a budget of $694,065 and went on to gross a mammoth $2,783,993 worldwide (Birchard: 368). The London *Times* (July 15, 1933) reported that Laughton was given the accolade of a waxwork of himself as Nero in a touring Madame Tussauds exhibition. Twenty-two years later, the film was satirized in the Bugs Bunny cartoon *Roman Legion-Hare* (Warner Bros., Friz Freleng, 1955); an animated version of Laughton's Nero was on prominent display just as he was in the original film. *The Sign of the Cross* was yet another fillip in Laughton's meteoric film career.

Island of Lost Souls (1932)

Tagline: "She Was His Masterpiece! Woman Out of Panther...."[19]

U.S. (Paramount Publix Corporation)

Credits: Directed by Erle C. Kenton; Screenplay: Waldemar Young and Philip Wylie; From a novel by H.G. Wells; Photography: Karl Struss; **Uncredited Technical Credits**: Art Director: Hans Dreier; Makeup: Wally Westmore, Charles Gemora; Music: Arthur Johnston, Sigmund

Krumgold; Visual Effects: Gordon Jennings; U.S. release: December 29, 1932; U.K. release: Banned on its initial release by the British Board of Film Censors, later passed on July 9, 1958; Genre: Horror; Black and White; Running Time: 70 minutes; DVD Region 1 and Blu-ray Region A, the Criterion Collection, released October 2011; Dual format edition: DVD Region 2 and Blu-ray Region B, Masters of Cinema, Eureka Entertainment, released May 2012; English subtitle captions for the deaf and hard of hearing are available on these discs.

Cast: Charles Laughton (*Dr. Moreau*); Richard Arlen (*Edward Parker*); Leila Hyams (*Ruth Parker*); Bela Lugosi (*Sayer of the Law*); Kathleen Burke (*The Panther Woman*); Arthur Hohl (*Montgomery*); Stanley Fields (*Captain Davies*); Paul Hurst (*Donahue*); Hans Steinke (*Ouran*); Tetsu Komai (*M'ling*); George Irving (*The Consul*); **Uncredited Cast**: Robert Kortman (*Hogan*); Harry Ekezian (*Gola*); Rosemary Grimes (*Samoan Girl*); Joe Bonomo, Constantine Romanoff, John George, Robert Milasch, Duke York (*Beasts*); Charles Gemora (*Gorilla on Pier*); Schlitze (*Furry Mammal*); Buster Brodie (*Pig Man*).

Synopsis: A trading ship, the S.S. *Covena*, en route to Apia, Samoa, finds a lifeboat afloat with an unconscious man, Edward Parker, aboard. When he recovers, the *Covena*'s medic, Montgomery, suggests they take a turn around the deck. On deck, Parker notices a cargo of cages containing wild lions, tigers, apes, monkeys and dogs. Montgomery introduces Parker to Captain Davies. The men of the *Covena* later begin unloading its animal cargo onto a waiting vessel captained by Dr. Moreau. Parker is kayoed by Davies and thrown overboard onto Moreau's vessel. Moreau offers Parker the chance to take a schooner with Montgomery to find his way back to the nearest port. Parker accepts the offer and also hospitality in the doctor's home. As well as wearing a belt and loaded revolver, Moreau carries a whip which he uses to assert his authority over the natives of the island. Moreau confides to Montgomery that Parker has been brought to the house to meet Lota; the doctor's latest experiment. Moreau says Lota is pure Polynesian and the only woman on the island. A shrieking sound of someone being tortured is heard from the house. When Parker asks what the noise is, Lota replies it is from the House of Pain. Parker rushes into the house to discover Dr. Moreau, assisted by Montgomery, in the middle of a vivisection operation. Parker decides Lota and he must escape from the island immediately. However, their way is barred by the natives who gather around the couple in a menacing manner. Moreau appears on a hillside where he strikes a gong, cracks a whip and shouts the question: "What is the law?" Moreau disperses the natives and brings Parker and Lota back to the house. He shows Parker around the extensive gardens and his laboratory where he explains his fantastic and diabolic bio-anthropological research. These began in London, where his experiments were picked up by the newspapers, who hounded Moreau out of England. Before leaving, he picked up Montgomery, a medical student facing a custodial sentence for professional misconduct. Parker is repulsed to learn that the natives are part of Moreau's attempt to make animals into humans. The

Stars break for lunch at the Paramount Studio commissary in November 1932. Left to right: Alison Skipworth, writer Aldous Huxley conversing with Laughton—in costume and makeup as Dr. Moreau in the studio's production of *Island of Lost Souls* (1932)—and Frances Dee.

(1932) Island of Lost Souls

following morning, the schooner that was to take Parker away lies wrecked in the water. Moreau blames this on the native beasts of the island. In Apia, Parker's fiancée Ruth Thomas asks the American consul to question Captain Davies. He admits "dropping" Parker off on a small island. The consul warns the captain that if he finds any irregularities, he will revoke his license. Captain Donahue is called into the consul's office and offers to sail to the island with Ruth. Back on Dr. Moreau's island, Parker has fallen in love with Lota. As they embrace after a kiss, he finds her hands are in fact claws. Confronting Moreau, he is told that Lota was his most successful experiment. Parker strikes Moreau and he falls to the floor. Moreau then visits Lota only to find that her hands are indeed reverting to "the stubborn beast flesh." His disappointment is suspended when Lota sheds tears; the first of his creatures to do so. He decides to take Lota back to the House of Pain to arrest her reversion to animal form. Before he has a chance to carry out this corrective surgery, Captain Donahue and Ruth arrive in search of Parker. Reunited with Ruth, Parker wants to leave the island immediately but is frustrated by Moreau, who suggests they accept his hospitality for the night and set off in the morning. During the night, a native beast-man tries to break into Ruth's bedroom. The attempt is thwarted, and Parker tells her to dress quickly to make their escape. Montgomery hears the commotion and decides to leave even if he will be arrested on his return to England. Captain Donahue intends to return to the ship and bring back his crew. Moreau instructs one of his creatures, Ouran, to follow and kill him. When he has killed the captain, Ouran takes the body to the natives' settlement. This causes unrest as he has broken the law by spilling blood. The creatures realize that if this man (Captain Donahue) can die, then so can Moreau. When Moreau finds that the creatures intend to kill him, he decides to subjugate them with his whip, but the creatures turn on him and he is overpowered. Parker, Ruth, Montgomery and Lota make their escape through the jungle. Lota and Ouran tangle, and kill each other in the struggle. In his laboratory, Moreau is killed by his creatures. Montgomery, Parker and Ruth row to safety and look back to see fires raging on the island. Moreau's perverse fiefdom is no more.

Selected Dialogue:

MOREAU: "What is the law?"

MOREAU: "I went on with this research just as it led me. I let my imagination run fantastically ahead."

MOREAU: "Mr. Parker, spare me these youthful horrors, please."

MOREAU: "Mr. Parker. Do you know what it means to feel like God?"

MOREAU: "The stubborn beast flesh creeping back. Well, it's no use. I may as well quit. Day by day, it creeps back. It creeps back."

MOREAU: "This time, I'll burn out all the animal in her! I'll make her completely human."

MOREAU: "The natives, they have a curious ceremony. Mr. Parker's witnessed it. They are restless tonight."

MOREAU: "They're more than usually restless tonight."

Production Commentary: Inspired by the commercial success of Universal's *Dracula* and *Frankenstein,* Paramount paid $15,000 for the rights to H.G. Wells 1896 novel *The Island of Dr. Moreau.* The casting of the crew and actors would be fraught with many changes as the studio sought ways of dealing with the unsavory nature of the novel's subject matter. *Film Daily* (June 13, 1932) announced a cast comprising Nancy Carroll, Fay Wray, Irving Pichel, Boris Karloff, Bela Lugosi and Noah Beery. *Film Daily* (June 16, 1932), Randolph Scott was announced as a cast member. *Hollywood Filmographic* (June 25, 1935) reported that Edward Venturini would direct. *Film Daily* (August 8, 1932) announced Norman Taurog as director with Philip Wylie and Garrett Fort assigned as scenarists. *Variety* (August 8, 1932) announced that Venturini and Philip Wylie were taken off the film. Wylie was replaced by Fort, who had worked on the *Dracula* and *Frankenstein* screenplays. Fort had a penchant for injecting wry comedy into horror material. *Film Daily* (August 20, 1932) announced another change to the scenarists: Waldemar Young in collaboration with Thomas Burtis would be scripting. *Variety* (September 20, 1932) announced that director Norman Taurog was taken off the film as it was not his type. He was replaced by Erle C. Kenton who would, it was hoped, inject a subdued comic element into the fantastic yarn. *Film Daily* (October 17, 1932) reported George Irving, having completed work on *Rasputin and the Empress* (MGM, Richard Boleslawski, 1932), would join the cast and also Paul Hurst. *Film Daily* (October 19, 1932) announced Bela Lugosi had been definitely assigned to appear in the film. *Film Daily* (September 28, 1932) announced the cast as Richard Arlen, Charles Laughton, Irving Pichel and Arthur Hohl. *The New Paramount Punch* (November 16, 1932) said that Leila Hyams had joined the cast along with Pichel and Bela Lugosi and Boris Karloff together.

Much to author Wells' chagrin, Paramount introduced ballyhoo and exploitation by devising a nationwide campaign to find a newcomer to play a panther woman to add sexual interest to Wells' problematic story. A 19-year-old Chicago model, Kathleen Burke, was chosen from among 60,000 candidates. (Her fiancé Glen R. Rardin, a Chicago photographer, had submitted photographs to Paramount.) The 5'6" brunette had never worked in films, but had appeared in amateur productions in high school.

On the main title credits Laughton's name is given alongside that of Richard Arlen, and Laughton heads the end cast credits. In a *Photoplay* interview (October 1934), Laughton claimed that Arlen and he detested each other mutually during the making of the picture. Arlen took to calling Laughton "Buster." Only after the finish of the picture, when Laughton was introduced to Arlen's wife Joby, did Laughton and Arlen patch up their differences and become friends. Laughton was paid $2250 per week for his work on the film.

Shooting began on September 26, 1932. A budget of $300,000 was allocated to this production. There were two weeks location shooting on board ship at Catalina Island off the Los Angeles coast. Laughton found the smell of the animals, who accompanied the actors on board, very disconcerting. The animals were often sick, wild and dangerous, cooped up in their cages. One member of the company was severely mauled by a tiger. Laughton refused to travel back to the coast on the boat and instead flew back on a seaplane. After this experience, he was none too keen about visiting zoos. The rest of the shoot was conducted on the Paramount ranch. Laughton decided on a trim goatee beard after visiting a Hollywood eye doctor who had one. In several scenes, Dr. Moreau was called upon to use a whip. When it was suggested a double would be used in long shot for these scenes, Laughton casually announced that he would like to try cracking the whip himself. He executed the cracking of the whip with great assurance. What he did not tell the director or crew was he had perfected the proficient use of a long lash back in 1928 when he performed the part of Crispin in the stage play *A Man with Red Hair* under the direction of James Whale.

Director Erle C. Kenton and his team rose to the logistical challenges such a complex project demanded. *Cinema Progress* (May–June 1938) reported that Paramount's director of sound recording, Loren L. Ryder, was able to conjure up a strange and horrifying sound required for the patois of the animal men. Ryder managed to blend animal cries with human language. The recording was then played backwards, and then as a "cincher" he alternated the sound loop by first speeding it up and then slowing it down. The room where the synchronization of sound occurred and where a master negative soundtrack was made became known among the Paramount sound technicians as "The House of Pain." *The New Movie Magazine* (May 1933) reported that the extras who played Moreau's creatures were selected from men with well-developed torsos: wrestlers, truck drivers and furniture movers. Their bodies were stained dark brown, then strands of crêpe hair were glued all over their bodies with spirit gum. During filming, some 20 gallons of spirit gum and 300 yards of crêpe hair were used.

The film ran into censorship trouble. *The Film Daily* (January 9, 1933) reported that it was banned twice in Richmond, Virginia, by chief censor R.C.L. Moncure, who considered it "too extreme." It suffered savage cuts before it was finally released in early 1933 to brisk business. Abroad, The British Board of Film Censors, banned *Island of Lost Souls* outright. Only in 1958, after substantive cuts, was it finally given an "X" certificate (anyone under 16 was forbidden to view the film). It was also banned in Denmark, Germany, Holland, Hungary, India, Italy, Latvia, the Netherlands, New Zealand, South Africa and

Sweden. The ban was a blow to Paramount, who counted on its British credentials, author H.G. Wells and actor Charles Laughton as valuable commodities in exploiting the film on the international market.

Inside the Paramount Publix studios, company bosses also had their disputes. *Variety* (January 17, 1933) reported that the New York head office differed from the West Coast in how to sell the film. One side said they should go for the traditional horror angle, another argued for capitalizing on the Panther Girl promotion. The latter prevailed, as it was felt that the usual horror pitch had been done to death. *The New York State Exhibitor* (December 10, 1932) advised exhibitors that *Island of Lost Souls* was, "the last word in mad imagination. Go to it." Norbert Lusk, writing in *Picture Play* (April 1933), felt that Laughton made the film worthwhile: "He dominates the picture by the originality of his portrayal. Scorning the methods of Hollywood's favorite exponent of horror roles, who dilate their eyes to frighten children, he masks his morbid mind with a charming amiability...." Arthur Forde, writing in *Hollywood Filmograph* (December 10, 1932), enthused,

> All that can be done in the way of horror films has now definitely been done. *Island of Lost Souls* tops all the rest. It out-Frankensteins *Frankenstein*, and relegates all other thrillers to the class of children's bedtime stories. For the part of the mad doctor, Charles Laughton was selected. This great, but unfortunately cast, actor had played four lunatics and one half-lunatic in the five pictures he has made. I cannot but wish he would be given a chance at something else, and I imagine he must feel the same way. Be that as it may, he makes a grand character of Dr. Moreau.

Motion Picture Reviews (January 1933) was condemnatory: "It is regrettable that so fine an actor as Charles Laughton should be cast in a picture which offers neither mental stimulus nor relaxation and will actually prove nerve-racking to the majority of people."[20] *Motion Picture Herald* (May 13, 1933) reported that J.J. Hoffman, manager of the Plainview Theatre in Plainview, Nebraska, was equally blunt: "Three cheers for the foreign countries who have banned this picture, and shame on us for allowing this to be shown anywhere. Words fail me."

Laughton's exquisitely paced performance consists of measured calm and brooding mixed with demented fanaticism. It enhances a troubling and yet utterly compelling film that has toxic political undertones even for this pre–Code era. Apart from issues of animal vivisection and social degeneration in the Wells' novel, the film's production and release took place against a background of the rise of fascism throughout Europe and the Third International Eugenics Conference held in New York on August 24, 1932.

Island of Lost Souls demonstrates, if proof were needed, Laughton's disposition for going way beyond just the memorizing and delivering of lines and providing blocking for the camera. For Laughton, anguish and pain were integral parts of the acting process. His acting is part of the sum of the film's striking attributes. These include stylized *mise en scène*, lighting and editing. In combination with Laughton's unassailable star performance, they deliver the crucial features of twisted perversion and diabolical mendacity which remain in the mind long after the final credits have faded.

White Woman (1933)

Tagline: "Ten Years—Since They'd Seen a Woman!"[21]

U.S. (Paramount Publix Corporation)

Credits: Directed by Stuart Walker; Screenplay: Samuel Hoffenstein and Gladys Lehman; From a play by Norman Reilly Raine and Frank Butler; Music: Harry Revel; Lyrics: Mack Gordon; Photography: Harry Fischbeck; **Uncredited Technical Credits**: Producer: E. Lloyd Sheldon; Music: Karl Hajos, John Leipold; Editor: Jane Loring; Art Directors: Hans Dreier, Harry Oliver; Costumer: Travis Banton; Background Photography: Dewey Wrigley; Stock Music Arranger: Rudolf G. Kopp; Sound: Joseph Foohey; U.S. release: November 10, 1933; Genre: Drama; Black and White; Running Time: 68 minutes; DVD Region 1 from Universal on the Universal Vault Series label released in November 2014; no English subtitle captions for the deaf and hard of hearing.

Cast: Carole Lombard (*Judith Denning*); **Charles Laughton (*Horace Prin*)**; Charles Bickford (*Ballister*); Kent Taylor (*David von Elst*); Percy Kilbride (*Jakey*); James Bell (*Hambly*); Charles B. Middleton (*Fenton*); Claude King (*Chisholm*); Ethel Griffies (*Mrs. Chisholm*); Jimmie Dime

(*Vaegi*); Marc Lawrence (*Connors*); **Uncredited Cast**: Noble Johnson (*First Native Chief*); Gregg Whitespear (*Second Native Chief*); Tetsu Komai (*Native*); Victor Wong (*Waiter*).

Synopsis: Beautiful American widow Judith Denning is a cabaret singer, singing torch songs in a native Malayan café. One day she receives a letter informing her that her presence in the Malayan outpost has become untenable and she is to be deported. Hurrying to the law office of G.M. Chisholm, she tries to prevent her imminent deportation, but to no avail. Her hidden past (her rubber planter husband committed suicide) has ensured that she is an outcast in her own society. Accompanied by a local trader, Horace H. Prin, Chisholm and his wife go to the café to hear Denning sing. Prin is besotted with her singing and much else besides. He proposes marriage if she will come to his jungle houseboat and keep it clean and tidy. Despite reservations, Judith decides to take a chance as it will save her being deported by the colonial elite. On boarding Prin's houseboat, a large, dilapidated river steamer adjacent to his jungle plantation, she is introduced to a retinue of his white crew, drawn from criminal exiles. These include chief overseer David von Elst; Jakey, Prin's faithful managerial servant, and Jakey's pet chimp Duke. Von Elst is attracted to Judith and they begin a relationship. Among the collection of social misfits is Hambly, who decides he wants to quit and go home. Warned by Prin of dire consequences should he do so, Hambly is soon killed by native poison arrows while escaping down river in a canoe. Prin delights in his culpability for this crime. Judith is appalled by Prin's sadistic, tyrannical rule over those around him. As the natives go about their work manufacturing raw rubber, David and Judith canoodle on the river, but their reverie is soon dispelled by disparaging remarks from Prin about Judith's past. As punishment, David is sent upriver by Prin. A replacement overseer, Ballister, appears to replace David. A Texan who has escaped from a chain gang, Ballister is undeterred by Prin's authoritarianism. He makes a play for Judith, but she spurns his advances. Two native chiefs arrive at Prin's door to complain, but Prin replies by spraying their faces with drink in contempt. Though Prin thinks he is still in control of events, native war drums begin beating as they plan their revenge. At an outpost further up the river, David and a colleague, Fenton, are shut up in their stockade. The decapitated head of a colleague, Connors, is thrown through the window. This incident galvanizes David into a determination to escape whatever the danger. He manages to reach the safety of Prin's houseboat by running through the jungle. Both Judith and Ballister call Prin a coward to his face. David decides to take the number one boat with Judith to make good their escape. Jakey also decides to leave. In conversation, Prin tells Ballister that he has drained the boat's gas so that Judith and Ballister will surely die at the hands of the natives. Ballister decides to warn the trio and substitutes another boat full with gas. He explains this to Prin. Resigned to their fate, the two lock themselves in the

In *White Woman* (1933) debauched trader Horace Prin (Laughton) overhears the dulcet tones of torch singer Judith Denning (Carole Lombard). His preliminary affectations towards her delectable allure are rebuffed with undisguised ennui.

houseboat, aware that the natives are closing in. Jakey has taken his revenge on Prin by dropping a stash of machine guns into the river and substituting the dead body of Duke and a note in the ammunition box. Prin and Ballister begin playing a game of poker. As they drink and play their hands, natives board the boat, and Ballister is killed by a poison dart. A defiant Prin harangues the dead Ballister, and then prepares to confront the waiting natives, shrieking his name and rank as he goes to meet his grisly death.

Selected Dialogue:

PRIN: "That's what I call a lady."

PRIN: "'Ere, m'lad, will you tell the beautiful lady that I want 'er to 'onor us with 'er company, when she's through with 'er warble."

PRIN: "'Ere's me with a royal flush for the first time in me life, and you goes and croaks on me! You ungrateful 'ound!"

PRIN: "I'm Prin! I'm king of the river! King of the river! And king of everything in it, under it, and alongside of it!"

Production Commentary: It is said that imitation is the sincerest form of flattery. This pre–Code "steamy tropic" melodrama was produced on the back of recent commercial successes involving adventure stories set in exotic climes. Paramount produced *Dangerous Paradise* (William A. Wellman, 1930), a loose adaptation of Joseph Conrad's *Victory*, plus *Thunder Below* (Richard Wallace, 1932) and the Josef von Sternberg hit *Shanghai Express* (1932). The *mise en scène* of a tropical atmosphere is captured via standing sets used in these three films and many others. Prior to the rigorous enforcement of censorial guidelines from the Hays Code in July 1934, film censorship was often flouted, and oversight was poor. *White Woman* is a torrid potboiler with inferences of moral depravity, miscegenation and prostitution. All these toxic subjects are put across with an insouciance typical of the pre–Code era.

Two torch songs, "He's a Cute Brute" and "Yes, My Dear," are sung by Lombard as a café singer with a dark past. Actually, she mimes to a singing voice provided by Mona Lowe. "Singer" Lombard, outwardly the epitome of sangfroid, wears a delectable Travis Banton dress, places her hand on her hip, pouts her lips and half-closes her eyes with weary resignation as she performs.

The film begins well enough in its scene-setting, but plot motivation soon begins to falter. Thereafter, there is an indifferent middle section and the narrative only regains momentum toward the end as it shifts towards its diabolic conclusions. Ballister, played in blustering fashion by Charles Bickford, is a character who is unafraid, or intimidated by the threats of trader Horace Prin. Writing in the *New York Times* (May 18, 1933), Andre Sennwald remarked of Laughton's acting, "[He] has an enormous variety of technical tricks of voice and expression, and he can enliven a performance even when it does not seem worth the trouble." Indeed, Laughton's playing of Prin is dependent on comic schtick, deploying props and quirky diction. He drops his aitches in the style of a London Cockney, and twirls a conspicuous walrus moustache. As he does so, he alternates and fidgets with his apparel: cane, straw boater and gloves. He also produces numerous facial twitches, and often cocks his head to the left as he lasciviously ogles Carole Lombard's Judith Denning. Laughton's Prin is alternately pompous, inflated and comic in his embarrassed attempts at polite banter. Then, as the reels go by, he becomes scheming, shifty, sly and malevolent. The final reel is worth the wait. Its somber doomed fatalism is redolent of Joseph Conrad's *Heart of Darkness* with Prin and Ballister shuttered in a riverboat playing a final game of cards before being killed by natives.

Laughton found Carole Lombard uncongenial. Whereas acting was a form of torture for Laughton, Lombard's approach to acting was always ever so relaxed and always focused. Acting for her was a joy. There was no agony in getting a performance out of her and she hardly ever made mistakes. True, she peppered her language with salty expressions, but there was no malice behind her use of expletives. Her "hands on" approach to acting and lack of finesse in her choice of language was both alien and threatening to Laughton. In consequence, the two actors display little screen rapport. Indeed, in their scenes together they act as though in separate rooms.

Writing in *Picture Play* (February 1934), Norbert Lusk declared, "The eminent Charles

Laughton is handicapped by inferior material in this, though he rises above it as much as he can. Again, he contributes a morbid, perverse character which, though fascinating, cannot be rated among his triumphs." *Variety* (November 21, 1933) summed up the film's deficiencies: "Artificial and hokey, this picture would be a complete dud were it not for the cast names, especially those of Charles Laughton and Carole Lombard. It's lesser second run material and more certain on double bills." *White Woman* may be a long way behind other tropic melodramas such as *Kongo* (MGM, William Cowen, 1932), *Red Dust* (MGM, Victor Fleming, 1932), *Seven Sinners* (Universal, Tay Garnett, 1940) and *Torrid Zone* (Warner Bros., William Keighley, 1940); and it certainly is no *African Queen* (Horizon, John Huston, 1951). However, it does contain an irresistible Laughton performance.

White Woman's high melodramatics made a remake impossible to pass up. The story reappeared, slightly altered, in 1939 as *Island of Lost Men* (Paramount, Kurt Neumann). The role of a cabaret singer was given to Chinese American actress Anna May Wong, and J. Carrol Naish played Prin.

The Private Life of Henry VIII (1933)

Tagline: "Good Pictures Like Good Books Never Grow Old!"[22]

U.K. (London Film Productions/United Artists/Korda-Toeplitz)

Credits: Directed by Alexander Korda; Story and Dialogue: Lajos Biro and Arthur Wimperis; Scenario: Arthur Wimperis; Editorial Supervisor: Harold Young; Photography: Georges Perinal; Settings Designer: Vincent Korda; Technical Advisor: Philip Lindsay; Costume Designer: John Armstrong; Production Manager: David B. Cunynghame; Camera: Osmond Borrodaile; Editor: Stephen Harrison; Assistant Director: Geoffrey Boothby; Music: Kurt Schroeder; Sound: A.W. Watkins; Costumiers: B.J. Simmons & Co.; Passed by the British Board of Censors on August 16, 1933; U.K. release: October 24, 1933; U.S. release: October 12, 1933; U.K. reissue: 1946, released by British Lion; Genre: Historical Drama; Black and White; Running Time: 97 minutes; DVD Region 1 Eclipse Box Set, *Alexander Korda's Private Lives*, The Criterion Collection, released May 2009; English subtitle captions for the deaf and hard of hearing are available on this disc.

Cast: **Charles Laughton (*Henry VIII*)**; Robert Donat (*Thomas Culpeper*); Franklin Dyall (*Thomas Cromwell*); Miles Mander (*Wriothesley*); Lawrence Hanray (*Archbishop Cranmer*); William Austin (*Duke of Cleves*); John Loder (*Peynell*); Claud Allister (*Cornell*); Gibb McLaughlin (*The French Executioner*); Sam Livesey (*The English Executioner*); Merle Oberon (*Anne Boleyn, the Second Wife*); Wendy Barrie (*Jane Seymour, the Third Wife*); Elsa Lanchester (*Anne of Cleves, the Fourth Wife*); Binnie Barnes (*Katherine Howard, the Fifth Wife*); Everley Gregg (*Catherine Parr, the Sixth Wife*); Lady Tree (*The King's Nurse*); **Uncredited Cast**: Frederick Culley (*Duke of Norfolk*); Annie Esmond (*The Cook's Wife*); William Heughan (*Kingston*); Arthur Howard (*Kitchen Helper*); Judy Kelly (*Lady Rochford*); Wally Patch (*Butcher in Kitchen*); Hay Petrie (*The King's Barber*); Terry Thomas (*Extra*); John Turnbull (*Hans Holbein*).

Awards: Academy Award: **Best Actor in a Leading Role**: **Charles Laughton**; Academy Award Nomination: Best Picture.

Synopsis: Anne of Cleves, King Henry VIII's first wife, was respectful, but not to his liking so he divorced her. His marriage to Anne Boleyn also proved unsuccessful,

On the studio backlot during filming of *The Private Life of Henry VIII* (1933) Merle Oberon accompanies Laughton, dressed in their costumes of Anne Boleyn and King Henry VIII.

but for different reasons. At the king's palace, ladies, maids and servants amuse themselves by admiring the king's bed. Outside the palace, an expectant crowd waits to witness the public execution of Anne Boleyn. Inside the palace, Anne waits, resigned to her fate. The public executioner sharpens his axe. Among the ladies in the royal palace is Jane Seymour, who is noticed by the king because of her forceful opinions and her striking beauty. As the platform for the public beheading is made ready, the assembled crowd murmurs with anticipation and impatience. King Henry is also exasperated by foreign affairs on the European continent. He demands that a fleet of ships be built to defend the English islands from invasion. Thomas Culpeper brings the Lady Jane to the king to discuss her wedding dress. They laugh together. The king gives Culpeper the benefit of his insights into matrimony. Following the regrettable spectacle of the public execution of Anne Boleyn, preparations are made for the marriage bed. Several months later it is announced that the king has sired a male heir to the throne. The king returns in haste from his hunting expedition to find his newborn son in good health, but his beloved Jane has died in childbirth.

At a state banquet, the king expresses himself with raucous gusto while belching and throwing the legs of a capon over his shoulder. As Henry bemoans his lot, the court remains silent, eating their meals. The king requests music be heard to liven the deadly silence. The Lady Kathryn Howard volunteers to sing a song composed by the king. The king is very pleased with her singing and makes a jest which everyone finds amusing. Cromwell advises the king to remarry to provide more heirs to the English throne. He suggests the Lady Anne of Cleves. Master Peynell is sent to see her and bring back a portrait of the Dutch queen. The king is intrigued by the portrait, but still has affection for Kathryn. Though the king manages to gain entrance to Kathryn's bedroom, his attempts to woo her are inept and his efforts are finally stymied by a message delivered by Kathryn's lover, Thomas Culpeper, that the Lady Anne of Cleves has crossed the channel and is on her way to Rochester. Alone with Peynell, the Lady Anne describes her dilemma of loving one man but being contracted to marry another. When Henry meets the Lady Anne, her plain demeanor and unregal gait repel him instantly. Though he reprimands his loyal lieutenant, Cromwell, he recognizes that failure to go through with the proposed marriage would risk war with Europe, and he reluctantly agrees to go through with the marriage. Their first night spent together is tense, but the king finds the Lady Anne has a penchant for playing cards. After shouting and misunderstandings, they agree to a divorce with all the Lady Anne's demands being met, including giving her Peynell as master to manage the two estates she has been given at her request. Following Henry's successful fifth marriage to Kathryn Howard, he decides to show his prowess and wrestles a professional wrestler to the floor. For a man of 50, this is his undoing. He collapses and is taken to his bed. As he recuperates in bed, the queen and Culpeper talk over their dilemma as secret lovers. As the months pass, Culpeper decides he should leave for America. The queen and Culpeper are interrupted by the appearance of the king, who is unaware of their liaisons. Members of the court hear rumors concerning their affair and apply pressure on the queen's lady-in-waiting to reveal all, on pain of being tortured on the rack. Members of the Privy Council gather and the truth of the queen's adultery with Culpeper is revealed to the king. He is reduced to sobbing. Again, the public gallows are made ready. The king, alone in his palace, expresses private remorse for the execution of Kathryn. By 1543, the king is in his dotage, but gains the loyalty and care of a sixth and final wife, Katherine Parr. She provides him with a measure of contentment and consolation in his old age.

Selected Dialogue:

HENRY: "There's no delicacy nowadays. No consideration for others. Refinement's a thing of the past. Manners are dead!"
HENRY: "Am I the king, or a breeding bull?"
HENRY: "The things I've done for England!"
HENRY: "Six wives and the best of them's the worst."

Production Commentary: It is often asserted that *The Private Life of Henry VIII* was the first British film to gain genuine international success in the U.S. This, as critic Anthony Slide correctly asserts, is erroneous

(Slide, 1985: 10). British producer Herbert Wilcox had success in the U.S. during the 1920s with such films as *Flames of Passion* (Astra, 1922), which used American star Mae Marsh in the lead to improve the sale of British films in the U.S. Just as fallacious is the claim that Laughton was the very first British actor to win a Best Actor Oscar. It was in fact British actor George Arliss who, four years before, at the 1930 Oscars, had won the Oscar as Best Actor in a leading role for his portrayal of a British prime minister in the historical drama *Disraeli* (Warner Bros., Alfred E. Green, 1929).

Nevertheless, *The Private Life of Henry VIII* is a landmark film in the Laughton canon. It's the first film in which he was top-billed above the title and received an Academy Award for Best Actor. And well deserved it was, for this film marked a triumph for British cinema by being bold in ambition and popular in its use of humor and pathos. For Laughton it was a defining film, giving him fertile material with which to stamp his own iconic and memorable performances on historical characters. Laughton attacks the role of the proud Tudor monarch with a vigor and gusto that surmounts a decidedly economic production.

At the helm was producer Alexander Korda. Although he later complained, "Charles needs a midwife, not a director" (Korda:100), he and Laughton hit it off, at least initially. Korda found Laughton both challenging and engrossing; an intellectual who exercised thought and feeling in his performances. At a commercial level, Laughton was now a bankable star because he was well-known on both sides of the pond. The acclaim and recognition the film generated became a double-edged sword for Laughton. His over-weening ego demanded it, but profound insecurity about his appearance made him loath the public adulation. It was the only time Laughton and Robert Donat appeared together on screen. Both actors were touched with genius, but also blighted in their careers by temperament, insecurity and self-doubt.

The film is a series of interconnecting vignettes charting the reign of the king from full maturity to old age. Whether Laughton is seen on horseback engaged in falconry or indulging himself in a wrestling match at Hampton Court, he is always the center of attention. His character evolves sedulously and Laughton never falters or repeats himself in his acting of the role. The film not only cemented his reputation in America, but other members of the supporting cast were also brought to the attention of Hollywood casting directors. These included Donat, Miles Mander, Wendy Barrie, Elsa Lanchester and Binnie Barnes. With the exception of Donat, they all forged substantive Hollywood careers. Aside from Laughton, the only other cast members who was familiar to audiences in the U.S. at this time were William Austin and Claud Allister. The former had been active in Hollywood since the early 1920s. The latter made his film debut in *The Trial of Mary Dugan* (MGM, Bayard Veiller, 1929) and had built a Hollywood career playing pompous, blundering upper-class idiots, complete with monocle and top hat.

Korda's direction is somewhat pedestrian. The film was shot economically in just five weeks for a modest price of some £60,000. But it transcends its shortcomings and boasts a grace and fascination that wins the day. Critics on both sides of the Atlantic were unanimous in their praise. The *Film Daily* (September 21, 1933) noted, "Aside from the characterization by Charles Laughton in the title role which is one of the grandest pieces of screen acting in a long while, this narrative about the notorious British ruler … has been adapted with a good eye to angles of appeal that will register with current audiences." *Variety* (October 17, 1933) in a capsule review raved, "History comes alive and, with Charles Laughton's vital, complete performance and the sure direction, makes robust, civilized entertainment. Overtones of sympathy created for the Merry Monarch who will appease the strait-laced provincials." Elsewhere, *Variety* also praised the absence of problematic "broad English accents," something which was held against Victor Saville's handsome musical production *The Good Companions* (Gaumont-British, 1932). This film's U.S. release was delayed due to its "foreign nature," by which the reviewer explained, "very English accent[s], characteristics, etc."

Assessing the legacy of *The Private Life of Henry VIII*, critic Pauline Kael gave it a backhanded compliment: "[T]his war-horse of the movie repertory … is still alive and in good spirits" (Kael: 473). Indeed, it has just been brought back to rude health. As a joint initiative between the British Film Institute and the Film Foundation, the film has undergone a full restoration. A new 4k digital restoration was shown at the sixty-second London Film Festival on October 20, 2018. It awaits rediscovery and appreciation in all its glory; warts and all.

The Barretts of Wimpole Street (1934) reissued as Forbidden Alliance

Tagline: "WITH PRIDE IN OUR HEART—Congratulations to NORMA SHEARER, FREDRIC MARCH, CHARLES LAUGHTON and all the others who together have given the world this glorious entertainment."[23]

U.S. (Metro-Goldwyn-Mayer)

Credits: From the play by Rudolf Besier; Directed by Sidney Franklin; Screenplay: Ernest Vajda, Claudine West and Donald Ogden Stewart; Musical Score: Herbert Stothart; Recording Director: Douglas Shearer; Art Director: Cedric Gibbons; Associates: Harry McAfee, Edwin B. Willis; Gowns by Adrian; Photography: William Daniels; Editor: Margaret Booth; U.S. release: September 21, 1934; U.K. release: December 31, 1934; Genre: Historical Drama; Black and White; Running Time: 110 minutes; 35mm print at George Eastman Museum; DVD from the Warner Archive Collection, released February 2014; no English subtitle captions for the deaf and hard of hearing.

Cast: Norma Shearer (*Elizabeth Barrett*); Fredric March (*Robert Browning*); **Charles Laughton** (*Edward Moulton-Barrett*); Maureen O'Sullivan (*Henrietta Barrett*); Katherine Alexander (*Anabel Barrett*); Ralph Forbes (*Captain Surface Cook*); Marion Clayton (*Bella Hedley*); Ian Wolfe (*Harry Bevan*); Ferdinand Munier (*Dr. Chambers*); Una O'Connor (*Wilson*); Leo Carroll (*Dr. Ford-Waterlow*); Vernon Downing (*Octavius Barrett*); Neville Clark (*Charles Barrett*); Matthew Smith (*George Barrett*); Robert Carleton (*Alfred Barrett*); Allan Conrad (*Henry Barrett*); Peter Hobbes (*Septimus Barrett*); Flush (*Cocker Spaniel Dog*); **Uncredited Cast**: Lowden Adams (*Butler*); Winter Hall (*Clergyman*); George Kirby (*Coachman*).

Awards: Academy Award Nomination: Best Picture; Academy Award Nomination: Best Actress in a Leading Role: Norma Shearer.

Synopsis: Wimpole Street, London 1845: the home of widower Edward Moulton-Barrett and his large family of children, headed by the poet Elizabeth Barrett. With her books and her dog Flush, Elizabeth is confined bedridden to her upstairs bedroom and seems resigned to life as an invalid. Though her father provides his family security and comfort, he denies them the right to live their own lives. Among the many works of poetry Elizabeth finds inspiring are those of Robert Browning. One day, Browning, an impetuous young man, pays Elizabeth a visit. His warmth, vitality and idealism have a profound impact on her. As a result of several more visits by Browning, her health improves and she begins to walk again. But more than this, she comes to understand that her rigid authoritarian father abuses his position of power to repress other members of the family; he has a subconscious incestuous fixation on her, as his favorite daughter, and he uses religion as justification for dispensing his cruelty. She decides she must disobey her father and leave the family home forever to marry her beloved Browning. When her father learns of the elopement from her

Laughton exposes the paternal cruelty of Edward Moulton-Barrett to the dismay of his beloved daughter, Elizabeth, played by Norma Shearer in *The Barretts of Wimpole Street* (1934).

brothers and sisters, he is crushed but decides to enact a cruel punishment for his daughter's aberrant behavior by demanding that Flush be destroyed. But Flush had accompanied her when she vacated the home and so Barrett must stew in his own vindictiveness.

Selected Dialogue:

MOULTON-BARRETT: "I am most displeased!"

MOULTON-BARRETT: "I am gravely displeased!"

MOULTON-BARRETT: "I shall never in any way reproach you. You shall never know by deed or word or hint of mine how much you have grieved and wounded your father by refusing to do the little thing he asked."

MOULTON-BARRETT: "So, clandestine meetings under my own roof and abetted by one whom I believed to be holy, chaste and good…."

MOULTON-BARRETT: "Now listen to me. Unless you give me your solemn word that you'll neither see, nor have any communication with this man again, you'll leave my house at once, as you are, with only the clothes you have on. Once outside my doors, you can go to perdition any way you please. You'll never be admitted again as long as I live. I think you know I never go back on my word. You have your choice. Take it."

Production Commentary: Thanks to the astute generosity of MGM producer Irving Thalberg, Laughton secured the role of Moulton-Barrett in *The Barretts of Wimpole Street*. In a *Modern Screen* interview (December 1934), the actor paid Thalberg a compliment:

> He possesses a balance that is rare in producers. He never knows it all. I talked with him by telephone from London for the part of Papa Barrett in *The Barretts of Wimpole Street*. He said it was a putrid part for me. He said people would continue to hate me for portraying that demonical old man. I answered that I didn't believe people associated players with the parts they portrayed and that I wasn't afraid of risking it. I won him over. I like working with Thalberg because he combines the action of the executive with a sensitiveness rarely found in producers. He really likes actors whereas most producers distrust and misunderstand them. He [is] always ready to talk over disputed points.

Laughton professed to be unconcerned with appearance, flattery, overnight success or high status, but in the same interview the insecure actor declared, "I don't know why they go to see me in pictures. I'm so ugly! Why would you want to see me when there's Bing Crosby, a perfectly delightful fellow, and with such a voice. I'm fat and dull. Only good for comedy—low comedy at that."

Apart from Laughton's commitment to the London stage and efforts to persuade Thalberg of his suitability for the role, contemporary sources show how different the film might have turned out. *Variety* (April 11, 1933) reported that William Randolph Hearst was determined to produce a film version of the celebrated play and give the lead to his protégé Marion Davies. But MGM executives were against it. *Variety* (February 19, 1934) then announced that Thalberg's wife Norma Shearer had secured the role, while Davies was busy appearing in *Operator 13* (MGM, Richard Boleslawski, 1934). Director Sidney Franklin had seen Cedric Hardwicke as Barrett on the London stage and suggested he be cast in the film. But Thalberg had seen Laughton in *Payment Deferred* and was mindful of his recent Best Actor Oscar win for *The Private Life of Henry VIII* and insisted that Laughton was ideal for the part. It was agreed that Laughton would begin filming following the finish of a season of Old Vic plays.

Laughton arrived in Hollywood in May 1934 to find the studio had already begun shooting some of Norma Shearer's scenes. Shearer was renowned for her careful use of rehearsals and thorough preparation of detail for her film scenes. Like Laughton, she had insecurities and troubles from eyesight problems, the mental health of her elder sister Athole, and the need to give an exacting performance in whatever role she was assigned. The two bonded and they relaxed on the set. The highlight of the film occurred when Moulton-Barrett forced his younger daughter to swear on the Bible not to communicate with her beloved suitor ever again. This solemn scene was ruined when Laughton began to laugh uncontrollably. Though they did not understand the joke, Shearer and Maureen

O'Sullivan joined in the hilarity. Laughton finally explained that he could not help remembering how during his schooldays, he had struggled with many of the Bible's more difficult passages. Unfortunately, the director, Sidney Franklin, was less than pleased when he had to explain to the front office why he had lost some $10,000 worth of shooting time. Franklin shared Thalberg's taste for bringing middlebrow literary classics to the screen; he also directed a scene-for-scene Metrocolor-CinemaScope remake in 1957. It starred John Gielgud as Moulton-Barrett, Jennifer Jones as Elizabeth and Bill Travers as Robert Browning.

Applying sideburns to his face and bearing a stern demeanor, Laughton gives a sinuous performance that is capped by a malevolent glint in his eyes. When told he was to wear a wig for the role of the tyrannical head of the Barrett household, Laughton refused and instead grew his hair long and dyed it. In an interview given to *Photoplay* (October 1934), he was asked if he preferred stage or screen, and replied, "Both. From one to the other, never lingering in a rut. Under conditions I enjoy, I really like movies best." His conditions were exacting, as was to be expected from a perfectionist who was never truly satisfied with his performances. *Variety* (June 19, 1934) reported that the picture took 14 weeks to shoot. Given a prime publicity campaign, *The Barretts of Wimpole Street* went on to make a profit of $668,000. Despite slight complaints regarding the film's length of nearly two hours and minor quibbles about its cast, this was very much a prestige item. *Variety* (October 2, 1934) was quick to spot the commercial potential of this historical drama:

> *The Barretts of Wimpole Street* for all its celluloid lethargy, is box-office; a box-office insured by Shearer, March and Laughton on the marquee.... The unnatural love of Papa Barrett [is] graphically depicted by Charles Laughton, in another of his outstanding screen portraits as the psychopathic hateful character whose twisted affections for his children, especially daughter Elizabeth, almost proves her physical and spiritual undoing.... Laughton's relentless abnormal assignment is played to the hilt and the [audience] will walk out hating the character and admiring the art which makes the antipathy so vivid.

Caroline Lejeune writing in the *Observer* (October 14, 1934), found that Laughton's performance as the tyrannical father went against her tenets of decorum and proportionate realism: She called it, "as thorough-going a case of psychopathic fixation as ever came out of the Greek drama or the pages of Freud.... [B]y consistently sharpening and itemizing the details of his part, [Laughton] has tended to throw the picture out of perspective." This was either a manifestation of, "Laughton's power to adapt himself to his medium or as a proof of the cinema's inability to accommodate genius." This was, she claimed, an unfortunate blemish on what was otherwise, "a pleasing, well-mannered, and occasionally distinguished photoplay, done with taste and thoroughness." Critic Graham Greene of *The Spectator* (September 6, 1935) found Laughton's film performance outdid the London stage version, opining that the movie was, "well worth seeing for the sake of Mr. Charles Laughton as Mr. Barrett, a more macabre and openly sensual Mr. Barrett than Sir Cedric Hardwicke's."[24]

Discussing with Irving Thalberg the incestuous obsession of Moulton-Barrett towards his daughter, Laughton assured the producer, "They can't censor the gleam in my eye" (Lambert: 208). Guilt about being gay, a repulsion toward his own perceived ugliness and drawing on masochistic feelings lent Laughton an affinity in playing outsiders or the vulnerable. Judging the film today, Shearer appears rather too agile for someone in fragile health and no attempt is made to disguise March's American accent. Laughton's fearsome presence steals the film. Just 35 years old and having made his professional stage debut only nine years previously, this is Laughton in his prime and at his memorable best. There were tribulations involved in pitching his performance at the appropriate level, but when he managed to hit his stride, he made it appear all so straightforward and easy.

Ruggles of Red Gap (1935)

Tagline: "Extra! *Ruggles of Red Gap* Breaking All Records! Read All About It!"[25]

U.S. (Paramount Pictures)

Ruggles of Red Gap (1935)

Credits: Produced by Arthur Hornblow, Jr.; Directed by Leo McCarey; Screenplay: Walter DeLeon and Harlan Thompson; Adaptation: Humphrey Pearson; Photography: Alfred Gilks; **Uncredited Technical Credits**: Art Directors: Hans Dreier, Robert Odell; Editor: Edward Dmytryk; Costumes: Travis Banton; Sound: Philip Wisdom; U.S. release: March 8, 1935; U.K. release: July 22, 1935; U.S. reissue: July 18, 1941; Genre: Western Comedy; Black and White; Running Time: 92 minutes; DVD Region 1, Universal Vault series label, released January 2010; no English subtitle captions for the deaf and hard of hearing; Dual format edition: DVD Region 2 and Blu-ray Region B, Masters of Cinema, Eureka Entertainment; English subtitle captions for the deaf and hard of hearing are available on these discs.

Cast: **Charles Laughton** (*Ruggles*); Mary Boland (*Effie Floud*); Charlie Ruggles (*Egbert Floud*); ZaSu Pitts (*Mrs. Judson*); Roland Young (*Earl of Burnstead*); Leila Hyams (*Nell Kenner*); Maude Eburne ("*Ma*" *Pettingill*); Lucien Littlefield (*Charles Belknap-Jackson*); Leota Lorraine (*Mrs. Belknap-Jackson*); James Burke (*Jeff Tuttle*); Dell Henderson (*Sam*); Clarence Wilson (*Jake Henshaw*); **Uncredited Cast**: Ernie Adams (*Dishwasher*); Augusta Anderson (*Mrs. Wallaby*); Alyce Ardell (*Lisette—French Maid*); Harry Bernard (*Harry—Bartender #2*); Harry Bowen (*Photographer*); George Burton (*Doc Squires*); Ricardo Lord Cezon (*Little Boy*); Alex Chivra (*Chef #1*); Heinie Conklin (*Waiter at the Grill*); Jim Corey (*Cowboy*); Carrie Daumery, Isabel La Mal (*Effie's Guests in Paris*); Sarah Edwards (*Mrs. Myron Carey*); Charles Fallon (*Max—Paris Café Waiter*); Brenda Fowler (*Judy Ballard*); Willie Fung (*Willie—Chinese Servant*); Armand Kaliz, Rafael Storm (*Clothing Salesmen*); Jane Keckley, Jane Kerr, Patsy O'Byrne (*Cooks*); Lee Kohlmar (*Jailer at Red Gap*); Edward LeSaint (*Diner at the Grill*); Sam Lufkin, Charles McAvoy, Frank Mills, Jack Norton (*Barflies*); Robert Milasch (*Driver*); Frank O'Connor (*Station Agent*); Albert Petit (*Waiter at Carousel*); Victor Potel (*Curly—Cowboy*); Frank Rice (*Hank Adams*); Henry Roquemore (*Fred—Diner at the Grill*); Rolfe Sedan (*Barber in Paris*); Genaro Spagnoli (*Frank—Cab Driver*); Libby Taylor (*Libby—Servant*); Jim Welch (*Man in Saloon*); William Welsh (*Eddie*).

Awards: Academy Award Nomination: Best Picture.

A gentleman's gentleman. Laughton as Marmaduke Ruggles: the personification of discretion, etiquette and savoir-faire in *Ruggles of Red Gap* (1935).

Synopsis: During the spring of 1908 in Paris, the Earl of Burnstead takes on the onerous duty of telling his manservant, Marmaduke Ruggles, he is to go to America. He explains he had dined with Mr. and Mrs. Floud, an American couple, and they had taught him their native card game, poker. Ruggles was the stake—and his lordship lost. At the Flouds' hotel, there is an altercation between Egbert and Effie Floud. He is against having an English valet, but she is intent on turning her apathetic husband into a gentleman, and insists they take Ruggles back with them to Red Gap, Washington. Mr. Floud goes to collect Ruggles. Ruggles and the Earl say their sad farewells. Back in her hotel room, Effie gathers all her husband's garish clothes and tells the maid to burn the lot. Her husband is to get an entirely new outfit. There follows a series of visits to a gentleman's outfitters and hairdresser. Effie leaves Egbert in the hands of Ruggles with instructions to show her husband the cultural sights of Paris. Egbert has other ideas and, treating Ruggles as an equal, they head to various cafes and soon become drunk. Upon their return, Effie decides they are to travel immediately back to Red Gap. When they arrive in the town by train, they are met by Effie's sister and brother-in-law, Mr. and Mrs. Belknap-Jackson. Egbert introduces Ruggles to everyone as "the colonel." An erroneous report appears in the

(1935) Ruggles of Red Gap

local paper that the Flouds are entertaining an honored guest, Colonel Ruggles, rather than employing a servant. As the leaders of local society, Effie and the Belknap-Jacksons are obliged to maintain the fiction of Ruggles as their guest. Finally, Belknap-Jackson decides to dismiss Ruggles. He packs his bags and waits for his train at the Silver Dollar Saloon. There he meets Egbert and his rich, plain-speaking mother-in-law, "Ma" Pettingill. They are annoyed to learn of his being discharged without their approval. There follows a discussion on egalitarianism. When no one in the saloon can remember President Lincoln's address at Gettysburg, Ruggles recites the whole speech to everyone's amazement. Ruggles then declares he will give up the family tradition of being a manservant and instead set up his own business. With assistance and help from widow Prunella Judson, a woman Ruggles has taken a shine to, and financial aid from Egbert and Ma Pettingill, he begins work on opening a restaurant. Effie tells Ruggles that the Earl of Burnstead is to visit Red Gap in order to retain his services. This causes Ruggles to consider where his loyalties lie. When the earl arrives, Ruggles cannot be found and the worst is feared. But Ruggles reappears and informs the earl that he is now independent from his service, and the earl congratulates him. Ruggles is now free to continue with the grand opening of the Anglo-American Grill. At the opening, the earl arrives with his new bride, Nell Kenner, a saloon entertainer. Belknap-Jackson insults the earl for marrying beneath his social station. Ruggles reacts by ejecting Belknap-Jackson. He then retires to the kitchens, fearing that the incident has ruined the reputation of his business. But the earl makes a speech in Ruggles' honor. There follows a rousing chorus of "For He's a Jolly Good Fellow." Ruggles is dragged from the kitchen to the floor of the restaurant where he realizes with delight that the singing is not for the earl but for him, Ruggles of Red Gap.

Selected Dialogue:

RUGGLES: "Spats, sir, mark the difference between a man well turned out and a man merely dressed."

RUGGLES: "There is a certain difference in our walks of life, sir, which makes it impossible for me to sit at the same table with yourself, sir…. It just doesn't do for a gentleman's servant to sit with his superiors, sir."

RUGGLES: "This is a land, sir, of great opportunity where all are created equal."

RUGGLES: "If I may say so, you're all a bit of okay."

Production Commentary: Leo McCarey's version of the often-filmed *Ruggles of Red Gap* contains much to admire. Harry Leon Wilson's celebrated 1915 book had already been filmed twice, first by Lawrence C. Windom for Essanay in 1918. Taylor Holmes played the lead. Next came James Cruze's 1923 Paramount film with Edward Everett Horton.[26] McCarey's comedy is created in a most democratic manner in the sense that the film is an ensemble piece comprised of character players rather than major stars. This gives every actor, whatever their status, a rare opportunity to stand out.

In late August 1934, prior to making the film, Laughton was taken ill with a rectal fistula. As a consequence, his figure on screen is lithe and trim. His physical movements are conspicuous for their sense of dexterity, energy and grace—all appropriate attributes in a role ingrained in servile behavior. His background in the hotel trade was something he drew heavily upon for portraying Ruggles. Laughton's observations of, and participation in, the hierarchical landscape of British social class during his early life intermingles with his recent experience of American meritocratic status. Laughton manifests the role by using his cadence and intonation of speech. At the beginning he is formal, staid and traditional. Then, little by little, there is a transformation of a servant turning into his own master by becoming informal, relaxed and subversive.

Film Daily (August 29, 1934) noted that the part of Egbert Floud was originally assigned to Sidney Toler, but he was replaced by Charlie Ruggles. This was the first and only collaboration between Laughton and acclaimed comedy director McCarey. Though they came from very different backgrounds, they shared a common desire for a greater creative autonomy in their film careers. As a British stage actor, Laughton was still making adjustments to the differing demands of a new medium, and after appearing in some indifferent film vehicles he was looking to ground himself in stronger material. His appearance in *Ruggles of Red Gap*, the final film of his Paramount contract, allowed him to achieve this goal. McCarey, too, had known great success early in his film career making comedy shorts at Hal Roach. He honed his filmmaking talent working with such comedians as Charley Chase, Max Davidson and Laurel and Hardy. He was now seeking a film to regain a measure of artistic integrity following a fallow period of lesser work. *Ruggles* was the film he needed.

Ruggles' tremendous success springs from the unlikely collaboration between McCarey and Laughton. McCarey ran an informal and relaxed ship. Scenes were often improvised on set and new dialogue jotted down. There was even a piano on hand for sing-a-longs! Such an unorthodox approach helped to ensure that McCarey could maintain creative control over his films. He cared little for an original written script; better instead to use improvisation to rewrite the script and then film these changes almost instantaneously and ensure that ideas were captured in the rushes at the end of a day.

In stark contrast, Laughton's approach was solitary, exacting and controlling. He concentrated solely on his own performance and then turned up on the set ready to perform in a precise manner of his own devising. He would often take other actors aside and try to impress upon them his own thoughts and feelings about the role he was playing. He often demanded they should oblige him by changing their approach to accommodate his wishes. It is therefore amazing to consider that by all accounts, filming went smoothly with no hold-ups or major incidents. Producer Arthur Hornblow, Jr., found they were in total rapport. For both Hornblow and Laughton, it was the first time in their careers that they had been able to exercise a degree of independence over the final product.

There is an episodic nature to the film's construction with inordinate use of long static takes, indicative of undercutting stylized spectacle, and leaving the audience to concentrate on the action on screen rather than being distracted by the camera. *Ruggles* is therefore a film based on dialogue and performance rather than any great reliance on camerawork or editing.

Prior to *Ruggles*, Laughton had returned from a less than satisfactory attempt to perform Shakespeare on the London stage, and then was ill in hospital. While convalescing after his operation, he met a man who had come to see his wife. The man asked if Laughton would go into her room and introduce himself to her and cheer her up. Afterwards, the man told Laughton it was the first time she had smiled. It was a salutary moment in which the actor realized that as an actor he possessed popular appeal with the public. Following the failure of his stab at high art, he now tried to concentrate on his growing status as a film star. *Ruggles* was his first attempt to tackle a comic role on film. His conversion from a serious actor devoted to high art to a film star devoted to the public was referenced in a *Film Weekly* interview (February 19, 1938):

> Being a film star for five years has altered my outlook.... Nowadays, I believe that Gary Cooper is doing a far greater service to mankind than the highly elocutionized Shakespearean actor playing to a handful of sophisticated Londoners. Playing Shakespeare is nothing more than a piece of scholarship. I began to see that the emotional sincerity of the masses was infinitely more important than the "correct" ideas of a few sophisticates.... By the time I made *Ruggles of Red Gap* I had lost my "correct" opinions and my sole concern was to loosen and stir the emotions of the rank and file of the film public.

Though Laughton here expresses a clear intent to change from a classic stage actor to a popular film star, he never embraced or accepted this change. This is apparent in his performance, which occasionally is somewhat flat, as though he was unsure of himself. Unlike the other players who used intuition to adopt the light, effortless touch required for comedy, Laughton tended to opt for deep characterization where the actor strives to lose himself in the part. Sometimes this works quite brilliantly as in the film's highlight of Laughton reciting the Gettysburg Address.

Critical reaction was positive. *Film Daily* (February 19, 1935) declared, "The production represents a distinct triumph for Charles Laughton, who essays the difficult role of the dignified gentleman's man absorbing the democratic ideas of the wild western mining town. Laughton delivers one of the outstanding performances of the screen...." *Variety* (March 13, 1935) was also complimentary and described the film as possessing "[p]lenty of marquee strength and dynamite on the inside. An A-1 comedy." It went on to suggest that Laughton's Ruggles would surprise some, and the actor's penchant for comedy would widen his appeal. His use of deadpan was commended. The reviewer also cites the recitation in full of Lincoln's Gettysburg Address as being "so dangerous and audacious that it almost startles.... It doesn't seem to belong in merely reading of it, but it's so deftly handled and beautifully done by Laughton that this serious moment turns into the high spot of the film." *Variety* did find one demerit: "[T]he timing is occasionally faulty, the laughs sometimes overlapping." In *Motion Picture Herald* (May 18, 1935), exhibitor Russell Anderson of the Casino Theatre, Gunnison, Utah, was enthusiastic: "The Gettysburg speech by Laughton deserves a cheer. Can't go too strongly on this one." The speech became a centerpiece of Laughton's repertoire whether on nationwide tours, for wartime service personnel, broadcasting on radio and television, or for any audience he took a shine to.

Mutiny on the Bounty (1935)

Tagline: "The flaming pages of history record the grandest adventure of all times!"[27]

U.S. (Metro-Goldwyn-Mayer)

Credits: Associate Producer: Albert Lewin; Produced and Directed by Frank Lloyd; Screenplay: Talbot Jennings, Jules Furthman and Carey Wilson; From the novel by Charles Nordhoff and James Norman Hall; Music Score: Herbert Stothart; Recording Director: Douglas Shearer; Art Director: Cedric Gibbons; Associate: Arnold Gillespie; Marine Director: James Havens; Photography: Arthur Edeson; Editor: Margaret Booth; U.S. release: November 1, 1935; U.K. release: September 21, 1936; U.S. reissue: May 5, 1939; Genre: Historical Drama; Black and White; Running Time: 132 minutes; 35mm print held at the George Eastman Museum; DVD Region 1 and Region 2 and Blu-ray Region A and Region B, Warner Home Video released November 2010; English subtitle captions for the deaf and hard of hearing are available on these discs.

Cast: Charles Laughton (*Captain Bligh*); Clark Gable (*Fletcher Christian*); Franchot Tone (*Byam*); Herbert Mundin (*Smith*); Eddie Quillan (*Ellison*); Dudley Digges (*Bacchus*); Donald Crisp (*Burkitt*); Henry Stephenson (*Sir Joseph Banks*); Francis Lister (*Captain Nelson*); Spring Byington (*Mrs. Byam*); Movita (*Tehani*); Mamo (*Maimiti*); Byron Russell (*Quintal*); Percy Waram (*Coleman*); David Torrence (*Lord Hood*); John Harrington (*Mr. Purcell*); Douglas Walton (*Stewart*); Ian Wolfe (*Maggs*); DeWitt Jennings (*Fryer*); Ivan Simpson (*Morgan*); Vernon Downing (*Hayward*); William Bambridge (*Hitihiti*); Marion Clayton (*Mary Ellison*); Stanley Fields (*Muspratt*); Wallis Clark (*Morrison*); Crauford Kent (*Lieutenant Edwards*); Pat Flaherty (*Churchill*); Alec Craig (*McCoy*); Charles Irwin (*Thompson*); Dick Winslow (*Tinkler*); **Uncredited Cast:** Robert Adair (*Warden*); Harry Allen (*Wherryman*); Lionel Belmore (*Innkeeper*); Nadine Beresford (*Ellison's Mother*); Julie Bescos (*Stunt Double*); Derek Blomfield (*Jeremy*); Lucy Chavarria (*Hina*); Harry Cording (*Soldier*); Ray Corrigan, Charles Dunbar, Edgar Edwards, Fred Graham, Clarke Jennings, Stubby Kruger, Gil Perkins, Jack Sterling, Harry Warren (*Able-Bodied Seamen*); Sam Wallace Driscoll (*Michael Byrne*); Harold Entwistle (*Captain Colpoys*); Sig Frohlich

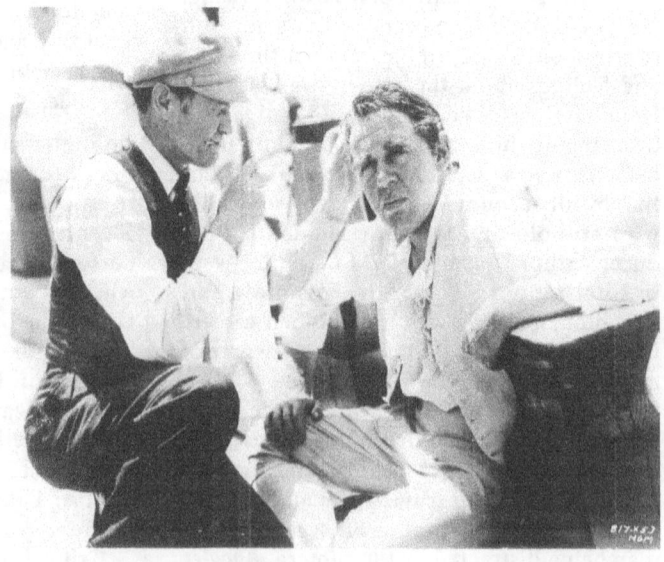

A makeup artist carefully applies the facial features that will give Laughton yet another outstanding role; that of Captain Bligh in *Mutiny on the Bounty* (1935).

(*Mutineer*); Mary Gordon (*Peddler*); Jon Hall, Charles Nauu, Satini Pualoa (*Tahitian Natives*); Winter Hall (*Chaplain*); Lilyan Irene. Vivien Oakland, Lotus Thompson (*Molls*); Tiny Jones (*Ship's Visitor at Portsmouth*); Hal Le Sueur (*Millard*); Robert Livingstone (*Lieutenant Young*); Doris Lloyd (*Cockney Moll*); King Mojave (*Richard Skinner*); John Power (*Hillebrand*); William Stack (*Judge Advocate*); Will Stanton (*Portsmouth Joe*); David Thursby (*McIntosh*); Eric Wilton (*Board Captain*).

Awards: Academy Award: Best Picture. Academy Award Nomination: Best Actor in a Leading Role: Clark Gable, **Charles Laughton**, Franchot Tone; Academy Award Nomination: Best Director: Frank Lloyd; Academy Award Nomination: Best Screenplay: Jules Furthman, Talbot Jennings, Carey Wilson; Academy Award Nomination: Best Film Editing: Margaret Booth; Academy Award Nomination: Best Music Score: Nat W. Finston and Herbert Stothart.

Synopsis: In December 1787, HMS *Bounty* begins preparation to sail from Portsmouth Harbour to the island of Tahiti to collect breadfruit plants. At the dockside, naval officer Fletcher Christian is at the head of a naval press gang. The party raids a tavern and six men are detained for two years mandatory service in the king's navy. Christian is later told that a press gang recruit, Tommy Ellison, has tried to break ship. Ellison explains that time away from his wife and expectant child is more than he can bear. Christian takes him in hand and arranges for his wife to be brought aboard so Ellison may say his farewells. Captain William Bligh arrives on board and orders all those who are not members of the crew to go ashore. Bligh receives written orders that a man who struck his captain be flogged. A new naval officer, Roger Byam, is to witness the harsh discipline. When Byam protests, Bligh launches into a tirade on the need for discipline in running a ship and reminds Byam that a midshipman is in no position to question his authority. Bligh orders that two dozen lashes be administered. However, the man is already dead. Bligh orders the punishment to proceed. The punishment is carried out and Bligh orders the crew to prepare to sail at once. In the captain's cabin, Christian discusses the lack of food aboard for such a long voyage. Bligh doesn't see the necessity of spending money on feeding common criminals. Bligh has his own method of dealing with seamen: the law of fear. An argument between Byam and another officer leads to a fight. Bligh intervenes and orders Byam to climb up to the masthead and remain there until he is called down. When the ship appears to be on the verge of keeling over, Christian goes on deck where Bligh is at the ship's wheel. Christian goes aloft to the masthead and retrieves a barely conscious Byam, who is taken below. Bligh sees his orders being disobeyed and commands that Byam resume his punishment aloft. Byam returns to the masthead, fortified with brandy and a cloak. Despite the weather, Byam manages to see his punishment through. Bligh later reprimands the crew for their laxity and shirking their duties. He reminds them that under the articles of war, he has the power to inflict any punishment he sees fit. Christian tries to persuade Bligh to let him deal with the men without resorting to harsh punishment, but Bligh refuses. The regime of cruel beatings and floggings continues. In conversation with Byam, Christian declares he may not last the two-year voyage with such a cruel superior. When Bligh asks Christian to sign the ship's stores book, Christian refuses. Bligh orders the ship's crew to assemble on deck where he reads the naval code and orders Christian to sign the book. This he does but under duress. Just as a stand-off between Bligh and Christian seems inevitable, land is sighted. The *Bounty* has reached Tahiti, and Hitihiti the tribal chief comes aboard. Bligh states they have come to the island to collect 1000 breadfruit plants. The chief takes a liking to midshipman Byam and requests that he come to the island as his personal guest. The rest of the crew members are ordered to bring the breadfruit plants aboard and to carry out repairs to the ship for the return voyage. Bligh forbids Christian from going to the island but Hitihiti intervenes, much to the pleasure of Byam. On the island, Christian falls in love with Hitihiti's granddaughter. The breadfruit plants need constant watering and Bligh vows to ration the water supply to the crew. After the interlude on the island, Bligh continues his tyrannical hold aboard ship. He orders a flogging when two crew members are accused of desertion. When the ailing ship's surgeon is ordered on deck to witness the punishment and dies, the crew and Christian begin to contemplate mutiny. Ultimately, Christian orders the men

(1935) *Mutiny on the Bounty*

to take over the ship, and Bligh is taken prisoner. Christian decides that Bligh and those loyal to him are to be cast adrift in a longboat. Despite atrocious conditions and little food, Bligh manages to steer a course to the island of Timor. While Christian and his mutineers celebrate Christmas in Tahiti, they spot a British ship, the *Pandora*. Christian orders his men to sail on the *Bounty*. Byam parts company with Christian as he wishes to return to England. When Byam goes aboard the *Pandora*, he finds Bligh in command. Byam is charged with mutiny and put in irons awaiting court-martial in England. Determined to capture Christian, Bligh recklessly loses his ship in rocky waters. Byam and the other prisoners are released and placed in a boat under Bligh's command. They manage to sail back to England. At Byam's court-martial, Bligh swears that Byam was planning mutiny with Christian. The court finds Byam and the other mutineers guilty. Byam's case is taken to the king for a royal pardon, which is granted. He resumes his naval career, serving under a new regime.

Selected Dialogue:

BLIGH: "Mr. Christian, clear the decks of this rabble."
BLIGH: "Discipline's the thing. A seaman's a seaman, captain's a captain. And a midshipman is the lowest form of animal life in the British navy."
BLIGH: "Look alive, you crawling caterpillar!"
BLIGH: "Won't eat cheese, eh? Before I'm done with you, I'll make you eat grass!"
BLIGH: "You mutinous dog!"
BLIGH: "Casting me adrift 3500 miles from a port of call. You're sending me to my doom, eh? Well, you're wrong, Christian! I'll take this boat as she floats to England if I must! I'll live to see you, all of you, hanging from the highest yardarm in the British fleet!"

Production Commentary: "Marvelous film, don't think we've seen a better one."[28] These ecstatic remarks were written by English middle-class filmgoer Adela Riddlesdale Stephenson (1899–1988) in her diary after seeing *Mutiny on the Bounty* in 1936. Mrs. Stephenson's superlatives were not misplaced. If the word "blockbuster" had been around in the 1930s, MGM's *Bounty* film would have fit the description precisely. *Mutiny on the Bounty* was, to use the vernacular of the day, a "super" or "special" production. It remains the apogee of producer Irving Thalberg's determination to combine artistic integrity with commercial acumen. It was star-studded, carefully crafted to appeal to all sectors of public taste and all shades of critical opinion, and boasted a final cut shaped by umpteen studio previews.

This justly celebrated film, still revered today, has spawned its own urban myth. James Cagney, David Niven and Dick Haymes are all allegedly to be found as extras in the picture. Try and spot them![29]

The plot begins to lose momentum in its second half when HMS *Bounty* anchors in Tahiti (process shots involving doubles and obvious use of back projection is much in evidence). But it still holds the attention with its sense of dramatic unity and star charisma. Even after over 80 years, Laughton's Captain Bligh still remains as captivating as ever. The actor contacted the same Savile Row tailor that had outfitted Bligh for measurements and type of material used to reproduce the captain's uniform for the film. In order to fit into the uniform, he shed over 55 pounds. With a scowl, a glare, a furrowed brow, a soupcon of makeup (bushy eyebrows) and an asymmetrical gait, Laughton becomes the martinet of all martinets.[30] Throughout the voyage, Bligh sadistically imposes a diet of corporal punishment to his recalcitrant crew. These public floggings, keelhaulings and severe reprimands were designed to instill discipline and unquestioning submission. The histrionics of maniacal authority is conveyed with perfect conviction by the actor—perhaps because Laughton understood so well the mindset of such a character from his schooldays at Stonyhurst College and army service during the First World War.

Interviewed by *Film Daily* (May 20, 1935), Laughton, hard at work on the picture, declared, "When you're a great actor you're entitled to have at least one hysterical scene in each picture." Production began on February 14, 1935, when a contingent of 60 MGM technical production staff, including directors Frank Lloyd and Richard Thorpe, sailed from San Pedro Harbor bound for the South Seas. A premier director of the era, Lloyd was director of *Mutiny on the Bounty*, and

Thorpe was directing an adaptation of Herman Melville's tropical novel *Typee* which in its final cut was re-titled *Last of the Pagans*. At this early stage of production, Robert Montgomery was slated to appear in *Mutiny on the Bounty*. By May 1935, he had been replaced by Franchot Tone. Again, as with *Island of Lost Souls*, Catalina Island was pressed into service. By the time of its completion, the film had cost nearly $2,000,000.

The filming of this epic did not pass without incident. On July 25, 1935, second unit assistant cameraman Glenn Strong drowned. As he tried to retrieve a camera, the vessel he was on capsized and sank. Added to this tragic accident was an unwelcome confrontation between Clark Gable and Laughton, who disliked each other. Gable felt the role of Christian would demean his masculinity in the eyes of his legion of fans. To appear "in character," he had to shave off his trademark moustache. For his part, Laughton's fears and phobias regarding his own appearance began to emerge when confronted with Gable's handsome physique. Gable complained that Laughton averted his gaze when they played a scene together. Careful viewing of the film in certain scenes where Bligh and Christian engage reveals that Laughton does appear to avoid eye contact with Gable. Camera set-ups, used in a standard two-shot when photographing the two principals, often appear more intricate and involved even by MGM's usual affluent production standards. The standoff between the two actors was only placated by the intervention of Irving Thalberg. This situation proved a double-edged sword. Although it held up production, the sense of antipathy displayed by the two actors lent a sense of authenticity to the two leading protagonists in the storyline. This was the last time that Laughton worked for Thalberg.

Praise for this historical adventure from both critics and the film trade was universal. *Film Daily* (November 1, 1935) declared, "It is grim, gripping, and pictorially perfect. Frank Lloyd's direction is of the best and he again demonstrates that he is a past master in the handling of stories of the sea. Laughton is masterful as the cruel sadistic captain...." *Harrison's Reports* (November 16, 1935) stated, "Powerful! It is a thrilling melodrama, brutal but exciting—realistic to the point where the suffering of the seamen will tear at one's heart. Although it is very long, the story is so fascinating that one's eyes do not wander from the screen for a second. Charles Laughton is excellent as the sadistic Captain of the *Bounty*, a combination of able seaman and fiend, who delights in seeing punishment meted out according to his instructions." *Independent Exhibitor's Bulletin* (November 20, 1935) also praised MGM's ability to delivering a first-class product. They admired the casting of Gable and Tone as "lure for feminine trade!" and then noted, "Charles Laughton has a role that is his juiciest to date and he does miracles with it." Also, they instructed exhibitors that the picture should be sold as "one of the great pictures of all time." The film was subsequently reissued. It remains a cornerstone of MGM production from this era. It was one of the biggest moneymakers of the 1930s, returning a gross of $4,460,000 during its initial run. For Laughton, the role of Bligh, like King Henry VIII, proved in the long term something of a millstone. The media of the day gave wide exposure to the film and this led to unending imitations from personalities in various arenas of the entertainment world such as vaudeville, cabaret, radio and film. However, far from being a form of flattery, it was for Laughton an unwelcome intrusion and brought on fears of being forever typecast as a villain; albeit an iconoclastic one.

Les Misérables (1935)

Tagline: "Some Have Seen It Twice ... Others Three Times."[31]

U.S. (Twentieth Century Pictures, Inc./United Artists)

Credits: Producer: Joseph M. Schenck; Directed by Richard Boleslawski; Associate Producers: William Goetz, Raymond Griffith; Screenplay: W.P. Lipscomb; Photography: Gregg Toland; Art Director: Richard Day; Editor: Barbara McLean; Musical Director: Alfred Newman; Sound: Frank Maher, Roger Heman; Costumes: Omar Kiam; Assistant Director: Eric Stacey; U.S. release: April 3, 1935; U.K. release: October 7, 1935; Genre: Historical Drama; Black and White; Running Time: 108 minutes; DVD all regions, Cinema Classics Collection, 20th Century–Fox, released December 2012; English subtitle captions for the deaf and hard of hearing are available on this disc.

Cast: Fredric March (*Jean Valjean/Champmathieu*); **Charles Laughton** (*Javert*); Sir Cedric Hardwicke (*Bishop Bienvenue*); Rochelle Hudson (*Cosette*); Frances Drake (*Eponine*); John

50 (1935) *Les Misérables*

Beal (*Marius*); Florence Eldridge (*Fantine*); Jessie Ralph (*Mme. Magloire*); Mary Forbes (*Mlle. Baptiseme*); Florence Roberts (*Toussaint*); Jane Kerr (*Mme. Thenardier*); Ferdinand Gottschalk (*Thenardier*); Charles Haefeli (*Brevet*); Marilynne [sic] Knowlden (*Little Cosette*); John Bleifer (*Chenildieu*); Leonid Kinskey (*Genflou*); Harry Semels (*Cochepaille*); Eily Malyon (*Mother Superior*); Ian MacLaren (*Head Gardener*); Vernon Downing (*Brissac*); Lyons Wickland (*Lamarque*); John Carradine (*Enjoiras*); **Uncredited Cast**: Herbert Ashley, Heinie Conklin, Robert R. Stephenson (*Drunks at Inn*); Sam Baker, Everett Brown (*Black Convicts*); Elmer Ballard (*Court Clerk*); Reginald Barlow (*Henri*); George Barraud (*Prosecutor in Arras*); Leon Beaumon, Stanley Blystone, Ray Burgess, Jack Curtis, David Dunbar, Lew Hicks, John Northpole, Robert St. Angelo (*Gendarmes in Prefect's Office*); Margaret Bloodgood (*Factory Forewoman*); Sidney Bracey (*Mayor's Clerk*); Herbert Bunston (*Judge at Favorelles*); William P. Carleton (*First Judge in Arras*); Philip Cash (*Galley Carpenter Warder*); Kathleen Chambers (*Jean's Paris Servant After Convent*); Stephen Chase, Ethan Laidlaw, Claude Payton (*Gendarmes at Bishop's Home*); Davison Clark (*Marcin*); Gilbert Clayton (*Duchaine*); Maxine Cook (*Thernardier's Child*); Edward Cooper (*Prison Clerk*); Harry Cording (*Beam Warder*); J. Gunnis Davis (*Defense Consul in Arras*); Joe de Stefani (*Usher in Arras Courtroom*); Lowell Drew (*Duval*); Cecil Elliott (*Concierge*); William Elmer (*Lawyer*); Arthur Evers (*Court Clerk*); Raul Figarola (*Lawyer*); Budd Fine (*Galley Fight Warder*); Olin Francis (*Galley Whip Warder*); Christian J. Frank (*Gendarme Investigator*); Roger Gray (*Gendarme at Inn*); Robert Greig (*Prison Governor at Jean's Release*); George Guhl (*Onlooker*); Frank Hagney (*Galley Prisoner*); Keith Hitchcock (*Senior Prefect Conducting Gendarme Appointments*); Gertrude Hoffman (*Nurse*); Virginia Howell (*Old Beggar Woman Directing Jean to Bishop*); Olaf Hytten (*Pierre*); John Ince (*Third Judge in Arras*); E. Midge Ingleton (*Peasant on Road*); Paul Irving (*Innkeeper Evicting Jean*); Perry Ivins (*Monsieur Devereaux*); T.C. Jack (*Galley Fight Warder*); J.J. Lentz (*Galley Carpenter*); Jacques Lory (*Prison Clerk*); Wilfred Lucas (*Onlooker*); Mary McLaren (*Nurse*); George MacQuarrie (*Doorman at Arras*); Murdock MacQuarrie (*Fauchelevant*); Jean Marion (*Peasant Child with Jean's Sister*); Jim Mason (*Galley Prisoner*); Frank McCarroll (*Javert's Aide in Chase*); Philo McCullough (*Galley Whip Warder*); J.P. McGowan (*Javert's Plainclothesman*); Al Ferguson, Hercules Mendez, Tony Merlo, Joe Rickson, Monte Vandergrift (*Gendarmes*); Art Miles (*Blacksmith Warder*); Thomas R. Mills (*L'Estrange*); Roberta Mountjoy (*Thernardier's Child*); Leonard Mudie (*Priest Counseling Released Prisoners*); G. Raymond Nye (*Jacques*);

In *Les Misérables* (1935), Laughton gives a powerful and memorable performance as the obsessive executor of the criminal law, Inspector Javert.

Billie Orlean (*Peasant Child with Jean's Sister*); Paul Palmer (*Javert's Aide in Chase*); Frederick Peters (*Galley Whip Warder*); Francis Powers (*Lawyer*); Albert Prisco (*Galley Prisoner*); Lorin Raker (*Valsin*); Gerald Rogers (*Onlooker*); Buddy Roosevelt (*Beggar*); Kai Schmidt (*Lawyer*); Nick Shaid (*Old Beggar in Road*); C. Montague Shaw (*Factory Foreman*); Clifford Smith (*Javert's Aide in Chase*); Pat Somerset (*François*); Pietro Sosso (*Jean's Valet Arranging Coach to Calais*); Walter Stegmeier (*Galley Carpenter*); Leo Sulky (*Galley Whip Warder*); Emma Tansey (*Peasant Woman in Road*); Cyril Thornton (*Javert's Plainclothesman*); Anders Van Haden (*Second Judge in Arras*); Perry N. Vekroff (*Clerk in Favorelles*); Bradley Ward (*Plainclothesman in Bois*); Harry Webberly (*Lawyer*); Lillian West (*Jean's Landlady*); Cecil Weston (*Lodging Housekeeper*); Robert Wilber (*Galley Prisoner*); Leo Willis, Harry Wilson (*Galley Fight Warders*); Eric Wilton (*Gendarme Investigator*).

Awards: Academy Award Nomination: Best Picture; Academy Award Nomination: Best Cinematography: Gregg Toland; Academy Award Nomination: Best Film Editing: Barbara McLean; Academy Award Nomination: Best Assistant Director: Eric Stacey.

Synopsis: At the beginning of the nineteenth century, in a court of law in Favorelles, France, Jean Valjean is sentenced to ten years as a galley slave for stealing a loaf of bread to feed his starving family. As Valjean endures his unjust prison stay, officer Emil Javert has served four years in the police service in the Landrecy District and has a good record, but he is denied promotion on the grounds of his family background (his father was a galley slave and he himelf was born in prison). He submits that he is a servant of the law and intends to carry out his duty to obey the rule of law to the letter. This appeal to his superior officer effects the confirmation of his appointment. During his sentence as a galley slave, Jean Valjean witnesses brutality, injustice and privation to himself and his fellow prisoners. On release from prison, he finds an inhospitable world ill disposed to a former convict. As he sits brooding in the pouring rain, a passerby suggests he pay a call on the local priest. Bishop Bienvenue offers him a meal and a bed for the night without any preconditions. During the night, Valjean makes off with several silver plates but is later apprehended by the police. When the police confront the bishop, he advises them that the silver plates were not stolen but were a gift to Valjean. The Bishop even asks why Valjean did not take the two candlesticks! Moved by the bishop's generosity of spirit, and his plea that life is for giving not taking. Valjean determines that he shall improve himself and keep on the right side of the law. Five years later, Valjean has taken on the identity of Monsieur Madeleine, owner of a thriving glass factory. He is renowned for paying good wages and is a model employer. The town council members pay a call on Madeleine and beg him to consider becoming mayor of the district. Although initially he declines, he is eventually won over by the high esteem his workers display towards him. As Madeleine is elected mayor, Javert is appointed inspector of police. The pair meet and Madeleine immediately asks for justice in Javert's administration of the law. A former employee, Fantine, visits Javert and appeals for reinstatement (she was dismissed because of rumors she had given birth to a child out of wedlock). When her appeal fails, she decides to take her case directly to Monsieur Madeleine and presents herself in a distraught manner to him. Though Javert would have her arrested, Madeleine demands justice and instructs that the sick woman be cared for while he searches for her young daughter Cosette, who he finds slaving at a local inn. While rescuing Cosette, he encounters a man trapped under a cart. He uses his back to lift the cart and this is witnessed by Javert, who is already suspicious of Madeleine. The policeman makes enquiries and learns that a convict known as Champmathieu has confessed in open court that he is none other than the wanted Jean Valjean. Javert goes to Madeleine and confesses his actions and requests that he be dismissed and that charges be pressed. Madeleine refuses, and his refusal greatly annoys Javert. Madeleine decides he must go to the court and reveal his true identity to the court. Following the revelation of his true identity, Valjean rushes to Fantine with a dowry of 20,000 francs to take care of Cosette. Javert, who witnesses the offer, confiscates the money. When Fantine dies a short time after, Valjean knocks Javert to the ground and makes good his escape to Cosette, whom he takes to a convent. He changes his identity to Monsieur Duval and succeeds in getting a position as a gardener in the convent. Many years later, following Cosette's confirmation, she meets a young law student, Marius, who is agitating for social reforms. They fall in love. Marius is being spied on by Javert. Cosette is followed back to the convent, where Valjean sees his tormentor. He packs at once and intends to take Cosette to England with him. When Cosette tells him she has fallen in love, he responds with jealousy and anger. Because of her love for him, Cosette reluctantly agrees to accompany him. However, a friend of Marius arrives bearing a message saying that Marius is heavily involved in fighting in street barricades. Her love for Marius is evident and, remembering the words of Bishop Bienvenue, Valjean accompanies Cosette to the student revolt on the streets. The students succeed in capturing Javert, but Valjean intervenes and appeals for the release of Javert. More than ever, Javert is outraged by the clemency offered by Valjean and pursues Valjean as he carries a wounded Marius in his arms in the Paris sewers. He finally brings Marius to Cosette and begs a few moments from Javert so he may say goodbye to Cosette. Javert agrees and overhears a prayer spoken by Valjean. When Valjean returns outside, he finds a pair of handcuffs on the ground: Javert has drowned himself by jumping in the river.

(1935) Les Misérables

Selected Dialogue:

JAVERT: "While I'm in charge here, regulations—good, bad or indifferent—must be carried out to the letter!"

JAVERT: "Give me a free hand. I promise you there'll soon be very few criminals in this community."

JAVERT: "The law allows you nothing."

Production Commentary: In his 1936 diary, actor Michael Redgrave mentioned going to a cinema in the city of Liverpool (he began his professional acting career at the Liverpool Playhouse) to see *Les Misérables*. He described audience reactions to Javert: "Audience follow closely and resent Javert: Mock groans at his 'redemption.'" Redgrave then gives a backhanded compliment to Laughton's acting abilities: "Laughton up to his old tricks, but impresses in spite of them."[32] At the time of writing, Redgrave had never set foot in a film studio so he went to the cinema to check out the latest screen acting. He could have done much worse in selecting a Laughton screen performance. Though this Hollywood version of the famous Victor Hugo novel is heavily condensed, it succeeds in capturing the spirit, if not the essence, of the novel. There was a heavy contender in terms of length and "authenticity" when a simultaneous film version was produced and released in France.[33]

Hugo's historical novel, published in 1862, is renowned for its voluminous prose, the prolixity of its narrative, and many digressions offering commentary on revolution, morality, justice and religion accompanied by a display of Hugo's autodidact tendencies in presenting layers of detail and selective factual historical information. Literary purists may be affronted by the truncation and leveling of W.P. Lipscomb's screenplay. However, the film scenario's use of compression and brevity brings a sense of inner momentum and dramatic sweep to the progress of the narrative and carries the action along at pace.

For the role of the police inspector, Laughton undertook what was for him a necessary, almost systematic process of submerging himself in a role via inner torment and private anguish. These efforts are translated on the screen in the form of intense close-ups showing a pained stillness of expression. The character of Javert is tortured by carrying out the letter-of-the-law as his own conscience begins to doubt the justice of the criminal law. Laughton took it upon himself to devise his own precise and self-contained costume. As in *Ruggles of Red Gap* and *Mutiny on the Bounty*, he maintains a trim physical figure. When Javert first appears, he is among new police recruits, waiting to pass out. When his turn comes, he stands rigidly to attention as his commander reads aloud his personal file—and casts doubt on Javert's suitability. At this point there is a cut from medium shot to a revelatory close-up as we see Javert's bottom lip quivering in anxiety at a moment of crisis. It hangs in the balance whether Javert will have his appointment confirmed. When his commander points out that Javert's father died as a prisoner on the galleys, Javert begins to speak with extreme concentration. He doesn't deny his ancestry, but in a wavering voice that perfectly matches his quivering lip he asserts his sense of duty. In this key moment, Javert is exposed as someone on a knife's edge who will be driven to self-destruction. This tense scene also captures a real sense of the power of speech beginning to disintegrate when a person is placed under pressure. Javert's vulnerability in the face of ambition and cruelty sets the tone for the ensuing drama.

To take on the verisimilitude of Javert's suffering even further, Laughton trudged through slime and mud for shots representing the Parisian sewers. When Javert finally catches up with Valjean and should be savoring a moment of vindictive triumph, the scene becomes a tragedy of torment and despair as Javert commits suicide by drowning. Director Richard Boleslawski refrains from showing his suicide directly and instead concentrates on the paraphernalia of fallible justice: abandoned manacles and police stick swirling in the current of the Seine. The use of ellipsis here is impeccable.

Laughton's Javert is a portrayal of an oppressor acted by someone who was himself oppressed. There have been over 50 film adaptations of Hugo's story, but the Laughton version still stands out for his towering central performance as Javert. Elsa Lanchester suggested that there was a strong sense of catharsis in Laughton's interpretation of the role: "As an actor he probed his personal, innermost pain to bring Javert to the screen

[and] he gave one of those cleansing performances that brought him a little peace" (Lanchester, 1983: 131). Laughton's attempt to set about finding his way into the role often took eccentric turns, as actress Marilyn Knowlden, playing little Cossette in the film, remembered in her autobiography. To prepare for one dramatic scene, Laughton threw chairs around the set. For a child of eight, this was frightening to watch. However, she also saw the lighter side of Laughton when he promised to make an appearance on one of Knowlden's sets. He turned up one day and struck up a friendship when the pair devised an impromptu wooden shoe dance on the set. She wearing wooden clogs and he in hip-length boots!

Production on the film began early in 1935; it was shot in 34 days. Alfred Newman's inspirational music theme was taken from a score composed the previous year for United Artists' *Our Daily Bread*. Both the film and Laughton drew excellent reviews. *Film Daily* (April 3, 1935) declared, "Superb production of Victor Hugo classic hits high mark in entertainment and artistry." Norbert Lusk of *Picture Play* (July 1935): "It is another of the great actor's great portrayals. More than Valjean's nemesis, he reduces to the status of apprentices those with whom he shares scenes. This is because Mr. Laughton makes Javert a man tortured by the discovery that the world he has created for himself is insecure." *Variety* (April 24, 1935): "His performance is much more on the quiet side, but equally powerful and always believable." In essence, Laughton was able to believe in Javert as an individual and then become the character on screen. To accomplish this, he searched deep and adapted his fertile imagination. Despite appearing little like the character in the novel and delivering his lines often in a broad Yorkshire accent, Laughton's blocking and control of body movement lends the film a credence that overrides all these deficiencies.

It was a process which actor James Mason referred to as "a method actor without the bullshit" (Callow: 80). Laughton was paid $100,000. It was money well spent. His screen portrayal as Javert carries due authority and severe gravitas in every scene. On a technical level, he was never more photogenic than when appearing in close-up in *Les Misérables*. The peerless cinematography of Gregg Toland made this possible. As far as the film is concerned, critic Leslie Halliwell was accurate when he remarked, "[I]n adaptation and performance it is hard to see how this film could be bettered" (Halliwell, 1977: 498).

Rembrandt (1936)

Tagline: "You Couldn't Have Better Reviews Even If Rembrandt Painted Them Himself!"[34]

U.K. (A London Film Production/Alexander Korda)

Credits: From the film play by Carl Zuckmayer; Photography: Georges Perinal; Settings Designer: Vincent Korda; Special Effects Director: Ned Mann; Production Manager: David B. Cunynghame; Scenario: June Head; Costume Designer: John Armstrong; Musical Director: Muir Mathieson; Recording Director: A.W. Watkins; Supervising Editor: William Hornbeck; Editor: Francis Lyon; Unit Manager: Geoffrey

Vincent Korda's distinctive art direction in *Rembrandt* (1936) complements Laughton's sensitive playing of the Dutch painter. Here Rembrandt van Rijn indulges himself with wine. As portrayed by Laughton, he is a dedicated but tortured genius of the canvas.

54 (1936) *Rembrandt*

Boothby; Technical Advisor: Johan De Meester; Musical Score: Geoffrey Toye; Camera Operator: Robert Krasker; Assistant Art Director: H.M. Walker; Sound Recordist: A. Fisher; Directed by Alexander Korda; U.K. release: Passed by the British Board of Film Censors on October 29, 1936; General release: November 4, 1936; U.S. release: December 25, 1936; U.K. reissue: 1943, released by British Lion; Genre: Historical Drama: Black and White; Running Time: 84 minutes; DVD Region 1 in Eclipse box set: *Alexander Korda's Private Lives* from the Criterion Collection, released May 2009; English subtitle captions for the deaf and hard of hearing are available on this disc; DVD Region 2 from Network, released August 2015; no English subtitle captions for the deaf and hard of hearing.

Cast: **Charles Laughton** (*Rembrandt van Rijn*); Gertrude Lawrence (*Geertie*); Elsa Lanchester (*Hendrickie*); Edward Chapman (*Fabrizius*); Walter Hudd (*Banning Cocq*); Roger Livesey (*Beggar Saul*); John Bryning (*Titus*); Sam Livesey (*Auctioneer*); Herbert Lomas (*Rembrandt's Father*); Allan Jeayes (*Tulp*); John Clements (*Flinck*); Raymond Huntley (*Ludwick*); Abraham Sofaer (*Menasseh*); Lawrence Hanray (*Heertsbeeke*); Austin Trevor (*Marquis*); Henry Hewitt (*Jan Six*); Gertrude Musgrove (*Girl at Inn*); Richard Gofe (*Titus, as a Child*); Basil Gill (*Rembrandt's Brother*); Barry Livesey (*Peasant Lad*), (*Peasant Lads*); Jack Livesey (*Journeyman*); John Turnbull (*Minister*); Edmund Willard (*Van Zeeland*); **Uncredited Cast**: Hector Abbas, Charles Paton, Leonard Sharp (*Burghers at Auction*); Evelyn Ankers (*Minor Role*); Baroness Barany (*Criada*); Lewis Broughton (*Saskia's Brother*); Rex Evans, Wilfrid Hyde White (*Civil Guardsmen*); William Fagan (*Burgomaster*); Marius Goring (*Baron Leivens*); Alexander Knox (*Ludwick's Assistant*); Quentin McPhearson (*Official*); George Merritt (*Church Warden*); Hay Petrie (*Jeweler*); Bellenden Powell (*Court Member*); George Pughe (*Museum Director*); Jerrold Robertshaw (*Museum Director*); Byron Webber (*Court Member*); Roger Wellesley (*Burgomaster's Secretary*).

Synopsis: In seventeenth century Holland, Rembrandt van Rijn, the son of a miller from Leyden, became the greatest painter of the age. Rembrandt goes to a painter's shop for materials to paint a portrait of his wife Saskia. A gathering crowd beckons Rembrandt over and they insist that he join them for a drink. In an artist's studio, two apprentice artists discuss with another trainee how much each pays for the privilege of being taught by Rembrandt. When Rembrandt's housekeeper Geertie enters, one of the student painters insists that Rembrandt be told how ill his wife is. Geertie brings doctors to the house. Meanwhile, at the local tavern, Rembrandt is being toasted. A servant enters and tells Rembrandt that his beloved Lady Saskia is ill. Rembrandt rushes back to his house, but his wife has died. An equerry to the Prince of Orange pays Rembrandt a visit in his studio where the painter is desperate to finish the portrait of his late wife. The equerry announces the condolences of the House of Orange, but Rembrandt pays scant attention and continues painting with intense concentration. Rembrandt finally puts the finishing touches to his masterpiece "The Night Watch." The huge painting is unveiled amid hilarity, embarrassment and incredulity. Several of his patrons voice their concerns and worries, and beg Rembrandt to explain himself and save the situation. Inflamed by their disregard for his artistic interpretation of a collection of members of the civic military guard, Rembrandt launches into a bitter denunciation of their high rank and distinguished position as viewed in the painting. At Rembrandt's home, an art student tells his servant her master is now a laughingstock. Rembrandt returns home and decides to drink his problems away. Geertie and the two young art students join him in drunken revelry. In a drunken stupor, Rembrandt reveals his need of a woman he can call his wife. Ten years later, Rembrandt is now married to Geertie. However, all is not well. Several debtors serve his family with a writ of bankruptcy. His wife is told that the young prince is due in court and that Rembrandt should petition him for a commission or a grant. With this, he will be solvent again. Rembrandt takes a walk and encounters a beggar. Rembrandt makes an offer for the beggar to pose in his studio for a portrait of the King of the Old Testament. In the middle of the sitting, there is a banging on the door. Geertie remonstrates with bailiffs threatening to repossess the house. Rembrandt must approach the prince. As he steps outside, he again meets the beggar, who suggests that as they are both impecunious, Rembrandt should accompany him and learn the tricks of begging. Rembrandt decides he should return to his home in Leyden, and the peasants who were his people. He returns to the family home where his elderly father still lives. In the local inn, Rembrandt encounters hostility and derision. He ends up brawling with some locals and decides to return to Amsterdam. Upon his return, his wife complains that he avoids her. Rembrandt meets the new maid, Hendrickje Stoffels, and paints her portrait. They express a liking for each other, and eventually are able to marry, but as a debtor Rembrandt is forced from his home. The couple retreats to a small house in the countryside. Hendrickje is terminally ill, and requests that members of the household do not reveal her condition as it would spoil the happiness of the couple's marriage. As they sit in the studio talking of their first meeting, Hendrickje collapses and dies in her sitting chair. Rembrandt is heartbroken. In his final years, an eccentric Rembrandt is still in poverty, but he encounters a crowd of young people who invite him to a tavern. There he dispenses the wisdom of old age, and an ex-pupil gives him money so he can buy food. Instead, Rembrandt heads to the art shop to buy painting materials, and returns to his studio to begin work on a final self-portrait.

Selected Dialogue:

REMBRANDT: "Your nose is painted by bad liquor. Your mouth is reeking with bawdy kisses. Vanity and stupidity are written all over your face. The only pretty thing about you are your ruffs and your breastplates. And the only distinguished thing about you are your hats."

REMBRANDT: "What is success? A soldier can reckon his success in victories. The merchant, in money. But my world is insubstantial. I live in a beautiful, blinding, swirling mist. The world can offer me nothing."

REMBRANDT: "The world is a narrow cage enclosed on four sides by iron bars. You can beat your head against those bars until you're sick. But you'll never get out, never as long as you live."

REMBRANDT: "Painters have a different way of looking at things. You must imagine I am looking at you in the same way as the water with which you wash yourself, or the air you move in or the light that shines on you."

REMBRANDT: "Vanity of vanities. All is vanity."

Production Commentary: *Rembrandt* has the distinction of being one of the first films to be shot at new film studios built at Denham, Buckinghamshire. Founded by Alexander Korda, the studios were financed by Prudential Insurance.

Director Vincente Minnelli's *Lust for Life* (MGM, 1956), a biopic of painter Vincent van Gogh, provides a pre-credit rider acknowledging various institutional galleries for their help in permitting the prodigious display of Van Gogh's work on screen. *Rembrandt* refrained, apart from a long shot of the famed "The Night Watch," from showing any of the artist's paintings on screen. Elsa Lanchester explained that the original plan was to use paintings on screen for dramatic emphasis. However, it was soon realized that dramatic interest existed in the inclinations which caused the man to paint. Besides, having self-portraits on screen would have reminded the public that Laughton was not the painter Rembrandt (Lanchester, 1938: 225–26). It can be argued that the absence of artwork allows audiences to concentrate solely on the drama itself.

As in *The Private Life of Henry VIII*, the story of Rembrandt is framed via the maturing of the central character. The story begins at the height of Rembrandt's powers as a painter and then covers his life until the onset of doting old age. Each episode of his life is consistent with a concentration of intimate dramatic detail and careful precision.

Preparations for the film begin in May 1936 when it was announced that Alexander Korda would direct. On May 8, 1936, it was reported that Laughton had left London for Amsterdam to make intensive searches for primary sources regarding the renowned master painter. The film was allocated a budget of $980,000 and production began in early June 1936 with Gertrude Lawrence and Elsa Lanchester cast in leading roles. By July 24, Lawrence had completed her work. With principal photography completed, a second unit left for Holland at the end of August to take exteriors in Amsterdam and at Rembrandt's former home.

On *Rembrandt*, director Korda had many distractions. He found himself juggling the incessant demands of a studio mogul pressured to attend various public relations and production meetings. Korda utilized not only press and radio to publicize *Rembrandt* but the film was included among seven film excerpts shown as part of experimental test transmissions on the inaugural broadcast of British television on August 26, 1936. Despite the heavy publicity drive, critical reaction was muted if respectful. On the one hand, the combination of Korda and Laughton was sure to fire speculative interest given their successful collaboration on *The Private Life of Henry VIII*. Korda had a track record of tackling historical subjects and bringing large-scale dramas to a wider public. Laughton had also proved, time and again, that he was able to bring to the screen difficult characterizations with verisimilitude. However, critics noted that there was no precedent for the subject matter of Rembrandt. For a large sector of the paying public, the fortunes of a painter set, in the remote locale of Holland, and the presentation of obscure Dutch laws would be a drag on its box office prospects. Nevertheless, it was felt that the very unfamiliarity of these weaknesses in *Rembrandt* could be overcome by "legitimate novelty." It was described by *Harrison's Reports* (December 12, 1936) as "fairly good" but the review went on to lament the deficiency of the story:

> [I]t is rambling and lacks dramatic power; Laughton goes into long speeches that at times are stirring and at other times dull. The most interesting events in Rembrandt's career are just sketched over. And the transition from one period of his life to another is handled too abruptly. As it stands, it is a picture that should entertain mostly cultured audiences, for it lacks mass appeal.

Independent Exhibitor's Film Bulletin (December 30, 1936) saw it for what it was, an art house film: "*Rembrandt* will hold interest for the masses only because of the presence of Charles Laughton—and he will not disappoint them—but, being a heavy costume play, it is safe to predict that even many of his followers will pass it up." Film exhibitors were advised: "Sell this as Laughton's greatest performance. Ignore the story and concentrate on the star!" The *Motion Picture Daily* (November 17, 1936) opined,

> This story of the life of one of the greatest of painters is, in fact, just a bit out of focus. It seems to have nearly every quality but the most important quality of all, conviction. The studio work is brilliant, but there is too much studio. Laughton is brilliant in his best moments, but there is too much Laughton; he is a magnificent elocutionist but why, except to prove that fact, give him two long biblical passages to deliver [...]?

According to *National Board Review Magazine* (January 1937),

> Laughton has made an astonishing gallery of screen portrayals.... But in every one of them was something of tour de force, remarkable cleverness and skill that excited admiration but rarely sympathy, always just that shade too theatrical that kept it from really touching the heart. Here in *Rembrandt* however, there is an inescapable increase in Laughton's stature as an actor. That oft-praised art that conceals art is at work and not now as so often before do we sit admiringly watching, conscious even as we watch that we are seeing something that we are inwardly labelling good acting.... It is easy to believe that Rembrandt was like that, like the painter Laughton makes live so vitally on the screen.

Graham Greene in *The Spectator* (November 20, 1936) wrote that he considered Korda's film as incidental in plot, and its subject depicted in a too reverential and pompous manner. He went on to complain, "[N]o amount of money spent on expensive sets, no careful photography, will atone for the lack of a story 'line,' the continuity and drive of a well-constructed plot." *Observer* critic Caroline Lejeune praised the film (November 8, 1936): "[The] film which Alexander Korda and Charles Laughton have made together with so much sweat and love and heart-searching is one of the finest films ever produced here or in any other country—but I am quite prepared to admit that this may be a matter of taste."

Laughton at this time was at the pinnacle of his acting career, and in *Rembrandt* he chose to turn his back on Hollywood and give what turned out to be a remarkable and considered account of the life and struggle of an inspired artist. As a total actor, he gave a strong impression of being the complete character (from the apex of his creative powers to the failing decline of his dotage) rather than just acting out the role. But critical opinion was mixed and the paying public, puzzled by it all, chose to stay away.

Undeterred, Laughton decided to continue in his personal quest to become independent as an artist and be able to create work according to his inclinations and on his own unique terms.

Vessel of Wrath also known as The Beachcomber (1938)

Tagline: "The Critics Cheer—The Magazines Rave! Acclaimed as the Grandest Role of Laughton's Film Career—and a Sure-fire Money-Maker for Theatres Everywhere."[35]

U.K. (Mayflower Pictures)

Credits: Written for the screen by Bartlett Cormack; A Pommer-Laughton Production; Photography: Jules Kruger; Settings: Tom Morahan; Music: Richard Addinsell; Musical Director: Muir Mathieson; Scenario: B. Van Thal; Editor: Robert Hamer; Sound Recordist: Jack Rogerson: Technical Advisor: C.M. Morrell; Assistant Director: Edward Baird; Camera Operator: Gus Drisse; Production Manager: Roland Gillett; Produced and Directed By Erich Pommer; U.K. release: February 24, 1938; U.K. reissue: 1949, released by Renown; U.S. release: March 10, 1939; Genre: Comedy; Black and White; Running Time: 92 minutes; DVD all regions from Reel Vault, released July 2015; no English subtitle captions for the deaf and hard of hearing.

Cast: Charles Laughton (*Ginger Ted/Edward Claude Wilson*); Elsa Lanchester (*Martha Jones*); Robert Newton (*The Controleur*); Tyrone Guthrie (*The Reverend Jones*); Eliot Makeham (*The Clerk*); Dolly Mollinger (*Lia*); D.A. Ward (*The Chieftain*); J. Solomon (*The Sergeant*); **Uncredited Cast**: S Alley (*Mechanic*); Dudley (*A Dog*); Mah Foo (*Ho*); Rosita Garcia (*Kati*); Fred Groves (*Dutch Sea Captain*); Ley On (*Ah King*).

Synopsis: In the Dutch Colonial South Seas, feckless reprobate Edward Claude Wilson, known as "Ginger Ted," is arrested when English missionary Martha Jones and her brother Owen accuse him of using a native girl, Lia, for his own lustful desires. The Controleur sentences Ginger Ted to three months of hard labor and sends him to alcohol-free Agor Island—the home of many native women. The Joneses decide to take him in hand and save him from his dissolute self. Martha insists on going to a nearby island to treat a medical emergency. The Controleur sends a staff member along to accompany her and gives covert orders that Ginger will be picked up on the return journey. As Martha and Ginger reluctantly sail together, the boat strikes its propeller on a reef. During the night despite initial antagonism the two eventually warm to each other. When Martha returns unscathed her brother congratulates Ted for his positive behavior towards his sister. When the Controleur hears this from Ted he laughs uncontrollably which prompts Ted to knock him down unconscious. Returning to his waterside shack he becomes drunk and passes out. When he wakes, he finds Martha has tidied up his dwelling. Incensed he tells her to leave. The Controleur asks that Ted accompany Dr. Jones to help while he innoculates natives on adjacent islands where a plague of typhoid has broken out. Reluctantly, Ted agrees. In the middle of his inoculation, Jones is stricken with malaria. The headsman's wife arrives bearing her sick child. Martha

Laughton as reprobate derelict "Ginger Ted" and Elsa Lanchester as schoolmistress Miss Martha Jones in the dramatic comedy *Vessel of Wrath*—known in the U.S. as *The Beachcomber* (1938).

innoculates the child, but when the headsman demands the return of his child and is refused, drums are heard ominously in the jungle. The pair begin to exchange confessions about their lives. Ginger tells Martha he had always wanted to marry a barmaid, run away and buy a pub despite being the son of a vicar. Martha then replies that her father had drunk himself to death. In the morning the inoculated child recovers and any danger from vengeful natives passes and they are free to leave the island. When Martha and Ted return to England they decide to run a local pub known as "The Fox and Rabbit Darts Club." In an effort to reform Ginger has taken the pledge and abstains from consuming any alcohol.

Selected Dialogue:

TED: "Aw, dry up, you blubbering monkey."
TED: "I was mad for the minute. I got over it. It does stick in my craw, you giving way to that twitty twerp."
TED: "I was the fat boy at school. They used to call me 'Jack Spratt.'"

Production Commentary: Laughton made few friends in Hollywood, but those he did befriend, he was excessively fond of. One of his closest Hollywood friends was director Josef von Sternberg. Laughton told *Photoplay* (October 1934) that, when offered a role in von Sternberg's *The Scarlet Empress* (Paramount, 1934), he refused, saying, "We wouldn't get along." Following the debacle of the aborted filming of Alexander Korda's *I, Claudius*, under von Sternberg's directorial baton, Laughton decided to take on the mantle of producer and actor and form a new film company, Mayflower Pictures.[36] The company was set up using facilities at Elstree Studios and Laughton had two business partners: German émigré Erich Pommer was co-producer and director, while financial backing came from executive John Maxwell. *Vessel of Wrath*, or *The Beachcomber* as it is known in the U.S., was the first of three films produced under the Mayflower banner.

Laughton found the role of producer-actor an exhausting experience. Like his mentor Irving Thalberg, he was on call virtually 24 hours a day seven days a week with production meetings and schedules as well as the rigors of filming itself. *Vessel of Wrath* was an expensive and ambitious film shot on location for four weeks in the South of France at Golfe Juan and St. Tropez. This was a complex logistical exercise involving location scouting to arrange for advanced transportation for a film crew of between 50 and 60 people, including sound and camera crew, makeup, wardrobe and catering. The interiors were shot at Elstree and these had to be matched up in a seamless fashion with the second unit exteriors already filmed.

Elsa Lanchester played the prim, sanctimonious missionary Miss Jones and Laughton was indolent reprobate Ginger Ted. Being both non-conformist in religious and morality, the parts were eminently suitable for them. They make an incongruous yet appealing couple. The differing backgrounds of the two protagonists is reminiscent of C.S. Forester's central characters in his 1935 novel *The African Queen*. Charlie Allnut and Rose Sayer were later played memorably by Humphrey Bogart and Katharine Hepburn in John Huston's excellent 1951 film adaptation.

Vessel of Wrath's adapted scenario, taken from the 1931 Somerset Maugham short story, was written by Bartlett Cormack (1898–1942). Cormack had a good track record of adapting scenarios for the screen (including his own stage play *The Racket*). He adapted Ben Hecht and Charles MacArthur's play *The Front Page* for Howard Hughes' 1931 movie, and wrote *This Day and Age* (Paramount, 1933), *Four Frightened People* (Paramount, 1934) and *Cleopatra* (Paramount, 1934) for Cecil B. DeMille.

Censorship thwarted the pretense of a realistic depiction of a lowlife character such as Ginger Ted. The presence of occasional idiomatic expression such as "twerp" are a reminder of the risible censorial compromises filmmakers had to endure at the behest of the British Board of Film Censors. This was the first of only two film performances by the English stage producer and actor Tyrone Guthrie (1900–1971) who, on both occasions, was persuaded by Laughton to appear in front of the camera. Here he played a gangling and somewhat eccentric missionary. It is also interesting that an early role was given to Robert Newton (1905–1956). He had worked with Laughton on the aborted *I, Claudius*, and after *Vessel of Wrath* appeared alongside him again in *Jamaica Inn*. His dramatic role of the Controleur is performed in an understated and restrained fashion, in direct contrast to his later role of pirate Long John Silver in *Treasure Island* (Walt Disney, Byron Haskin, 1950). Newton appeared in the 1954 remake *The Beachcomber* (United Artists/London Films, Muriel Box, 1954) as Ginger Ted, using all his exaggerated and flamboyant vocal delivery and acting persona.

Critical reaction to *The Vessel of Wrath* was distinctly mixed. Critic John Grierson in *World Film News* (April 1938) stated, "Like any first film from a new production unit *Vessel of Wrath* is a problem child.... The trouble with Laughton is that he is good at several very different things. Add to these talents the equally various ones of being good at comedy and quite brilliant in slapstick and you have a deadly mixture of virtues." According to *The Motion Picture Herald* (March 26, 1938):

> Whether directorial treatment, script confusion or editorial indifference has translated coherence into a rather cacophonous mass, it is difficult to estimate, but in its present form Pommer's film is less a social or psychological essay than an effort at half-hearted burlesque. Laughton's "Ginger Ted" is broadly enough designed, but his missionary opposite savors rather of revue than real life.... There is the nucleus of something bigger than normal in the Laughton-Pommer team, but until star and producer no longer share other burdens than those for which they are equipped, we may have to wait.

In a capsule review, *Silver Screen* (February 1939) was also doubtful about the film: "So-so. This one may be a bit hard for some of you to swallow.... [It] does not live up to the promise of its original, in spite of the casting of Charles Laughton and his wife, Elsa Lanchester, in the principal roles. The incidental music and the photography are things to rave about, however." By contrast, *Variety* (March 16, 1938) was upbeat:

> Moment this film starts you recognize the master touch. Laughton has a flair for film producing and in cooperation with such an experienced topnotcher as Erich Pommer, a well-turned-out picture is assured. This one should be a hit of no mean proportion here, and should do well in America.... Laughton has an ideal role. He plays a lovable derelict, better than a ruthless ship's commander, getting more out of comedy than drama. His humor is invigorating, even when bordering on the indelicate, and his character portrayal is unctuously persuasive. Elsa Lanchester makes an excellent foil for him.... Characterization is amusing without undue caricature.... Thoroughly ingratiating comedy, and the entertainment unfailing.

Though *Vessel of Wrath* was a good effort, none of the three Mayflower films were unequivocal artistic triumphs or instant commercial hits. As a group they remain stylized hybrids. The ghost of UFA studios hangs in all three of these films. Laughton can be compared to Emil Jannings in playing characters such as Ginger Ted, whose self-respect is disadvantaged by the fate of their circumstances. Dramatic self-abasement and comic pathos are difficult attributes to convey successfully though Laughton is to be commended for trying.

St. Martin's Lane also known as *Sidewalks of London* (1938)

Tagline: "When VIVIEN LEIGH Swings It ... and CHARLES LAUGHTON Sings It ... (WOW!)"[37]

U.K. (Mayflower Pictures)

Credits: Written by Clemence Dane; Directed by Tim Whelan; Photography: Jules Kruger; Settings: Tom Morahan; Music: Arthur Johnston; Costumes: John Armstrong; Lyrics: Eddie Pola; Musical Director: Muir Mathieson; Film Editors: Hugh Stewart, Robert Hamer; Dance Director: Philip Buchel; Sound Recordist: Jack Rogerson; Assistant Director: Philip Brandon; Camera Operator: Gus Drisse; Musical Assistant: Fred Lewis; Production Manager: Roland Gillett; Produced by Erich Pommer; U.K. release: Passed by the British Board of Film Censors on June 20, 1938; General release: July 30, 1938; U.K. reissue: 1949, released by Renown; U.S. release: February 16, 1940; Genre: Romantic Drama; Black and White; Running Time: 84 minutes; Blu-ray Region A and DVD Region 1, *The Vivien Leigh Anniversary Collection* box set, Cohen Film Collection, released November 2013; no English subtitle captions for the deaf and hard of hearing.

Cast: Charles Laughton (*Charles Staggers*); Vivien Leigh (*Libby*); Rex Harrison (*Harley Prentiss*); Larry Adler (*Constantine*); Tyrone Guthrie (*Gentry*); Maire O'Neill (*Mrs. Such*); Gus McNaughton (*Arthur Smith*); Polly Ward (*Frankie*); Basil Gill (*Magistrate*); Helen Haye (*Selina*); David Burns (*Hackett*); Phyllis Stanley

(1938) St. Martin's Lane

(*Della*); Edward Lexy (*Mr. Such*); Clare Greet (*Old Maud*); Alf Goddard (*Doggie*); Cyril Smith (*Blackface*); Romilly Lunge (*Duchesi*); Ronald Ward (*Temperley*); Carroll Gibbons and His Orchestra; The Luna Boys and Other London Street Entertainers; **Uncredited Cast**: Clifford Buckton (*Man Outside Theater*); Bartlett Cormack (*Strang*); Edie Martin (*Libby's Dresser*); Ronald Shiner (*Barman*); John Singer (*Autograph Hunter*); Jerry Verno (*Drunk*).

Working Titles: *Partners of the Night*; *London After Dark*

Synopsis: In London, entertainers ("buskers") in the street outside the many theaters and cinemas are part of city life in the evening. A well-known actor steps out of his car at a theater and is mobbed for his autograph. A young woman, Libby, is disappointed not to obtain his autograph, and then is drawn to a recitation performed by busker Charles Staggers. A pickpocket, she steals a small tip given to Staggers by a passerby and goes to a coffee stall to spend it. There she meets a songwriter, Hartley Prentiss, who offers her a cigarette which she gladly accepts. Staggers appears and demands that she return his tip. His loud protestations attract the attention of a policeman. Prentiss is bemused by all the commotion, but Staggers catches sight of Libby stealing Prentiss' cigarette case. She runs off. Staggers tracks her down to a deserted property where she begins an impromptu dance. When Staggers challenges her about absconding with his tip, their argument is heard in the street outside by a policeman who whistles for assistance. They both slip away, and Libby finds herself in Staggers' lodgings. The following morning, Staggers' landlord becomes aware that Staggers has a female in his room. Staggers locks the ill-tempered Libby in his room while he tries to straighten things out. When he returns to his room, now wrecked by the distraught Libby, he calms her down and offers the prospect of Libby becoming his leading lady in a new busker routine. With a newfound confidence, she bakes Staggers a birthday cake. Staggers, Libby and two other buskers form a street singing quartet, with Libby dancing. Prentiss arrives to thank Staggers for finding his cigarette case. False modesty forbids Staggers from rejecting the offer of a financial reward. Libby appears and invites Prentiss into Staggers' apartment, where she gives a partial and potted account of her life and plans which include a new production outside the Holborn Empire. As they perform, Prentiss appears with influential friends. A police constable shoos away the street performers as a public nuisance, and the troupe repairs to a local pub. Libby decides to make contact with Prentiss at his penthouse. Next, Libby--or Liberty, as she is known on the stage—rises from bit parts to leading lady in a succession of plays. Prentiss' is searching for a new, catchy song. Liberty remembers the tune from her street theater days and

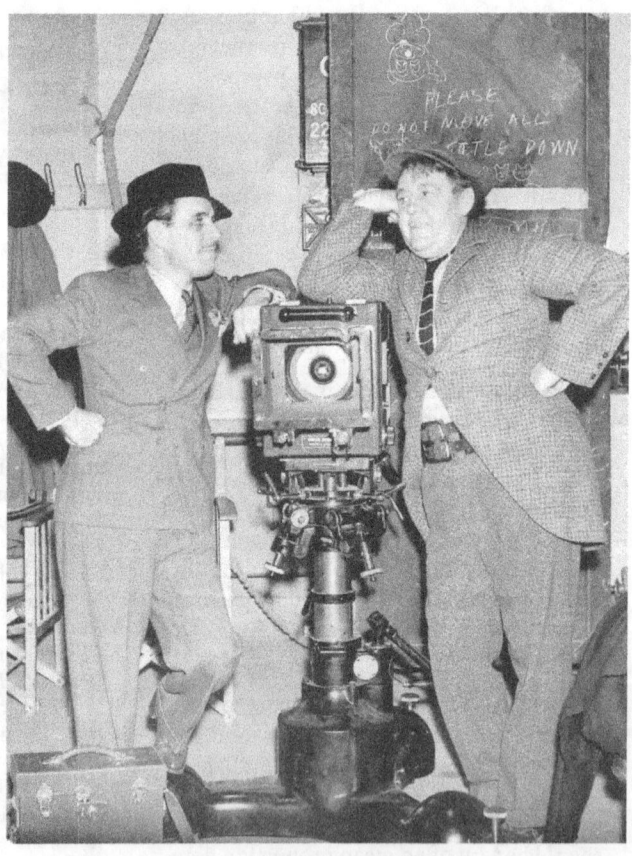

Director Tim Whelan and Laughton (right) relax on the soundstages of the British film *St. Martin's Lane*—known in the U.S. as *Sidewalks of London* (1938).

picks it out on the piano. The tune is reorchestrated and forms the centerpiece of her new musical. As she prepares to dress backstage, through an open window comes the familiar sound of buskers in the street. Following her triumph on stage, Liberty is mobbed by autograph seekers. At the back of the large crowd is a drunken Staggers, who tries to attract Liberty's attention, but only succeeds in appearing antisocial and is arrested by the police. After his trial and sentencing, Staggers wanders the street pretending to be blind. He encounters Libby, who takes him in a taxi to her apartment. She has hopes that she can find a place for Staggers in the theater. But his audition does not go well, and he decides that being an actor on the legitimate stage is not for him. As he leaves the stage, Libby tries to persuade him to stay, to no avail. In the street, he encounters his old busker friends, and he joins them, performing his favorite recitation again.

Selected Dialogue:

STAGGERS: "There ain't no answer. You're after justice and logic. There ain't no justice and there ain't no logic. The world ain't made that way. Everything's luck, see. And good temper. And if you can take a joke. The whole of life's a joke."

STAGGERS: "I'm a man, I am. There's some of yeh thinks it funny I should say so. I think it's funny myself. I'm fed up with the union office. Dear old Charles, good old Charles. Yes, he's good enough to fetch and carry good enough to feed the cat when the rest of you can't spare the time, but when it comes to give and take, work and play, men and women, then it's good morning to you, Charles, keep on your own side of the street; the gutter side."

STAGGERS: "This isn't any good, darling. You can't make an actor out of me. I've been outside. Why, I'm a busker, see, I'm all right."

Production Commentary: This second film produced by Laughton's Mayflower Films has occasional passages of brilliance but is otherwise variable. Like the main title which is missing an apostrophe, the film lacks coherence and unity. It required firmer direction than import Tim Whelan was able to deliver. But then again, with Laughton and producer Erich Pommer constantly looking over his shoulder, who can be surprised if a sense of disarray appears on the screen from time to time? Whelan had a background as a writer of silent comedy, including Harold Lloyd and Harry Langdon films. There are occasional flashes of this surfacing, such as the chase when Libby is being pursued for the theft of money. In *World Film News* (November 1938), critic Basil Wright called it "a throwback to the deep glamour of the Golden days of the German cinema: the genius of Pommer." Wright also noted that Pommer handled Laughton in the manner of a previous German star, Emil Jannings: Both tended to act with their backs.

Laughton throughout his life was fascinated by entertainers. Street performers or buskers in the open streets entertaining direct to the public chimed with Laughton's credo of bringing art and entertainment to the masses. For Laughton, this was of great significance. A tale in which a natural talent is discovered and nurtured also appealed to the teacher in him. He hoped to cast his wife Elsa Lanchester in the role of Libby, but to gain the necessary finance from Alexander Korda he had to acquiesce to Korda's insistence that Vivien Leigh be cast. Laughton found Leigh, like Carole Lombard, unbearable. Leigh too had a penchant for spewing invective and obscenities at the drop of a hat.

The film was released in the U.S. in 1940 after the media furor of *Gone with the Wind*, and reviewers were keen to contrast Libby with Scarlett O'Hara. The two characters were said to be intent on fame rather than morality. In the States, the film was distributed under the title *Sidewalks of London*. The *New York Times* (February 15, 1940) was doubtful about its appeal for the average American audience:

> Mr. Laughton and his buskery troupe seem never quite up to the job of convincing us that busker, as a peculiarly British institution, deserves our sympathy. But, much as we should like to have been affected, we remained, to the end, singularly unmoved by Mr. Laughton's buskered, bewhiskered drama. And this we will admit, was not entirely the fault [of] script or director. Mr. Laughton, Miss Leigh, Rex Harrison and

the others have performed their stints most gracefully, and Tim Whelan...has kept his picture moving—perceptibly anyway. But chiefly, we feel, the film was not meant for us. It is not our language at all, and it hasn't been sufficiently well handled to speak coherently in the universal terms of drama. Dullish is the word for it.

Film Daily (January 31, 1940) saw Laughton's role as a street entertainer as, "turning from his usual cruel and terrifying roles" and an attempt to avoid typecasting and seize a new opportunity in his acting career. *Variety* (January 24, 1940) thought Laughton's performance was "excellent," but also noted, "For class audiences it's amusing, but general audiences will [find it] decidedly colloquial.... Tim Whelan's direction delves into human characterization, but is too slowly paced to hit wide American audience reaction."

Laughton's Staggers is yet another character at odds with society. He gets by using his own gifts of intuition and the power of performance to deceive ("blag") his way into a situation and then out again with his pride and prejudice both intact. For Laughton, high art and low life were intertwined inextricably.

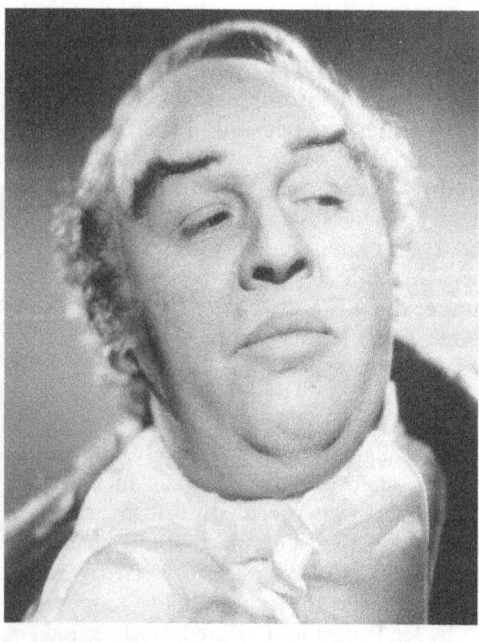

Laughton in heavy disguise as Sir Humphrey Pengallan: a gentleman and a blaggard in *Jamaica Inn* (1939).

Jamaica Inn (1939)

Tagline: "The one and only Charles Laughton as that monster in human form—Sir Humphrey Pengallan who holds six trembling lives within his evil net!"[38]

U.K. (Mayflower Pictures)

Credits: Adapted from the novel by Daphne Du Maurier; Screenplay: Sidney Gilliat and Joan Harrison; Dialogue: Sidney Gilliat; Continuity: Alma Reville; Additional Dialogue: J.B. Priestley; Photography: Harry Stradling in collaboration with Bernard Knowles; Settings: Tom Morahan; Costumes: Molly McArthur; Music: Eric Fenby; Musical Director: Frederic Lewis; Sound Recordist: Jack Rogerson; Editor: Robert Hamer; Special Effects: Harry Watt; Makeup: Ern Westmore; Production Manager: Hugh Perceval; Directed by Alfred Hitchcock; Produced by Erich Pommer; **Uncredited Technical Credits**: Visual Effects: W. Percy Day; Dialogue Coach: J. Lee Thompson; U.K. release: Passed by the British Board of Film Censors on May 8, 1939; General release: May 25, 1939; U.K. reissues: 1944 and 1948, both released by Renown; U.S. release: October 12, 1939; Genre: Crime–Costume Drama; Black and White; Running Time: 107 minutes; U.S. release cut to 98 minutes; 35mm print at British Film Institute, National Film and Television Archive; Blu-ray Region A and DVD Region 1, Cohen Collection, in a new digital restoration released May 2015; no English subtitle captions for the deaf and hard of hearing; Blu-ray Region B and DVD Region 2, Arrow Academy (same restoration) released November 2016; English subtitle captions for the deaf and hard of hearing are available on these discs.

Cast: Charles Laughton (*Sir Humphrey Pengallan*); Horace Hodges (*Pengallan's Butler*); Hay Petrie (*Pengallan's Groom*); Frederick Piper (*Pengallan's Agent*); Herbert Lomas, Clare Greet, William Devlin (*Pengallan's Tenants*); Jeanne De Casalis, Mabel Terry Lewis, Bromley Davenport, George Curzon, Basil Radford (*Pengallan's Friends*); Leslie Banks (*Joss Merlyn*); Marie Ney (*Patience—Joss' Wife*); Maureen O'Hara (*Mary—Joss' Niece*); Emlyn Williams (*Harry the Peddler*); Wylie Watson (*Salvation Watkins*); Morland Graham (*Sea Lawyer Sydney*); Edwin Greenwood (*Dandy*); Mervyn Johns (*Thomas*); Stephen Haggard (*The Boy*); Robert Newton (*Jem Trehearne*); **Uncredited Cast**: Robert Adair (*Captain Murray*); Marie Ault, O.B. Clarence (*Coach Passengers*); Mary Jerrold (*Miss Black—Housekeeper*); John Longden (*Captain Johnson*); Aubrey Mather (*Coachman*).

Synopsis: In the early nineteenth century, the isolated tavern of Jamaica Inn, on the Cornish seacoast, is the headquarters of a band of cutthroat pirates who extinguish beacon lights (warning passing ships of rocks ahead), then murder the crews of damaged ships and pilfer the cargo. Mary Yellan, a passenger on a coach, is dropped off near the home of the local squire. She requests a horse to ride to Jamaica Inn where she intends to live with her Aunt Patience, sister of her dead mother. Despite warnings about staying at Jamaica Inn, she insists. On her arrival, she finds her aunt subservient to her brutish husband, Joss Merlyn. The inn is occupied by Joss' smuggling gang. There is dissent within their ranks as they receive little money for their illicit escapades. They suspect a recent recruit to the gang, Jem Trehearne, as the source of their discontent; after deciding that he must hang, they string him up. After the gang leaves, Mary cuts the rope and she and Jem escape from the inn together. The following morning, the pair are pursued by the gang, but manage to escape into the protection of the local squire Sir Humphrey Pengallan. They inform him of what is taking place at Jamaica Inn, unaware that Pengallan is the mastermind behind the shipwrecks. Mary slips away and returns to the inn to warn her aunt that the authorities are coming to apprehend the gang and that she must escape. The aunt refuses to leave her husband. When Trehearne and Pengallan arrive at the inn, the latter reveals his criminal identity. Trehearne is tied up and placed under guard. Mary is able to stop a potential wreck by hoisting a warning flag but is later abducted by Pengallan. She is taken a ship docked in the harbor. Trehearne manages to alert the local army garrison. They arrive in time to rescue Mary from the deranged squire, who is cornered on the topsail of the ship. He commits suicide by throwing himself to the deck below.

Selected Dialogue:

PENGALLAN: "Chadwick! Chadwick!"
PENGALLAN: "I'd transport all the riffraff in Bristol to Botany Bay to save one beautiful woman a single headache. Something you don't understand. Never will. Because you're neither a philosopher nor a gentleman."
PENGALLAN: "These outbursts of mine are quite inexcusable. I can't think what comes over me."
PENGALLAN: "I never really cared for wrecking. After all, not my kind of thing, hobnobbing with cutthroats. It had to be done. Half my friends living like paupers. But I'm living like a prince. Drowned hundreds of sailors to do it."
PENGALLAN: "Well, you have to be hard now. The age of chivalry has gone."
PENGALLAN: "What are you all waiting for? A spectacle? You shall have it. And tell your children how the great age ended! Make way for Pengallan!"

Production Commentary: Based on Daphne du Maurier's best-selling 1936 novel, *Jamaica Inn* is a lurid story of violence and brutality, lavishly staged. Its opening sequence of a wrecking is most effective, and the night scene is outstandingly photographed by ace cinematographer Harry Stradling.[39] The score was written by a native of Scarborough, musician Eric Fenby (1906–1997) a close friend of composer Frederick Delius (1862–1934). Fenby wrote a complete music score for the film, and paid for this work, but the finished film contains only three brief pieces (running just three minutes and 15 seconds) heard over the opening and closing credits.

Laughton's Sir Humphrey Pengallan is not a character to be found in the novel; it was conceived by scenarists Sidney Gilliat and Joan Harrison in response to objections by film censors of the day. In the novel, the head of the wrecking gang was a clergyman, Francis Davy. Producer Erich Pommer was informed that the depiction of a parson as a madman involved in shipwrecking and murder would not pass the watchful eye of the Hollywood censor, the Hays Office.[40] Therefore, scenarists took a minor character in the novel, Squire Bassett, and altered this character to that of Sir Humphrey Pengallan. At the time of the film's release, it was suggested that the Jekyll and Hyde role of Squire Pengallan gave Laughton ample scope for a display of virtuosity. His roguish sense of humor relishes exaggeration which comes near caricature. He suggests skillfully the development of an inherent streak of madness in the man's makeup. Sir Humphrey thinks little of murder if it supplies him with the money necessary for him to live as a gentleman should. Yet he is kind and considerate to his tenants. Since the film plays in the style of a blood-and-thunder melodrama, the story makes little claim for plausibility.

Shooting began at Elstree Studios on September 1, 1938, and wrapped in mid–October. Though a newcomer to film, 18-year-old Maureen O'Hara had already displayed promise as an actress. Indeed, it was Laughton who had been responsible for giving the young Irish actress (real name: Maureen Fitz-Simons) her first big break in films. He had seen a screen test she had made and was intrigued. He suggested she change her name from FitzSimons to the shorter O'Hara. Like many leading actresses in Hitchcock films, O'Hara found herself susceptible to the suspenseful perversities of its director. In several sequences, her character is humiliated. In one scene, she is bound and gagged.

For all the unquestionable expertise behind the camera and on screen, Laughton's playing of Pengallan is problematic. Throughout the film, he indulges in pouting, grimacing and preening before the camera. Yet he struggles and fails to connect successfully to the part one way or the other. He never seems to have quite found out what he was looking for. Should he play the role as a star lead, or as a character player? Should he adjust his performance style for the camera or fall back on a familiar theatrical manner? For all its amusement, Laughton's performance is indecisive and indigestible, undermining any real sense of suspense or dramatic momentum. Laughton substitutes melodramatic indulgence and a sense of rollicking adventure.

The sets are opulent and well-lit and Laughton as the star and producer cossets himself in a very expensive wardrobe.[41] He submits himself to the extravagances of caricature. Wearing a false nose, and adopting an affected Regency foppishness, he sacrifices subtlety for spectacle. Fans of Laughton were much amused by all this pantomime, but the director had other ideas. Hitchcock was famed for his fastidiousness in commanding and controlling every phase of the film process. Scripts were pre-planned, storyboarded and pored over in minute detail, as were the cinematography, the décor, the editing and even the promotion of a film. This meant improvisation or ad-libbing from his actors was, at best, frowned on and, at worst, nigh on impossible. In later years, Hitchcock became his own producer, but when assigned *Jamaica Inn* he was still a contract director. As executive producers of Mayflower Pictures, Laughton and Pommer held the reins of artistic control and responsibility for the film's overall production. On the studio floor, Hitchcock found Laughton to be an actor who lacked the discipline and control he considered essential. Hitchcock said of Laughton, "There are many, many great artists in the world who are extremely talented and are geniuses, but they never become a pro [...] Charles never became a craft professional. He was always an artist and a genius, and he worked that way, so it became a disordered lack of control...." (Lanchester, 1983: 160). Hitchcock gave a further damning verdict of working with Laughton: "You can't direct a Laughton picture. The best you can hope for is to referee" (Halliwell, 1973: 112). Although *Jamaica Inn* was a box office success, Hitchcock was dismissive, calling it "an absurd thing to undertake" (Truffaut: 167). For Hitchcock, the script was incongruous as the story was a whodunit and spoiled by casting Laughton in the key role of the respectable justice of the peace. For Hitchcock, logic dictated that as the criminal mastermind behind all the treachery and violence, the justice of the peace should have appeared at the end of the picture.

There are just a few directorial touches which can be construed as characteristically Hitchcock. The crowd scenes are handled with his usual dexterity. Yet, despite Hitchcock's complaints to François Truffaut of Laughton being very unprofessional, *Jamaica Inn* was popular with Laughton fans and audiences of the day. Prints of the film were sent to troops stationed in France at the outbreak of World War II. In March 1939, just a few months before the film's U.K. premiere in May 1939, a BBC radio play of the novel was broadcast. The film was reissued twice in Britain during the 1940s.

Critical reaction was, on the whole, favorable. However, the novelist Graham Greene, in his capacity as film critic for *The Spectator* (1935–1940), was consistently tendentious and hostile towards Hitchcock and his films. In a *Spectator* review (May 19, 1939), he gave *Jamaica Inn* the thumbs-down: "The unsatisfactory picture has been lavishly produced though the whole set of the sinister inn creaks like its own signboard. No expense has been spared, and I was irresistibility reminded of an all-star charity matinée." *Variety* (May 31, 1939) was, despite some qualms, upbeat in its assessment: "Superb direction, excellent casting, expressive playing offset an uneven screenplay to make *Jamaica Inn* a gripping version of the Daphne du Maurier novel." *Harrison's Reports* (September 30, 1939) gave the film a cautious welcome: "This British-made production will probably do good business, not because the picture itself merits it, but because of the popularity of Charles Laughton, the star, and Alfred Hitchcock, the director; also because of the fame of the novel.... Laughton overacts a bit; but his performance is colorful and amusing; he dominates the picture."

Film Bulletin (October 7, 1939) was laudatory: "Superbly acted and magnificently directed.... It combines the best features of English mystery-drama with American action. Because it is an English production, no exhibitor should stamp it as a film of limited appeal. It is first-rate motion picture entertainment. Charles Laughton is virtually the whole show. Expertly he creates a fascinating madman whose insanity becomes more intense, more apparent as he comprehends his approaching doom." *Film Daily* (October 12, 1939) thought it had "a typically good Laughton performance" and went on to assert, "Devotees of the more rugged melodramas, and the large coterie of Charles Laughton admirers will find the present production satisfying, particularly from the standpoint of the star's performance...." The *Motion Picture Daily* (October 12, 1939) congratulated Laughton and Pommer: "The sullen, grim atmosphere of the novel...has been admirably translated into celluloid terms...." The trade magazine, *The Movies ... and the People Who Make Them* (November 10, 1939) cited Laughton's performance as something to savor: "Laughton's portrait of Pengallan is a fascinating and colorful study, at once genteel and murderous, gallant and ruthless, polite and egotistical."

If you take *Jamaica Inn* as a simple smuggling yarn, it is enjoyable and fascinating, but as a dramatic suspense story it does not bear too close an examination. Similarly, Laughton's performance can be construed as either watchable for its campiness or an awful warning of what happens when a star is given carte blanche to perform as he sees fit. The latter is all the more noticeable in the film given the director's antipathy towards the story material and disapproval of its star. However, at the time of the film's release, its popularity ensured that neither career of its star or director were diminished in any way. Many seeing *Jamaica Inn* today might conclude with Graham Greene that it shows Laughton as a "ham actor—the very best 'ham'" (Parkinson: 158).[42]

The Hunchback of Notre Dame (1939)

Tagline: "BIG Beyond Words! ... Wonderous Beyond Belief! ... Magnificent Beyond Compare!"[43]

U.S. (RKO Radio Pictures)

Credits: Produced by Pandro S. Berman; Screenplay: Sonia Levien; Adaptation: Bruno Frank; Musical Adaptation and Original Composition by Alfred Newman; Photography: Joseph H. August; Special Effects: Vernon L. Walker; Art Director: Van Nest Polglase; Associate: Al Herman; Costumes: Walter Plunkett; Set Decorator: Darrell Silvera; Recorder: John E. Tribby; Editor: William Hamilton, Robert Wise; Assistant Directors: Argyle Nelson, Edward Killy; Dance Director: Ernst Matray; Technical Advisor: Louis Vandenecker; Dialogue Director: Will Price; Assistant to Mr. Dieterle: Peter Berneis; Directed by William Dieterle; U.S. release: December 29, 1939; U.K. release: Passed by the British Board of Film Censors on January 23, 1940; Genre: Historical Drama; Black and White; Running Time: 115 minutes; 35mm print held at the Library of Congress; Warner Bros. did a new digital restoration in 2015; Blu-ray Region A, Warner Bros., released June 2015; Blu-ray Region B, HMV Premium Collection, released October 2018; Blu-ray Region A, box set, *The Golden Year: 5 Classic Films from 1939*, Warner Bros., released June 2015; English subtitle captions for the deaf and hard of hearing are available on these discs; DVD Region 2 (unrestored), Odeon Entertainment, released April 2014; no English subtitle captions for the deaf and hard of hearing.

Cast: Charles Laughton (*Quasimodo*); Sir Cedric Hardwicke (*Frollo*); Thomas Mitchell (*Clopin*); Maureen O'Hara (*Esmeralda*); Edmond O'Brien (*Gringoire*); Alan Marshal (*Phoebus*); Walter Hampden (*Archdeacon*); Harry Davenport (*King Louis XI*); Katherine Alexander (*Madame de Lys*); George Zucco (*Procurator*); Fritz Leiber (*Old Nobleman*); Etienne Girardot (*Doctor*); Helene Whitney (*Fleur de Lys*); Minna

(1939) The Hunchback of Notre Dame

Gombell (*Queen of Beggars*); Arthur Hohl (*Olivier*); Curt Bois (*Student*); George Tobias (*Beggar*); Rod LaRocque (*Phillippe*); Spencer Charters (*Court Clerk*); Kathryn Adams, Dianne Hunter (*Fleur's Companions*); Siegfried Arno (*Tailor*); **Uncredited Cast**: Eddie Abdo, Consuelo Melendez (*Singers*); Louis Adlon (*Venus*); Vangie Beilby (*Contestant*); Lionel Belmore (*Judge at Esmeralda's Trial*); Barlowe Borland (*Dubois*); Earl Clyde (*Juggler*); Edmund Cobb, Alexander Granach (*Soldiers*); Alan Copeland (*Choirboy*); Harry Cording (*Guard*); Harold DeGarro (*Stilt Walker*); Dick Dickinson (*Wooden-Leg Man*); Charles Drake (*Young Priest*); Arthur Dulac (*Mars*); Ralph Dunn (*Soldier*); Gretl Dupont (*Lissy*); James Fawcett (*Festival Ball-Walker*); J.C. Fowler (*Nobleman*); Thom Fox (*Jupiter*); Vallejo Ganter (*Merchant*); Peter Godfrey (*Monk*); Edward Groag (*Moon*); Charlie Hall (*Mercury*); Charles Halton (*Printer*); Rondo Hatton (*Ugly Man*); Al Herman (*Short Fat Soldier*); Otto Hoffman (*Deaf Judge*); Kenner G. Kemp (*Townsman*); Cy Kendall (*Nobleman Signing Petition*); Victor Kilian (*Esmeralda's Hangman*); Ann Kunde (*Townswoman*); Mike Lally (*Beggar*); Ray Long (*Festival Skeleton Dancer*); Joseph P. Mack (*Workman in Play*); Frank Mazzola (*Child*); Margaret McWade (*Younger Sister*); Robert Milasch (*Townsman*); Arthur Millett (*Count Graville*); Frank Mills (*Beggar*); Angela Mulinos (*Helena*); Ferdinand Munier (*Defense Attorney*); Paul Newlan (*Whipper*); Lillian Nicholson (*DeLys' Servant*); Nestor Paiva (*Man in Street When Gypsies Arrive*); Tempe Pigott (*Madeleine*); Antonio Pina (*Ladder Man*); Russ Powell (*Second "Ugly Man" Contestant*); Elsie Prescott (*Contestant*); Dewey Robinson (*Butcher*); Hector V. Sarno (*Knight*); Norbert Schiller (*Saturn*); Margaret Seddon (*Older Sister*); Ward Shattuck (*Festival Juggler*); Alan Spear (*Festival Contortionist*); Rudolf Steinboeck (*Peasant in Play*); Ann G. Sterling (*Gypsy Girl*); Louis Valaris (*Tightrope Man*); Harry J. Vejar (*Noble*); Gisela Werbisek (*Grandmother*); Louis Zamperini (*Street Urchin*).

Awards: Nominated Academy Award: Best Sound Recording: RKO Radio Studio Sound Department, John Aalberg; Nominated Academy Award: Best Music Scoring: Alfred Newman.

Synopsis: In fifteenth-century France, King Louis XI and Jehan Frollo, the king's high justice, inspect a new invention, the printing press. The king decides it is a miracle, but Frollo contends that it could destroy a kingdom. The king is not convinced and tells Frollo he is exaggerating. The king examines a new book written by Pierre Gringoire, a French poet. Again, Frollo speaks out, calling Gringoire a heretic. The king takes the opposite view, seeing books and reading as a blessing. Frollo's attitude hardens and he asserts that the press must be broken and the printer hanged. He sees it as his mission to protect France from these books

Left to right: Maureen O'Hara as gypsy girl Esmeralda, Laughton in the shadows as Quasimodo, the Hunchback of Notre Dame Cathedral, and Cedric Hardwicke as the villainous High Justice, Jehan Frollo. All these fine performances in *The Hunchback of Notre Dame* (1939) were underpinned by a strong script, impressive cinematography, art direction and topped by firm direction from émigré director William Dieterle.

just as he would protect it from witches, sorcerers, gypsies and other outcasts. On the outskirts of Paris, gypsy caravans are driven back as soldiers guard a city crossing. A young gypsy girl, Esmeralda, manages to slip past, and guards give chase. Mingling with the crowd, she goes to the city center where the annual celebration of the Festival of Fools is taking place, presided over by the king. Quasimodo, the bell-ringer of Notre Dame Cathedral, is crowned the king of fools. At the height of Quasimodo's coronation, Frollo stops the proceedings. Esmeralda decides she must appeal to the king. When guards threaten her, she runs into Notre Dame Cathedral and claims sanctuary. Frollo brands her a witch and says she will hang. Esmeralda meets Quasimodo, and her screams arouse the king's guards. Quasimodo is brought to trial. For disturbing the peace, abducting a woman, and resisting the king's guards, the city magistrate sentences Quasimodo to a lashing of 50 strokes. After his flogging, he calls for water. Moved by his call for help, Esmeralda brings it to him. Cathedral workmen soon notice a change in Quasimodo: The hunchback has fallen in love since Esmeralda's act of kindness. Frollo confronts Esmeralda and confesses he wants her for himself. She manages to break free and performs her dance much to the delight of Phoebus, captain of the king's guards, who professes his love for her. He is later found murdered and Esmeralda is accused of the crime. Frollo admits to the murder to his brother the archbishop and blames the satanic gypsy girl for his actions. He asks his brother to help him, but he refuses. Frollo declares that Esmeralda must die and accuses her of bewitching him to kill. Hearing this, the archbishop declares that it is his duty to help Esmeralda. At Esmeralda's trial, Gringoire's defense is overruled and he is removed from the court. Frollo asks Esmeralda to confess her sorcery. Quasimodo bursts into the court and confesses to the murder of Captain Phoebus. His confession is greeted with derision and he is taken away. Esmeralda is shown instruments of torture, but she still protests her innocence. The court is suspended while she is tortured. Frollo observes and hears her screams of agony. When the court re-convenes, Esmeralda, under the duress of torture, confesses to her "crime." The death penalty is read out, but the king intervenes and orders she should be tried by ordeal. She is blindfolded and told to choose from her own dagger (guilt) or the king's dagger (innocence). The outcome tells against her and she is sentenced to death by hanging. Quasimodo sees Esmeralda being brought to the scaffold and, as the hangman prepares to place the rope around her neck, Quasimodo swings across and rescues her. Triumphant, Quasimodo carries Esmeralda up to the bell tower. The king's noblemen are enraged that an imbecilic hunchback can take the law into his own hands and decide to petition the king to suspend sanctuary. Despite the kindness of the monks and Quasimodo, Esmeralda pines for Gringoire. Gringoire publishes a pamphlet to sway public opinion for the release of Esmeralda. The king is read the pamphlet by Frollo. The king understands that Gringoire has used the printing press to sway public opinion. It's an impertinence, but the king rather admires the use of this new tactic in powerbroking. The archbishop brings news that the people are threatening to storm the cathedral. The king reacts in anger and blames the archbishop. When the archbishop protests the girl's innocence, the king replies that if he is so sure of her innocence, then he must know who the real murderer is. Frollo confesses that he killed Captain Phoebus. The archbishop explains that Frollo is in love with Esmeralda but condemned her to death because she does not love him. The king orders the arrest of Frollo. Clopin demands that the gypsy girl be released. His demands are ignored and a retinue of Parisian craftsmen, who have read Gringoire's pamphlet, appear in front of the cathedral door to defend the sanctuary of the church. Quasimodo sees the commotion below and wakes Esmeralda. He uses various methods to fight the crowds until the king's guards arrive. Quasimodo finds Esmeralda is being pursued by Frollo, who is bent on killing her. He confronts Frollo in the bell tower and throws him to his death. Gringoire announces to the crowd that Esmeralda is safe and has been pardoned by the king. Gringoire says his farewell to Clopin, who has been fatally injured. Arm in arm, Esmeralda and Gringoire walk off to begin a new life together. Quasimodo remains alone

(1939) The Hunchback of Notre Dame

and misunderstood in the Notre Dame bell tower, clinging to a gargoyle in despair and torment as he ponders an indifferent world.

Selected Dialogue:

QUASIMODO: "She gave me water."
QUASIMODO: "Sanctuary! Sanctuary! Sanctuary! Sanctuary! Sanctuary!"
QUASIMODO: "I never realized 'til now how ugly I am because you're so beautiful. I'm not a man. I'm not a beast. I'm about as shapeless as the man in the moon."
QUASIMODO: "Why was I not made of stone like thee?"

Production Commentary: Laughton rounded off the decade with his never-to-be forgotten Quasimodo, the disabled bellringer of Notre Dame Cathedral. As in his skilled playing of Javert in Hugo's *Les Misérables*, Laughton exerts on screen another vivid and compelling portrait, this time a grotesque deformed body within which beats a brave and tender heart.

The Hunchback of Notre Dame is a triumph of Hollywood studio production, featuring a hand-picked cast assisted by faultless technical backup. This large-scale prestigious RKO production cost $1,826,000 to produce and earned $3,155,000 in rentals. It was Oscar-nominated for Best Sound Recording (John Aalberg) (but lost to *When Tomorrow Comes*) and Best Music Score (Alfred Newman) (but lost to *Stagecoach*).

Interviewed by *Modern Screen* (December 1940), director William Dieterle (1893–1972) spoke about Laughton's demanding and difficult approach to acting:

> Charles Laughton is the most eccentric person I have ever met. He's full of unusual ideas about his scenes. And you have to hold the reins on him, or soon you find him not only acting in his pictures, but also directing them. He never plays a scene the same way twice. And because the only time he relaxes is at rehearsals, I feel he often gives his best performance then when, unfortunately, the camera isn't looking. Laughton has one curious quirk. Whenever I approach him to begin a scene, he replies, "I am not in the mood." This, I learned, is not temperament, but fear. He actually has an inferiority complex about getting in front of the camera. He always thinks he won't be good enough. Yet he's touched with genius…. Like [Paul] Muni, he, too, believes he must feel and experience an emotion before he can portray it. When we were shooting the final scene of *The Hunchback of Notre Dame*, Laughton was supposed to be on top of a 350-foot cathedral, looking down. Naturally, we intended to fake the shot, by shooting a close-up on the ground with Laughton on a platform ten feet high. Well, before the scene, Laughton strolled up to me and said, "Bill, I can't feel the scene. I've got to experience it. I've got to get up on top of that 350-foot cathedral for a few hours and get the feeling. Then you can fake it, after I'm in the mood." I knew better than to argue with him. So, Laughton began climbing up the 350-foot structure. A big eater, he had just completed an enormous lunch, and when he had climbed halfway up, I saw him waver, look down, sway—and suddenly he was ill to his stomach. We helped him down and put him on a cot. And take it from me, sir, Mr. Laughton didn't have to feel the scene that afternoon. He was happy to have it faked!

Warner Bros. makeup wizard Perc Westmore (1904–1970) was loaned to RKO for a hefty $10,0000. In the 1923 Universal *Hunchback* directed by Wallace Worsley, star Lon Chaney devised his own makeup. The hump he created weighed some 40 pounds. Westmore found he could duplicate a hump using six pounds of sponge rubber. Laughton wouldn't hear of using it, as he wished to suffer the same pain endured by Chaney. When Westmore suggested he feign agony, Laughton was outraged and insulted and called Westmore "a hired hand." Producer Pandro S. Berman had the unenviable task of adjudicating on the affair. Laughton was sent back to England on a two-week vacation.

Despite all these tantrums, the film remains an imperishable achievement showing the Hollywood studio system at full capability in its astounding scale, audacity, enchantment and with an unerring showmanship in providing quality entertainment for a mass audience. Every member of the cast is superb, providing many memorable moments to savor.

Central to this triumph is Laughton's performance. The script is remarkable for its compression of Victor Hugo's vast, meandering story. There are immense set pieces such as the Feast of Fools and Esmeralda on the gallows. Cedric Hardwicke excels as the silent, frozen-lipped and perverted Frollo. Apparently, Claude Rains, who had tutored Laughton during his days at RADA, was approached by Laughton to play the role of Frollo, but Laughton was so patronizing in his manner (speaking as though he was now the teacher and Rains his pupil) that the actor instantly rejected the offer. George Zucco, as the prosecutor at Esmeralda's trial, relishes the atmosphere of medieval superstitious and barbarity (at one point, he says, "My lord, surely it's time to use the tortures on this stubborn wench!").

The film failed to receive any major Academy Awards due to stiff competition from *Gone with the Wind* but it was a popular success with both critics and the public. *Film Bulletin* (December 30, 1939) was typical in its praise: "From start to finish it is absorbing, fascinating entertainment—spectacular, vivid and breathtaking." However, it went on to cite a few flaws: "Criticism might be levelled at the abrupt cutting in many of the sequences as well as at the variety of accents used by members of the cast but such flaws are not likely to distract the masses who will find [the film] entertainment very much to their liking." According to *Variety* (December 20, 1939), "Laughton, despite his over-playing in the early stages to make Quasimodo a most repellent character, tones down the bestial characteristics of the role in the latter half to emerge as the victor, rather than the victim, of audience reaction." The *Film Daily* (December 15, 1939) gave this verdict on its central player: "Charles Laughton's grasp upon the character of the unhappy Quasimodo, grotesque, misshapen, deaf almost inarticulate bellringer of the Cathedral, is no less firm; it was a tailored-to-fit role despite the fact that a century separates novel and star. Laughton's few lines are the more effective for it."

Hugo's gargantuan tale of fate, abandonment and intolerance was something Laughton was attracted to, Quasimodo being a protagonist who endures social opprobrium, pain and the ostracism of disability. Laughton's troubled background and demons (his Catholicism, masochism, sexuality, and physical repulsion) are all, to a degree, on display throughout the film: The medieval institution of the Catholic cathedral Notre-Dame de Paris, the humiliation and pain of Quasimodo's public flagellation, the unrequited love for Esmeralda and a grotesque deformed body all have their parallels in Laughton's difficult life. In the concluding shot of the film, the camera registers on the figure of the Hunchback clinging to a gargoyle on the cathedral ramparts, and then pulls back so the pathetic figure becomes indistinguishable from the supreme architecture of Notre Dame. Simultaneously Quasimodo appears to dissolve into Laughton and vice versa.

The 1939 *Hunchback of Notre Dame* remains unsurpassed and represents Laughton and the Hollywood studio system at its finest.

They Knew What They Wanted (1940)

Tagline: "Daring! Exciting! Sensational!"[44]
U.S. (RKO Radio Pictures)

Left to right: Director Garson Kanin, and stars Carole Lombard and Laughton all look miserable in a studio screening room. As well they might. The filming of *They Knew What They Wanted* (1940) was fraught with difficulty and the final result on screen was indifferent, to say the least.

(1940) They Knew What They Wanted

Credits: Executive Producer: Harry E. Edington; Produced by Erich Pommer; Screenplay: Robert Ardrey; From the Pulitzer Prize Play by Sidney Howard; Music: Alfred Newman; Photography: Harry Stradling; Special Effects: Vernon L. Walker; Art Director: Van Nest Polglase; Associate: Mark-Lee Kirk; Wardrobe: Edward Stevenson; Set Decorator: Darrell Silvera; Recorder: John L. Cass; Editor: John Sturges; Assistant Director: Ruby Rosenberg; Directed by Garson Kanin; U.S. release: October 25, 1940; U.K. release: December 27, 1941; Genre: Drama; Black and White; Running Time: 96 minutes; Not commercially available on DVD or Blu-ray.

Cast: **Charles Laughton** (*Tony Patucci*); Carole Lombard (*Amy Peters*); William Gargan (*Joe*); Harry Carey (*A Doctor*); Frank Fay (*Father McKee*); **Uncredited Cast**: Joseph E. Bernard (*The R.F.D.*); Janet Fox (*Mildred*); Lee Tung Foo (*Ah Gee—Cook*); Karl Malden (*Red*); Victor Kilian (*The Photographer*); Demetrius Alexis, Bobbie Hale, Stephen Soldi (*Restaurant Customers*); Ricca Allen (*Mrs. Thing*); Effie Anderson (*Nurse*); Bobby Barber (*Tony's Pal at Table*); Tom Ewell (*New Hired Hand*); Nestor Paiva (*Tony's Pal at Restaurant Table*); Antonio Filauri (*Customer*); Marie Blake, Millicent Green, Grace Lenard, Patricia Oakley (*Waitresses*); Paul Le Pere (*Hired Hand*); Paul Panzer (*Proprietor of Italian Restaurant*); Joe Sully (*Father of Family*).

Working Title: *The Other Man*

Awards: Academy Award Nomination: Best Actor in a Supporting Role: William Gargan.

Synopsis: Napa Valley grape grower Tony Patucci, a simple Italian, goes into the nearest town to find himself a bride. After some difficulty in putting on new patent leather shoes, he takes them off in a restaurant. One shoe is found on the floor by a waitress and returned to Tony, who is smitten by her. A priest, Father McKee, pays a visit to the grape farm and inquiries when the head foreman, Joe, will settle down, but he is non-committal on the issue of matrimony. Tony appears riding his horse in high spirits, telling Father McKee and Joe he is to marry soon. He has decided to write a letter proposing to the waitress. Reading the letter aloud in front of her work colleagues, she is ribbed. She gets one of her friends to type out a reply. When Tony receives an answer, he brings the letter to Joe for him to read. In her reply, she identifies herself as Amy Peters. There follows a flurry of letters which culminate in an offer to come and meet him. Instead of sending a photograph of himself, Tony decides to send one of Joe. Driving to the railway depot, Amy greets Joe with a sensual kiss, thinking he is Patucci. As the truck pulls into Tony's ranch, he makes small talk before he tells Amy the truth. Despite her shock, she agrees to marry Tony. To celebrate, Tony throws a party and invites everyone in the district. Tony performs deeds of strength and stamina to demonstrate his masculine potency. In the middle of all this exhibitionism, a minor fight breaks out. This makes Tony all the more determined to demonstrate his machismo. In a drunken state, he climbs onto the roof of his ranch house, loses his footing and falls from the roof, breaking his legs. While he is incapacitated, Amy is seduced by Joe. When Amy faints during a meal, the doctor determines that she is pregnant and breaks the news to Joe. Amy admits her betrayal to Tony and decides she must leave immediately. A vengeful Tony beats Joe badly, and Joe disappears in shame. When Father McKee arrives to drive Amy and Tony to their wedding, Tony tells the priest the bad news. Tony decides to forgive Amy and asks her to reconsider and marry him. Full of repentance, she declines and leaves with Father McKee. As the truck disappears into the distance, Tony looks on in the forlorn hope she will return to him one day.

Selected Dialogue:

PATUCCI: "Looka me, Tony!"
PATUCCI: "Peoples dey know whata dey want, but peoples dey no usa da head. We usa da head."

Production Commentary: In the *New York Times* (October 11, 1940), Bosley Crowther complained about Laughton's lack of restraint in performing the role of Tony, citing a tendency towards "creep" and commandeering his talent to show "more and more of the renowned and accomplished character actor, than of a genial and generous Italian-American...." Crowther went on to accuse the actor of going "just a bit too far in this film ... [giving] little more than an actor's expansive imitation of a big dummy with a thick Italian accent."

There is more than a little justification in these accusations. Essentially, Laughton had not wanted to take on the role, but was contractually obliged to make another film for RKO. In a search for prestige, RKO had purchased the rights to Sidney Howard's 1925 Pulitzer Prize–winning play for $50,000. The story had been filmed twice before, first as a silent, *The Secret Hour* (Paramount, Rowland V. Lee, 1928) with Jean Hersholt, then as an early talkie, *A Lady to Love* (MGM, Victor Sjostrom, 1930) with Edward G. Robinson and Vilma Banky. In his memoir, director Garson Kanin devoted a chapter of some 24 pages detailing his encounter with Laughton and the making of this film. Though edifying, it does not make pleasant reading. Laughton's behavior was nothing if not outrageous from the very start through to its final cut and edit. At various times, the actor had occasion to prevaricate, procrastinate, obfuscate, stonewall, make unreasonable demands, become irritable, selfish and sulk in silence.

Kanin had first seen Laughton on the New York stage in the thriller *Payment Deferred*. Thereafter he was, like millions of others, enthralled by Laughton's film work, as Henry VIII and Rembrandt and in his many Hollywood films. Feeling Laughton could play any role, and despite opposition from the front office, he decided to cast him as Tony in *They Knew What They Wanted*. He was sure Laughton would relish the challenge and be more than able to deliver a perfect performance during the allotted 42-day schedule.

At their first meeting, Kanin was soon disabused of any notion of a collegial approach to the project. Laughton brusquely rebuffed suggestions of assistance in achieving a suitable Italian accent. He was also disdainful of his co-star Carole Lombard. Apart from casual use of profanities on the set, her intuitive approach to acting and the filming process grated on Laughton. She could handle any script changes, whether large or small, and improvise on the spot with promptness and a minimum of fuss. Her visceral professionalism earned deep respect from film crews at every studio. But for Laughton, whose creative methodology was based on cerebral inspiration and creative control, it was an unwanted burden. It also didn't help when Laughton's earnings during this period were reported as $116,170 and Carole Lombard's a colossal $211,111.[45] Laughton also had to swallow his pride as both their names were given equal billing above the title in the opening credits. Kanin also had Erich Pommer to contend with. Pommer, a Laughton loyalist, passionately defended Laughton's whimsical, difficult and often impossible demands.

Kanin was able to extract a two-week rehearsal period from the studio. It soon became apparent during rehearsals that Laughton's attempt to come up with a credible accent for the part using his own idiosyncratic methods had not yielded tangible results. Laughton belatedly realized that he needed the help he had so arrogantly rejected seven weeks previously. Kanin put him in touch with a voice coach and Laughton soon learned all the necessary inflections of a native Italian-American accent. Before shooting began, the *New York Times* did an interview with Laughton. Kanin overheard the interviewer congratulating Laughton on the authenticity of his accent. Laughton deliberately avoided mentioning the vital work of the voice coach. Instead, he fabricated a self-serving tale of the accent being inspired by studying the paintings of Michelangelo, listening to the works of Vivaldi and reading Dante in the original language, rather than admitting to consulting a translator. During a location trip to the Napa Valley, Laughton presented a difficult problem to Kanin, but he was able to offer a solution there and then. In gratitude, Laughton suggested they go for a drink somewhere. When they found a suitable place, Laughton began to give forth comments about his whole approach to acting. He hated the success that stardom brought. He only wanted to be an actor. He talked at interminable length about the ups and downs of his career and seemed to grow to like Kanin. However, the following morning on set, he recoiled when Kanin greeted him cheerfully as a valued colleague.

In examining Laughton's playing opposite Carole Lombard's relaxed style, it is soon apparent how natural and uncomplicated she is, despite a facial scar which required careful lighting during close-ups. Ace cinematographer Harry Stradling was more than up to the job of carrying out such demanding work. As with Stradling's work in *Jamaica Inn*, there is a fluidity and intensity often lacking in the dramatic performances of its principal actors. As Amy, the San Francisco hash house waitress, Lombard carries off this unglamorous dramatic role skillfully. Never was a single take spoiled on account of her temperament. In contrast, Laughton agonizes, rationalizes and intellectualizes the part until he is little more than a staged caricature. Laughton was full of his own ideas, but when offered advice by others, he could not bear to accept any. He required nothing less than total control so that he could investigate, probe and dissect a role. In one key scene, Amy meets Tony who, fearful she might not come, has sent a photograph of his handsome foreman rather than his own photograph. A feast has been prepared in the center of a large ranch room. The table holds a large bowl of churned butter. During the initial take, everything was going fine until Laughton succeeded in sitting down in the butter. Not only was the take ruined but the wardrobe department had to supply another pair of pants. During the second take, Laughton again contrived to sit in the butter. When Kanin protested, Laughton told him he had prepared the scene in his mind and therefore had to sit exactly where the butter was. On the third take, the butter was moved and, sure enough, Laughton sat in the same spot where the butter had been! Interviewed by Allan Eyles in *Focus on Film* (Spring 1974), Kanin recalled, "Charles Laughton was a difficult man but ... if someone's good they're not like anyone else, they see things their way and it's hard for them to see it anybody else's way. Actors who simply bring their bodies and do as they're told are not difficult. But they're not very good."

William Gargan, who played Joe the foreman, gave a performance of sufficient substance to earn a Best Supporting Actor Oscar nomination. However, Frank Fay as the priest comes across as too sanctimonious. This was Karl Malden's film debut. During the 1950s, Malden gave acclaimed performances in *A Streetcar Named Desire* and *On the Waterfront* under the direction of Elia Kazan. Another screen actor of the 1950s destined for brief fame during the decade was Tom Ewell. He also made his screen debut in a minor unbilled role in the film.

They Knew What They Wanted did not perform well at the box office and left a $291,000 loss in the studio's profits. Compared to William Wyler's early mature melodrama *A House Divided* (Universal, 1931), which manages a distinctive and cinematic variant on the mail-order bride plot, *They Knew What They Wanted* never manages to escape its stage origins. In 1956, a Broadway musical was produced by songwriter Frank Loesser based on the Sidney Howard play. *The Most Happy Fella* did good business and was nominated for several Tony Awards.

The last word on this Laughton film belongs to Elsa Lanchester: "I thought they [Laughton and Lombard] were both miscast" (Lanchester: 1983, 166).

It Started with Eve (1941)

Tagline: "A showman's dream of casting come true!"[46]

U.S. (Universal Pictures)

Credits: Screenplay: Norman Krasna, Leo Townsend; Original Story: Hans Kraly; Photography: Rudolph Maté; Art Director: Jack Otterson; Associate: Martin Obzina; Editor: Bernard W. Burton; Assistant Director: Phil Karlson; Gowns: Vera West; Set Decorator: R.A. Gausman; Musical Director: Charles Previn; Musical Score: H.J. Salter; Vocal Coach: Andres de Segurola; Sound

In *It Started with Eve* (1941), Laughton plays dying millionaire, Jonathan Reynolds. As part of his careful preparation for the role, he adopts an amusing shuffling gait. Throughout the film his performance is suggestive of the manner and style of a Walt Disney animated figure.

It Started with Eve (1941)

Director: Bernard B. Brown; Technician: Joseph Lapis; Produced by Joe Pasternak; Directed by Henry Koster; U.S. release: September 26, 1941; U.K. release: January 5, 1942; Genre: Musical Comedy; Black and White; Running Time: 90 minutes; DVD Region 1, *Deanna Durbin Sweetheart Pack*, released August 2004; English subtitle captions for the deaf and hard of hearing are available on this disc. DVD Region 1, Universal Vault series label, released March 2013; DVD Region 2, Simply Media, released April 2011 and *Deanna Durbin Box Set Three*, Simply Media, released October 2011; no English subtitle captions for the deaf and hard of hearing; Blu-ray Region A, *Deanna Durbin Collection*, Kino Lorber, released June 2020; English subtitle captions for the deaf and hard of hearing are available on this disc.

Cast: Deanna Durbin (*Anne Terry*); **Charles Laughton (*Jonathan Reynolds*)**; Robert Cummings (*J. Reynolds Jr.*); Guy Kibbee (*Bishop*); Margaret Tallichet (*Gloria Pennington*); Catherine Doucet (*Mrs. Pennington*); Walter Catlett (*Dr. Harvey*); Charles Coleman (*Roberts*); Leonard Elliott (*Reverend Stebbins*); Irving Bacon, Gus Schilling (*Ravens*); Wade Boteler (*Newspaper Editor*); Dorothea Kent (*Jackie*); Clara Blandick (*Nurse*); **Uncredited Cast**: Sig Arno (*Captain of Waiters*); John Banner, Mary Currier, Jack W. Johnston, Mira McKinney, Edmund Mortimer, Ferdinand Munier, Broderick O'Farrell, Herbert Rawlinson, Larry Steers, Charlotte Treadway, Florence Wix (*Party Guests*); Leon Belasco (*Couturier*); Wilson Benge (*Williams—Butler*); Ralph Brooks, Jack Byron, Sonia Darrin, Bess Flowers, James Ford, Sam Harris, Helen Parrish, Ronald R. Rondell (*Nightclub Patrons*); Nora Cecil (*Mrs. Fields—Hotel Guest*); Chick Chandler (*Frank—Reporter*); Jack Chefe (*Commuter at Train Station*); Dora Clement (*Nurse*); Dorothy Darrell (*Girl*); George Davis (*Waiter*); Lowell Drew (*Plump Man*); Gretl Dupont (*Young Woman*); John Eldredge (*Clerk*); Mary Gordon (*Mrs. O'Toole*); Alexander Granach (*Popalard*); Jesse Graves (*Red Cap Porter*); Ernest Grooney (*Orchestra Leader*); John Hamilton (*Manager*); Robert Homans (*Conductor*); Rosalind Ivan (*Mrs. Mulligan*); Selmer Jackson (*Henry—Hotel Guest*); Lew Kelly (*Old Man Mose, Apartment Tenant*); George Lessey (*Johnson—Hotel Guest*); George J. Lewis (*Maître d'*); Adolf E. Licho (*Sigoni*); Marie MacDonald (*Cigarette Girl*); Bert Moorhouse (*Mr. Duncan*); Mantan Moreland (*Railway Porter*); Jack Mulhall (*Nightclub Photographer*); William H. O'Brien (*Nightclub Waiter*); Sarah Padden (*Jenny—Overcoat Check Girl*); Jack Perrin (*Chauffeur*); Jessie Perry (*Elderly Woman*); Paul Porcasi (*Armand—Chef*); Tim Ryan (*Tom—Assistant Editor*); Tom Seidel (*Assistant Clerk*); Ray Spiker (*Ice Man*); Leonard Sues (*Sidney*); Walter Tetley (*Messenger*); Ray Walker (*Slim--Reporter*); Lucille Ward (*Nurse*).

Working Titles: *Almost an Angel*; *It Started with Adam*

Awards: Academy Award Nomination: Best Music Scoring of a Musical Picture: Charles Previn, Hans J. Salter.

Synopsis: On a rainswept night at the offices of the *New York Daily Star Press*, editors are brought a front-page copy of their latest lead story. The death of millionaire Jonathan Reynolds will make banner headlines for both the *Daily Star* and their rivals at the *Daily Herald*. Each is vying to break the news first, but though his death is imminent, no official announcement has been made. In frustration, the chief editor phones one of the *Star*'s reporters outside Reynolds' mansion who watches eagerly for any confirmation of the millionaire's demise. As the millionaire's son Johnny Jr. races to see his ailing father, the family physician advises him to prepare for the worst. Despite Johnny's pretense at being upbeat, his father groans and asks what the girl he will marry is like. Following Johnny's brief description of his fiancée, Gloria Pennington, the eccentric millionaire suggests he bring her immediately to see him. But when Johnny goes to her hotel, Gloria is unavailable. While in the hotel lobby, he meets a coat check girl, Anne Terry, who offers to take his overcoat. He declines, but he later approaches her on impulse and in a moment of panic asks her to pose as his fiancée. Somewhat bewildered, she agrees. When she is presented to the old man, he is so delighted that he recovers almost instantaneously. Anne assists his miraculous recovery by playing an invigorating waltz, "When I Sing," on the piano downstairs. Reynolds sneaks out of bed and goes to the landing to see and hear Anne. Thereafter, Reynolds tries to acquire supplies of his personal cigars so he may enjoy the pleasure of a furtive smoke which his physician forbids. When the real fiancée arrives at the house, Johnny wants the imposter to go, but Anne wishes to continue the masquerade in order to meet the old man's musical friends such as Jascha Heifetz and Leopold Stokowski, who might be interested in her voice. Reynolds soon learns the truth about the masquerade and begins the role of matchmaker behind the scenes. He organizes a grand party with a full orchestra and exquisite cuisine, all designed to culminate in the announcement of the engagement of Anne and Johnny. However, Johnny persuades Anne not to attend. Reynolds is so disappointed at her absence that he goes to Anne's apartment where with some sadness she sings "Goin' Home." To cheer her up, Reynolds suggests they go to a nice quiet place where nobody will know who he is and then they can talk things over. In fact, he picks a prominent night spot where everyone recognizes him. A press photographer snaps a picture of them at their table. He introduces Anne to the Reynolds Special, a concoction of coconut milk and vegetable juices. She takes a sip and almost immediately begins to suffer the effects of high intoxication. She begins to cry and he offers her a handkerchief, but it turns out to be a lamb chop he stole at the party. This sets the pair off on a spate of giggling and uncontrolled hilarity. They decide to hit the dance floor where Anne introduces Reynolds to the dancing of the conga. After some hesitation, Reynolds enters into a high-spirited rendition of the conga to an appreciative audience that eggs the couple on. Johnny arrives with Dr. Harvey and ushers the couple from the dance floor. Anne and Johnny have an altercation which ends with Anne throwing the Reynolds Special in Johnny's face. When Reynolds sees the couple embraced in affection, he finally retreats back upstairs to his bed wearing a wry smile and smoking an illicit cigar.

Selected Dialogue:

REYNOLDS: "Trouble with being sick is you've got to associate with doctors."

REYNOLDS: "They said they were taking the first train back to Mexico City. I advised them to take a plane. It's quicker."

Production Commentary: Laughton had signed an MGM contract, but now that Irving Thalberg was dead, studio chief Louis B. Mayer decided to fulfill its contractual obligations by loaning Laughton out to various studios. The first picture for another studio was Universal's *It Started with Eve*. This film was the last musical comedy produced by Joe Pasternak for Universal, featuring the studio's popular singing star Deanna Durbin, before leaving for a 24-year stint as producer of MGM musicals and comedies. The lucrative partnership between Pasternak and Durbin from 1936 to 1941 produced nine musical films. Of these, *Three Smart Girls, One Hundred Men and a Girl, Three Smart Girls Grow Up, First Love, Spring Parade* and *It Started with Eve* were all directed by Henry Koster. The Durbin vehicles had their roots in European movies Koster had worked on in the early 1930s back at Universal's European (German-based) company. Durbin's films were always more popular in Europe than in the U.S. (*It Started with Eve* was itself remade by the studio in 1964 as *I'd Rather be Rich* with Sandra Dee and Maurice Chevalier.)

Filming began during May 1941. To allow for plot development, the pace is slow and, regrettably, there's less emphasis on music and songs. But the film does have distinctive settings and photography. Historian William K. Everson has drawn attention to certain sequences which show a marked similarity to Orson Welles' *Citizen Kane*, released while *It Started with Eve* was in production. The opening montage of the dying millionaire appears a takeoff of the faux newsreel in the Welles film. The interior of the Reynolds mansion is comparable with the empty spaces of Xanadu occupied by Charles Foster Kane and Susan Alexander.

During the opening of the film, there is a reference to Captain Kidd, a role Laughton would play some four years later. There is also a running gag involving the illicit smoking and concealment of cigars, something which would reappear to great comic effect in Laughton's playing of Sir Wilfrid Robarts in *Witness for the Prosecution*. Laughton approaches the role of the elderly millionaire with a winning combination of glee and a sense of the picaresque. Indeed, he manifests the appearance of a Disneyish animated character as he shuffles around in a nightshirt, a cross between Dopey the dwarf in *Snow White and the Seven Dwarfs* and Old Geppetto the wood-carver in *Pinocchio*. Laughton would have been at home as one of the eccentric professors in Howard Hawks' delightful screwball iteration of the *Snow White* legend, *Ball of Fire* (Samuel Goldwyn, 1941).

It Started with Eve is a diverting film, if shorn of those lilting Durbin songs so beloved by fans of the adolescent coloratura singer. Among the musical highlights is Durbin's rendering of "When I Sing," taken from Tchaikovsky's "Sleeping Beauty Waltz." At its best, *It Started with Eve* is the cinematic equivalent of a soufflé that begins with a dramatic opening and then settles down to a frothy fairy tale plot involving assumed identities and complications. Durbin, now 20, was transitioning from adolescent to leading lady. In typical scriptwriting fashion, several misunderstandings and confrontations are followed by the main characters realizing their true feelings for one another; Laughton as the eccentric millionaire derives newfound purpose and can contemplate death as a happy man.

In an April 1990 letter to Everson, the reclusive Deanna Durbin wrote of Laughton, "He was marvelous in the picture and the fact that we remained very close friends even though we were both aware of *Eve* being a Laughton not a Durbin film, shows how fond we were of each other."[47]

If the sight of Laughton dancing the conga with Durbin at a nightclub, followed by jiving on the dance floor while inebriated, invites the charge of compromising his talent, then there are plenty of other examples of thespian talent misapplying itself. Consider two flagrant examples of English actors indulging themselves in their later careers. Sir John Gielgud as the manservant Hobson in *Arthur* (Orion Pictures, Steve Gordon, 1981) gives forth with expletives at the drop of a hat; Laurence Olivier indulges in sexual shenanigans in such high trash as *The Betsy* (Allied Artists, Daniel Petrie, 1978). By comparison, Laughton's gyrations and cavorting seems mild stuff.

According to the *New York Times'* Bosley Crowther (October 27, 1941), "Henry Koster ... certainly knew how to get the best out of Mr. Laughton, that man of great renown. For this is one of his sharpest performances the old boy has given in years. Mr. Laughton plays with flavor, mischief, humor and great inventiveness. He knows how an old man would behave—and he never carries it too far. Under a perfect makeup you'd hardly know it was Mr. Laughton—which is saying a lot…. It's the perfect '8-to-80' picture." Not everyone found the film so agreeable. In his memoir, Garson Kanin remembered going to see the film with playwright Robert Sherwood. During a long deathbed scene, Laughton's character uttered the line, "I'm—so—so—happy!" At this point, Sherwood leaned over to Kanin and whispered, "For 'happy,' read 'hammy'" (Kanin: 252–53).

The Tuttles of Tahiti (1942)

Tagline: "Meet the Tuttles—they were never meant to have money—just fun."[48]

U.S. (RKO Radio Pictures/Sol Lesser)

Credits: Screenplay: S. Lewis Meltzer and Robert Carson; Adaptation: James Hilton; From the Novel *No More Gas* by Charles Nordhoff and James Norman Hall; Music: Roy Webb; Musical Director: C. Bakaleinikoff; Photography: Nicholas Musuraca; Special Effects: Vernon L. Walker; Art Directors: Albert S. D'Agostino, Carroll Clark; Wardrobe: Renié; Recorder: John E. Tribby; Editor: Fredric Knudtson; Dialogue Director: J. Edward Killy; Directed by Charles Vidor; U.S. release: May 1, 1942; Genre: Comedy; Black and White; Running Time: 91 minutes; DVD from Warner Archive Collection, released January 2019; no English subtitle captions for the deaf and hard of hearing.

Cast: Charles Laughton (*Jonas*); Jon Hall (*Chester*); Peggy Drake (*Tamara*); Victor Francen (*Dr. Blondin*); Gene Reynolds (*Ru*); Florence Bates (*Emily*); Curt Bois (*Jensen*); Adeline de Walt Reynolds (*Mama Ruau*); Mala (*Nat*); Leonard Sues (*Fana*); Jody Gilbert (*Effie*); Tommy Cook (*Riki*); Jack Carr (*Rapoti*); Jimmy Ames (*Manu*); Ernie Adams (*Paki*); Jim Spencer (*Tupa*); Alma Ross (*Hio*); Teddy Infuhr (*Ala*); **Uncredited Cast**: Philip Ahn (*Emily's Servant*); John Bagni (*Ben*); Bobby Barber (*Tinsmith*); Peggy Lou

Florence Bates and Laughton in costume, with script to hand, on the set of *The Tuttles of Tahiti* (1942).

(1942) The Tuttles of Tahiti

Bianco (*Georgette*); Frank Bruno (*Islander*); Spencer Chan (*Chauffeur—Chinese Servant*); Birdie De Bolt (*Tupa's Wife*); Nellie Duran (*Islander*); Fern Emmett (*Martha*); Lee Tung Foo (*Islander*); Byron Foulger (*Assistant Bank Manager*); Willie Fung (*Creditor*); Chester Gan (*Emily's Servant*); Nancy Gates (*Tupa's Daughter—Aged 14*); Irene Gay (*Ben's Wife*); My Lee Haulani (*Tupa's Daughter—Aged Eight*); George Kaluna (*Cola*); Al Kikume (*Postman*); Grace Lem (*Woman in Dress Shop*); James B. Leong (*Candy Salesman*); Tani Marsh (*Andrew's Wife*); Billy Moya (*Andre's Son—Aged 11*); Steven Muller (*Rapoti's Son*); George Piltz (*Andrew*); Robin Raymond (*Maitu*); Max Reid (*Rapoti's Son—Aged 11*); Linda Rivas (*Islander*); Mary Shaw (*Rapoti's Wife*); Ignacio Saenz (*Tupa's Son—Aged 16*).

Working Titles: *Out of Gas*; *No More Gas*; *The Gay Tuttles of Tahiti*

Synopsis: Chester Tuttle returns from service in the merchant navy to his home in the South Sea Islands. He brings a cockerel which he hopes will beat other contenders on the island and provide financial security for his impecunious family. His excitable father, Jonas Tuttle, is overjoyed and reintroduces his son to the extended Tuttle family he left behind. Jonas shows Chester a stash of cash saved to pay back the local physician, Dr. Blondin, for his assistance to the family over the years. Chester announces he has a solution to their financial problems. He introduces his cockerel, the Black Eagle, from San Francisco. Exulted by the bird, Jonas manages to get his old jalopy car started and pays a call on a neighbor, Emily, a wealthy contestant in cockfights on the island. He proposes to enter his bird against her rooster at a cockfight. To raise money to finance the fight, Jonas sends his sons out fishing on a motorboat, but they run out of gas and are stranded on the sea. Jonas is forced to borrow more money from the kindly Dr. Blondin. The doctor's devious housekeeper, Jensen, persuades the doctor to ask Jonas for a mortgage on his house as security. Jonas bets all his savings and property on the bird winning. When the bird loses ignominiously, Jonas is warned that he has forfeited everything. Realizing their predicament, Dr. Blondin advances the Tuttles just enough money to buy gas for their fishing boat in the hope they will earn enough money to repay the mortgage. During a fishing trip, Chester and his brothers run out of gas just as a storm is brewing. When they are missing for over a week, they are presumed to be lost. While drifting, the boys come across a huge ship abandoned during the storm, and with gas found aboard they start their fishing boat and tow the ship to port. The salvage money enables the Tuttles to spend lavishly for new furniture and Chester's marriage to Tamara, Emily's daughter. Soon all they have left is the money to pay the mortgage, which Jonas carelessly hides in a catalogue. The creditors come to remove all the unpaid furniture and in the confusion the catalogue is lost. They recover the money just as they face eviction and are able to pay the mortgage. Even so, Jonas is again forced to approach Dr. Blondin to borrow money to pay for gas.

Selected Dialogue:

TUTTLE: "There's so many of them. What's the difference? They're all Tuttles!"

TUTTLE: "You know sometimes I think that a nice drink is one of man's greatest inventions."

Production Commentary: At the height of his cinematic fame in 1935, Laughton was quoted in *Film Daily* (February 26, 1935) as saying, "Hollywood is a goofy place, but I like it." Due to Laughton's unconventional approach to acting, there were many within the Hollywood film community who might have suggested that "goofy" was an apt description for the actor.

At first glance, his decision to take on this piece of South Seas moonshine may appear a trifle wacky. However, the film's screenplay was based on a *Saturday Evening Post* story, "Out of Gas." This was followed by a successful novel, *No More Gas*. Charles Nordhoff and James Norman Hall were the writers, and their previous historical novel had been the source of one of Laughton's greatest successes, *Mutiny on the Bounty*. In that film, the ship's crew set foot on a South Seas Island island paradise and Laughton's Captain Bligh shakes hands with the chieftain. Now seven years later, Laughton had taken on the mantle of a poor person's overlord of an insignificant atoll. Thus, *The Tuttles of Tahiti* can be explained as Laughton revisiting *Mutiny on the Bounty* by the back door as it were.

The film draws upon another previous role: Laughton's island wastrel, Ginger Ted, in *Vessel of Wrath/The Beachcomber*. Indeed, the exotic South Seas setting was both topical and indicative of the era. Dorothy Lamour's South Seas escapades at Paramount during the 1930s were now joined by Betty Grable in *Song of the Islands* (Walter Lang, 1942) at Twentieth Century–Fox. Later, Maria Montez turned up on a Pacific isle in Universal's *Cobra Woman* (Robert Siodmak, 1944). Other dramatic representations of the South Seas during this period include *The Moon and Sixpence* (United Artists, Albert Lewin, 1942); *South of Pago Pago* (United Artists, Alfred E. Green, 1940) and *Aloma of the South Seas* (Paramount, Alfred Santell, 1941). The last two films featured Jon Hall as the male lead.

Bit part actress Peggy Drake made her star feature debut in *The Tuttles of Tahiti* playing Tamara and was signed to a seven-year $1000-a-week RKO contract. Her bid for stardom came to an abrupt end. The cavernous soundstages were converted into Tahiti. The actors had to walk barefoot on cold earth which grips hosed down twice a day. South Seas breezes were fabricated using industrial fans. Halfway through the shooting, these conditions resulted in Peggy Drake falling ill with pneumonia and being hospitalized. This held up production for two months. These travails added costs of $847,000. This was never recouped and Drake's RKO contract was terminated. The 20-year-old found Laughton a willing teacher, full of suggestions on how to improve her acting technique. As she explained in an article, "Promotion for Peggy," in *Hollywood* (May 1942), "Mr. Laughton was very helpful, after we started shooting. When I'd give my lines the wrong intonation, for instance, he'd take my aside and say, 'Why don't you try it this way, my dear?' He's been wonderful!"

In participating in this film, Laughton chose to disregard the axiom, "Never work with children or animals." As the patriarch, he is surrounded by passels of kids and cockerels at every turn. Though his acting can be read as a standard cute comic performance which aims to be funny and charming, the overriding impression given is of Laughton slumming his performance on dubious material and riding on a novelty ticket. "Paying for ice for father's piles" (Callow: 147), as Laughton colloquially put it.

Critical response to the film was generally positive, although there was some disquiet concerning the suitability of the role for an actor of Laughton's stature. The *New York Times* (April 30, 1942) implied there was uniqueness in seeing Laughton in this South Seas comic drama: "Charles Laughton is to the life drawn as Jonas, the wily, sporting head of the clan." Caroline Lejeune of the *Observer* (February 28, 1943) wrote about his venture into unworthy material: "Charles Laughton, in his time, can give some magnificent performances, yet he seems equally happy to give a perfect travesty of Charles Laughton, the performer." The *Showmen's Trade Review* (March 21, 1942) saw much to exploit for film exhibitors: "Play up Laughton and Hall and if you haven't had a South Sea lobby in some time this is one that will stand that kind of advertising." The reviewer also commended Laughton for taking on the role: "He makes the character of Jonas…so real that the spectator is moved to understanding sympathy while at the same time wanting to kick his pants for the inconsiderate acts he perpetrates on his family and friends."

Though it does have a superficial and congenial charm, the film suffers from B picture content, and struggles to maintain its A picture status. Depending on your inclinations, Laughton's performance in *The Tuttles of Tahiti* can be read in either of two ways: as a lighthearted departure, *or* a manifestation of Laughton's indifference to the quality of script material and an object lesson in the misuse of his acting talent. In the end, the choice is yours.

Tales of Manhattan (1942)

Tagline: "A Story as Thrilling as Its Stars!"[49]

U.S. (Twentieth Century–Fox)

Credits: Original Stories and Screenplay: Ben Hecht, Ferenc Molnar, Donald Ogden Stewart, Samuel Hoffenstein, Alan Campbell, Ladislas Fodor, L. Vadnai, L. Gorog, Lamar Trotti, Henry Blankfort; Musical Director: Edward Paul; Original Music: Sol Kaplan; "Glory Day" by Leo Robin and Ralph Rainger; Orchestrations: Clarence Wheeler, Charles Bradshaw and Hugo Friedhofer; Vocal Arrangements: Hall Johnson; Photography: Joseph Walker; Art Directors: Richard Day, Boris Leven; Editor: Robert Bischoff; Unit Manager: J.H. Nadel; Assistant Director: Robert Stillman; Set Decorator: Thomas Little; Costumes: Dolly Tree, Bernard Newman, Gwen Wakeling, Irene; Makeup: Guy Pearce; Sound: W.D. Flick, Roger Heman; Directed by Julien Duvivier; U.S. release: October 30, 1942; Genre: Multi-Drama; Black

(1942) Tales of Manhattan

and White; Running Time: 118 minutes; DVD from Twentieth Century–Fox Cinema Archives, released August 2013; no English subtitle captions for the deaf and hard of hearing.

Cast: Charles Boyer (*Orman*); Rita Hayworth (*Ethel*); Ginger Rogers (*Diane*); Henry Fonda (*George*); **Charles Laughton (*Charles Smith*)**; Edward G. Robinson (*Browne*); Paul Robeson (*Luke*); Ethel Waters (*Esther*); "Rochester" (*The Reverend Lazarus*); Thomas Mitchell (*Halloway*); Cesar Romero (*Harry*); Roland Young (*Edgar*); Gail Patrick (*Ellen*); Eugene Pallette (*Luther*); Victor Francen (*Arturo Bellini*); George Sanders (*Williams*); James Gleason ("*Father*" *Joe*); Marion Martin (*Squirrel*); Elsa Lanchester (*Mrs. Smith*); Harry Davenport (*Professor Lyons*); James Rennie (*Hank Bronson*); J. Carrol Naish (*Costello*); and The Hall Johnson Choir (*Themselves*); Frank Orth (*Second-Hand Clothes Dealer*); Christian Rub (*Wilson*); Sig Arno (*Piccolo Player*); Harry Hayden (*David*); Morris Ankrum (*Judge*); Don Douglas (*Henderson*); Mae Marsh (*Molly*); Clarence Muse (*Grandpa*); George Reed (*Christopher*); Cordell Hickman (*Nicodemus*); Paul Renay ("*Spud*" *Johnson*); Barbara Lynn (*Mary*); Adeline DeWalt Reynolds (*Grandmother*); Helene Reynolds (*Actress*); **Uncredited Cast**: Eric Wilton (*Halloway's Butler*); Jack Chefe (*Mr. Martelli*); Robert Greig (*Lazar the Tailor*); Cyril Ring, Bert Stevens (*Assistant Tailors*); William Halligan (*Oliver Webb*); Charles Williams (*Orman's Bespectacled Agent*); Buster Brodie (*Call Boy*); Rene Austin (*Susan*); Gino Corrado (*Spectator at Concert*); Frank Dae (*Elderly Man*); Frank Darien (*Elsa's Old Father*); Bess Flowers, Colin Kenny, Bert Moorhouse, Count Stefenelli (*Concertgoers*); Frank Jaquet (*Oboist*); Forbes Murray (*Dignified Man*); Tom O'Grady (*Latecomer to Concert*); Dewey Robinson (*Smith's Bullying Boss*); Curly Twiford (*Birdman*); Will Wright (*Old Concertgoer*); Esther Howard (*Woman Taking Cigarette from Joe*); Joseph E. Bernard (*Wally—Postman*); Ted Billings (*Man at City Mission*); Don Brodie (*Whistler at Mission*); Ralph Brooks (*Man at Reunion*); Sayre Dearing, Harold Miller (*Men at Reunion*); Maggie Dorsey (*Woman*); Ted Stanhope (*Henderson's Chauffeur*); Rita Christiani (*Young Woman in Embrace*); Olive Ball (*Shantytown Woman*); Jerry Bergen (*Little Man*); Chester Clute (*Mr. Langehanke*); Marcel Dalio (*Second Salesman at Santelli's*); Margaret Dumont (*Madame Langehanke*); W.C. Fields (*Professor Pufflewhistle*); Dot Farley, Rondo Hatton, Ellinor Vanderveer, Dorothy Vernon (*Party Guests*); William Irving (*Victim of Drink*); Edgar Norton (*Jessup—Langehanke's Butler*); Phil Silvers (*First Salesman at Santelli's*).

Working Title: *Tails of Manhattan*

Synopsis: An anthology of five stories in which a tuxedo tailcoat passes through the hands of several diverse individuals living in and around New York. **Story #1**: An actor and his lover are confronted by her sadistic husband, with tragic consequences. **Story #2**: A diffident fellow tries to help his friend when his suspicious fiancée creates havoc. **Story #3**: Talented composer Charles Smith is forced to eke out a living as a pianist playing boogie woogie at a downtown café. After an audition with a temperamental conductor, he secures a commission to conduct his own work at a public concert. With minutes to spare, his wife finds an old tailcoat for the occasion, but it proves too tight a fit. As he conducts vigorously, disaster strikes as his tailcoat tears apart. Smith is oblivious to his plight and continues to conduct while the audience breaks into convulsions of laughter. When he is told the cause of the commotion, he takes off the coat and throws it on the floor in despair. Smith's mentor, the regular conductor, then removes his coat and instructs his protégé to continue the concert. To show solidarity, all the men in the audience remove their jackets as

Laughton takes the baton as composer Charles Smith in the all-star anthology film, *Tales of Manhattan* (1942).

well. At the conclusion of the concert, Smith and his wife go on the town to celebrate his success. Smith gives the coat to a Salvation Army representative on the street, telling her it brought him luck in a roundabout fashion. **Story #4**: A disbarred lawyer is now down-and-out in a flophouse. When he receives an invitation for a college reunion at the Waldorf-Astoria, the flophouse owner presents him with the battered tailcoat. **Story #5**: A shantytown full of impoverished farmers finds the tailcoat—the pockets full of money—after it literally falls from the sky (from a plane, actually).

Selected Dialogue:

SMITH: "It's too small."
SMITH: "It's a rabbit's foot!"

Production Commentary: *Tales of Manhattan* dusted off the vogue for portmanteau films and remains a good example of the genre. It benefits from the Continental input of French director Julien Duvivier, who five years previously, in *Un Carnet de Bal* (Sigma, 1937), had used a similar framing device, a dance program, to connect seven short dramas.

In *Tales of Manhattan*, a dress coat acts as the link for five dramas. The episode starring Laughton as a luckless composer finds him in top form and he delivers a priceless character performance as everyman Charles Smith. The vignette is both concise in construction and effective in its playing. The role of a frustrated composer who yearns to play his "serious" compositions on a public platform, instead of knocking out boogie woogie tunes on a honkytonk piano, appealed to Laughton. He too was motivated by a desire to create and present "good art" fit for mass consumption. Doubtless, playing a would-be music conductor charged with unifying an orchestra also appealed to his artistic vanity. Laughton's playing in this vignette is executed with relish and he has excellent support from Elsa Lanchester as his wife and Victor Francen as a musical maestro Arturo Bellini, a Hollywood caricature of famous Italian conductor Arturo Toscanini. The sketch is pure Hollywood hokum, but it is presented and played with impeccable assurance.

Producers Boris Morros and Sam Spiegel (using his S.P. Eagle *nom de screen*) managed to bring the film in on a budget of slightly more than $1,000,000. This was achieved by selling the idea they were producing episodes rather than a conventional complete film. Consequently, they were able to arrange relatively low salary deals for star players and writers.

At the time of its release, the film got a lukewarm reception from the critics. Caroline Lejeune in the *Observer* (April 4, 1943) wrote of the Laughton sketch, "[T]he whole unfortunate episode ends in a triumph of mugging by all." The *New York Times* (September 25, 1942) thought Laughton's pianist was "overplayed." Other critics were supportive of Laughton's endeavors in the film. *Variety* (August 5, 1942) was congratulatory: "This scene ranks among the ... best in the picture.... Laughton just about carries off all the acting honors." The London *Times* (April 1, 1943) felt Laughton managed to achieve "more humorous and pathetic [traits] by the sheer physical energy and facial expressiveness of his acting—no man can lose, and find, his dignity on the screen with such endearing abandon."

In the preview print, there was a nine-minute W.C. Fields sequence which was deleted because of concerns about the film's length. This was originally inserted between the Edward G. Robinson and Paul Robeson episodes. In this deleted story, a second-hand clothes dealer sells the coat to an eccentric professor who then gives a temperance lecture, unaware that the coconut milk he passes around has been spiked. The episode was rediscovered in the Twentieth Century–Fox vaults in the 1990s and included as a supplement on a studio video release in 1996.

The success of *Tales of Manhattan* led to director Duvivier undertaking an anthology film for Universal, *Flesh and Fantasy* (1943). *Tales of Manhattan* players Charles Boyer, Edward G. Robinson and Thomas Mitchell were again cast in this production. Alas, Laughton was unavailable. On the evidence of Laughton's performance in *Tales of Manhattan* this was a missed opportunity. A further collaboration with Duvivier could have resulted in another satisfying film performance.

Stand By for Action aka *Cargo of Innocents* (1942)

Tagline: "There's Action in the Pacific and It's Terrific!"[50]

U.S. (Metro-Goldwyn-Mayer)

(1942) Stand By for Action

Cast members from *Stand By for Action* (1942) on the back lot of the vast MGM Studios in Culver City. Left to right: Walter Brennan, Robert Taylor, Laughton and Brian Donlevy.

Credits: Produced by Robert Z. Leonard and Orville O. Dull; Screenlay: George Bruce, John L. Balderston and Herman J. Mankiewicz; Original Story: Captain Harvey Haislip, U.S.N., and R.C. Sherriff; Suggested by the Story "A Cargo of Innocence" by Laurence Kirk; Photography: Charles Rosher; Musical Score: Lennie Hayton; Recording Director: Douglas Shearer; Art Director: Cedric Gibbons; Associate: Urie McCleary; Set Decorator: Edwin B. Willis; Associate: Edward G. Boyle; Special Effects: Arnold Gillespie, Don Jahraus; Technical Advisor: Lieut. Comdr. H.D. Smith, U.S.N.; Editor: George Boemler; Directed by Robert Z. Leonard; U.S. release: December 31, 1942; Genre: War Drama; Black and White; Running Time: 109 minutes; DVD from the Warner Archive Collection, released June 2012; no English subtitle captions for the deaf and hard of hearing.

Cast: Robert Taylor (*Lieut. Gregg Masterman*); **Charles Laughton** (*Rear Admiral Stephen Thomas*); Brian Donlevy (*Lieut. Comdr. Martin J. Roberts*); Walter Brennan (*Chief Yeoman Henry Johnson*); Marilyn Maxwell (*Audrey Carr*); Henry O'Neill (*Comdr. Stone, M.C.*); Marta Linden (*Mary Collins*); Chill Wills (*Chief Boatswain's Mate Jenks*); Douglass Dumbrille (*Captain Ludlow*); Richard Quine (*Ensign Lindsay*); William Tannen (*Flag Lieut. Dudley*); Douglas Fowley (*Ensign Martin*); Tim Ryan (*Lieut. Tim Ryan*); Dick Simmons (*Lieut. J.G. Royce*); Byron Foulger (*Pharmacist's Mate "Doc" Miller*); Hobart Cavanaugh (*Carpenter's Mate "Chips"*); Inez Cooper (*Susan Garrison*); Ben Welden (*Chief Quartermaster Rankin*); Harry Fleischmann (*Chief Signalman*); **Uncredited Cast**: Frank Whitbeck (*Narrator*); Ernie Alexander, Ralph McCullough (*Sailors in Boat*); Will Armstrong, Billy Bletcher, Frank Hagney, Oscar "Dutch" Hendrian, "Snub" Pollard, Pat West, Harry Wilson, Duke York (*Sailors*); Wally Cassell, Jim Davis, James Millican (*Talkers*); Jay Eaton (*Party Guest*); Calvin Emery (*Lookout*); Sam Harris (*Senator at Party*); Robert Kent (*Hank Nels*); Hal Le Sueur (*Lookout*); Frank McLure (*Ship Officer*); Bea Nigro (*Senator's Wife*); Spec O'Donnell (*Jason*); William Roberts (*Marine Messenger*); Elizabeth Russell (*Expectant Mother*); Theodore von Eltz (*Commander*); Douglas Wood (*Senior Masterman*).

Working Titles: *Cargo of Innocence*; *A Cargo of Innocents*; *Men o' War*; *Clear for Action*; *Navy Convoy*; *This Man's Navy*; *Pacific Task Force*

Awards: Academy Award Nomination: Special Effects: A. Arnold Gillespie, Donald Jahraus, Michael Steinore.

Synopsis: Following the attack on the Pacific Fleet at Pearl Harbor, U.S. Navy sailors at a West Coast base are put on a war footing. Lieut. Comdr. Martin J. Roberts complains to his superior, Rear Admiral Stephan "Iron Pants" Thomas, when repair work on his ship is unduly delayed. Thomas promotes Roberts to command a mothballed destroyer, the U.S.S. *Warren*. Lieut. Gregg Masterman, aide to Roberts, is promoted to second in command aboard the *Warren*. When Roberts and Masterman board the *Warren*, they encounter former chief yeoman Henry Johnson, who had served on the ship during World War I; now a civilian caretaker, he tells the officers about the ship's proud history. Roberts tells Johnson that he cannot serve again because the war will be "too tough for gray hairs." Masterman suggests to Johnson he dye his hair to look much younger and manages to help in get him back into the Navy. While on its shakedown cruise, the *Warren* is ordered to join a Navy convoy. A short time later, a violent storm arises, and Johnson is himself knocked unconscious. Then the *Warren* spots a lifeboat with two women and 20 infants aboard. As executive officer, Masterman is put in charge of their welfare. His troubles increase when the two women give birth. When the *Warren* reaches the convoy, Thomas aboard his flagship, the *Chattanooga*, is amazed to see a baby crawling on the *Warren*'s deck. A Japanese plane attacks the *Warren* and Masterman, in charge of the ship's gun crew, shoots the plane down. A Japanese battleship shells the *Chattanooga* and puts it out of commission. Roberts orders a smoke screen to protect the convoy, planning to double back through the smoke and to attack the battleship. Masterman objects to the plan but, after Roberts is wounded, carries out his orders. The battleship is taken by surprise and sunk. During the fighting, Johnson leaves his sickbed and pilots the *Warren* to victory. When the convoy arrives in San Francisco, the *Chattanooga* is towed by the *Warren*. For their gallantry during action against the enemy, Roberts, Masterman and Johnson are each awarded the Navy Cross.

Selected Dialogue:

THOMAS: "Don't shout! Don't shout!"

THOMAS: "Do you realize, sir, that I am an island entirely surrounded by bright young men known as aides just to prevent people from taking the enemy? There is an old custom, sir, which demands that an officer should be announced to his commanding officer."

Production Commentary: "The Mightiest Sea-Epic Since *Mutiny on the Bounty*" boasted the theatrical trailer. The movie and Laughton's performance are just that: serviceable and very little else.

Laughton was now on his sixth nautical role. This wartime drama with comic overtones finds Laughton kicked upstairs and promoted to a mock-heroic rear admiral. Laughton seems nothing more than jolly at best and dutiful at worse. We first hear him blustering before we see him ensconced in his braid, sat behind a service desk receiving his orders over the phone. Without even trying, he appeared to be mugging the part. As Peter Ustinov commented, "When Laughton was sitting quietly in a chair, not speaking, he was doing too much" (Callow: 156).

The film offers a conservative depiction of the American wartime navy. In this early stage of the war, critics tended to get behind any flag-waver that appeared on the screen. Hence, reviews stressed the collaborative team efforts of the production crew and cast members in putting together a morale raiser. *Film Daily* (December 10, 1942) typically aggregated patriotism and heroics with notions of truth and authenticity. "Romance be damned! Here is a production that can stand its ground and win its public without becoming a slave to boy-meets-girl formula." In Britain where the title was changed to *Cargo of Innocents*, Caroline Lejeune in her weekly *Observer* column (March 21, 1943) lamented, "They've played *Cargo of Innocents* light, and if it's of practically of no interest to Orson Welles fans, it will give a lot of people a satisfactory show, besides intriguing a few who like to see the quick brain behind Charles Laughton mugging." Bosley Crowther writing in the *New York Times* (March 12, 1943) was anything but impressed: "This is the type of war film which breeds complacency. This is the sort of mock heroics which insults our fighting men."

When *Variety* published its list of the Top Grossers of 1943 (January 5, 1944), *Stand By for Action* ranked eighth position of 16 MGM releases. It earned a respectable $1,900,000. Laughton shows no embarrassment in performing mediocre material, written below his skill set as an actor. Though he is, as always, worth watching, there appears a disconnect throughout most of the film except in one scene where the screenwriters have him launch into a speech exalting the spirit of John Paul Jones. Here his renowned oratory comes into its own and is conveyed with sincere and intense feeling. In conclusion, Laughton gets behind the war effort and gives a plausible performance and milks every scene for all its worth. However, for all the stellar cast and production values, the net result is well below par. The promised action sequences are held in abeyance and when they do arrive on screen they are muted and disappointing with no U.S. service personnel casualties shown on screen. The film is often unfocused as it tries too hard to cram so much in. It laid the template for service comedies such as *The Baby and the Battleship* (British Lion, Jay Lewis, 1956) and *Operation Petticoat* (Universal-International, Blake

Edwards, 1959) but *Stand By for Action* makes for tepid entertainment.

Forever and a Day (1943)

Tagline: "78 Stars and a Great Story as Big as the Cast!"[51]

U.S. (RKO Radio Pictures)

Credits: Writers: Charles Bennett, Alan Campbell, Norman Corwin, C.S. Forester, Peter Godfrey, Jack Hartfield, Lawrence Hazard, S.M. Herzig, James Hilton, Michael Hogan, Christopher Isherwood, Emmet Lavery, W.P. Lipscomb, Gene Lockhart, Frederick Lonsdale, Alice Duer Miller, R.C. Sherriff, Donald Ogden Stewart, John Van Druten, Claudine West, Keith Winter; Directors: Rene Clair, Edmund Goulding, Cedric Hardwicke, Frank Lloyd, Victor Saville, Robert Stevenson, Herbert Wilcox; **Uncredited Technical Credits**: Photography: Robert De Grasse, Lee Garmes, Nicholas Musuraca, Russell Metty; Art Directors: Albert S. D'Agostino, Lawrence P. Williams, Al Herman; Editors: Elmo Williams, George Crone; Set Decorators: Darrell Silvera, Claude Carpenter; Costumes: Walter Plunkett, Renie, Edward Stevenson; Music: Anthony Collins; Sound: Bailey Fesler, John C. Grubb, John Tribby, Richard Van Hessen, Earl Wolcott; Special Effects: Vernon L. Walker, Douglas Travers; Production Co-Coordinator: Lloyd Richards; Technical Advisor: C.S. Ramsay-Hill; U.S. release: March 26, 1943; U.K. release: August 2, 1943; Genre: Multi-Drama; Black and White; Running Time: 104 minutes; DVD Region 2 from Simply Media, released May 2015; no English subtitle captions for the deaf and hard of hearing.

Cast: Kent Smith (*Gates T. Pomfret*); Reginald Gardiner (*Assistant Hotel Manager*); Victor McLaglen (*Spavin*); Billy Bevan (*Cabby*); Arthur Treacher (*Second Watcher*); Ruth Warrick (*Lesley Trimble*); Herbert Marshall (*Curate*); C. Aubrey Smith (*Admiral Trimble*); Edmund Gwenn (*Stubbs*); Ray Milland (*Bill*); Dame May Whitty (*Mrs. Trimble*); Gene Lockhart (*Cobblewick*); Anna Neagle (*Susan*); Claude Rains (*Pomfret*); Jessie Matthews (*Mildred Trimble*); Reginald Owen (*Simpson*); Ian Hunter (*Dexter*); **Charles Laughton** (*Bellamy*); Sir Cedric Hardwicke (*Dabb*); Anna Lee (*Bride*); Patric Knowles (*Son*); Edward Everett Horton (*Sir Anthony*); Isobel Elsom (*Lady Trimble-Pomfret*); June Duprez (*Julia*); Wendell Hulett (*Augustus*); Ida Lupino (*Jenny*); Brian Aherne (*Jim*); Merle Oberon (*Marjorie*); Una O'Connor (*Mrs. Ismay*); Nigel Bruce (*Major Garrow*); Elsa Lanchester (*Mamie*); Robert Coote (*Blind Officer*); June (*V.A.D. Girl*); Roland Young (*Barringer*); Gladys Cooper (*Mrs. Barringer*); Robert Cummings (*Ned Trimble*); Donald Crisp (*Captain Martin*); **Uncredited Cast**: George Kirby (*News Vendor*); Doreen Monroe, Connie Leon (*Wartime Londoners*); May Beatty (*London Cook*); Joy Harrington (*Wartime Bus Conductor*); Ernest Grooney (*Hotel Manager*); Harry Allen (*Cockney Air Raid Warden*); Aubrey Mather (*Man in Air Raid Shelter*); Ethel Griffies (*Wife of Man in Air Raid Shelter*); June Lockhart (*Girl in Air Raid Shelter*); Barbara Everest (*Girl's Mother in Air Raid Shelter*); Stuart Robertson (*Air Raid Warden*); Charles Irwin (*Corporal Charlie*); Gerald Oliver Smith, Snub Pollard (*Men in Air Raid Shelter*); Mary Gordon (*Woman in Air Raid Shelter*); Lumsden Hare (*Fitch*); Ben Webster (*Vicar*); Claud Allister (*William Barstow*); Alan Edmiston (*Tripp Pomfret's Lawyer*); Doris Lloyd (*Trimble Maid*); Helena Pickard (*Trimble Maid*); Halliwell Hobbes (*Doctor*); Clifford Severn (*Nelson Trimble*); Alec Craig (*Ambrose Pomfret's Butler*); Buster Keaton (*Wilkins*); Montague Love (*Sir John Bunn*); Daphne

With a large British cast, *Forever and a Day* (1943) was produced for war charities in Hollywood. The portmanteau story followed the historical fortunes of a middle-class London family, the Pomfrets. Left to right: Laughton as the Pomfrets' butler, Bellamy, Ian Hunter as Dexter Pomfret and, in her only Hollywood role, Jessie Matthews as Mildred Pomfret née Trimble.

Moore (*Elizabeth Trimble-Pomfret*); Cecil Kellaway (*Dinner Guest*); Wendy Barrie (*Edith Trimble-Pomfret*); Queenie Leonard (*Maid*); Eric Blore (*Charles*); Walter Kingsford (*Estate Lawyer*); Dennis Hoey (*Mover*); Emily Fitzroy (*Ms. Fulcher*); Richard Haydn (*Mr. Fulcher*); Odette Myrtil (*Madame Gaby*); Ivan Simpson (*Dexter*); Anita Bolster (*Mrs. Garrow*); Pax Walker (*Waitress*); Marta Gale (*Miss Garrow*); Arthur Mulliner (*Elderly Bachelor*); Jean Prescott (*A.T.S. Girl*); Clyde Cook (*Cabby*).

Working Title: *This Changing World*

Synopsis: During the wartime London blackout, an American journalist, Gates T. Pomfret, is staying at a London hotel. He receives a wire instructing him to sell the family home on Pomfret Street. When he calls, the occupant of the house, Lesley Trimble, is too busy to answer the doorbell as she is taking refreshments to the public air raid shelter next door. Gates eventually gains access to the house and he has cross words with Lesley about his financial offer and lack of courtesy towards the house. As Lesley and Gates look out on a firebombed London, she begins her recollections concerning the history of the house. In 804, Admiral Trimble buys a plot of land to build a home for his family. When the house is built, he shows his son Bill a plaque in the cellar which shows the ownership of the house as residing with Pomfret and his descendants. Soon after, a young woman appears drenched by a nighttime storm. She is being pursued by two men who inform Bill and his family that she is the ward of Ambrose Pomfret, who has decided she shall be married to one of the men, William Barstow. Bill and his mother decide to remove the men from the house and take Susan Trenchard into their home for the time being. When Ambrose Pomfret later appears at the house, Susan tells him she is to be married to Bill Pomfret. To her surprise, Bill agrees to marry her. Shortly after their marriage, Bill leaves to fight in the Napoleonic Wars. On the day of Napoleon's defeat at Trafalgar, the death of Bill in battle is announced. Their son is also born on the same day. As a widow, Susan finds her financial situation is precarious. With malicious intent, Ambrose Pomfret decides to purchase the Trimble home. One night in a pique of rage he attempts to deface the portrait of old Admiral Trimble. The following morning, he is found dead at the foot of the painting. Gates interrupts Lesley's story to ask if all the Pomfrets were unjust. She continues her family history with the story of Dexter Pomfret, a successful ironmonger and butterfly collector. The old admiral's great granddaughter, Mildred Trimble, appears at the front door of the house. She wishes to purchase the portrait of the old admiral. Dexter and Mildred find they have much in common and they later marry. Mrs. Pomfret decides to install a new iron bath with shower, but this causes upset with her husband until Mrs. Pomfret persuades a respected businessman that he should take up the bath as a business proposition. Dexter likes her idea of building iron bathtubs and the ensuing business is a success. In the following 15 years, the Pomfret family expands to include two daughters and one son. While the daughters are obedient, the Pomfret son, Anthony, has his own ideas and rebels against his father. Anthony acquires a knighthood, but pretension and wealth ensures that his family heritage is lost. During the 1897 Diamond Jubilee parade, Jenny Jones, the Pomfrets' maid, is unable to see Queen Victoria passing. She meets Jim Trimble, a modest coal man who lifts her up so she can see the queen as she goes by. Jim has pride in his ancestor Eustace, who had helped to build the house where Jenny is now in service. When Jim decides to emigrate to America to begin a new life, he asks Jenny to join him and she accepts the offer gladly. Following the death of Lord and Lady Pomfret, their son and heir Augustus Pomfret, having moved to New York, decides to sell the house. During the First World War, the house serves as a residential hotel. During 1917, an American doughboy, Ned Trimble, is billeted there at the home of his ancestors for 24 hours. The hotel is run by Mrs. Ismay and her daughter Marjorie. A couple, the Barringers, are expecting their son, Captain Archibald Barringer, to arrive home on leave and join them in celebration of his recent military decorations. They invite Ned to their table and as Mrs. Barringer tells him about her beloved son Archie, a telegram arrives informing them of his death. Mrs. Barringer retires to her room and her husband offers Ned a place at the table for dinner and they drink a solemn toast to Archie's memory. Following dinner, Marjorie gives Ned a tour of the premises. The next morning, Ned proposes to Marjorie and they are wed before Ned embarks on his tour of duty. After the November armistice, Marjorie returns to the cellar of the house where Ned spoke his first endearment to her following his reading of the plaque of ownership put there by old Admiral Pomfret over a century before. Back in the present day, Lesley concludes her reminiscences by telling how she and her mother had restored the hotel with money bequeathed by her father. As Lesley and Gates ponder about their ancestors and how they have put down roots in the house, another air raid starts and they take shelter in the cellar. A direct hit demolishes the property, but the pair emerge safe from the cellar after the all-clear. Lesley and Gates see the old house is in ruins—but the painting of old Admiral Pomfret still survives, and with it the indomitable spirit of the Pomfret ancestors lives on.

Production Commentary: In the middle of World War II, Laughton did a cameo for British war relief in *Forever and a Day*. All the British artists in Hollywood gave their services free and RKO provided facilities and distribution. All profits generated were donated to two charitable concerns, the British Red Cross and the United States National Foundation for Infantile Paralysis. The idea of putting on such a vast propaganda exercise from British and European expatriates in Hollywood to assist the war effort came from actor Cedric Hardwicke. Apart from being seen to be doing their patriotic duty, there was also the question of assuaging the charge that British ex-pats were "basking" in the Hollywood sun while Britain suffered strategic bombing by the German Luftwaffe in the Blitz on British cities.

The portmanteau story featuring over 70 stars is structured around a London house and several generations of one family, the Pomfrets. The story owes its genesis to Noël Coward's popular play *Cavalcade*. Like Coward's play, written during the Great Depression, the aim of *Forever and a Day* was to instill a sense of national pride and unity during a period of crisis and upheaval. *Forever and a Day* is a rally to arms and an effective piece of wartime flag-waving.

Laughton's vignette is efficient and effervescent, and he does a successful piece of character playing as a tippling butler. He acts opposite Jesse Matthews (in a dramatic role) and Ian Hunter. Matthews and Hunter were last-minute replacements for Greer Garson and Ronald Colman, who proved unavailable. Cedric Hardwicke and Buster Keaton also appear in the sketch as a pair of plumbers indulging themselves in slapstick. This episode was directed by Victor Saville, who had directed some of Jesse Matthews' best musical films of the 1930s.

Laughton's butler Bellamy, though amusing in itself, appears somewhat derivative and not only because it is a concoction borne of Marmaduke Ruggles. During this period, there were several actors and comics who portrayed congenial alcoholics. Arthur Housman (1889–1942) and Jack Norton (1882–1958) were two small-part actors who spent their time portraying Hollywood screen souses. In Britain, Jimmy James (1892–1965) and Freddie Frinton (1909–1968) built their comic careers playing inebriates on stage and screen.

The logistics of such a large-scale enterprise was formidable and Bosley Crowther of the *New York Times* (March 13, 1943) spoke for many when he wrote, "Under [the] circumstances, it is surprising that the film was actually made and also that it should be as agreeable as it is…. It should be a pleasant entertainment—especially for those who dote on the past." He went on to describe the second episode as "a bright and gay bit of comedy." Caroline Lejeune, writing in the *Observer* (June 20, 1943), was underwhelmed: "The most imposing thing about *Forever and a Day*…is its harmonious consistency—the fact that so many diverse talents could work together to achieve something so monumentally and homogeneously dull." Laughton's small cameo impersonating an inebriated servant is certainly amiable, yet hardly enthralling. The film's running time of 104 minutes is crammed full of British film personnel. As a consequence, there isn't the space for anything especially extreme, grandiloquent or memorable for Laughton (or anyone else) to commit to the screen before passing on to the next sketch.

This Land Is Mine (1943)

Tagline: "I Don't Dare Believe in Anyone…. Even the Man I Love!"[52]

U.S. (RKO Radio Pictures/Jean Renoir-Dudley Nichols)

This Land Is Mine (1943)

Credits: Music: Lothar Perl; Musical Director: C. Bakaleinikoff; Art Directors: Albert S. D'Agostino, Walter E. Keller; Special Effects: Vernon L. Walker; Editor: Frederic Knudtson; Dialogue Director: Leo Bulgakov; Set Decorators: Darrell Silvera, Al Fields; Recorder: John E. Tribby; Rerecorded by James G. Stewart; Gowns: Renié; Directed by Jean Renoir; Screenplay: Dudley Nichols; Photography: Frank Redman; Production Designer: Eugene Lourié; Assistant Director: Edward Donahoe; U.S. release: May 7, 1943; U.K. release: July 19, 1943; Genre: War Drama; Black and White; Running Time: 103 minutes; DVD from the Warner Archive Collection, released December 2012; no English subtitle captions for the deaf and hard of hearing.

Cast: Charles Laughton (*Albert Lory*); Maureen O'Hara (*Louise Martin*); George Sanders (*George Lambert*); Walter Slezak (*Major von Keller*); Kent Smith (*Paul Martin*); Una O'Connor (*Mrs. Emma Lory*); Philip Merivale (*Professor Sorel*); Thurston Hall (*Mayor Henry Manville*); George Coulouris (*Prosecutor*); Nancy Gates (*Julie Grant*); Ivan Simpson (*Judge*); John Donat (*Edmund Lorraine*); **Uncredited Cast**: Philip Ahlm (*German Second Lieutenant*); Frank Alten (*Captain Schwartz*); Louis V. Arco, John Banner (*German Sergeants*); Joan Barclay (*Young Woman*); Trevor Bardette (*Courtroom Guard who Brings Albert's Notes*); Linda Bieber (*Emily—Schoolgirl*); Tommy Bond (*Pug-nosed School Bully*); Sven Hugo Borg (*German Soldier*); Leo Bulgakov (*Little Fat Man*); Bobby Burns (*Courtroom Spectator*); George M. Carleton (*Mr. Noble—Jury Foreman and Butcher*); Wheaton Chambers (*Mr. Lorraine*); Gordon B. Clarke (*First Lieutenant*); Albert D'Arno, Russell Hoyt (*German Soldiers*); John Dilson (*Mayor's Secretary*); Ludwig Donath (*German Captain*); Margaret Fealy (*Old Woman*); Hans Fuerberg (*Kurt—German Soldier*); Ernest Grooney (*Priest*); Mary Halsey (*Girl*); Mildred Hardy (*Old Woman*); Sam Harris (*Man Knocked Down on Sidewalk/Townsman Shot by Firing Squad*); Hallene Hill (*Woman in Window*); Otto Hoffman (*Victor—Printer*); Lloyd Ingraham (*Man with Paper on Street*); Elmer Jerome (*Man in Window*); Casey Johnson (*Boy*); Terrellyne Johnson (*Girl*); P.J. Kelly, David Kirkland (*Judges*); Jeanne Lafayette (*Woman on Street*); Gabriel Lenoff (*German First Lieutenant*); Oscar Loraine (*Clerk*); Theodore Lorch (*Juror*); George MacQuarrie (*Chief of Police*); Hal Malone (*Man in Courtroom*); Jack Martin (*German Captain*); Claire McDowell (*Woman in Bathroom*); Ed McNamara (*Policeman*); Freddie Mercer (*Boy in Classroom*); Hans Moebus (*German Chauffeur*); Rudolf Myzet (*German Soldier*); O'Neill Nolan (*Henry*); William J. O'Brien (*Nightswitchman*); Frank O'Connor (*Juror*); Lillian O'Malley (*Woman in Street*); June Pickerell (*Woman in Window*); Lon Poff (*Old Man*); John Rice (*Burly Cop*); Ferdinand Schumann-Heink (*Karl—German Soldier*); Hans Schumm (*German Sergeant Who Pushes Albert*); Lester Sharpe (*German Soldier*); Jack Shea (*Burly Cop*); Ida Shoemaker (*Woman in Street*); George Sorel (*German Sergeant*); Robert R. Stephenson (*German Sergeant on Street*); Gus Taillon (*Newsman*); Walter Thiele, Nicholas Vehr (*German Soldiers*); Hans von Morhart (*Soldier Who Gets

Left to right: Laughton as the shy schoolmaster Albert Lory, Maureen O'Hara as school colleague Louise Martin, and John Donat as schoolboy Edmund Lorraine in Jean Renoir's wartime resistance drama *This Land is Mine* (1943).

(1943) *This Land Is Mine*

Slapped); Cecil Weston (*Mrs. Lorraine*); William Yetter Sr. (*Otto—German Soldier*).

Working Title: *Monsieur Thomas*

Awards: Academy Award for Best Sound Recording: Stephen Dunn.

Synopsis: Somewhere in an unspecified European country, a town square war memorial commemorates the 1914–1918 war with the inscription "In memory of those who died to bring peace to the world." The headline of a newspaper on the ground: "Hitler invades." German troops begin their occupation of the town and Major von Keller, the district commandant, shakes hands with Henry Manville, the town's mayor. Posters adorn the walls of the town informing the locals what to expect in the event of resistance or sabotage. In the home of the schoolmaster, the meek, cat-loving Albert Lory, his domineering mother Emma calls him down to breakfast. As they sit at the table, a resistance pamphlet is pushed under the front door. Though he attempts to burn the pamphlet, the heading *Liberty* catches his eye and he decides to retrieve the document from destruction. On his way to school, he meets schoolteacher Louise Martin, whom he secretly loves. She is arguing with her brother Paul. She becomes upset when Paul shows passing German soldiers a copy of the resistance leaflet. The mayor sees collaboration as the best option and orders the head of the school, Professor Sorel, to cut selective passages from various classical literature texts, such as Plato and Aristotle. After discussion of where the cuts should be made, Lory and Louise retire to their classrooms and instruct their pupils to remove those passages from their copies of the books. An air raid begins and Albert races across the street to fetch his elderly mother. In the school cellar, Lory quivers in fright as the action reaches its full intensity. Louise decides to instigate a sing-along, and this raises the morale of the children. After the raid, Lory tells Professor Sorel he is a coward. Sorel cautions him against defeatism and points out that in this environment of sacrifice, the role of the schoolteacher is needed more than ever. News of a train derailment outside the town brings Major von Keller to investigate. He calls on the chief train depot superintendent, George Lambert, to assist in tracking down the saboteurs. When Lory is arrested in his home, his indefatigable mother appeals to the mayor for his release. Following the death of Louise's brother (shot while evading a posse of German troops), Lory is released from jail. Lory learns of the death of Paul and is accused by Louise of informing the Germans. Lory later learns that his own mother told the Germans about Paul. Lambert commits suicide and Lory stumbles in to find the body. When Lory is discovered holding the suicide gun, he is arrested and put on trial. Lory waives his right to a lawyer and in open court he gives an impassioned account of his own cowardice and weakness. While in his cell, he is visited by von Keller, who wishes to save him. Von Keller proposes that a suicide note will be found on the body and Lory is half convinced until he sees Professor Sorel with nine other men being executed. Following this, he delivers a heartfelt indictment of his own culpability and that of his fellow townspeople. When he has finished his own defense, the jury delivers a unanimous verdict of not guilty. Following his acquittal, he returns to the school and recites the *Rights of Man* to his admiring pupils. When the Germans arrive to arrest him, he passes the book to Louise, who continues reading the book aloud to the schoolchildren.

Selected Dialogue:

LORY: "Goodbye, citizens!"

Production Commentary: Though Laughton never appeared in a French film, he was directed by one of France's top directors although, alas, in compromised circumstances. *This Land Is Mine* is a contentious film which divides critics and audiences. Towards the end of 1935, Laughton purchased the Pierre-Auguste Renoir masterpiece "The Judgment of Paris" for a reported $36,000. It had a prized place in his private collection. Laughton had first met Jean Renoir briefly on the set of *Vessel of Wrath* during the winter of 1937. Not only did they share similar tastes in art appreciation, but it has been noted by Renoir biographer Pascal Mérigeau that Laughton and Renoir bore a striking physical resemblance, and also shared a shambolic sense of dress. Both wore loose-fitting trousers in which their potbellies bulged above their belts.

However, their inclination towards neglect revealed fundamental differences. For Renoir, it was intentional. For Laughton, this indifference towards clothes derived from sheer revulsion concerning his physical appearance and body. This caused the actor to be inattentive regarding his personal appearance and revel in grime. Moreover, Laughton's self-image was volatile, to say the least. He doubted his sense of self-worth and capabilities and indulged himself in masochistic tendencies. Despite this, the two became firm friends. When in 1941 the exiled Renoir settled in Los Angeles, he was a frequent visitor to Laughton's Pacific Palisades home. There Laughton gave readings of Shakespeare and the Bible, acting out all the roles for the amusement and enlightenment of his friends. Such was the intensity of these recitals that Laughton was driven to fury should his performances be interrupted by extraneous sounds such as ticking clocks, ringing telephones or the barking of Renoir's pet dogs. Laughton later attended Renoir's wedding to Dido Freire.

Laughton was eager to collaborate with Renoir on a film project. During the spring of 1941, Renoir sent him a script. Laughton readily accepted and sent a confirmatory telegram in which he wrote, "[J]ust read the script which is truly wonderful but what a challenge for a tired old ham Stop Hope I can live up to half of what is in it" (Mérigeau: 480). This message confirms that Laughton had serious misgivings about his own abilities as an actor. His film career was beginning to flounder as he took whatever was offered to him, however unsuited or poor the material. The role of a milquetoast and mother-fixated schoolmaster came as a welcome shot in the arm. It also helped that he was again teamed with Maureen O'Hara and Una O'Connor. The role of the German officer was offered to Erich von Stroheim, but reluctantly he had to turn the role down as he was contracted to appear on stage in *Arsenic and Old Lace*. The role of Major von Keller was instead assigned to Walter Slezak, who delivers a memorable performance of a Nazi commandant possessed of a deadly charm. In his only film appearance, Robert Donat's son John (1933–2004) played the small role of Edmund Sorel. Like his father, he found the filmmaking process tedious, but when eventually he was called upon to perform, he did his scenes professionally in one take.

Among Renoir's friends was veteran screenwriter (and now producer) Dudley Nichols. During his career, Nichols had collaborated with John Ford, Howard Hawks and Fritz Lang. *This Land Is Mine* was Renoir's second American film. His first, Fox's *Swamp Water* (1941), although a financial success, had caused Renoir many problems. He soon learned from studio chief Darryl F. Zanuck that his methods of improvisation, long takes and lengthy script conferences were anathema in Hollywood film production processes. Although it had been a baptism of fire, Renoir came from the experience having met senior screenwriter Nichols. Renoir was eager to adapt to the Hollywood manner of directing in terms of numbers of shots used and less camera movement. He saw Nichols as an ally in adapting to Hollywood's systemic processes. They worked on the script together, but as producer and screenwriter Nichols came to exert a pivotal influence on how the film was conceived, shot and edited.

Nichols used a twin track approach in exerting his influence, calling upon his authority as producer and also claiming creative rights as screenwriter. For instance, he forbade Renoir to use a crane for a tracking shot at the opening of the film on grounds of cost. This made Renoir decide to use static shots overall to lend stylistic continuity to the film. Any attempt by Renoir to change the script, even in a minor way, was met with a sharp reminder from Nichols that they had already discussed and settled script issues. Renoir was also reminded of the challenging demands of censorship from the front office.

As it turned out, Nichols influence-interference proved a detriment to the final film. His interventions go some way to explain why some of the fundamentals in the film, such as continuity, are problematic. In an opening scene at the breakfast table, Lory pours himself a glass of milk from a bottle and drinks from the glass. In a subsequent shot, the half-empty glass is suddenly full again!

The film began shooting on October 11, 1942, and ended 54 days later on December 11, 1942. *Variety* (January 5, 1944) in the 1943 "Top Grossers of the Season" reported the film as no big commercial hit, but it performed moderately well at the box office. *This Land Is Mine* ranked 14 out of 17 RKO releases, earning $1,400,000 in domestic film rentals. Above, ranked 13, was the first of the studio's Tarzan series, *Tarzan Triumphs*, with earnings of $1,500,000, and below, ranked twelfth, was Val Lewton's horror sleeper *Cat People* with earnings of $1,200,000.

Some see *This Land Is Mine* as a heartfelt plea for acts of resistance against the tyranny of foreign occupation. For others, it remains a rather obvious and heavy-handed piece of anti–Nazi propaganda replete with polemical speeches and didactic messages. Its hybrid style and structure are both a key virtue and also a major disadvantage. It was directed by an exiled French director more attuned to creative autonomy than the commercial imperative of mainstream Hollywood. Gone are Renoir's signature style of fluid camerawork distinguished by use of long takes using deep focus to allow actors a degree of flexibility to achieve convincing characterizations. Such a dazzling aesthetic is here repudiated and replaced by a static camera, short workaday takes, and use of two-shot editing. This was the dominant style adhered to in Hollywood film production at that time.

For critic Leo Braudy, the film failed: "Although Renoir's intention, and the intention of Dudley Nichols' script may have been to portray the spirit of a society under occupation, *This Land Is Mine* rises only occasionally above hollow message" (Braudy: 139). Laughton biographer Simon Callow suggests that the actor's performance is "the most simply human, as opposed to projected or heightened, he ever gave" (Callow: 158). The *Photoplay* reviewer (June 1943) thought Laughton's portrayal of a shrinking, timid schoolmaster surpassed anything he had achieved since playing Captain Bligh, and it called the film "an oratorical masterpiece." The review went on: "We think you will come away from this picture not with a feeling of hate and revenge but a holocaust of honest humility and definite determination raging within." The *Exhibitor* (March 24, 1943) had an equally positive opinion of Laughton and the film: "It has been ideally cast, handled with restraint, but it is Laughton's picture…." *Variety* (March 17, 1943) took a more cautious view: "Charles Laughton gives a shrewdly conceived and developed portrayal, although he occasionally mugs a bit." The trade paper also cast a critical eye on several of Laughton's outstanding speeches, such as the defiant schoolroom reading of *Rights of Man*. The review noted that though magnificently put across, these speeches were still suspiciously theatrical in tone. *Variety* then took issue with the artificiality of the production values: the obvious use of standard studio sets with little attempt to disguise their origins due to government restrictions. Bosley Crowther of *The New York Times* (May 28, 1943) congratulated Renoir and Nichols for producing "a sincere and responsible effort to penetrate beneath the melodramatic aspects of Nazi occupation of a foreign land… [It's] a sane, courageous film, marked only by occasional violences…."

Erskine Johnson of *Hollywood* (March 1943) described an incident during filming which revealed Laughton's constant striving for authenticity and perfection when approaching a role—in this instance, Laughton's attempt to register an authentically startled look for the camera. Instead of the usual pistol shot or sudden shout used for such scenes, the sound people decided to rig up a loudspeaker system playing a record of a train wreck. Then they set up a siren. Both sounds were set off together at their maximum limit. Laughton was indeed startled!

The central character of Albert Lory finds Laughton giving a brilliant if uneven performance. There can be little doubt that he wanted very much to take on the role, and his performance is a reminder of how gifted he was. Even so, neither director, star nor scenarist, either individually or collectively, bring the project off. Nichols' script, though wearing its heart on its sleeve, is too often prone to displays of didactic exhibitionism. Such asymmetrical qualities are featured throughout the film and are never quite reconciled with the result that the film lacks the usual fluidity found in more traditional Hollywood productions. Another factor which worked against the intentions of Nichols, Renoir and Laughton was the glut of anti–Nazi propaganda films being produced at this time. Émigré Fritz Lang had directed both *Man Hunt* (Twentieth Century–Fox, 1941) and *Hangman Also Die!* (United Artists/Arnold Pressburger, 1943) for example. However, Renoir's film does possess a unique quality. Namely, of being on the periphery and showing insights into human frailty. This gives the film a minor edge on traditional propaganda of the period. George Sanders performance as a Quisling who believes appeasement is the only answer is shown in a compassionate light. He later has a crisis of conscience and commits suicide. Eugène Lourié's unadorned *mise en scène* (using basic standing sets from RKO's *The Hunchback of Notre Dame*) as background for the unspecified European town lends a sense of ambivalence to the film. This is consistent with a narrative preoccupied by notions of resistance and collaboration during wartime occupation.

Despite good intent, *This Land Is Mine* did little to enhance Laughton's reputation and halt his perceived decline. Even though imperfect, his collaboration with the legendary Jean Renoir is still significant in terms of dispelling the myth that Laughton had given up on serious acting in films. Along with his later collaboration with Bertolt Brecht, the film is a salutary reminder of how progressive Laughton's acting range and capabilities were even in the face of personal torment, professional turmoil and financial difficulties. For this reason, if no other, *This Land Is Mine* is deserving of our attention.

The Man from Down Under (1943)

Tagline: "A Socko Combination! Leo and Laughton."[53]

U.S. (Metro-Goldwyn-Mayer)

Credits: Produced by Robert Z. Leonard and Orville O. Dull; Screenplay: Wells Root and Thomas Seller; Story: Bogart Rogers and Mark Kelly; Photography: Sidney Wagner; Musical Score: David Snell; "'E Pinched Me" by Earl Brent; Recording Director: Douglas Shearer; Art Director: Cedric Gibbons, Associate: Stephen Goosson; Set Decorator: Edwin B. Willis; Associate: Glen Barner; Special Effects: A. Arnold Gillespie; Costume Supervisor: Irene; Men's Costumes: Gile Steele; Makeup Creator: Jack Dawn; Technical Advisor: Lon Jones; Editor: George White; Directed by Robert Z. Leonard; U.S. release: August 4, 1943; U.K. release: November 29, 1943; Genre: Comedy; Black and White; Running Time: 103 minutes; The theatrical trailer is available to download and view on Turner Classic Movies. DVD from the Warner Archive Collection, released June 2018; no English subtitle captions for the deaf and hard of hearing.

Cast: **Charles Laughton** (*Jocko Wilson*); Binnie Barnes (*Aggie Dawlins*); Richard Carlson ("*Nipper*" *Wilson*); Donna Reed (*Mary Wilson*); Christopher Severn ("*Nipper*" *as a Child*); Clyde Cook (*Ginger Gaffney*); Horace McNally ("*Dusty*" *Rhodes*); Arthur Shields (*Father Polycarp*); Evelyn Falke (*Mary as a Child*); Hobart Cavanaugh ("*Boots*"); Andre Charlot (*Father Antoine*); **Uncredited Cast**: Philip Ahn (*English-Speaking Japanese Aviator*); Richard Ainley (*Military Doctor*); Luis Alberni (*Dino Piza*); Eric Alden, Harry Fleischmann (*Newsmen*); Harry Allen (*Laborer*); Jimmy Aubrey (*Tipsy—Anzac Soldier*); Martha Bamattre (*Fat Woman*); Charles Bates (*French Boy*); Louise Bates (*Minister's Wife*); Ted Billings (*Pub Patron*); Charles Bimbo (*Man in Sydney Pub*); Luke Chan (*Japanese Gunner*); Wallis Clark (*Major*); James Conaty (*Ringside*); Clancy Cooper (*Foreman*); Harry Cording, Gibson Gowland, George Magrill, Will Stanton (*Bettors*); Hal Craig (*Police Sergeant*); Harold De Becker (*Private Roberts*); Kay Deslys (*Beefy Blonde*); Eddie Dew, Al Ferguson (*Soldiers*); Rex Evans (*Doyle*); E.L. Fisher-Smith (*Officer*); Wing Foo (*Japanese Soldier*); Christian J. Frank (*French Mug*); Albert Godderis (*Bartender*); Mickey Golden, George Levine, Charles Schaeffer (*Fighters in Montage*); Roland Got (*Japanese Soldier*); Fred Graham, Frank Hagney, Jack Stoney, Harry Warren (*Military Policemen*); Bobbie Hale (*Aggie's Dancing Partner*); Lumsden Hare, Holmes Herbert, Brandon Hurst (*Government Officials at Train Station*); Sam Harris

A raucous couple: Binnie Barnes as Aggie Dawlins and Laughton as Jocko Wilson in *The Man from Down Under* (1943).

(1943) The Man from Down Under

(*Man at Station/Boxing Spectator*); Joe Hartman (*Photographer*); Leyland Hodgson (*Labor Crew's Clerk*); E. Mason Hopper (*Desk Clerk*); Anne Howard (*Girl*); Boyd Irwin (*Colonel*); Charles Irwin (*Ring Announcer*); Ethan Laidlaw (*Parade Spectator*); Peter Lawford (*Mr. Jones*); Dorothy Lawrence, Mary McLeod (*Nurses*); Nelson Leigh (*Man in Sydney Pub*); Eily Malyon (*Sarah—Aggie's Maid*); Bert Moorhouse (*Ringsider*); Pat Moran (*Australian Soldier*); Carol Nugent, Judy Nugent (*Young Girls*); George O'Flaherty (*Aircraft Officer*); Pat O'Malley (*Priest*); Alfred Paix (*French Priest*); Ezra Paulette (*French Mug*); Gil Perkins (*Australian Soldier/Bartender in Sydney Pub*); Cynthia Randolph (*Girl*); Ernest Severn (*Tough Boy*); Raymond Severn (*"Nipper" at Age 12*); Reginald Sheffield (*Recruit*); Leslie Sketchley (*Officer*); Arthur Space (*Bailey*); Robert St. Angelo (*French Mug*); Freddie Steele (*Terry McGroth—Boxer*); Art Foster, Charles Sullivan (*Referees*); Robert Tait (*Soloist for "'E Pinched Me"*); Frank Tang (*Japanese Soldier*); Maurice Tauzin (*Jean—Boy*); Evan Thomas (*Doctor*); David Thursby (*Newsman*); Harry Tozer (*Australian Soldier*); Russell Wade (*Ringsider*); Constance Weiler (*Girl at Station*); Catherine Wallace, Elizabeth Williams, Florence Wix (*Minister's Wives*); Ian Wolfe (*Returning Soldier Seeking Father Antoine*); Beal Wong (*Japanese Soldier*).

Working Title: *The Man Down Under*

Synopsis: At a French port of embarkation in 1919, Australian soldier Jocko Wilson pays a visit to a local music hall where his sweetheart, entertainer Aggie Dawlins, is at the top of the bill. He befriends two Belgian orphans, a boy and his younger sister, and decides to adopt them. Realizing he knows nothing about raising children, he proposes to Aggie and she accepts. Jocko gets in a fight and lands in the brig, and Aggie is left ashore unmarried and infuriated. In Sydney, Jocko becomes a famous pub owner and raises the boy, now called Nipper, to be a boxer. The girl, Mary, is sent to boarding school. Nipper wins the boxing championship of the British Empire, but a badly injured shoulder puts an end to his boxing career. With the prize money, Jocko buys a remote hotel in the country and takes Nipper and Mary to live with him. Aggie, now a rich widow, visits the hotel. Seeking revenge for Jocko's mistreatment of her, she lures him into a gambling game and wins the hotel from him. "Dusty" Rhodes, an American newspaperman, has fallen in love with Mary and wants her to go to Europe as his wife, much to the chagrin of Nipper whose affections for Mary are strong. Mary does not love Dusty. Realizing that Nipper's love for Mary is more than brotherly affection, Dusty decides to leave. War is declared and the hotel is turned into a shelter for evacuated children. Jocko, too old to join the services, joins a work battalion. Nipper is wounded in the Malayan campaign and returns to Australia at a point near the hotel. During an air raid in which the hotel is bombed, a Japanese plane is shot down. The uninjured Japanese air crew members take possession of the hotel. Jocko and Nipper rush to the rescue and retake the hotel in a fierce fight. Reunited, Nipper and Mary's happiness is complete when they learn from a friendly priest, Father Polycarp, that an investigation of their parentage shows that they were foster brother and sister, with no blood ties. Jocko is also happy when he learns he has gained a captain's commission and Aggie's affection as well.

Selected Dialogue:

WILSON: "If you stick your sniveling face in here again, I'll bash it in!"

Production Commentary: *The Man from Down Under* is one among many undistinguished flag-wavers produced by Hollywood during the war years. For his efforts of presenting unrelenting exuberance on the screen, Laughton receives star billing. He begged British star Gracie Fields to take the role of Aggie Dawlins, but she expressed little interest and turned it down. Instead, Binnie Barnes was cast and is mostly boisterous and dull-witted in her characterization throughout.

A weak and mechanical script tends to accentuate contrived plotting with facetious situations. The film's content and delivery both have a sense of insistent boisterousness with only the usual MGM production values left to carry it along. As a veteran Anzac, Laughton just blows and bellows his way through the shenanigans of farcical malarkey. It comes as little surprise to learn from *Showmen's Trade Review* (June 6, 1942) that MGM had purchased *The Man Down Under* intending it to be a Wallace Beery vehicle. If Laughton had decided to pass on the role, it's the type of lead part the stolid actor Lionel Atwill might have considered. As it is, Laughton supplies ham in a raucous and unattractive fashion. He was once quoted as saying (*Film Daily*, August 12, 1935), "I don't act except when I'm paid for it; other times I like to forget that I'm an actor." In *The Man from Down Under* he appears to have decided to give wit and grace a backseat in favor of 103 minutes of unremitting mugging to camera.

Jocko Wilson is based on the Australian larrikin, a rowdy bloke given to gambling, drinking and hanging out with belligerent gangs. Redeemed by courtship and marriage, Jocko becomes a contented husband and father. However, he retains a sense of aggression and disdain for social propriety and authority. The larrikin was celebrated in C.J. Dennis' humorous verse poem "The Songs of a Sentimental Bloke" (1915). A silent feature adaptation, *The Sentimental Bloke* (Southern Cross Feature Film Company), was released in Australia in 1919. Directed by the prolific Raymond Longford, it was popular in Australia, New Zealand and Britain.

Australian journalist Lon Jones was called in to act as technical advisor on Australian life and dialogue director for *Man from Down Under*. In the *Sydney Morning Herald* (June 12, 1943), he provided an invaluable insight into Laughton's idiosyncrasies in attaining (he hoped) the correct impression for the character he was playing. Laughton had read the script and liked it, but from the very start he began to doubt his abilities. Would he be able to look and sound the part of an Anzac soldier and be convincing? In some desperation, he confessed, "I am just a fat ugly pig in real life, and nothing can change that rather deplorable fact. I am one of those unfortunate actors who have to depend solely on their dramatic ability to create a transition on the stage or screen." Realizing that the Australian public and the rest of the world regarded the Anzacs as the greatest fighting force of modern times, he began to contemplate his suitability for the role. "I realize only too well that if I should fail in this role, I will make enemies of millions of Australians and that is something I do not look forward to." When Laughton first agreed to take on the role, the studio had assigned the film to a young director. Instead, Laughton requested Robert Z. Leonard, the director of *Stand By for Action*. Only Leonard would be able to deal with the various issues he was having difficulty with. The studio complied with this request.

For the majority of screen actors, the usual method of working involved going straight into a scene and relying on the director to put things right if problems arose. With Laughton, this did not apply. He took each scene with deep introspection and seriousness. He often stayed up past midnight rehearsing each scene several different ways until he felt he had mastered it. Always early on the set, he began by discussing the scenes to be shot that day with director Leonard and asking for suggestions. Sometimes Leonard would alter lines to fit in with his interpretations. This would necessitate dialogue alterations. Before the cameras begin rolling, Laughton insisted on rehearsing each scene often up to half a dozen times, slowly at first until he felt the scene was smooth and natural. If need be, he would spend up to 15 minutes on one particular gesture or line trying to get the action or inflection accurate. Crucially, "When he begins his rehearsal, he invariably apologizes to Leonard for the fact that he is going to 'ham it up' until he feels he is *sliding* [my italics] into the character."

Viewing the film today, it feels as though Laughton is "plunging" rather than sliding his way into the role. Throughout there is little modulation or variability in his performance; it just remains full on. The film began shooting on March 6, 1943, and was completed by May 15. It went into general release on August 4, 1943. Critical approbation for this film was in short supply. Caroline Lejeune felt that Laughton had forsaken any pretense to artistic endeavor in films and had settled instead for the second-rate. Writing in the *Observer* (November 28, 1943), she was moved to providing an amusing clerihew:

> The art of Mr. Charles Laughton
> Has indubitably caught on.
> The Yorkshireman's made good—
> In Hollywood.
> But I wonder
> If our friends from down under
> Will find him quite de rigueur
> As a digger?

The *New York Times* (September 27, 1943) reviewer opined, "In the curious, clumsy and oddly lifeless story ... even Mr. Laughton's outrageously ebullient spirit seems tamed and listless. Perhaps it is his comment upon the naïvetés of the story, but the fact is for once in his life Mr. Laughton is giving a performance that is simply ordinary. And certainly, the film has little else to recommend it." *Showmen's Trade Review* (August 7, 1943) cut to the chase: "Weak on comedy, long on tears, and spotted with artificial action climaxes, this is far below the Laughton artistic standard, but will please those who like their pathos and thrills laid on with a shovel." *The Motion Picture Daily* (August 4, 1943) declared,

> Two highlights are in evidence.... In between are barren spaces which fail to compensate for the long wait between Highlight 1 and Highlight 2. The end result is an attraction of fair interest. That's all. Performances are led off by Laughton in one of those blustering roustabout roles of his. It is inconsequential detail and listless development of the story throughout limitless footage which cause *The Man from Down Under* to bog down, thereby suggesting the film would be better by far if it were sharply edited.

Critic David Thomson aptly summed up Laughton's decline during this period: "He passed from 'greatness' to junk with surprising ease" (Thomson: 741).

The Canterville Ghost (1944)

Tagline: "The Story of a Fearless Phantom Who Lost His Spirit!"[54]

U.S. (Metro-Goldwyn-Mayer)

Credits: Producer: Arthur L. Field; Screenplay: Edwin Harvey Blum; Based on "The Canterville Ghost" by Oscar Wilde; Photography: Robert Planck; Music Score: George Bassman; Dance Director: Jack Donohue; Recording Director: Douglas Shearer: Art Directors: Cedric Gibbons; Edward Carfagno; Set Decorator: Edwin B. Willis; Associate: Mildred Griffiths; Costume Supervisor: Irene; Men's Costumes: Valles; Makeup Created by Jack Dawn; Editor: Chester W. Schaeffer; Directed by Jules Dassin; U.S. release: July 20, 1944; U.K. release: September 25, 1944; Genre: Historical Fantasy Drama; Black and White; Running Time: 96 minutes; 35mm print available at George Eastman Museum; DVD from the Warner Archive Collection, released February 2006; no English subtitle captions for the deaf and hard of hearing.

Cast: Charles Laughton (*Sir Simon de Canterville/The Ghost*); Robert Young (*Cuffy Williams*); Margaret O'Brien (*Lady Jessica de Canterville*); William Gargan (*Sergeant Benson*); Reginald Owen (*Lord Canterville*); "Rags" Ragland (*Big Harry*); Una O'Connor (*Mrs. Umney*); Donald Stuart (*Sir Valentine Williams*); Elisabeth Risdon (*Mrs. Polverdine*); Frank Faylen (*Lieutenant Kane*); Lumsden Hare (*Mr. Potts*); Mike Mazurki (*Metropolus*); William Moss (*Hector*); Bobby Readick (*Eddie*); Marc Cramer (*Bugsy McDougle*); William Tannen (*Jordan*); Peter Lawford (*Anthony de Canterville*); **Uncredited Cast**: Brandon Hurst (*Mr. Peabody*); Tor Johnson (*Bold Sir Guy*); Frances Raeburn (*Eleanor*); David Thursby (*Carpenter*); Gordon Richards, Tom Stevenson, Colin Kenny (*Noblemen*); John Rogers (*Simon's Squire*); Charles Hall, Syd Dawon (*Bold Sir Guy's Squires*); Charles Irwin (*Marshall of the Hunt*); Larry Wheat (*Doctor*); James Aubrey (*Chimney Sweep*); Billy Bletcher (*Window Washer*); Elspeth Dudgeon (*Aged Woman at Party*); Patsy O'Byrne (*Servant at Party*); Harry Allen (*Mr. Cawthorne*); Colin Campbell (*Vicar*); Anna Marie Stewart (*Buxom Lass at Party*); Guy Kingsford (*British Tommy*); Viola Moore (*Girl*); Herberta Williams (*Matron at Party*); Herbert Clifton, Frank Benson (*Men in Village Hall*); Aina Constant (*Factory Girl at Party*); Vernon Downing (*Officer*); Roy Seager (*Roly Poly Man*); Dale Easton (*Sergeant in Village Hall*); Robert Schuler (*Stanley*); Brent Richards (*Arthur*); Jack Lambert (*Trigger—Machine Gunner*); Mary McLeod (*Girl at Party*).

Synopsis: In 1634 England, Sir Simon de Canterville shows cowardice during a duel

Laughton strikes a suitable imperious attitude combined with a mischievous twinkle in his eyes as Sir Simon de Canterville in *The Canterville Ghost* (1944).

and hides in an alcove in Canterville Castle. Simon's proud father, Lord Canterville, orders the alcove bricked up with Simon inside, and Simon's ghost is condemned to roam until one of his kinsmen performs a brave deed. In consequence, Sir Simon de Canterville haunts Canterville Castle for more than three centuries, vainly waiting for a brave kinsman to free him. With the coming of World War II, platoons of American Rangers are billeted in the castle. Six-year-old Lady Jessica de Canterville greets the Rangers and warns them about the ghost. One night the ghost appears, but is frightened off by the Rangers. Noticing young Jessica's fear of her ancestor, Ranger Cuffy Williams suggests they visit the ghost. They enter Sir Simon's chamber and find him in a dejected mood because of his inability to frighten the Rangers. He is an almost human ghost, weary of the curse that befell him. Sir Simon and Jessica discover that Cuffy is a de Canterville descendant. Delighted, Sir Simon looks to Cuffy to perform an act of bravery in his name. However, the realization that all the de Cantervilles for three centuries have been cowards has a psychological effect on Cuffy, and he disgraces himself during a commando raid. As Cuffy prepares to quit the Rangers at the suggestion of his commanding officer, Jessica discovers a delayed action bomb, which had been dropped by parachute by a Nazi plane. Encouraged by Jessica, and aided by Sir Simon, Cuffy hitches the bomb to an army Jeep and hauls it to a ravine, where it explodes harmlessly. Cuffy's heroic act restores his confidence and permits the ghost to go to his grave in honor and peace.

Selected Dialogue:

DE CANTERVILLE: "Excuse me, I really must gibber at the oriel window."

DE CANTERVILLE: "Am I a saucy antelope?"

Production Commentary: In 1939, MGM purchased Oscar Wilde's short story "The Canterville Ghost" and the *Exhibitor* (January 28, 1939) announced that it would be brought to the screen by producer Milton Bren and would feature such MGM stars as Margaret Sullavan, James Stewart and Frank Morgan. The advent of World War II put paid to these plans. Four years later, *Film Daily* (July 13, 1943) revealed that child actress Margaret O'Brien was cast to star in the production. *Film Daily* (August 13, 1943) alerted readers that Robert Young and Laughton had been cast. *Motion Picture Herald* (August 28, 1943) reported that shooting on a modernized version of Wilde's story had commenced at MGM with Norman Z. McLeod assigned directing and Arthur L. Field producing.

Following 38 days of shooting, *Motion Picture Daily* (September 30, 1943) announced, "Norman McLeod didn't like his stint on *The Canterville Ghost* at MGM so he asked for a change which was granted." *Showmen's Trade Review* (October 30, 1943) published confirmation of the replacement director: Jules Dassin. According to Charles Higham, McLeod was replaced after five weeks spent shooting because he failed to win the confidence of Laughton. Though MGM was no longer granting Laughton star billing above the title of his films, this change in personnel seemed to offer a temporary boost to his confidence. He spent a considerable amount of time off-camera submitting various suggestions to Dassin, who seemed appreciative of the star's attention. Margaret O'Brien remembered Laughton's insecurity, his worry about being upstaged by his young co-star, and his feeling that he was not being good enough in whatever scene they were filming.

What appears on the screen is entertaining enough and Laughton strikes a rapport with the material and the actors. This is one of the more appealing efforts from his checkered output at MGM during this period. Critics were in the main appreciative of his comic burlesque of ghostly apparitions. *Variety* (May 31, 1944) had no hesitation in declaring that he and O'Brien "come through with top-notch performances...." *Showmen's Trade Review* (June 3, 1944) was also complimentary: "The role, with its opportunity for burlesquing, is well played by Charles Laughton and he can exaggerate the characterization to his heart's content without being adjudged guilty of overacting. After all, there are no limits to what ghosts can do." Meanwhile, the *Manchester Guardian* (November 21, 1944) regretted the unfortunate vulgarization of Wilde's story: "The trifle to which the whimsical personality of the ghost lent its chief charm has been spattered with such incongruous artifices as topicality (American Rangers and a block-buster), sob-stuff, 'hot' music (in one sequence), slick comedy, and

94 (1945) The Suspect

sheer slapstick. The best passages are those of slapstick, but in an accompanying 'short' the Three Stooges, though they are no challenge to the undoubted talents of Robert Young, Charles Laughton and little Margaret O'Brien, stick to the same medium throughout and succeed better." In *Hollywood* (January 1941), Laughton was quoted as saying, "I am the incurable ham and Hollywood is a ham's paradise. I'm always acting even when I'm alone in a room. Then I go prancing about." There is quite a bit of slapstick "prancing" by Laughton in *The Canterville Ghost*, but if the viewer is in the right mood, it can be very winning in its appeal.

The Suspect (1945)

Tagline: "Rising in Terrifying Suspense! Crashing with Shattering Impact!"[55]

U.S. (Universal Pictures)

Credits: Screenplay: Bertram Millhauser; Adaptation by Arthur T. Horman; From a Novel by James Ronald; Photography: Paul Ivano; Music Score and Direction: Frank Skinner; Art Directors: John B. Goodman, Martin Obzina; Director of Sound: Bernard B. Brown; Technician: Charles Carroll; Set Decorators: Russell A. Gausman, E.R. Robinson; Editor: Arthur Hilton; Gowns: Vera West; Assistant Director: William Tummel; Produced by Islin Auster; Directed by Robert Siodmak; U.S. release: January 26, 1945; U.K. release: July 2, 1945; Genre: Crime–Film Noir; Black and White; Running Time: 85 minutes; DVD Region 2 Koch Media (Germany), released May 2014; no English subtitle captions for the deaf and hard of hearing.

Cast: **Charles Laughton** (*Philip Marshall*); Ella Raines (*Mary*); Dean Harens (*John*); Stanley Ridges (*Huxley*); Henry Daniell (*Mr. Simmons*); Rosalind Ivan (*Cora*); Molly Lamont (*Mrs. Simmons*); Raymond Severn (*Merridew*); Eve Amber (*Sybil*); Maude Eburne (*Mrs. Packer*); Clifford Brooke (*Mr. Packer*); **Uncredited Cast**: Keith Hitchcock (*William Crummit*); Ernie Adams (*Cabbie*); Jimmy Aubrey (*Pogson*); Helena Grant (*Miss Pomfret*); Lillian Bronson (*Miss Crevy*); John Rogers (*Mr. Margett*); Cecil Weston (*Mrs. Chadwick*); Charles Knight (*Mr. Chadwick*); Hilda Plowright (*Mrs. Margett*); Sally Shepherd (*Mrs. Brown*); Elspeth Dudgeon (*Pauline Barlow*); Kate McKenna (*Mrs. Jevne*); Olaf Hytten (*Mr. Jevne*); Vera Lewis (*Hannah Barlow*); Grace Hampton (*Margaret*); Sidney Lawford (*Lord Eldon*); Gerald Hamer (*Griswold*); Johnny Berkes (*Detective Sergeant Pennyfeather*); Frank Dawson (*Jarvis*); Edgar Norton (*Mr. Frazer*); Katherine Yorke, Rebel Randall, Keith Ferguson, Barbara Gray, Sheila Roberts (*Models*); Charles McNaughton, Tony Santoro (*Waiters*); Nina Campana (*Cashier at Luigi's*); Tommy Cook (*Child Violinist*).

Synopsis: In 1902 London, a mild-mannered shopkeeper, Philip Marshall, finds his life is blighted by his shrewish and nagging wife Cora. He becomes acquainted with a pleasant young girl, Mary Gray. When their relationship develops into love, Marshall decides to kill his wife. He clubs her to death with a cane and tells the authorities that her injuries were the result of a fall downstairs. Harboring doubts: Inspector Huxley of Scotland Yard and a vicious blackmailer, neighbor Gilbert Simmons. Marshall realizes that Gilbert will never cease his blackmailing demands and is forced to silence him by the use of poison administered in a drink of whiskey. Marshall then decides that Mary and he should emigrate to Canada. But as they board a ship, Inspector Huxley brings news that Gilbert's wife Edith has been charged with his murder. Marshall decides to hand himself over to the authorities.

Laughton (left) on the set of the thriller *The Suspect* (1945) with director Robert Siodmak offering resolve and assistance. Laughton delivers an understated performance as the subdued Philip Marshall who commits murder.

Selected Dialogue:

MARSHALL: "You are a swine, a filthy, blackmailing swine."

Production Commentary: Discussing aspects of his acting career, Robert Powell recalled that for his portrayal of Jesus in the miniseries *Jesus of Nazareth* (ITC, Franco Zeffirelli, 1977), he was called upon to do the hardest and most difficult thing an actor can be asked to do: To achieve acceptance in such a challenging role, he had to disregard and otherwise shed all the formal training and informal idiosyncrasies that years of acting produces. He withdrew and concentrated on doing precisely *nothing*.[56] For those who are convinced that Laughton always contrived to present himself using tricks of the acting trade including: makeup, physiological peculiarities based on facial tics and the mimicking of accents, *The Suspect* comes as a revelation.

The story was based loosely on the Dr. Crippen case and Laughton is the acme of restraint as the downtrodden husband playing against the hateful possessiveness of his wife, memorably played by Rosalind Ivan. Only in the arms of a young stenographer (Ella Raines) does he find contentment and happiness. His Philip Marshall has none of the unpleasantness he had delivered to such effect on screen during the 1930s. In this film we find Laughton devoid of the usual props, schtick, ham or anything else to hinder or distract him, turning in a positive, unobtrusive, likable performance.

Good though his performance is, the script does not provide sufficient psychological torment as found in Javert in *Les Misérables*, or true suspense as that supplied by the likes of Alfred Hitchcock and Henri-Georges Clouzot. There is no sense of a violent mood in Laughton's character. Laughton's biographer Simon Callow observed that the film is deficient in motivation and plausibility. The *New York Times* (February 1, 1945) describes the flaws in its approach to suspense as: too "genteel," "innocent" and "overburdened with politeness." However, the reviewer went on to describe Laughton as having "seldom portrayed a more likable character or performed with more restraint...." *Variety* (December 27, 1944) found Laughton to be excellent: "This is practically a new Laughton. There is less of the bluster and none of the villainy of previous vehicles. He gives an impeccable performance.... [I]t's Laughton's picture and he makes the most of it." *Harrison's Reports* (December 30, 1944) agreed: "[Laughton] gives one of the best portrayals of his career, managing to win one's sympathy despite his murderous deeds." The *Monthly Film Bulletin* (April 1945, Vol. 12, No. 136) declared, "Reminiscent in some respects of *Payment Deferred*, this drama gives Laughton another role of the sort he revels in. He is at his best in presenting this respectable middle-aged businessman who was capable of gentleness and love on one hand and cold hate and desperate action on the other." The London *Times* critic (May 7, 1945) praised Laughton and also singled out another actor as outstanding: "Miss Rosalind Ivan, as Cora, steals the film. Her shrewishness and malice are terrifying in their intensity, but Miss Ivan makes it clear that she remains in her own eyes a virtuous and badly treated woman—a remarkable performance."

The film does convey a sense of subdued anxiety as Laughton is driven to kill his

Ella Raines as Mary Gray and Laughton as middle-aged shopkeeper Philip Marshall in *The Suspect* (1945).

wife and suffers at the hands of an neighbor turned blackmailer. His ordered and genteel world collapses as he is plunged into fearful circumstances. Émigré director Robert Siodmak had already cleverly cast Deanna Durbin and Gene Kelly against type in *Christmas Holiday* (Universal, 1944). Siodmak managed to provide a select group of supporting actors who gave excellent performances, in particular Ivan as the shrew (a role she repeated in Fritz Lang's *Scarlet Street* [Universal, 1945]), Henry Daniell as the vulpine blackmailer and Stanley Ridges as the methodical Scotland Yard inspector. Also making a rare appearance was Sidney Lawford, father of actor Peter Lawford, as Lord Eldon.

Laughton biographer Charles Higham has related how Siodmak handled the actor's instability with calculated support and determination. He did not give Laughton the complete script, preferring to give him relevant sections with face-to-face discussions the day before filming. Laughton was kept fully occupied during the film's production by being permitted to rehearse the other actors. Warned that Laughton would at some point be prone to spells of indecision, the director threw a prepared outburst. Laughton sought to mollify him and the rest of the film progressed without incident. Siodmak later became part of Laughton's inner circle of friends.

Even with its flaws, this is a must-see Laughton film for its unassuming central performance. *The Suspect* is a corrective to the charge that Laughton perpetually indulged himself in his film performances.

Captain Kidd (1945)

Tagline: "He loved to loot and looted for love!"[57]

U.S. (United Artists/Benedict Bogeaus/Rowland V. Lee)

Credits: Screenplay: Norman Reilly Raine; Original Story: Robert N. Lee; Production Associate: Arthur M. Landau; Photographer: Archie Stout; Art Director: Charles Odds; Set Decorator: Maurice Yates; Costumes: Greta; Supervising Editor: James Smith; Sound Technician: Frank Webster; Special Effects: Lee Zavitz; Hair Stylist: Scotty Rackin; Musical Supervisor: David Chudnow; Assistant Director: Joseph Depew; Musical Score: Werner Janssen conducting the Janssen Symphony Orchestra; Executive Producer: James Nasser; Assistant to Producer: Carley Harriman; Produced by Benedict Bogeaus; Directed by Rowland V. Lee; U.S. release: August 24, 1945; U.K. release: January 21, 1946; Genre: Historical Swashbuckler; Black and White; Running Time: 89 minutes; DVD all regions from Alpha Video and the Roan Archival Group; no English subtitle captions for the deaf and hard of hearing.

Cast: Charles Laughton (*Captain William Kidd*); Randolph Scott (*Adam Mercy*); Barbara Britton (*Lady Anne Falconer*); John Carradine (*Orange Povey*); Gilbert Roland (*Jose Lorenzo*); John Qualen (*Bart Blivens*); Sheldon Leonard (*Cyprian Boyle*); William Farnum (*Rawson*); Henry Daniell (*King William III*); Reginald Owen (*Cary Shadwell*); **Uncredited Cast**: Abner Biberman (*Theodore Blades*); Harry Cording (*Newgate Prison Warder*); James Dime, Jack Kenny, Cap Somers (*Pirates*); Lumsden Hare (*Lord Fallsworth*); Al Hill (*Peter Sharfstone*); Frank Mills (*Ship's Sailor Waiter*); Edgar Norton (*Nobleman with King William III*); Reginald Sheffield (*Captain of the King's Guard*); Ray Teal (*Michael O'Shawn*); Eric Wilton (*Nobleman with King William III*); Frederick Worlock (*Landers—Newgate Prison Governor*).

Awards: Academy Award Nomination: Best Music Score of a Dramatic or Comedy Picture: Werner Janssen.

Synopsis: In 1699 Madagascar, ruthless pirate Captain William Kidd meets the frigate *The Twelve Apostles*, commanded by Admiral Lord Blayne. The latter is soon a burning wreck and Kidd and his crew bury their ill-gotten booty. When Kidd returns to London, he is given an audience with King William. Despite Kidd's dubious reputation, he is instructed to sail and escort a British treasure ship through the pirate-infested Madagascar waters. Kidd is able to convince the king to grant a royal pardon to former pirates, now condemned prisoners, so he can raise a crew. Kidd visits Newgate Prison to enlist men to serve on his ship. Among those selected is Adam Mercy, who is appointed an officer on his ship. To Kidd's surprise, a former pirate, Orange Povey, appears on the dockside and insists on signing up for the voyage. Povey warns Kidd that should anything happen to him, he has instructed a friend to reveal all about Kidd's piratical activities. Once the voyage begins, a captain's valet, Cary Shadwell, begins to instruct Kidd on the manners and mores of a gentleman. Kidd begin to suspect that Mercy is a spy in the service of the king and tells Shadwell to find out more about him. Shadwell reports back to Kidd that Mercy is a "nobody" who

Captain Kidd (1945)

learned his manners from employers of quality. Kidd decides to kill a fellow pirate, Boyle, by having a topsail fall on him. Mercy detects that someone has tampered with the lines. He searches Kidd's cabin and, in a secret compartment in the captain's desk, discovers a skull-and-crossbones pirate flag. When Kidd confronts Mercy, Mercy "admits" to being sent by the king. He offers to turn against the crown in return for a share in the buried treasure. Kidd decides a "partnership" with Mercy will be useful. Afterwards, in Kidd's quarters, he tells them that the galleon *The Queda Merchant* is sailing from Calcutta to England. When they intercept her to guarantee safe passage, the galleon will be carrying treasure. As this will be the king's ship, they are to take possession of her in a "legal" and "honest" fashion. Eventually, *The Queda Merchant* is spotted, and Kidd goes aboard to introduce himself to Captain Rawson, Lord Fallsworth and his daughter, the Lady Anne Dunstan. Lord Fallsworth and Lady Anne are to transfer to Kidd's ship with a treasure chest. Just after Lady Anne has boarded, her father suffers a fatal accident instigated by Kidd's crew. *The Queda Merchant* explodes and everyone on board is killed. Mercy enters the cabin of Lady Anne and informs her of his true identity: Adam Blayne, son of Lord Blayne. He explains that his father was killed and accused of piracy. The accusation was believed by the king and so Adam took to the sea and turned pirate. By doing so, he hoped to uncover the truth. Lady Anne guesses, correctly, that Adam's father, like her own father, had been killed by Kidd. Adam asks her to court Kidd's friendship to ensure her personal safety. He then tells her that, when they return to London, she must go to the Lord of the Admiralty and the king. When pirate Lorenzo enters Lady Anne's cabin, Adam intervenes, and emerges victorious after a fencing duel. Kidd picks up Adam's medallion, which bears the crest of the Blayne dynasty, and now realizes who Adam is. When Adam realizes that his medallion is missing, he guesses that Kidd may have found it and made the connection. Adam knows that Kidd will kill him should a suitable opportunity occur. The ship docks in the lagoon which harbors the pirate treasure. Povey, Kidd and Adam go to a cave where the treasure is buried, and Povey and Adam dig it up. Adam finds a chest and Kidd instructs him to open it. The Blayne family jewels are inside. Kidd confronts him with the Blayne medallion, which Adam says he obtained in exchange for a ring. A dramatic fight follows, during which Adam falls into the sea. Satisfied that Adam has been killed, Povey and Kidd return to the ship. Adam is able to slip aboard ship and escape with Lady Anne. They board a boat but are spotted by a member of the crew. Kidd orders their boat be shelled by cannon and assumes they have perished. On his return to England, Kidd is presented to the king. Instead of being received with great honor, he finds that Lady Anne and Adam have reached England and have provided the king with proof of his villainy. Kidd is tried in a court of law, found guilty and executed. The king bestows a frigate, to be named Lady Anne, as a wedding gift for Anne and Adam's loyalty and service to king and country.

Laughton's quirky performance as seafaring rapscallion Captain William Kidd is a surprising delight in Benedict Bogeaus otherwise cheapskate production, *Captain Kidd* (1945).

Selected Dialogue:

KIDD: "Your neck will be stretched as long as your memory, one of these days."

KIDD: "Now then, me bullies! Would you

rather do the gallows dance, and hang in chains 'til the crows pick your eyes from your rotting skulls? Or would you feel the roll of a stout ship beneath your feet again? ... Look you then! I want men with iron in their blood, and steel in their sinews!"

KIDD: "You blundering ass! Your presence is getting increasingly irksome to me. Get you below."

KIDD: "Of all the slumocky blaggards."

KIDD: "Everybody wants to bargain with me.... Who do you think I am a stinking sausage merchant?"

Production Commentary: Laughton was shrewd enough to know that independent producer Benedict Bogeaus (1904–1968) was no Irving Thalberg and *Captain Kidd* would be no *Mutiny on the Bounty*. Bogeaus had acquired the General Service studio located on Hollywood's Santa Monica Boulevard in early 1942. He soon established himself at the forefront of independent film production. His first film, *The Bridge of San Luis Rey* (United Artists, Rowland V. Lee, 1944), was not a commercial success, but his next production, *Dark Waters* (United Artists, André de Toth, 1944) proved a hit. Bogeaus followed up with *Captain Kidd*. Laughton's performance as the famed rogue mariner transcends what otherwise is a ramshackle film with very obvious budgetary constraints. The situation is now complicated by the poor quality of master material available on current digital releases. The film is today relegated to the abject status of "public domain" due to non-renewal of copyright during the early 1970s.

In *Captain Kidd*, there is none of the finesse or intelligence of scripting achieved in, say, Laughton's RKO films or the independent Mayflower productions. Likewise, there is an absence of attractive décor common to the Paramount and MGM productions. But Laughton provides an intriguing performance as a reprobate who behaves, or more accurately *mis*behaves, above his social station. It is tempting to pass his performance off as an example of a triumph of style over substance. However, this does a disservice to his acting abilities and neglects the circumstances by which he approached the role.

When production began in February 1945, Laughton was in the middle of translating the play *Galileo* with his collaborator, playwright Bertolt Brecht. It seems feasible to suggest that working with Brecht rekindled his creative interest in acting. This comes across in viewing *Captain Kidd*. A Brechtian actor must always be in control of their emotions, and there is a real sense of discipline here with any tendency towards flamboyance held in check. The usual ostentation found in many of his film performances is gone, replaced by a sense of delight. Laughton acts in quotation marks as he demonstrates the protagonist's social circumstance and class aspirations. Several scenes involving Laughton and John Carradine, as Orange Povey, are compelling and dynamic in their awareness of social status and social improvement. In particular, Brecht's notion of distancing or "verfredungseffekt" is pertinent to several scenes. That is to say, stripping events of their self-evident, familiar, obvious qualities and creating a sense of curiosity and astonishment about them. This is especially applicable to those scenes in which Laughton plays opposite Reginald Owen (they had also played together in *The Canterville Ghost*) as the valet, Shadwell. These scenes are memorable for their potent mix of comic rapport with undertones of social class, behavior and manners.

Laughton delivers his lines in a minor sub–Cockney accent which might imply a tongue-in-cheek attitude, but the performance is no burlesque. Laughton shows Kidd as being ambivalent about an inclination to learn or an instinct to murder his mentor. Laughton in a return to form gives an edge to a character torn between plain speaking, deadly, cruel intent and giving no hostages to fortune. The very flatness of the production allows little distraction from the significance of the leading screen performance.

The romantic leads are disappointing. Randolph Scott as Mercy lacks the charisma so evident in his many Westerns and remains throughout wooden. Barbara Britton's Lady Anne is decorative in appearance, but otherwise very anodyne. There are comparisons to be made between Laughton's previous incarnation of nautical disobedience in his rendering of Captain Bligh, Bligh being, "a universal symbol of the cruelty bred by repression" (Callow: 175). In contrast, Kidd is linear, "the character laid out for examination, a prototype rather than an archetype of behavior" (Callow: 175). Unlike say Laughton's Henry Hobson in *Hobson's Choice*, which is spun out and offers little in the way of surprise, his Captain William Kidd is unpredictable in the sense that one is never quite sure where the performance is taking us. All of which provides an odd paradox: an unexpected fine performance in an otherwise lackluster film.

The film is often derided by critics. David Shipman refers to *Captain Kidd* as "a cardboard kiddie epic" (Shipman: 340). Yet the public is savvy about such matters. Consider cinema patron and Laughton fan Betty Toles of Colorado Springs, Colorado, who enthused in *Screenland* (June 1946), "There is no other actor quite like Charles Laughton—when he has a part he can really sink his teeth into." She has a point. The *Monthly Film Bulletin* (December 1945, Vol. 12, No. 144) described Laughton's command of the role: "[He] makes a nasty oily rogue of Kidd." The *New York Times* (November 23, 1945) was mindful of the singularity of the leading role: "*Captain Kidd* is strictly Charles Laughton's vehicle. The rest of the crew are merely along for the ride." The *Box Office Digest* (August 11, 1945) was perplexed, finding the interpretation of the role "a trifle aslant from any that your reviewer has met in research, or fiction, but it is a Captain Kidd tailored for Laughton, and that is the pirate whom the audience will enjoy.... He is a tough hombre, but a slightly mean clown. So his character sets the menace, while the 'business' of the role gives the entertainment." The *Photoplay* reviewer (November 1945) summed up the film as "[a] tongue-in-cheek bit of malarkey." A succinct description which nevertheless is remiss in neglecting the nuances of the acting itself.

Harrison's Reports (August 4, 1945) was more on the mark: "The performances are superior to the story values, and are the main reason for one's interest in the picture." *Film Bulletin* (August 20, 1945) described Laughton's performance as "outstanding." *Variety* (August 1, 1945) dismissed the film as an "OK pirate actioner," but thought Laughton's performance was "capital." Carolyn Harrow of *Film and Radio Guide* (Vol. XII, No. 1, October 1945) described Laughton's Kidd as a role which "one feels he keenly enjoys depicting. He is as masterly as ever as the arch-hypocrite and ruffian who is as big a coward as he is a bully. Laughton makes the most of every bit of irony. He deserves the gratitude of author, producer and director." Gratitude was in short supply when Caroline Lejeune wrote in the *Observer* (November 25, 1945), "Mr. Laughton's performance is made up of lines and touches broken off from all his old parts, and combined with the facility of a good actor who has long since stopped trying to get down to the core of a character, and is content to amuse himself with surface decoration." All very well no doubt, but Laughton deserves a sporting chance to show his mettle rather than be written off or derided as here. The London *Times* (November 26, 1945) was altogether more assiduous and forgiving when it declared,

> Kidd is a man with an eye on respectability and a title even while he is proving himself the terror of the Madagascar waters, and Mr. Laughton magnificently conveys the yeasty mingling of contradictory elements. Kidd's satirical enjoyment of his own villainy is immense, and his wistful snobbery binds him in a curious spiritual relationship with that old Etonian pirate, Captain Hook. *Captain Kidd* does not rollick enough and is by no means another *Mutiny on the Bounty*, but Mr. Laughton's acting gives it distinction.

He does indeed. A solo tour de force being at once doughty and yet sardonic, and lending *Captain Kidd* a certain sparkle. This exists because of the strength and purpose Laughton is able to provide as a total actor of exceptional range. Quite simply, he manages to create something from very little and succeeds in doing it rather well.

Because of Him (1946)

Tagline: "Business was Never So *Beautiful*! And It's All *Because of Him*"[58]

U.S. (Universal Pictures)

Credits: Associate Producer: Howard Christie; Screenplay: Edmund Beloin; Original Story: Edmund Beloin and Sig Herzig; Musical Score: Miklos Rozsa; Musical Direction for Miss Durbin: Edgar Fairchild; Photography: Hal Mohr; Art Directors: John B. Goodman, Robert Clatworthy; Director of Sound: Bernard B. Brown; Technician: Joe Lapis. Vocal Coach: Al Proctor; Editor: Ted J. Kent; Hair Stylist: Carmen Dirigo; Director of Makeup: Jack P. Pierce; Costumes: Travis Banton;

(1946) Because of Him

Assistant Director: William Holland; Set Decorators: R.A. Gausman, Oliver Emert; Produced by Felix Jackson; Directed by Richard Wallace; U.S. release: January 18, 1946; U.K. release: March 11, 1946; Genre: Musical; Black and White; Running Time: 88 minutes; DVD Region 1 from TCM, released February 2011; DVD Region 2 from Simply Media, released March 2011; no English subtitle captions for the deaf and hard of hearing.

Cast: Deanna Durbin (*Kim Walker*); **Charles Laughton (*John Sheridan*)**; Franchot Tone (*Paul Taylor*); Helen Broderick (*Nora Bartlett*); Stanley Ridges (*Charles Gilbert*); Donald Meek (*Martin*); Regina Wallace (*Head Nurse*); Charles Halton (*Mr. Dunlop*); Douglas Wood (*Samuel Hapgood*); **Uncredited Cast**: Joan Fulton [Joan Shawlee], Karen Randle (*Autograph Seekers*); George Anderson (*Detective*); Brooks Benedict, Mary Currier, Bess Flowers, Stuart Holmes (*Playgoers*); Helen Bennett, George Eldredge, John Kellogg, George J. Lewis, Bert Moorhouse, James Nolan, Tom Quinn, Janet Shaw, John Shay, Emmett Vogan, Billy Wayne (*Reporters*); Gladys Blake (*Mabel*); George Chandler, Steve Wayne (*Busboys*); Gwen Donovan, Mabel Forrest (*Actresses*); Ralph Dunn (*Cop*); Mary Field, Ethyl May Halls (*Maids*); Ed Fury, Gene Garrick (*Young Men*); Phil Garris (*Usher*); Wilton Graff (*Stage Manager*); James Bush, Gus Glassmire, John Hamilton (*Critics*); Robert Homans (*Police Sergeant*); Teddy Infuhr (*Boy*); Jimmy Kelly (*Fat Man*); Perc Launders (*Cop*); Eve March (*Secretary*); Mary McLeod (*Young Girl*); Billy Nelson (*Elevator Operator*); Rebel Randall (*Roxanne*); Jack Rice (*Florist*); Beatrice Roberts (*Wife*); Charles Sherlock (*Photographer*); Charles Sullivan (*Ambulance Driver*); Jean Trent (*Blonde*); John Vosper (*Toastmaster*); Ray Walker (*Daniels*); Eddy Waller (*Gubbins*); Lynn Whitney (*Martha Manners*); Charles C. Wilson (*City Editor*).

Working Title: *Catherine the Last*

Synopsis: A young waitress, Kim Walker, dreams of becoming a big Hollywood star. She comes to the attention of famous stage actor John Sheridan, who has his heart set on casting an unknown actress in his next play, *Strange Laughter*. Using a ruse, Kim manages to obtain Sheridan's signature on a letter of introduction to the producer of the play. When they meet, the producer is charmed and decides to hire Kim as the lead in the play. But the playwright, Paul, views Kim as an untried amateur and is determined to keep her from appearing in his play. After returning from a vacation cut short due to poor weather, Sheridan finds his apartment is being used for a party to celebrate Kim's casting. Bemused, Sheridan plays along with her deception. He escorts Kim home only to advise her not to proceed with her desire to become an actress. Kim's friend Nora plants a story in the press saying that Sheridan's rejection drove Kim to attempt suicide. The actor, sensitive to adverse publicity, takes Kim out the following day and is enchanted when he hears her rendition of the song "Danny Boy." Suitably impressed, he offers her the lead in the new play. Paul, contrite on hearing about Kim's attempted suicide, also offers her the lead. Hearing that she already has the role, and her confession that she has fallen in love with him, is more than Paul can bear and he mistakes her sincerity for a hoax. Through all the rehearsals, Paul is spiteful and cruel to Kim. Sheridan threatens to quit the play. Instead, Paul leaves the play; Sheridan takes over as producer. The day before the opening, Paul threatens to sabotage the production

Laughton as ham actor John Sheridan takes a bow and steals the limelight from Deanna Durbin as aspiring actress Kim Walker in *Because of Him* (1946).

by demanding his name be removed from all credits. Kim has become so distracted by Paul's misbehavior that Sheridan decides to pretend that he is in love with Kim in the hope of calming her nerves. Her opening night is a huge success. Reading the critical raves in the papers, Paul decides to slip into the theater unannounced to see Kim's performance. Sheridan sees Paul and decides to change the ending of the play so that Kim and Paul can be reunited on stage.

Selected Dialogue:

> SHERIDAN: "That may be art, ladies and gentlemen, but it gets monotonous."

Production Commentary: *Because of Him* was the seventeenth Deanna Durbin film in a filmography of 21 feature films and one short. This was the second and final Laughton-Durbin pairing, after *It Started with Eve* (1941).

Produced in 1945 but not released until early in 1946, *Because of You* did nothing to halt Durbin's decline at the box office. Despite solid production values, a Miklós Rózsa score and a first-rate supporting cast, the film suffers from a weak script that lacks the lightness of touch so evident in the Joe Pasternak and Henry Koster era at Universal.

The film takes itself all too seriously, but Laughton doesn't and, in an odd way, the film is the better for it. He steals just about every scene he appears in. Also cast as a romantic lead was Franchot Tone, who had appeared opposite Durbin in *Nice Girl?* (Universal, William A. Seiter, 1941). A selection from contemporary trade papers reveals some background to the film's production. On February 28, 1945, the *Exhibitor* announced that Durbin's next production would be *Catherine the Last*, a modern comedy drama to co-star Laughton. By August 15, 1945, Thalia Bell of *Motion Picture Daily* revealed that Franchot Tone had been cast in the picture, which was now retitled *Because of Him*. Between 1943 and 1947, Felix Jackson had produced seven of Durbin's films. Durbin was married to Jackson at the time of this production and was pregnant with her first child. The working title *Catherine the Last* came from a successful 1936 Austrian romantic comedy film which Jackson had written.

There is for Laughton aficionados an array of compensatory tidbits. The opening finds ham actor John Sheridan taking a bow upon the end of a long engagement playing the lead in *Cyrano de Bergerac*. He removes his false nose and declaims in hammy style his ethos of the theatrical experience. This was the role Laughton had considered and prepared for in a proposed film for Korda during the 1930s. Later in the film, there are quotations from *King Lear* and a scene where Laughton rehearses a play.

Critics agreed that Durbin had been dealt a bad hand and that Laughton scooped the acting honors, using all the traits of ham acting. The *New York Times* (January 25, 1946) wrote of Laughton, "His performance is magnificently expansive. In less polite society it might be whispered that Mr. Laughton is hamming up all over the screen ... but his grandiose acting is in keeping with the general exaggerations of the plot." *Showmen's Trade Review* (January 12, 1946) stated, "In spite of good production, Miss Durbin's delightful singing and good acting on the part of the star, Franchot Tone and, of course, Charles Laughton, this picture is slow moving and apparently written with little inspiration with the result that it provides but few moments of real entertainment. The comedy throughout the action seems forced, lacks the feeling of spontaneity and imparts a mood of restlessness to audiences." *Variety* (January 9, 1946) wrote, "Laughton grabs the acting honors in a sterling portrayal of the actor whose every gesture would look well between two slices of rye. Way he poses for the newspaper photos, goes into lengthy quotations from his stage successes etc. should bring the house down." The London *Times* (January 28, 1946) spoke for many when by suggesting that Laughton stole the film from Durbin, "Miss Deanna Durbin may have her name first on the programme, but this is Mr. Charles Laughton's film. Florid of phrase, self-conscious in pose, he revels in this good-natured satire of a popular actor who might well be Mr. Laughton himself, and the pity is that a performance so full of style and gusto should be thrown away on a misguided film."

Because of Him does have its moments, but in contrast to *It Started with Eve* it provides only moderate entertainment value. With the exception of "Danny Boy," Deanna Durbin's three songs are forgettable. Durbin took to calling Laughton by the pet name of "Ducky" during production and there is still a sense of synergy between the two. Laughton carries the film along, offering a rich comic performance even though audiences are invited to laugh at him rather than with him. To accuse Laughton of carrying an incidental film, giving a tokenistic performance, propping up a diminishing star does carry more than a grain of truth.

Laughton's increasing commitment to translate and perform Bertolt Brecht's *Galileo* was beginning to cause him serious concern. Not least was the lack of finance necessary for this project to be completed. Laughton decided to cough up $25,000 of his own money, half the production costs, to underwrite a four-week run of the play at the small Coronet Theater in Los Angeles. It is not fanciful to suggest that Laughton, in spending time away from the exertions of *Galileo*, was regaining a new outlook on the art of acting. It is a mistake to conclude his self-parody in the film was an act of some desperation by an actor irredeemably down on his luck. His flamboyance throughout the film does not equate to a loss of appetite for learning and a lessening of his commitment to the ideal of acting. Laughton still had much to do, give and say. *Because of Him* offered him an advantageous if tangential interlude in which aspects of his acting unrelated to the film are shown. Indeed, more substantive work from Laughton was to follow in several future films.

The Paradine Case (1947)

Tagline: "A Seven-Star HIT by the Producer and Director of *Spellbound*"[59]

U.S. (David O. Selznick/Vanguard Films)

Credits: From the novel by Robert Hichens; Adaptation by Alma Reville; Screenplay: David O. Selznick; Photography: Lee Garmes; Music: Franz Waxman; Production Designer: J. McMillan Johnson; Art Director: Thomas Morahan; Gowns: Travis Banton; Supervising Editor: Hal C. Kern; Associate: John Faure; Scenario Assistant: Lydia Schiller; Sound Director: James G. Stewart; Recorder: Richard Van Hessen; Interiors: Joseph B. Platt; Set Decorator: Emile Kuri; Assistant Director: Lowell J. Farrell; Unit Manager: Fred Ahern; Special Effects: Clarence Slifer; Hair Styles: Larry Germain; Directed by Alfred Hitchcock; U.S. release: December 29, 1947; Genre: Suspense Drama; Black and White; Running Time: 116 minutes (premiered at 132 minutes and later shortened by Selznick for general release); Blu-ray Region A and DVD Region 1, Kino Lorber, released May 2017; English subtitle captions for the deaf and hard of hearing are available on this disc; DVD Region 2, Freemantle Home Entertainment, released December 2008; no English subtitle captions for the deaf and hard of hearing.

Cast: Gregory Peck (*Anthony Keane*); Ann Todd [Miss Todd appears by arrangement with J. Arthur Rank Organization] (*Gay Keane*); **Charles Laughton (Lord Thomas Horfield)**; Charles Coburn (*Sir Simon Flaquer*); Ethel Barrymore (*Lady Sophie Horfield*); and introducing two new stars: Louis Jourdan (*Andre Latour*) and [Alida] Valli (*Maddalena Anna Paradine*); Leo G. Carroll (*Sir Joseph Farrell*); Joan Tetzel (*Judy Flaquer*); Isobel Elsom (*Innkeeper*); **Uncredited Cast**: Patrick Aherne (*Police Sergeant Leggett*); Leonard Carey (*Courtroom Stenographer*); Elspeth Dudgeon (*Second Matron*); John Goldsworthy (*Lakin*); Lumsden Hare, Edgar Norton (*Courtroom Attendants*); Sam Harris, Kenner G. Kemp, Thomas Martin, Arthur Tovey (*Courtroom Spectators*); Alfred Hitchcock (*Man Carrying Cello Case*); Colin Hunter (*Baker*); Boyd Irwin (*Courtroom Observer*); Colin Keith-Johnston (*Clerk of the Court*); Colin Kenny (*Juror*); Lester Matthews (*Police Inspector Ambrose*); Phyllis Morris (*Mrs. Carr—Housekeeper at Hindley Hall*); "Snub" Pollard (*Cabby*); Bert Stevens (*Barrister in Courtroom*); John Williams (*Barrister Collins*).

Working Titles: *Mrs. Paradine Takes the Stand*; *The Lie*; *Heartbreak*; *The Grand Passion*; *A Question of Life and Death*; *A Woman of Experience*; *The Dark Hour*; *A Crime of Passion*; *This Is No Ordinary Woman*; *Guilty?*; *The Indelible Stain*; *Guilty!*; *The Woman Who Did the Killing*; *Hanging Is Easy*; *The Accused*; *Bewildered*; *The Green-Eyed Monster*; *Woman and Wife*

Awards: Nominated Academy Award: Best Actress in a Supporting Role: Ethel Barrymore.

Synopsis: In 1946 London, Maddalena Anna Paradine is arrested for poisoning her blind husband, Colonel Richard Paradine. The family solicitor, Sir Simon Flaquer, arranges for her to be defended by Tony Keane, whose wife Gay thinks that Mrs. Paradine is probably innocent. When Simon and Tony visit Mrs. Paradine in prison, she tells them that she is concerned that people will think that she married a helpless blind man so that she could kill him for his money. Tony impresses upon her to believe that she had made a considerable sacrifice in marrying Richard. Tony and Gay attend a dinner party at the home of the presiding judge in the

Paradine case, Lord Thomas Horfield, who offends Gay with his lecherous behavior. Mrs. Paradine reluctantly admits to Tony that she had been involved with several men before her marriage but says that her husband knew all about her past. When Tony and Flaquer discuss whether to present the argument that Richard committed suicide, possibly assisted by his valet André Latour, Flaquer is unimpressed by Tony's reasoning and feels that their client may well be guilty. Tony passionately defends her and is overheard by Gay. Later, when Tony asks Mrs. Paradine about Latour, she protects him as if he might be her lover. Gay confronts Tony with her suspicions that he is becoming infatuated with Mrs. Paradine. He offers to give up the case and take her to Switzerland, and she confidently insists that he continue. Tony decides to do some investigating at the Paradine country home, Hindley Hall, in Cumberland, and takes a room at a nearby hotel. Latour greets him at the house and allows him to wander around, accompanied by the housekeeper. That evening, Latour tells Tony that he was not involved with Mrs. Paradine and describes her as an evil woman. Disturbed by his words, Tony asks Latour to leave. Back in London, when Tony tells Mrs. Paradine of Latour's accusation and suggests that they were lovers, she asks Tony to remove himself from the case. After he apologizes, she agrees to let him continue. Sir Simon's daughter Judy, who is Gay's best friend, asks her about the rumors regarding Tony being in love with Mrs. Paradine. Gay tells Tony that she does not want to lose him and that she wants Mrs. Paradine to be found innocent for, if she were executed, Tony would imagine her as a great lost love. When the trial starts at the Old Bailey, the Crown's prosecutor, Sir Joseph Farrell, portrays Richard as a true gentleman and establishes that Latour had been his devoted manservant before and during the war, and had won a medal for gallantry. After stating that the colonel was the best man he ever knew, Latour testifies that Mrs. Paradine lied to the colonel that he, Latour, intended to leave, causing the colonel to become very upset with him. Although Tony proves that Latour had put the colonel's old dog to death with poison, Latour denies any involvement in his employer's death. During a recess, Mrs. Paradine tells Tony that she will not forgive him for accusing Latour of murder and states that she wishes to be found innocent, but not at the cost of Latour being destroyed. When Tony admits to having romantic feelings for her, she asserts that their relationship is only one of client and lawyer. After the prosecution establishes that Latour and Mrs. Paradine did engage in an adulterous relationship, Tony puts her in the witness box. She states that she asked her husband to find another position for Latour, as he had been taking liberties with her and had tried to make love to her. When Mrs. Paradine implicates herself in her husband's death, Tony requests a recess. That evening, Judy tells Tony that she feels that Mrs. Paradine will be found

Though producer David O. Selznick's *The Paradine Case* (1947) has a starry cast and boasts a top director (Alfred Hitchcock) it is not considered to be among the very best of either producer or director. Nevertheless, it has its moments. Here, sexual impropriety is on display when Gay Keane (Ann Todd) is petted in an inappropriate and deviant manner by a lecherous judge, Lord Thomas Horfield, played with aplomb by Laughton.

guilty and that his career will be over. The next day, as the prosecutor interrogates Mrs. Paradine, word comes that Latour has committed suicide, whereupon a devastated Mrs. Paradine admits that she killed her husband as she had wanted to go away with Latour, insisting that he was not involved in the murder but had guessed that she was responsible. Mrs. Paradine angrily denounces Tony from the witness stand, accusing him of causing Latour's death. Tony humbly confesses to errors of judgment he has made in conducting her defense and, after imploring the jury not to hold his "incompetence" against Mrs. Paradine, asks to be excused from the case. Tony then returns to the forgiving Gay, while Mrs. Paradine faces execution by hanging.

Selected Dialogue:

HORFIELD: "Remarkable old girl, Lady Millicent. We used to have great times together at Deauville back in the '20s. I persuaded her to go in swimming at 70. I watched her frolicking in the surf and had sad thoughts about the impermanence of beauty."

HORFIELD: "I do not like to be interrupted in the middle of an insult."

HORFIELD: "Do not bandy words with me, Mr. Keane."

HORFIELD: "Surprising how closely the convolutions of a walnut resemble those of the human brain."

Production Commentary: Production of *The Paradine Case* was beset with problems. Alfred Hitchcock was riding high following his successful (artistically and financially) *Notorious* (RKO, 1946). Unfortunately for Hitchcock, he found that working on *The Paradine Case* meant contending with producer David O. Selznick. In *Notorious*, Hitchcock had been successful in casting all the main parts with actors of first choice. Not so with *The Paradine Case*. Laurence Olivier had been offered the star part of the barrister but turned it down. Greta Garbo had been assigned to play Mrs. Paradine and even shot a test, but this did not entice her out of retirement. Instead, Selznick's latest discovery, Italian actress Alida Valli, was cast as Mrs. Paradine. She was subjected to an intense Hollywood makeover. This being her first English-language film, she was assigned a voice coach, placed on a diet and had her teeth capped. She was coiffured in Garboesque makeup and fashion. All this was carried out via Selznick's precise instructions contained in his flurry of voluminous memos. Robert Newton had been considered for the role of the lover but was unavailable and Louis Jourdan took the part. Claude Rains was also announced for the Laughton role. The film began shooting on December 19, 1946, and concluded in May 7, 1947. Retakes were ordered in November 1947.

The scenario was based on the 1933 novel by Robert Smythe Hichens (1864–1950). In this long multifaceted thriller, the wife of a military hero murders her husband. Her defense counsel falls in love with her and jeopardizes his own marriage. If remade today, *The Paradine Case* would have all the attributes of a TV mini-series. Hitchcock and his wife Alma had written a draft script, but Selznick was dissatisfied. Hitchcock suggested the script be given to Scottish playwright James Bridie, but Bridie preferred to write the script in England rather than travel to the United States. This proved unsuccessful and so Ben Hecht was engaged to write additional dialogue. When the shoot began, there was still no finalized script and Selznick took to his own rewrites on a daily basis. This haphazard approach did not make for an organized shoot. This was Hitchcock's last film under Selznick's seven-year contract, and he was eager to get it done and direct his energies to other projects. Hitchcock resented Selznick's interference on the script, re-cutting the film and demanding retakes of key sequences. Artistic control and financial freedom obsessed Hitchcock just as much as it did Laughton.

Selznick was still putting the finishing touches to his psychological Western epic *Duel in the Sun* (King Vidor, 1946) as shooting began on *The Paradine Case*. In addition to having a heavy workload, he was undergoing a messy divorce from his first wife Irene, having fallen in love with actress Jennifer Jones. Much of his hyperactivity was assisted by dependence on the pharmaceutical drug Benzedrine. Unsurprisingly, his decision-making at this time was erratic and this encroached on the film. For example, Selznick's name appears some five times during the opening credits. He was still undecided on what to call the film only hours before the premiere: see above for the 18 working film titles considered. In ad hoc fashion, he chose to retain the original title of the novel. The main title credit is conspicuous by the plain font used rather than the otherwise ornate font that appears throughout the rest of the opening credits. This was the second and last time Laughton and Hitchcock worked together. Since their previous frosty encounter on *Jamaica Inn*, Laughton had relinquished the role of film producer, and although he has billing above the title it is preceded by Gregory Peck and Ann Todd. He was now reduced to the status of character player rather than nominal star. As a freelance actor, Laughton took Hitchcock's direction amicably enough. His portrayal of Lord Justice Thomas Horfield as administering severe justice with a dash of licentious perversion is both menacing and amusing. His fee was used to finance the long gestation of Brecht's *Galileo*.

According to *Variety* (December 31, 1947), "*The Paradine Case* offers two hours and 11 minutes of high dramatics. Because of the long running time and deliberate pace, it has slow spots but still maintains interest both for technical achievements and story content." The original rough cut was three hours long and this was edited down to just over two hours for its initial premiere. But producer Selznick (who had the final say in script and editing) must have taken the accusation of "long running time" and "slow spots" to heart for he cut the film again to a release length of just under two hours. Today many critics are perplexed as to why Ethel Barrymore was nominated for a Best Supporting Actress Oscar, given she appears in the film a mere three to four minutes. The answer is there was a deleted scene that appeared in the film before the beginning of the trial. Lady Sophie Horfield goes to an art gallery in a museum to a meeting with barrister Anthony Keane to plead for the life of Mrs. Paradine.[60] Despite the visual flamboyance of the courtroom scenes in a studio reconstruction of the Old Bailey in which multiple cameras and extended takes were employed to dazzling effect, the overall impression is one of detached and brittle characters, impervious to their impact upon one another.

Although the film on its initial release raked in $2,200,000 in domestic rentals at the U.S. box office (*Variety*, January 5, 1948), this covered only half of the $4,258,000 lavished on the production. The cost of the Old Bailey set was over $80,000 due to low ceilings constructed to allow for shooting with low camera angles. Critics applauded Hitchcock's usual technical brilliance and skill but were dismissive of the casting of both Gregory Peck and Laughton. The *Manchester Guardian* (January 15, 1949) wrote, "[T]he director has had to cope with the two quite unnecessary difficulties that Gregory Peck cannot sound or behave at all like the eminent K.C. he is meant to be and that Charles Laughton, given the part of a judge, persists in giving yet another impersonation of Charles Laughton." From The London *Times* (January 17, 1949): "A moderate Hitchcock; no more, no less…. Mr. Charles Laughton is, magnificently, the judge—ripeness is all, ripeness and the relishing of it—and it is well he is there to preside for Mr. Peck is never quite convincing…." Bosley Crowther in the *New York Times* (January 9, 1948) opined, "A bit too much flutter and flourish are in Charles Laughton's decoration of the judge…."

Laughton as a debauched judge manages to scene-steal whether presiding over the trial or fretting over his miserable marriage to the long-suffering Sophie who may, or may not, be half-mad. It is suggested that if she is the former, then it is Horfield himself who is the instigator. Barrymore and Laughton may be secondary characters, but their scenes together personify the double binary of justice: warm compassion vs. cold dispassion.

Hitchcock uses precise mathematical ingenuity in the angles and movement of the camera. Despite this professionalism, the overall effect is too often cold and calculating in its approach and is used as an expensive exercise in technical bravura. A similar dilemma is presented throughout the film, for in spite of outstanding photography by Lee Garmes, a lush Franz Waxman score, and fabulous gowns by Travis Banton, the film is eaten away by censorial restrictions and Selznick's penchant for script changes and extensive retakes. In the case of Laughton, his Lord Horfield is a grotesque; his misogyny, sadism and perversity are inferred, but apprehensions of censorship results in the character's motives and intentions being skated over. On the one hand, all that remains in the surviving final cut are a few *bon mots*, and an atmosphere of unpleasantness accompanied by soporific eccentricity. On the other hand, while Laughton's surviving scenes are fragmentary, their adult content is very apparent for knowing audiences. The film, like Laughton, is fascinating to watch.

There are numerous compromises and flaws concerning casting, a lethargic script, and a too-radical approach in the use of high expressionism involving *mise en scène*, editing and photography. They undermine the impact of the drama. In particular, the latter point serves to highlight a violation of the dominant Hollywood convention of the linear narrative rooted in notions of coherence and unity. There is a causal link common to a trio of Hitchcock films produced during the late 1940s. Both *The Paradine Case* and *Under Capricorn* (Warner Bros./Transatlantic Pictures, 1949) involve Hitchcock's use of the extended take. This preoccupation with the perspective of subjectivity would reach its apotheosis in *Rope* (Warner Bros./Transatlantic Pictures, 1948) where Hitchcock explores the allusion of shooting in "real time" and editing the film to appear as though shot via a single take.

In 1962, during lengthy discussions with critic and director François Truffaut, Hitchcock was complimentary about Laughton's performance as the judge:

> At [a] point in the picture there's a scene between Laughton [the judge] and Ann Todd [Mrs. Keane] to show he's a lustful man. First, there's the look in his eyes, with the camera then traveling over Ann Todd's bare shoulders. Now in front of her husband and his wife, he walks over to the couch, sits down next to her and coolly puts his hand on top of hers. This little episode is handled discreetly, yet the impact is outrageous [Truffaut: 252].

Although cast in a supporting role and despite interference from Selznick and Hays Office censorship issues, Laughton managed to overcome all obstacles and execute another enticing film performance.

Arch of Triumph (1948)

Tagline: "She looked out on the rooftops of a sleeping city. It was the second night ... the dangerous night!"[61]

U.S. (Enterprise Studios/United Artists/Lewis Milestone)

Credits: Screenplay: Lewis Milestone and Harry Brown; From the novel by Erich Maria Remarque, serialized in *Collier's* magazine; Music Composed by Louis Gruenberg; Music Conducter: Morris Stoloff; Production Designer: William Cameron Menzies; Associate Producer: Otto Klement; Executive Production Manager: Joseph C. Gilpin; Photography: Russell Metty; Art Director: William E. Flannery; Set Decorator: Edward G. Boyle; Second Unit Director: Nate Watt; Assistant Director: Robert Aldrich; Sound Engineer: Frank Webster; Special Scenic Effects: Robert M. Moreland; Makeup Supervisor: Gustaf M. Norin; Process Department: Mario Castegnaro; Editor: Duncan Mansfield; Musical Director: Rudolph Polk; Technical Advisor: Michel Bernheim; Wardrobe Designer: Marion Herwood Keyes; Costumes for Ingrid Bergman Designed by Edith Head; Technical Advice: French Research Foundation; Produced by David Lewis; Directed by Lewis Milestone; U.S. release: February 17, 1948; Genre: Drama; Black and White; Running Time: 135 minutes; Blu-ray Region A and DVD Region 1, Olive Films, released July 2014; Blu-ray Region B, Soul Media (Sweden), released August 2010; no English subtitle captions for the deaf and hard of hearing.

Cast: Ingrid Bergman (*Joan Madou*); Charles Boyer (*Dr. Ravic*); **Charles Laughton** (***Ivoni Haake***); Louis Calhern (*"Col" Boris Morosov*); Ruth Warrick (*Kate Bergstroem*); Roman Bohnen (*Dr. Veber*); J. Edward Bromberg (*Hotel Manager*); Ruth Nelson (*Madame Fessier*); Stephen Bekassy (*Alex*); Curt Bois (*Waiter*); Art Smith (*Inspector*); Michael Romanoff (*Captain Alidze*); **Uncredited Cast**: Richard Alexander, Robert Culler, William Yetter Sr. (*Gestapo Agents*); Sylvia Andrew (*Milan Charwoman*); Frank Arnold, Joe LeBlanc, Jacques Villon (*Newsboys*); Jessie Arnold (*Cashier*); George Balooi, Vladimir Dubinsky, Joseph Marievsky, Walter Rode (*Scheherazade's Waiters*); Griff Barnett (*Fernand*); Richard Bartell, Peter Cusanelli (*Taxi Drivers*); Claude Bayard, Walter DeCardo, Guy D'Ennery, Alex Melesh, George Root, Hal Stout, Tony Taurent (*Waiters*); Carmen Beretta (*Woman Injured by Crane*); Oliver Blake (*Albert*); Helen Boyce (*German Woman*); Hazel Brooks (*Sybil*); Feodor Chaliapin Jr., Boris Chmara (*Scheherazade's Chefs*); Neville Chamberlain (*Himself, Newsreel Archive*); Gordon B. Clarke (*Drunk*); William Conrad (*Policeman at Accident*); Gino Corrado (*Sommelier*); Franco Corsaro (*Lieutenant Navarro*); George Davis (*Alois*); Al Eben (*Worker*); Fernanda Eliscu (*Flower Woman*); Katherine Emery (*Grim Nurse*); Joe Espitallier (*Workman*); Adolph Faylauer (*Gambling House Patron*); Bess Flowers (*Gambler at Roulette Table*);

Byron Foulger (*Policeman at Accident*); Jay Gilpin (*Refugee Boy*); Alvin Hammer (*Albert*); Carl Hanson (*Taxi Driver*); Sam Harris (*Gambling House Patron*); Beba Holzer (*Casino Player*); Willy Kaufman (*Rappaport*); Ilia Khmara (*Russian Singer*); John Laurenz (*Colonel Gomez*); Carl M. Leviness (*Accident Witness*); George Magrill (*Taxi Driver*); Paul Marion (*Anesthetist*); Patricia Marlowe (*Scrub Nurse*); Andre Marsaudon (*Roulette Croupier*); Anthony Natale (*Milan Porter*); Bob O'Connor (*Policeman*); Manuel Paris (*Bartender*); Paule Pascal (*Refugee Mother*); Nino Pipitone (*General's Aide*); Joe Ploski (*Man at Party/Man in Line*); Marie Rabasse (*Bistro Owner's Wife*); Emil Rameau (*Mr. Schultz*); Vladimir Rashevsky (*Nugent*); Suzanne Ridgway (*Girl at Sidewalk Cafe*); Gene Roth (*Gestapo Agent*); William Roy (*Chasseur*); Irene Ryan (*Irate Wife*); Fred Santley (*Hotel Waiter at the Verdun*); Leonardo Scavino (*Captain Gonzales*); Peter Seal (*Scheherazade's Waiter*); Muni Seroff (*Krings*); Gwynne Shipman (*Nurse*); Sundar Singh, Kalu K. Sonkur (*Rug Peddlers*); Bob Stebbins (*Bellboy*); Larry Steers (*Man at Gambling House*); Helga Storme (*Telephone Operator*); Joyce Tucker (*Bistro Waitress*); Harry J. Vejar (*Bistro Owner*); Peter Virgo (*Vladislaus Polyanski*); Fay Wall (*Clarisse*); Joe Warfield (*Fouquet's Waiter*); Kay Williams (*Mrs. Green*); Barbara Woodell (*Eugenie*); Lilo Yarson (*Alvarez*).

An expressionist flashback at the beginning of Lewis Milestone's refugee drama *Arch of Triumph* (1948). Left to right: Victim Hazel Brooks tortured by Nazi gestapo chief Laughton accompanied by unidentified player. Political prisoner Charles Boyer looks on in abject terror. An unidentified player stands impassive to the spectacle of barbarism.

Synopsis: Paris in the winter of 1938. European refugees arrive in the city as a result of Nazi Germany's aggressive foreign expansionism in Central Europe. Among them is world-weary Dr. Ravic, who spends his time practicing medicine illegally, helping other refugees and also searching for his Nazi persecutor, Gestapo chief Ivoni Haake. Haake had tortured him and killed his girlfriend Sybil in Germany. Sitting in a restaurant, Ravic sees Haake outside. This triggers flashbacks of his torture and Sybil's death. He runs outside but is too late: Haake has vanished. On a dark, rainy night, Ravic comes upon a prostitute, Joan Madou, who is suicidal following the sudden death of her pimp-lover. With the assistance of Ravic, Joan is able to go to the police and sort matters out. Ravic then finds her a job in the Scheherazade café through a friend, Maurice, who, like Ravic, has fallen on hard times. Ravic and Joan spend time drinking together and find themselves falling in love. They later take a short trip to the French Riviera, where Ravic reveals that because he is classed as an undesirable alien and has no legal passport, he can never marry Joan. On his return, he stops to help at the scene of an accident on a construction site. A French official becomes suspicious and demands to see Ravic's identity papers. Ravic is then arrested and deported from France. Upon his return several months later, Ravic finds Joan is in a relationship with a wealthy young playboy; they had met on the Riviera. Though she cares little for her new lover, he is determined to marry her. Ravic offers her the chance to break off the affair and return to him. One night, Ravic again sees Herr Haake and they sit together at a café table where they engage in conversation. Haake fails to recognize Ravic. Ravic offers to show Haake Paris during his next visit to the city. Following the declaration of war by France on Germany, Haake returns to the city. While riding in Ravic's car in the French countryside, Ravic kills the German in a brutal attack. When Ravic returns to his apartment, he falls into a deep sleep and is woken by a frantic phone call from Joan. He rushes to her apartment and finds she has been mortally wounded by her rich lover. He carries out an emergency operation, but Joan dies on the operating table. He returns to his hotel only to find all refugees are being asked to produce their identity papers. Ravic joins the queue with his refugee friend Maurice, in the knowledge that both will be taken to an internment camp.

Selected Dialogue:

HAAKE: "That is one good thing they have here, it is cognac. Otherwise, all is decadent. These people who only wish an easy life."

Production Commentary: The theatrical trailer lauded this misconceived drama with the words, "So compelling is the emotional impact *Arch of Triumph*, so great its performances, so sustained its suspense, that mere excerpts cannot do justice to its story and its stars." The hyperbole continues, "It was two years in the making at the Enterprise Studios." Yet despite lavish set designs supplied by William Cameron Menzies (the film cost over four million dollars) and adroit camera set-ups, accompanied by low-key chiaroscuro lighting from leading cinematographer Russell Metty, these were not enough to save this expensive misfire.

Hindered by the pedestrian direction of Lewis Milestone, the scenario fails to offer sufficient character motivation or dramatic progression and all too soon stalls and dissolves into a studio-bound artifice that becomes inconsequential, meandering, pedantic and unconvincing. The original directorial cut was much longer, but the studio decided the length was detrimental to the film's potential commercial viability and so began a process of drastic cutting and re-editing. The studio cut was disowned by Milestone. Following Ingrid Bergman's appearance in *Arch of Triumph*, she played the title role in the disastrous *Joan of Arc* (Walter Wanger, Victor Fleming, 1948), which killed her Hollywood career for several years. Charles Boyer had little luck either with being cast in Milestone's film as he too was absent from the screen for three years.

Arch of Triumph was produced under the banner of the independent company Enterprise Films, formed in 1946 by star John Garfield, producers David L. Loew and Charles Enfield. Nine films were made by Enterprise Films over three years: *Arch of Triumph* plus *Ramrod* (André de Toth, 1947), *The Other Love* (André de Toth, 1947), *Body and Soul* (Robert Rossen, 1947), *So This Is New York* (Richard Fleischer, 1948), *Four Faces West* (Alfred E. Green, 1948), *No Minor Vices* (Lewis Milestone, 1948), *Force of Evil* (Abraham Polansky, 1949) and *Caught* (Max Ophuls, 1949).

It is useful to compare *Arch of Triumph* with *So Ends Our Night* (United Artists, John Cromwell, 1941): The films share similar, if not identical, contexts. They were both produced by independent producer David L. Loew, based on stories written by Erich Maria Remarque, and feature notable contributions from legendary production designer William Cameron Menzies, as well as music scores by Louis Gruenberg. Both films also contain contributions from two individuals who would later excel under the rise of independent production during the 1950s: Robert Aldrich was assistant director on *Arch of Triumph* and Stanley Kramer worked as production assistant on *So Ends Our Night*. Each film tackles the sensitive subject of European refugees and political persecution. *So Ends Our Night* has a visual panache which ably carries a sense of real danger and dramatic suspense, essential qualities which are sadly lacking throughout the duration of *Arch of Triumph*. Though *Arch of Triumph* has an obvious sumptuousness and expensive sheen in terms of décor and design, it ends up woefully misplacing the sense of ambition it so artfully seeks to construct for itself.

Where does third-billed Charles Laughton fit into all this? The producers were obviously hoping that his name would help sell the film. In this assumption, they were to be proven wide of the mark. Unlike Erich von Stroheim in *So Ends Our Night* (billed sixth) who brings a compelling menace to the role of Gestapo official Brenner, Laughton's playing of Ivoni Haake is disappointing and lacks any real sense of malevolence or menace. In *So Ends Our Night*, von Stroheim first appears to great advantage early on during a police interrogation and provides the viewer with an immediate sense of intrigue and danger. By contrast, Laughton's Gestapo chief makes his screen debut in a brief hyper-real montage flashback depicting mental and physical interrogation. The scene, though mesmerizing, is too momentary and deflates the crucial entrance of the character later in the film. Similarly, unlike von Stroheim's violent and dramatic demise in *So Ends Our Night* (he is pushed over a flight of stairs and falls through a glass roof), Laughton's killing in *Arch of Triumph* is too restrained and lacks dramatic tension. Though this was due to the imposition of censorship strictures typical of the time, it does more broadly demonstrate the difficulties of translating a major novel successfully to the screen. Unlike *So Ends Our Night*, there is little humor on display with which to revitalize the flaccid narrative and stop it ossifying. Not even Laughton's cameo appearance achieved any significant level of inspiration, and while his performance may appear as a welcome respite from the torturous relationship of the two main protagonists, he merely "slums" his role. Laughton's portrayal of the Gestapo chief is delivered with similar facial tics as seen in his previous role of the judge in *The Paradine Case* and is reliant on heavy caricature. One is given to conjecture how the film would have turned out if it had been produced in France with Laughton among a native French cast and crew. Laughton speaking fluent French (something he was well able to do) would have been an intriguing proposition. As it is, the mismatch of personnel and material appears complete, with *Arch of Triumph* being a victim of its own high aspirations.

Critics were candid in their dismay. *Variety* (February 18, 1948) remarked, "Charles Laughton is rather wasted as a Nazi menace, obviously the victim of the cutting room shears...." The *Monthly Film Bulletin* (November 1948, Vol. 15, No. 179) registered similar disappointment in Laughton's role: "Charles Laughton gives a competent performance which falls far short of a former greatness." Bosley Crowther in the *New York Times* (April 21, 1948) found Laughton "absurd as the Nazi brute."

In 1984, the film was remade as a TV movie with Anthony Hopkins as Ravic and Lesley-Anne Down as Joan Madou. Donald Pleasence took on the role of Haake.

While *Arch of Triumph* remains watchable, it would be stretching credulity somewhat to describe it in the laudatory terms expressed in the theatrical trailer: "The most eagerly awaited screen event of our times." *Variety* (January 5, 1948) noted that the film grossed $1,700,000 in domestic rentals but did not cover its production costs. When all is said and done, the film is stymied by an overwritten and overelaborate script accompanied by a disproportionate unease due to miscasting. *Arch of Triumph* is an example of Laughton being caught out by censorial interference resulting in a severe editing of his characterization, lessening his role and weakening its impact. As *Focus: A Film Review* (April 1949) succinctly put it, "Charles Laughton ... deserves better material."

The Big Clock (1948)

Tagline: "Rock with Excitement Round...."[62]
U.S. (Paramount Pictures)

Laughton plays megalomaniac publisher tycoon Earl Janoth in John Farrow's consistently engaging Paramount thriller, *The Big Clock* (1948).

(1948) The Big Clock

Credits: Screenplay: Jonathan Latimer; Based on the Novel by Kenneth Fearing; Photography: John F. Seitz; Art Directors: Hans Dreier, Roland Anderson and Albert Nozaki; Special Photographic Effects: Gordon Jennings; Process Photography: Farciot Edouart; Set Decorators: Sam Comer and Ross Dowd; Music Score: Victor Young; Editorial Supervisor: Eda Warren; Costumes: Edith Head; Makeup Supervision: Wally Westmore; Sound Recording: Hugo Grenzbach and Gene Garvin; Assistant Director: William H. Coleman; Produced by Richard Maibaum; Directed by John Farrow; U.S. release: April 9, 1948; U.K. release: April 19, 1948; Genre: Crime–Film Noir; Black and White; Running Time: 95 minutes; DVD Region 1, Universal Home Entertainment, released July 2004; Blu-ray Region A and Region B, Arrow Academy, released May 2019; English subtitle captions for the deaf and hard of hearing are available on these discs.

Cast: Ray Milland (*George Stroud*); **Charles Laughton** (*Earl Janoth*); Maureen O'Sullivan (*Georgette Stroud*); George Macready (*Steve Hagen*); Rita Johnson (*Pauline York*); Elsa Lanchester (*Louise Patterson*); Harold Vermilyea (*Don Klausmeyer*); Dan Tobin (*Roy Cordette*); Henry Morgan (*Bill Womack*); Richard Webb (*Nat Sperling*); Elaine Riley (*Lily Gold*); Luis Van Rooten (*Edwin Orlin*); Lloyd Corrigan (*McKinley*); Frank Orth (*Burt*); Margaret Field (*Second Secretary*); Philip Van Zandt (*Sidney Kislav*); Henri Letondal (*Antique Dealer*); Douglas Spencer (*Bert Finch*); Bobby Watson (*Morton Spaulding*); B.G. Norman (*George Jr.*); Joey Ray (*Joe Talbot*); Frances Morris (*Grace Adams*); Charlie (*Harry Rosenthal*); Erno Verebes (*Waiter*); James Burke (*O'Brien*); Lucille Barkley (*Hatcheck Girl*); **Uncredited Cast**: Dick Anderson (*Clarinetist—Ernie Felice Quartet*); Ernie Felice (*Accordionist—Ernie Felice Quartet*); Dick Fisher (*Guitarist—Ernie Felice Quartet*); Chick Parnell (*Bassist—Ernie Felice Quartet*); Marlene Aames (*Rosa O'Flynn*); Eric Alden, Harry Anderson, Jim Drum, Ralph Dunn, Bob Kortman (*Guards*); Bea Allen (*Betty—Newsstand Operator*); Dorothy Barrett (*Secretary*); Brooks Benedict, Paul Bradley (*Men at Van Barth's*); Bill Burt, Jim Davies (*Bartenders*); James Carlisle (*Van Spove*); Lane Chandler (*Apartment House Doorman*); Bob Coleman (*Messenger*); Frances Conley (*Miss Conley—Secretary*); Mary Currier (*Ivy Temple*); Mary Donovan (*Woman in Conference Room*); Mike Donovan, Al Ferguson, Chuck Hamilton, Pat Lane, Max Wagner (*Guards at Janoth Building*); Lester Dorr (*Cabby*); Virginia Duffy (*Secretary*); Skippy Elliott (*Miss Blanchard—Hagan's Secretary*); Lee Emery, Wally Earl, Kathy Young (*Elevator Operators*); John Farrell (*Drunk*); Julia Faye (*Secretary*); Bess Flowers (*Stylist in Conference Room*); Robbie Franks (*Secretary*); Robert Riordan, Franklyn Farnum, John Sheehan, Richard Gordon, George Hoagland, Stuart Holmes

A final confrontation between George Stroud (Ray Milland; in foreground) and villain Earl Janoth (Laughton) during the climax of *The Big Clock* (1948).

(*Men in Identification Line*); Henry Guttman (*Man at Van Barth's*); Frank Hagney (*Ice Man*); Theresa Harris (*Daisy—Stroud's Maid*); Cliff Heard (*Cab Driver*); Len Hendry (*Bill Morgan*); Earle Hodgins (*Tour Guide at Janoth Building*); Fred Howard (*Baxter James*); Jerry James (*Man with Fish*); Richard Keene (*Hamburger Cook*); Lucy Knoch (*Secretary*); Norman Leavitt (*Tourist*); Lillian Lindsco (*Elevator Operator*); Jean Marshall (*Secretary*); Don McGill (*Kiska*); William Meader (*Man from Airways in Elevator*); Lee Miller (*Man from Airways in Elevator*); Hans Moebus (*Man at Van Barth's*); Darlene Mohlief (*Elevator Starter*); Sheila Raven (*Elevator Starter*); Bert Moorhouse (*Editor at Conference Table*); Noel Neill (*Elevator Operator*); Barry Norton (*Man at Van Barth's*); Judy Nugent (*Penelope Patterson*); Broderick O'Farrell (*Flavin*); Garry Owen (*Cab Driver*); Pepito Perez (*Head Waiter at Van Barth's*); Gordon Richards (*Warren Parks*); Robert Robertson (*Security Guard*); Ruth Roman (*Secretary at Meeting*); Helen Spring (*Woman*); Robert Stevenson (*Cab Driver*); Diane Stewart (*Girl*); Harland Tucker (*Seymour Roberts*); Tad Van Brunt (*Tony Watson*); Nicholas Vehr (*Doorman at Van Barth's*); Robert Wegner (*Man at Van Barth's*); Joe Whitehead (*Fisher*); Napoleon Whiting (*Bootblack*).

Working Title: *Judas Picture*

Synopsis: At night in the Janoth building in New York City, George Stroud, hiding from security guards, takes refuge inside the giant clock in the lobby. He thinks back on the previous 36 hours (now seen in flashbacks) when he was looking forward to his first vacation in several years. Stroud is told by boss Earl Janoth that his assistance is required on a missing persons case. When he refuses, Janoth dismisses him. To console himself, Stroud goes to a bar where he meets Janoth's mistress Pauline York. Stroud loses track of the time there so his wife Georgette decides to go on vacation without him. Stroud and Pauline hit various night spots, bars and an antique shop where he purchases an avant-garde painting and a sundial. Stroud ends up going to York's apartment, but seeing Janoth arriving she urges him to leave immediately. As he dashes out into the hall, Janoth catches a brief glimpse of him and does not recognize him. In Pauline's apartment, she and Janoth accuse one another of misbehavior. In a fit of rage, Janoth kills her. When Janoth confesses what he did to colleague Steve Hagen, Hagen offers to fix things so that the murder is blamed on the unidentified man. Stroud catches up with his wife on vacation and tells her he has been fired but leaves out his adventures with Pauline. He receives a phone call from Janoth, who rehires him to track down the mysterious man. Stroud soon realizes that *he* is the man Janoth is after. To Georgette's disappointment, Stroud reluctantly returns to his old job and lead the manhunt. This places Stroud in an impossible situation. Apart from appearing to lead the hunt, he has to prevent the team from realizing that he, Stroud, is the one they're seeking. He must also carry on his own investigation to prove Janoth was the real murderer. Several people who saw Stroud and Pauline are located and brought to the Janoth Building. They include Louise Patterson an eccentric artist. One of the witnesses spots Stroud at a distance and Janoth orders the building locked down. As the dragnet tightens, Stroud devises an elaborate subterfuge that involves having McKinley, an actor, pose as a police inspector. When Stroud confronts Hagen and Janoth, Hagen cracks and reveals Janoth is the killer. Janoth tries to escape in a private elevator only to find to his cost that the elevator is stuck between floors. Janoth plunges to his death down the shaft. Artist Louise Patterson recognizes McKinley as her long-lost husband. Stroud and Georgette embrace in happy relief.

Selected Dialogue:

JANOTH: "There are 2,081,376,000 seconds in the average man's life, each tick of the clock the beat of a heart, and yet you sit here uselessly ticking your lives away because certain members are not on schedule."

JANOTH: "We live in a dynamic age with dynamic competitors—radio, newspapers, newsreels—and we must anticipate trends before they are trends. We are, in effect, clairvoyants."

JANOTH: "On the fourth floor in the broom closet, a bulb has been burning for several days. Find the man responsible. Dock his pay."

JANOTH: "Do you know that in some countries, after a murderer confesses, the police let him run and shoot him in the back?"

Production Commentary: *The Big Clock* reunited Laughton with Ray Milland and Maureen O'Sullivan. In contrast to their previous cinematic encounter in *Payment

Deferred 16 years before, Milland was now at the top of his game, having scored commercially and critically with his dramatic role in the ground-breaking *The Lost Weekend* (Paramount, Billy Wilder, 1945). Under Wilder's hard-hitting direction, Milland's depiction of chronic alcoholic Don Birnam earned him an Oscar for Best Actor.

Milland and Laughton offer excellent performances as hero and villain in *The Big Clock*. The film benefits from director John Farrow who, like Laughton, was very exacting and challenging in his craft and artistry. Farrow's camera uses a succession of demanding long takes and the editing of the film is executed with symmetry and precision. His emphasis on command and control of all aspects of the production aligned with Laughton's artistic temperament based on assiduous motivation and pedantic preparation. Farrow directs with authority and brings momentum to Kenneth Fearing's original story. *The Big Clock* was remade as *No Way Out* (Orion, Roger Donaldson, 1987).

The saturnine character of Earl Janoth invites Laughton to give a splendid examination of megalomania. Laughton plays a grotesque villain, and he uses delicate physical gestures throughout the film to demonstrate this. Examples include touching his lip and moustache with his fingers, and perpetual blinking. These inflections are doubtless an amalgam of previous characterizations on stage and screen, but nonetheless effective for that.

Producer Richard Maibaum's greatest gift to cinema: In later years, he became synonymous with the James Bond franchise. There is enough Bond-style material on display in *The Big Clock* to invite the supposition that had Laughton lived, he would have been a prime candidate for casting as a Bond supervillain. The title role in *Dr. No* (United Artists/Eon, Terence Young, 1962) perhaps, or maybe Blofeld stroking a white feline in *You Only Live Twice* (United Artists/Eon, Lewis Gilbert, 1967). Laughton clearly had the capacity to understand and enact the mentality of the fictional supervillain, having impersonated very successfully successions of martinets, emperors, kings and other would-be rulers and figures of authority. Laughton's Janoth has many of the attributes of the later Bond villains. He is clearly a megalomaniac, whose lust for power and perfection are his undoing. His sybaritic lifestyle exudes perversity and ruthlessness as he undergoes steam baths and massages. Bill Womack, Janoth's silent masseur-bodyguard, also acts as Janoth's hit man and is played with assurance by Henry Morgan. This character is reminiscent of the unspeaking and lethal manservant Oddjob in *Goldfinger* (United Artists/Eon, Guy Hamilton, 1964).

Another supporting player in the *Big Clock* cast, Elsa Lanchester, brings a delightful screwball comedic approach as an idiosyncratic artist who confronts the commercial world with her surreal observations. Though the film is classed today as an example of film noir, *The Big Clock* is too diffused in plot content and narrative method to be passed off as such. As the narrative unfolds, it displays affiliations to other well-defined genres, such as the suspense thriller and screwball comedy. Its sense of hybridity is what makes the film so accessible and interesting to a contemporary audience.

Variety (January 22, 1947) noted that *The Big Clock* would begin shooting on February 177. *Variety* (March 26, 1947) also cited Laughton as "bicycling between Paramount's *The Big Clock* and Selznick's *The Paradine Case*." *Variety* (April 16, 1947) reported that former silent star and protégé of Cecil B. DeMille, Julia Faye, had signed on for an uncredited role of a secretary in the film. According to *Variety* (January 5, 1949), the film grossed a respectable $2,000,000 at the U.S. box office. *Modern Screen* (April 1950) revealed up-and-coming star Ruth Roman had been up for the lead opposite Laughton but was passed over.

At the time of its release, *The Big Clock* received mixed reviews. The *Manchester Guardian* (March 20, 1948) was complimentary about Laughton's performance: "It is a long time since Charles Laughton was seen in a good film, so it is worth recording that *The Big Clock* is an extremely entertaining melodrama, which is not spoilt by Mr. Laughton's overacting." *Variety* (February 18, 1948) thought Laughton's part had "a familiar touch. It's a fair enough approximation to Sydney Greenstreet's domineering tycoon in *The Hucksters* [MGM, Jack Conway, 1947] to make the similarity striking." *Focus: A Film*

Review (May 1948) admired Laughton's performance, noting that he "looks the part and plays the part with sinister realism." Bosley Crowther in the New York Times (April 22, 1948) opined, "Charles Laughton is characteristically odious as the sadistic publisher."

In *Boxoffice* (October 9, 1948), exhibitor D.W. Trisko of the Ritz Theatre, Jerome, Arizona, gave it a scathing assessment: "If Paramount makes many more of these, the company had better quit. The picture smells."

Following an unproductive period in his film career, Laughton makes a return, albeit briefly, to stellar form playing Earl Janoth. The following year, Paramount gathered some of the talent from *The Big Clock* and used it in *Alias Nick Beal* aka *The Contact Man*. This adaptation of the Faust legend was directed by John Farrow, scripted by Jonathan Latimer, and starred Ray Milland and George Macready. Sadly, Laughton was not included. Too bad, it could have been interesting.

The Girl from Manhattan (1948)

Tagline: "SHE'S A BIG CITY GAL WHO KNOWS HER WAY AROUND … around men!—What she does to the home talent isn't meant to keep the home fires burning … but it keeps the home boys learning…."[63]

U.S. (United Artists/Benedict Bogeaus)

Credits: Original Story and Screenplay: Howard Estabrook; Assistants to the Producer: Lewis J. Rachmil, James Stacy; Music: Heinz Roemheld; Production Associate: Arthur M. Landau; Photographer: Ernest Laszlo; Associate Director: Harold Godsoe; Art Director: Jerome Pycha Jr.; Musical Supervisor: David Chudnow; Musical Arrangements: Wally Heglin; Women's Wardrobe: Greta; Man's Wardrobe: Earl Moser; Makeup: Robert Cowan; Hair Stylist: Doris M. Harris; Special Effects: Lee Zavitz; Set Decorations: Robert Priestley; Sound Technician: John Carter; Editor: James E. Smith; Produced by Benedict Bogeaus; Directed by Alfred E. Green; U.S. release: October 1, 1948; U.K. release: October 25, 1948; Genre: Drama; Black and White; Running Time: 81 minutes; Not commercially available on digital media.

Cast: Dorothy Lamour (*Carol Maynard*); George Montgomery (*Reverend Tom Walker*); **Charles Laughton** (*The Bishop*); Ernest Truex (*Homer Purdy*); Hugh Herbert (*Aaron Goss*); Constance Collier (*Mrs. Brooke*); William Frawley (*Mr. Bernouti*); Sara Allgood (*Mrs. Beeler*); Frank Orth (*Oscar Newsome*); Howard Freeman (*Sam Griffin*); Raymond Largay (*Wilbur J. Birth*); George Chandler (*Monty*); Selmer Jackson (*Dr. Moseby*); Adeline de Walt Reynolds (*Old Woman*); Maurice Cass (*Mr. Merkle*); Eddy Waller (*Jim Allison*); **Uncredited Cast**: Marie Blake, Everett Glass (*Committee Members*).

Working Titles: *All's Well That Ends Well*; *All's Well*

Synopsis: Tom Walker, a former Yale football player, gives up a promising gridiron career to become a priest under the guidance of his father's former friend, the Bishop of Pittsfield. His former girlfriend Carol Maynard, now a famous Manhattan model, is also in Pittsfield visiting her uncle, Homer Purdy. Homer runs a boarding house and Carol has been sending him money to pay off the mortgage. But the money has instead been used to assist the eccentric assortment of endearing residents. Tom rents a room and his romance with Carol is soon revived. Tom finds himself being manipulated by the lay church leader and real estate dealer Wilbur J. Birch, who plans to sell the old church property and with it the piece of land occupied by Homer's boarding house. Tom refrains from informing Carol of her uncle's predicament. But Carol eventually finds out and Homer suggests that a rich friend, Jim Allison, will be able to help him out. But he soon collapses under the burden of his financial circumstances. During the night, Tom hears the voice of his father asking him to solve Homer's problems. The following day, Carol receives the $3000 required for full payment of the outstanding mortgage debt. On hearing this, Homer assumes that his friend Allison has come to his aid and regains his health. Birch refuses the money. Carol is at a low ebb when Mr. Bernouti, a hotelier, arrives and informs her Birch has plans to make a substantial profit from the sale of the church and boarding house real estate. Carol realizes Tom is innocent and decides to confront Birch: Either he cancels his crooked deal, or she will ensure his reputation will be ruined. Faced with this ultimatum, he agrees. Allison tells Carol and Homer he was not responsible for sending the $3000. Carol then realizes Tom had given them his life savings. In gratitude, she readily accepts Tom's proposal of marriage.

Selected Dialogue:

BISHOP: "The good book says nothing whatever against apple pie and cowden."

Production Commentary: This modest comedy drama was another independent production from the stable of Benedict Bogeaus. Laughton gives a nonchalant performance as the bishop who is partial to eating pie. The script is somewhat anemic and there are few redeeming moments of amusement or entertainment. The romantic leads, Dorothy Lamour and George Montgomery, seem wasted in this ill-advised attempt to tap into the popularity of such 1940s Hollywood religiosity as *Going My Way* (Paramount, Leo McCarey, 1944) and *The Bells of St. Mary's* (RKO, Leo McCarey, 1945). The distinguished supporting cast of Laughton, Constance Collier, William Frawley, Ernest Truex *et al.* take it all in their stride.

Because Laughton's is making a supporting role, he cannot be held responsible for the pedestrian nature of story and dialogue. Such a small part, though hardly challenging in terms of acting, was doubtless irresistible for his bank balance.

The industry trade press was underwhelmed by this slow and ponderous film. Typical was *Showmen's Trade Review* (September 18, 1948):

> *The Girl from Manhattan* can most likely get by in the average situation with the aid of a stronger feature, and average moviegoers may accept it with little complaint. However, it would be unwise to promise a lot in advance advertising.... The cast and title should prove good initial draws, but more or less adverse word-of-mouth may cancel their effectiveness once the engagement has gotten under way. Don't go overboard on this one.

The *Independent Exhibitors Film Bulletin* (September 27, 1948) was unsparing in its criticism:

> There will be few pictures this season to match it for sheer ineptitude. Patrons are going to be attracted by its strong cast and they will expect a certain amount of amusement, but they will find the proceedings about as funny as a crutch. *The Girl from Manhattan* just doesn't deliver the entertainment promised by its title and cast, and grosses will zoom down once the word gets around. Exhibitors would be wise to avoid it, but if they must play it, confine it to the lower half of the double bill.

Harrison's Reports (September 18, 1948) added further brickbats: "*The Girl from Manhattan* shapes up as so dull and tedious an entertainment that it will try the patience of most picture-goers. There is not one kind word that can be said for the production; the story is trite, the dialogue is inept, and the acting substandard." *Variety* (September 15, 1948) provided another nail in the coffin: "[It] is one of the weakest sisters out of Hollywood in some time.... [I]t's difficult to figure how a producer with the experience of Benedict Bogeaus could come up with so dull a production. It's probably one of those things that looked good on paper but just couldn't make out on the screen." The review also says that Laughton as the bishop "overacts."

One of the few reviews supportive of Laughton, if not the film, was in *Monthly Film Bulletin* (October 1948, Vol. 15, No. 178): "Except for a delightful cameo of the Bishop by Charles Laughton, this film has no outstanding qualities."

Given the mediocrity of the film's script, it is legitimate to absolve Laughton of blame by countering he was able to come up with something...if not exceptional or remarkable, then at least palatable. It's a somewhat parochial film produced for a target audience of the small-town American market. Today, its interest lies primarily with those who are seeking to view all of Laughton's extant films.

The Bribe (1949)

Tagline: "5 Great Stars in a Daring Drama of Love and Adventure!"[64]

U.S. (Metro-Goldwyn-Mayer)

Credits: Screenplay: Marguerite Roberts; Based on the Short Story by Frederick Nebel; Musical Score: Miklos Rozsa; Photography: Joseph Ruttenberg; Art Directors: Cedric Gibbons, Malcolm Brown; Editor: Gene Ruggiero; Song "Situation Wanted": Nacio Herb Brown and William Katz; Recording Director: Douglas Shearer; Set Decorator: Edwin B. Willis; Associate: Hugh Hunt; Special Effects: Warren Newcombe; A. Arnold Gillespie; Miss Gardner's Costumes: Irene; Hair Styles Designed by Sydney Guilaroff; Makeup Created by Jack Dawn; Produced by Pandro S. Berman; Directed by Robert Z. Leonard; U.S. release: February 3, 1949; U.K. release: June 27, 1949; Genre: Crime–Film Noir; Black and White; Running Time: 98 minutes; DVD from the Warner Archive Collection, released January 2010; no

English subtitle captions for the deaf and hard of hearing.

Cast: Robert Taylor (*Rigby*); Ava Gardner (*Elizabeth Hintten*); **Charles Laughton (*J.J. Bealer*)**; Vincent Price (*Carwood*); John Hodiak (*Tug Hintten*); Samuel S. Hinds (*Dr. Warren*); John Hoyt (*Gibbs*); Tito Renaldo (*Emilio Gomez*); Martin Garralaga (*Pablo Gomez*); **Uncredited Cast**: Fernando Alvarado (*Flute Player*); Robert Cabal, David Cota, Pepe Hernandez, Richard Lopez (*Bellboys*); Gene Coogan, Elias Gamboa (*Club Patrons*); Peter Cusanelli (*Rhumba Dancer*); Marcel De la Brosse, Albert Pollet (*French Tourists*); Joe Dominquez, Juan Duval (*Waiters*); Nacho Galindo (*Second Hotel Clerk*); Charles Gonzales (*Bouncer*); William Haade (*Walker*); Bob Lugo (*Peon*); Frank Mayo, Walter Merrill (*American Tourists*); Ernesto Morelli (*Bartender*); Phyllis Graffeo, Alex Montoya, George Navarro, Paul Regas, Florita Romero, Roque Ybarra (*Peons*); Mike Morelli (*Townsman*); Alberto Morin (*Jose—Waiter*); Alfonso Pedrosa (*Hotel Proprietor*); Julian Rivero (*Diego—Boatman*); Felipe Turich (*First Hotel Clerk*); Harry J. Vejar (*Indian Tourist*); Tony Roux (*Businessman*); Harry Johnson, Duke Johnson (*Jugglers*).

Synopsis: A storm sweeps over Carlotta, a town in the Los Tranos fishing resort off the Central American coast. Rigby, a cop turned government agent, sent by Washington to investigate a war surplus supply racket, smokes and drinks as he reflects anxiously on his current, somewhat precarious circumstances. On his typewriter is a wire addressed to his superior, Police Chief Gibbs, requesting that government operatives fly in as soon as weather permits and conduct a raid on the racketeers. He now thinks back to the start of his assignment. Posing as an American sportsman, he flies from Washington to the island. The passenger in the next seat is Carwood, a mine owner. On landing, Rigby sets out to track down two American suspects, Tug Hintten and his wife Elizabeth. As he sits alone at Pedro's, a nightclub, the lights darken and Elizabeth begins to sing a sultry torch song, "Situation Wanted." Rigby visits her in her dressing room; irritated at his impertinence, she leaves the room. Rigby notices a man loitering outside. Upon her return, she is soon joined by her alcoholic husband Tug, an ex-pilot and now nightclub owner. He is the worse for his habitual drinking and eventually collapses. During the next few days, Rigby adopts the role of a tourist keen on fishing. He charters a speedboat and begins to reconnoiter the islands around Los Tranos. He also makes discreet inquiries about Tug's movements. Rigby soon falls in love with Elizabeth. J.J. Bealer, a derelict who hangs around the waterfront, has been tailing Rigby. Bealer offers him $10,000 to leave town. Rigby continues to pursue the case by befriending Carwood, who is staying at the same hotel. They go fishing together. In an attempt to kill Rigby, Carwood only succeeds in killing a local, Emilio Gomez, who is mauled by a shark. At the club, Rigby finds Bealer upping his offer to $12,000. Rigby walks away in contempt. As Elizabeth nurses her ailing husband, Bealer offers her the chance to save him. Elizabeth decides to tie in with Bealer after she learns that Rigby is a federal operative who is there to apprehend her husband. She visits Rigby and drugs his drink. Before falling unconscious, he tells her his true feelings for her. As he lies unconscious, she expresses regret that their relationship

Laughton (left) as a dissolute go-between, J.J. Bealer, trying to bribe undercover agent Rigby played by Robert Taylor in *The Bribe* (1949).

has to end this way. Carwood pays off Tug, then suffocates him with a pillow when he threatens to talk. Elizabeth and Bealer return to the room and Carwood hides. Rigby regains consciousness and, thanks to the intervention of Emilio's father, is able to ring for help. Members of the smuggling gang are apprehended. Carwood and Bealer run into Rigby, who tries to arrest Carwood. He escapes amidst the revelry of a local fiesta and walks into the middle of a spectacular firework carnival. After exchange of a few shots, Rigby shoots and kills Carwood. His death leaves Rigby and Elizabeth free to resume their romantic affair. Bealer looks on with oily glee.

Vincent Price (left) as criminal mastermind Carwood cuts deals with Laughton as payoff man J.J. Bealer in *The Bribe* (1949).

Selected Dialogue:

BEALER: "Get smart, Mr. Rigby. Everybody grafts nowadays, that's the way people operate."

BEALER: "I got a good nose for a deal. I can smell one on this sofa."

BEALER: "My feet may hurt, but they ain't noisy."

Production Commentary: At the time of release, MGM's *The Bribe* had considerable marquee value. It was expected that the film would draw audiences because of its five-star cast and the high-gloss production values associated with MGM, the Tiffany of Hollywood studios. Yet although the film is proficient technically, with excellent translucent cinematography supplied by award-winning Joseph Ruttenberg and an evocative Miklós Rózsa score, in terms of entertainment it was felt to be only adequate.[65]

Producer Pandro S. Berman had helmed an earlier Robert Taylor vehicle: *Undercurrent* (MGM, Vincente Minnelli, 1946), the star's first since returning from active service in the Navy during World War II. Ava Gardner was being given the star build-up following several years at the studio spent doing walk-on parts. Her career took off rapidly when she appeared as the femme fatale Kitty Collins in *The Killers* (Universal, Robert Siodmak, 1946). *The Bribe* was based on a short story by the prolific Frederick Nebel, published in *Cosmopolitan* magazine in September 1947.

The plot of *The Bribe* does not bear close inspection. It lacks both plausibility and realism, its two protagonists are superficial, and dramatic situations often fail to develop into any real significance. The film scenario has little by way of surprise beyond showing the central character, a federal agent, has his principles and honor compromised by his affection for a café singer and his confrontations with a gallery of rogues. Taylor walks through the part wearily. However, there is the odd moment of intrigue such as the sequence in which the agent is almost mauled by a shark, and a climactic shootout between the hero and villain (Vincent Price) during an eye-catching display of pyrotechnics in the middle of a fiesta. It has been inferred by biographer Simon Callow and others that this impressive highpoint is attributable to Vincente Minnelli, who was drafted in to give the film some much needed élan. It certainly achieves a gaudy excess.

The film tackles a familiar theme, private emotions vs. public duty, and its tone is one of earnestness delivered without any major pretense or ironic humor. These attributes would come later when copious footage from the film was edited into the neo-noir *Dead Men Don't Wear Plaid* (Universal, Carl Reiner, 1982), a mixture of homage, pastiche and parody. Director Reiner used the exotic period ambience of *The Bribe* for the recreation of a "retro look" belonging to a narrative that is rich with comic borrowings, conjunctions, references and bricolage: vintage footage being integrated in a contemporary (if contrived) storyline immersed with subversion and subterfuge (traits common to the destabilizing universe found in film noir). A hybrid offshoot, noir came from a fusion (or some would say disconnect) of the legacy of World War II, the literary subgenre of hard-boiled crime fiction and an influx of émigré technical talent behind the camera.

The Bribe's production history can be traced: *Variety* (December 3, 1947) noted, "Pandro S. Berman draws producer reins on *The Bribe*...." *Box Office* (May 8, 1948) announced that Laughton would appear with Ava Gardner and Robert Taylor under Berman and director Robert Z. Leonard. Filming would start in early June. *Variety* (June 2, 1948) announced four productions to begin at Metro during June and July, beginning with *The Bribe*. (The others were *Little Women*, *Take Me Out to the Ball Game* and *Easter Parade*.) *Box Office* (June 12, 1948) announced that Joseph Ruttenberg had been assigned as chief cinematographer. *Variety* noted on June 23 that filming had commenced and added on June 30: "Metro signed Nacio Herb Brown and William Katz to do song number for Ava Gardner to warble in *The Bribe*." *Box Office* (July 24, 1948) announced actor Samuel S. Hinds had joined the cast. This would turn out to be Hinds' final screen appearance as he died on October 13 in Pasadena of pneumonia. *Variety* (December 8, 1948) announced that *The Bribe* was part of a package of 16 MGM films now completed.

Laughton, billed third after Taylor and Gardner, plays Bealer, an anxious weasel-like waterfront criminal. Bealer is unlike Walter Brennan's Eddie, the alcoholic, comic sidekick to Humphrey Bogart in *To Have and Have Not* (Warner Bros., Howard Hawks, 1944), and Laughton's previous waterfront degenerate, the redeemed Ginger Ted, in *Vessel of Wrath*. The character is neither burlesque in manner nor capable of redemption. He is, rather, a sleazy, grubby, small-time derelict, a fixer who connives to survive and mitigate the pain of his craven existence. Laughton scene-steals from the other actors throughout the film. Notwithstanding Ava Gardner's star femme fatale (she has none of the wild abandon of Rita Hayworth in *Gilda* or the insolence of Lauren Bacall in *To Have and Have Not*), Laughton's only competitor for attention is Vincent Price, whose drooping walk and camp overacting makes Laughton's tics seem all the more subtle. Their eyeballing, as they try to outdo the other during their scenes together, is a sight to behold. It is Laughton who appears on screen speaking the final words at the end of the picture: While Taylor and Gardner are in a romantic embrace, Laughton hovers on a staircase looking down at the couple. Stammering and coughing, he splutters a question asking the whereabouts of Carswell. Receiving no reply (the couple, locked in their smoldering clinch, are oblivious), he suggests that when Rigby "gets around to it," he might call up "a cop." This can be taken as just sly eccentric humor or an ironic barb on the traditional star fadeout.

The combination of Laughton and the high-tone gloss of this MGM mood piece—call it noir if you want—keeps you watching and perhaps from asking searching questions of the script which, as has already been implied, is somewhat schematic and deficient in several respects. Contemporary critical reaction was, on the whole, disdainful. *Focus: A Film Review* (June 1949) viewed the film with ennui: "The story follows a well-worn formula…. The stock situations are played out with wearying inevitability. There is nothing original here." The critic then turns his attention to Laughton: "Charles Laughton now gives us extracts from his repertory. A wink, a grimace, a leer, a shuffle, and that's his latest character that was. How Hollywood has desiccated this great actor!" *Variety* (February 9, 1949) viewed Laughton's role in a more sanguine light: "Laughton has the meatiest role and socks it home. He's a broken-down beachcomber type with aching feet, sly and sleazy with a slightly humorous shading." Cynics might say it's just another retread of Ginger Ted with attitude, but Laughton does his best to infuse a psychological depth to his character, that in itself does not conceal the artificiality of the plot. *Variety* also noted,

118 (1949) The Man on the Eiffel Tower

"Robert Z. Leonard's direction does a good pacing job on the story and keeps its action hard and brittle."

Because MGM was building the career of their latest star Ava Gardner, the studio offered *The Bribe* to the experienced Leonard. It was something of a change of pace for the stolid style of Leonard, who was usually to be found directing projects passed over by the discerning George Cukor or substituting for the likes of prolific house director Richard Thorpe. As it is, Leonard turns in a satisfactory film but nothing more than that. There is no real sight of the divine spark in its 98 minutes. All of which is superfluous because, as already indicated, the film has been given retro cult status due to its extensive inclusion in *Dead Men Don't Wear Plaid*. The private detective, played in that film by comedian Steve Martin, is named Rigby and Laughton's character is addressed as "The Fat One Who Sweats a Lot."

The Bribe is a minor film in which there is less than meets the eye, but it does contain a noteworthy Laughton performance with its emphasis on the aging and degenerating process of body and psyche accompanied by a yearning to survive in whatever debased form that takes. Now in late middle age, Laughton's phobia about his physique provided the key for his characterization of J.J. Bealer, Laughton being one of the few actors who could make a discussion of his feet x-rays sound interesting!

The Man on the Eiffel Tower (1949)

Tagline: "PARIS ... Gay, Alluring ... Masking a Strange Adventure!"[66]

U.S./France (RKO Radio Pictures/A&T Film Productions)

Credits: Screenplay: Harry Brown; From the story "Battle of Nerves" by Georges Simenon; Photography: Stanley Cortez; Associate: Tony Braun; Music: Michel Michelet; Musical Director: C. Bakaleinkoff; Assistant to Producer: Ruby Rosenberg; Assistant Director: Mary Evans; Editor: Louis H. Sackin; Art Director: Rene Renoux; Recorder: Josh Westmoreland; Gowns for Miss Roc and Miss Wallace: Robert Piguet and Jacques Griffe; Hats for Miss Roc and Miss Wallace: Paulette; Produced by Irving Allen; Directed by Burgess Meredith; U.S. release: February 4, 1950; Genre: Crime; Ansco Color; Running Time: 97 minutes; DVD Region 1 Kino Video, released September 2008; DVD Region 2 Odeon Cinema released March 2012; no English subtitle captions for the deaf and hard of hearing.

Cast: Charles Laughton (*Inspector Maigret*); Franchot Tone (*Johann Radek*); Burgess Meredith (*Joseph Huertin*); Robert Hutton (*Bill Kirby*); Jean Wallace (*Edna Warren*); Patricia Roc (*Helen Kirby*); Belita (*Gisella*); George Thorpe (*Comelieu*); William Phipps (*Janvier*); William Cottrell (*Moers*); Chaz Chase (*Waiter*); Wilfrid Hyde White (*Professor Grollet*); **Uncredited Cast**: Howard Vernon (*Inspector*).

Synopsis: In a Parisian café, an impoverished medical student, Johann Radek, overhears American Bill Kirby say that he would pay a million francs to have his elderly aunt murdered. Radek decides to offer his services. He leaves a cryptic note at Bill's feet. Bill responds to by rolling a pair of dice, which come up "aces." During the night, a myopic knife grinder, Joseph Huertin, breaks into the home of Bill's aunt only to find the elderly woman and her maid have been murdered. Terrified, Huertin falls and his glasses drop to the floor. The attacker crushes the spectacles with his foot. Outside, the short-sighted Huertin meets his accomplice, Johann Radek.

Laughton as the thoughtful Inspector Jules Maigret, complete with smoking pipe, in *The Man on the Eiffel Tower* (1949).

As Radek escorts him home, he tells Huertin that he is certain to be arrested for the murders. The next day, Inspector Maigret arrests Huertin using his broken glasses as evidence. Maigret is convinced that Huertin did not act alone but is unable to get the name of his accomplice. He therefore allows Huertin to escape and has a plainclothes detective follow him. The following morning, a letter appears in the newspaper, claiming that Huertin had been freed by the police authorities in desperation. Huertin disappears and Maigret's superior questions his approach to the case. Maigret responds by sending the original letter for forensic examination. There is a coffee stain on the note. Maigret goes to the café where Bill received the note and waits. He sees Huertin at the window looking at Radek, who is eating and drinking. Radek decides Maigret is a policeman and, to frighten Huertin away, decides to get himself arrested. Under questioning, Radek discloses that he had studied medicine while being supported by his mother. Maigret then interviews one of Radek's professors and is informed that Radek is bipolar, talented but unstable. Radek is released but evades the plainclothesmen who follow him. He reaches the home of his mother, who turns out to be very much alive. She agrees to house Huertin, and Radek orders him to remain in the cellar. Maigret obtains the serial numbers of bank notes that Bill receives at his hotel and later finds Radek at the café. Feeling himself superior to the detective, Radek invites Maigret to lunch at the Eiffel Tower. An elated Radek insists on paying for the meal with Bill's money and declares the police investigation incompetent. Radek then contacts Bill, telling him the police are to reopen the case and will search for the murder weapon, a knife with fingerprints. He convinces the American to look for the weapon himself. Maigret turns up at the Henderson house to find Bill shot, an apparent suicide. The police arrive at Radek's mother's house in time to stop Huertin from hanging himself. Radek, unaware of Huertin's capture, continues to provoke Maigret, and as he is shadowed by the detective, he writes threatening letters. At the Henderson house, Maigret has Huertin confront the psychopath, and Radek is identified as his double-crossing accomplice. Maigret also informs Radek that his threatening letters have been intercepted and their recipients are assisting police. Radek escapes to the Eiffel Tower where he is pursued to the top by Huertin and the police. He considers jumping from the top, but then turns himself in. Now vindicated, Huertin is reunited with his repentant wife Gisella. Radek is last seen facing execution by guillotine.

Production Commentary: Laughton's performance as Inspector Maigret in *The Man on the Eiffel Tower* is somewhat subdued and introverted. As usual, he was trying to discover the key to the role. He also had the added distraction of being immersed in matters behind the cameras. The offer to return to postwar Paris and film on location enticed Laughton, but he found the designated director, Irving Allen, unbearable. Co-star–producer Franchot Tone stepped in with a solution: Directorial tasks were delegated to various stars of the film, including Tone, Laughton and Burgess Meredith, who has his name as director on the credits. It is not clear who directed which scenes, but exposure to the directorial process stimulated Laughton's quest for perfection in matters beyond his role as Maigret. He spent a great deal of time coaching the former Olympic figure skater turned actress Belita in matters of dress and acting technique. Laughton's biographer Simon Callow suggests that the arrangement for "group direction" was for Meredith to direct all the scenes he wasn't in with the same applying to Laughton, and anything left over assigned to Tone. It is suggested that Laughton directed the opening and closing scenes (Callow: 202). The opening scenes are notable for their display of pace and suspense, qualities missing from the rest of the film, and the chase at the finale is certainly well staged.

There are many distractions (including Belita) throughout the film, but Laughton's performance isn't among them. Because the character of Maigret is constantly thinking ahead, Laughton plays the role close to the chest. The film's production history bears greater examination than Laughton's performance. *The Man on the Eiffel Tower* was an early example of an independent production produced in Europe. It was the brainchild of Irving Allen and Tone, who formed a production company, A&T Film

(1949) The Man on the Eiffel Tower

Production. Together the pair had purchased Georges Simenon's mystery thriller. Production began during June 1948. All the exteriors were filmed on location in Paris with the cooperation of police authorities. Tone not only starred in the film but was principal producer. During July 1948, it was announced that Charles Laughton and Peter Lorre were also to be cast. A French company, Safia Films, would also be involved. There would be English and French versions with Safia Films arranging distribution in Europe and the United Kingdom, while Allen would make distribution arrangements in the U.S. During August 1948, William Phipps was announced as cast for a leading role. On September 20, 1948, the film started production and it was announced that it would be released by MGM. The six-week shoot was a difficult one. At one stage, a power shortage at the Billancourt Studio halted production for two days. French film technicians approved a resolution which insisted that the national government protect the film industry against the influx of foreign producers, despite the fact that filmmakers from abroad paid higher wages. Studio space in two Paris districts was used so that if power went off in one section, shooting could continue in the other. This helped to bring the film in for under $1,000,000. The budget would have cost up to $2,500,000 if it had been shot in the U.S. Irving Allen felt the authentic locations more than offset the disadvantages. The use of Ansco Color also saved up to 50 percent compared to Technicolor. It required no special camera, and rushes could be inspected 24 hours after shooting. Unfortunately, the processing facilities in Paris proved inadequate, but good service was obtained by shipping film by air to Metro-Goldwyn-Mayer's Ansco lab in Hollywood. By February 1949, Tone was in New York to arrange a releasing deal for the completed film. *Eiffel Tower* ended up released by RKO, not MGM. It was announced that another Ansco Color film, *The Man from Monte Carlo*, to be filmed in Monte Carlo, would be Tone's company's next production. (The first Ansco Color 35mm release won an Academy Award: It was a two-reel short released through Monogram, *Climbing the Matterhorn*, shot in 1946 by Irving Allen while he was producing a feature in Switzerland. In 1947, producer-director Allen's Florida-made *16 Fathoms Deep* was a feature made in Ansco Color, also released through Monogram.)

The Man on the Eiffel Tower was based on Georges Simenon's 1931 novel *La Tête d'un homme*, also known as *A Man's Head*. It was translated and published in English in 1939 under the title *A Battle of Nerves*. The novel had already been filmed before (1933) under its original title by veteran director Julien Duvivier (1896–1967).[67] Duvivier's approach to the 1933 version was radical and innovative. He decided to divulge the identity of the killer very early on in the narrative. Instead of standard linear exposition, he concentrated on the psychological drives and motives of the central characters and allowed photographer Armand Thirard's camera to become extremely mobile, subjective and probing. Similarly, the sound also has a surreal quality, revealing a state of mind and mood. *La Tête d'un homme* possesses a sense of intrigue and repeatability which *The Man on the Eiffel Tower* doesn't come close to. Hollywood cameraman Stanley Cortez found conditions on *Eiffel Tower* "weird." He recalled,

> We climbed the Eiffel Tower girder by girder, and at one stage Franchot Tone actually risked his life. To get out of the lens for one particular shot, he had to walk behind a railing onto a tiny narrow ledge with a drop of about 100 feet below him. He had to hang at one stage by his fingers so that he wouldn't be in a particular shot. He was very brave. The film was released on Ansco Reversal film, and it looked odd. It went through nine emulsions, and I was none too pleased [Higham: 110].

Working at the two studios used in the film's production, Billancourt and Joinville, was challenging for the Hollywood d.p. As he explained in *American Cinematographer* (February 1949), "The two studios which we used ... had been occupied by the Germans during the war. When they retreated, they sacked both studios of every available piece of equipment, leaving only the bare walls. It has been a heartbreaking job ever since for the gallant French technicians who are trying to refurbish their studios with the modern equipment necessary to full-scale motion picture production." He had to approach *Eiffel Tower* "cold," which is to say, without shooting tests to check for lighting and makeup. At that time, there were no Ansco laboratories in Europe. This meant a delay the company could ill afford because any tests had to be sent back to the U.S. for developing and printing.

Despite all these difficulties, Cortez managed to complete as many as 17 setups on some days. Burgess Meredith told interviewer Allen Eyles for *Focus on Film* (April 1979) that Franchot Tone had to secure the rights from author Georges Simenon. This came with the stipulation that after 15 years Simenon could revoke the rights. After 15 years, the film vanished. For many years, the film circulated in either black and white or poor color copies. When the UCLA Film and Television Archive undertook a restoration of the film, it was found that "no original elements exist today. The film has been preserved from two worn and scratched nitrate projection prints, the only 35mm color copies known to survive."[68]

The critics gave the film a mixed reception. The Catholic Film Institute periodical *Focus: A Film Review* (January 1951) did not pull its punches: "Here is a sad waste of talent. I fear that, like me, you will be unmoved until towards the end of the film. Not even the city of Paris, listed as a star and appearing as frequently as the others, seems to be giving its best. The film is not contemptible, but it misfires and is hardly above second feature standard." *Film Bulletin* (February 13, 1950) quoted Archer Winsten of the *New York Post*: "Has a tendency to lag behind its audience and anyway the audience doesn't care too much what happens.... Doesn't amount to much more than a color travelogue of Paris with familiar actors' faces doing a foreground story in accompaniment." in its own review (January 2, 1950), *Film Bulletin* rated it as a "tense thriller should be fair grosser." It went on to suggest that, "as [a] dualler," it should be "coupled with a comedy or musical feature." It also asserted, "[I]t should attract slightly above average grosses, although it will require support in most theaters." *Screenland* (February 1950) was succinct and positive: "Definitely a superior mystery." The *New York Times* (January 30, 1950) said of Laughton's performance, "[His] Maigret is a corpulent, sly, pipe-smoking sleuth complete with sweeping moustaches and all the answers, whose noted acting mannerisms are not hidden by makeup or locale."

Despite the lukewarm reception given to the film and Laughton's role, this project paid dividends for his future career. He established rapports with both Burgess Meredith, who he would continue to work with both on screen and stage, and Stanley Cortez, whose versatility and tenacity were put to vital use for the distinctive black-and-white cinematography of the astonishing *The Night of the Hunter* six years later.

The Blue Veil (1951)

Tagline: "The Blue Veil or the Wedding Veil ... which should she choose?"[69]

U.S. (RKO Radio Pictures/Krasna Productions)

Credits: Screenplay: Norman Corwin; Story: François Campaux; Music: Franz Waxman; Photography: Franz Planer; Art Directors: Albert D'Agostino, Carroll Clark; Musical Director: C. Bakaleinikoff; Editor: George J. Amy; Set Decorators: Darrell Silvera, Al Orenbach; Sound: Jean L. Speak, Clem Portman; Gowns: Milo Anderson; Creation of Miss Wyman's Makeup and Hair Styles: Perc Westmore; Associate Producer:

Laughton as a widowed corset manufacturer shows his wares to Vivian Vance (left) and Jane Wyman in *The Blue Veil* (1951)

(1951) *The Blue Veil*

Raymond Hakim; Produced by Jerry Wald and Norman Krasna; Directed by Curtis Bernhardt; U.S. release: October 26, 1951; Genre: Drama; Black and White; Running Time: 113 minutes; 35mm Print stored at the Library of Congress; Not commercially available on digital media.

Cast: Jane Wyman (*Louise Mason*); **Charles Laughton** (*Frederick K. Begley*); Joan Blondell (*Annie Rawlins*); Richard Carlson (*Jerry Kean*); Agnes Moorehead (*Fleur Palfrey*); Don Taylor (*Dr. Robbie Taylor*); Audrey Totter (*Helen Williams Hall*); Cyril Cusack (*Frank Hutchins*); Everett Sloane (*District Attorney*); Natalie Wood (*Stephanie Rawlins*); Warner Anderson (*Bill Parker*); Alan Napier (*Professor George Carter*); Harry Morgan (*Charles Hall*); Vivian Vance (*Alicia*); Les Tremayne (*Joplin*); John Ridgely (*Doctor*); Dan O'Herlihy (*Hugh Williams*); Carleton G. Young (*Henry Palfrey*); Dan Seymour (*Pelt*); **Uncredited Cast**: Lillian Albertson (*Mrs. Lipscott*); James Anderson (*Jim Tappan*); Charles Anthony (*Fred Begley Jr. as a Baby*); Genevieve Bell (*Head Nurse*); Lovyss Bradley (*Beverly*); Jack Chefe (*Cousin*); Allison Daniell (*Sue*); Frank Gerstle (*Doctor*); Jo Gilbert (*Miss Dunlop*); Lisa Golm (*Elsa*); James Griffith (*Joplin's Agent*); Joy Hallward (*Miss Golub*); Kenneth Harmon (*LouLou's Baby*); Kristine Harmon (*LouLou's Baby*); Jimmy Hawkins (*Tommy*); Jimmy Hunt (*Boy in Shop*); Patricia Joiner (*Phyllis*); Hazel Keener (*Nurse*); Roberta Lee (*Actress*); Edith Leslie (*Gussie*); Jane Liddell (*Denis' Wife*); Muriel Maddox (*Mrs. Tappan*); Lewis Martin (*Archbishop*); Patrick Michael McDonald (*Fred Begley Jr. as a Baby*); Mira McKinney (*Customer*); Torben Meyer (*Photographer*); Anne Moore (*Sarah*); Robert Nichols (*Fred Begley Jr.*); Karen Norris (*Jane Palfrey*); Richard Norris (*Denis*); Frank O'Connor (*Train Conductor*); Ruth Packard (*Sue's Mother*); Richard Reeves (*Detective*); Sammy Shack (*Cabbie*); Kathryn Sheldon (*Mrs. Chalmers*); Miles Shepard (*Guard*); Harry Strang (*Traffic Cop*); Sylvia Simms (*Miss Quimby*); Irene Vernon (*Adult Stephanie*); Mack Williams (*Detective*).

Awards: Academy Award Nomination: Best Actress in a Leading Role: Jane Wyman.

Academy Award Nomination: Best Actress in a Supporting Role: Joan Blondell.

Synopsis: Young widow Louise Mason, who lost her only child, decides to offer her services as a nanny to a local employment agency. The stories unfold of the many children (and their parents) she has reared in various households. First is widower Frederick Begley, a corset manufacturer with an infant son. He becomes fond of Louise and soon decides to keep her on a permanent basis. When he plucks up the courage to make a proposal of marriage, she turns him down, and explains that the love of her children must prevail above everything. Stung by this rebuff, he finds emotional security in his secretary, who becomes the second Mrs. Begley. Following their return from a European honeymoon, the new Mrs. Begley makes it plain to Louise that she (Mrs. Begley) will now be looking after the welfare of the child. So reluctantly Louise bids the Begleys adieu. Her second employers: a wealthy couple who have two children (a young son and an older brother who is tutored by a young and ambitious teacher). Louise and the teacher becomes friendly, and when he secures a teaching post overseas, he asks Louise to marry him. She accepts. But the teacher becomes hesitant about their future together and Louise decides such procrastination in their relationship does not bode well and breaks off the engagement. Louise returns to her work and is given charge of an adolescent girl, the daughter of a singer. The singer places her career above all else and fails to care for her daughter. When she misses the girl's confirmation at school, the girl introduces Louise to the other pupils as her mother. At this point Louise decides it is time to quit her position, but not before telling the singer about her lack of responsibility. On the eve of World War II, Louise begins looking after the welfare of the son of a young couple. When war is declared and the husband is injured in Europe, the young wife leaves the son in the care of Louise while she goes to her husband. Several years pass and she does not return and the money she had been sending for her son's care stops. Despite hardship, Louise continues to take care of the boy, who she loves dearly. Then, unexpectedly a letter arrives informing Louise that the mother has remarried and will be returning to New York to claim her son. Fearful of what the future may hold for the boy, Louise flees to Florida, but is soon apprehended. Although sympathetic, the district attorney is duty bound to return the boy to his natural mother. By now elderly and poor, Louise decides to return to the employment agency, but is informed that she is now too old to be a nanny. Instead, she takes a job in an elementary school so she can continue to look after children. She visits an optician to check on her failing eyesight and finds the optician was one of the many children she had nursed. She shows him photographs of her "children." Moved by her circumstances, he invites her to dinner the following week. When she arrives, she is amazed to find her former charges and their spouses have been invited as well. The optician introduces Louise to his two young children and tells her she will be their new nanny.

Selected Dialogue:

BEGLEY: "I'm a man of some standing in the community. I own a big concern; it's the fourth largest corset house in the East. I have the good will of my employees; most of the good things in life I have at my beck and call."

Production Commentary: There was a two-year gap in Laughton's film career which was filled by commitments to the theater and particularly his touring production *Don Juan in Hell*. This hiatus was broken by an offer from the multi-talented Norman Corwin. Corwin's stellar career in American radio had come to a sudden halt: He was ousted from the industry due to being blacklisted for expressing leftist views.

The Blue Veil is a remake of a French original, *Le Voile Bleu* (Compagnie Générale Cinématographique, Jean Stelli, 1942) with Gaby Morlay. Due to rights issues, the remake is all but forgotten today, which is a pity. Of RKO's 38 releases during 1951, *The Blue Veil* was a solid box office winner, bringing in a healthy $3,550,000 in rentals and $450,000 in profits for the studio.[70] The film achieves a delicate balancing act of staying on the right side of sentimentality without tipping over into something maudlin and unpalatable. The title refers to the traditional dress worn by governesses.

Laughton appears in the first of four vignettes that structure the film narrative. In a space of just a few minutes, he brings high comedy down to earth in a touching portrait of a lonely widower who is rejected by the one he adores.

The public flocked to see the film even after the critical reaction was distinctly lukewarm. *Focus: A Film Review (1950–1951)* (December 1951) came up with a droll assessment of Laughton's performance: "[He] is somewhat too reminiscent of the doting Henry VIII."

This little-discussed film demonstrates yet again Laughton's versatility and delicacy in bringing to the fore all the necessary attributes to shape a role into something beyond that stated in the script. There is a certain toughness and rigor in delivering what is essentially a performance of compression. He segues from farcical comedy to poignant tragedy in a relatively short period of time and never misses a beat. All the energy and poignancy are up there on the screen and executed on point. To see Laughton at work in this movie is to watch a master class of acting technique.

The Strange Door (1951)

Tagline: "Enter This Door at Your Peril ... For in This Gloomy Castle ... Live Horror and Fear!"[71]

U.S. (Universal-International)

Credits: Screenplay: Jerry Sackheim; Based on Robert Louis Stevenson's story "The Sire de Maletroit's Door"; Photography: Irving Glassberg; Art Directors: Bernard Herzbrun, Eric Orbom; Set Decorators: Russell A. Gausman, Julia Heron; Sound: Leslie I. Carey, Glenn E. Anderson; Musical

Excess abounds as Laughton dines on ham while playing crazed French nobleman, Sire Alan de Maletroit in *The Strange Door* (1951).

(1951) The Strange Door

Director: Joseph Gershenson; Editor: Edward Curtiss; Costumes: Rosemary Odell; Hair Stylist: Joan St. Oegger; Makeup: Bud Westmore; Produced by Ted Richmond; Directed by Joseph Pevney; U.S. release: October 30, 1951; Genre: Horror; Black and White; Running Time: 81 minutes; DVD Region 1, *The Boris Karloff Collection* box set in The Universal Franchise Collection, released September 2006; Blu-ray Region A, Kino Lorber, released April 2019; English subtitle captions for the deaf and hard of hearing are available on these discs.

Cast: **Charles Laughton** (*Sire Alan de Maletroit*); Boris Karloff (*Voltan*); Sally Forrest (*Blanche de Maletroit*); Richard Stapley (*Denis de Beaulieu*); William Cottrell (*Corbeau*); Alan Napier (*Count Grassin*); Morgan Farley (*Rinville*); Paul Cavanagh (*Edmond de Maletroit*); Michael Pate (*Talon*); **Uncredited Cast**: George Bruggeman, Forest Burns, Stanley Mann (*Servants*); Monique Chantal, Tao Porchon (*Barmaids*); Jack Chefe, Barry Norton, Albert Petit, Joe Phillips (*Townsmen*); Harry Cording (*Guard*); Herbert Evans (*Clergyman*); George Calliga, Franklyn Farnum, Joe Gilbert, Forbes Murray, Frank O'Connor. Scott Seaton, Hal Taggart, Elinor Vanderveer (*Wedding Guests*); Michael Hadlow (*Flunkey*); Charles Horvath (*Turec*); Claudia Jordon (*Singer*); George Kirby (*Cook*); Keith McConnell (*Courier*); Jennings Miles (*Coachman*); William H. O'Brien (*Bartender*); Eddie Parker (*Moret*); Bruce Riley (*Footman*); Patrick Whyte (*Butcher*); Sailor Vincent (*Stunt Double for Charles Laughton*); Don Turner (*Stunt Double for Boris Karloff*).

Working Title: *The Door*

Synopsis: In eighteenth-century France, nobleman Alan de Maletroit uses a past family quarrel as a pretext to exact a crazed revenge on members of his own family. When a woman he adored deserts him in favor of his brother Edmond, and then dies in childbirth, he maliciously imprisons his brother. He now raises their surviving daughter Blanche, who is unaware that her father is a prisoner beneath their chateau. As Blanche is about to come of age, de Maletroit decides to exact further revenge by marrying her off to an irresponsible wastrel, Denis de Beaulieu. Via an elaborate stratagem, de Maletroit succeeds in luring de Beaulieu to his chateau by framing him for murder at a tavern. However, Blanche and Denis fall in love before they are forced to marry. Following the marriage ceremony, they are imprisoned in a dungeon cell with Blanche's father. De Maletroit delights in informing his prisoners that they are all to be crushed to death by slowly encroaching walls in their cell. Voltan, a servant faithful to Blanche, decides to rescue the prisoners from agonizing death. Despite receiving wounds from gunshots and a knife, Voltan is able to acquire keys to the cell and throw them on the floor near the door before he dies. Denis manages to drag the keys to make good their escape. Blanche and her father Edmond reunite, and Edmond gives his blessing as Blanche and Denis embrace.

Selected Dialogue:

DE MALETROIT: "Life hangs by a slender thread."

DE MALETROIT: "In my secluded dominion, villainy binds men together."

DE MALETROIT: "I'm in the mood for relaxation. Let's visit the dungeons."

Production Commentary: There are two salient aspects to Laughton's appearance in *The Strange Door*. First, he is unashamedly over the top, but that is not by itself a major fault. Second, it doesn't take too long to realize that Laughton and Boris Karloff hardly appear together in the film. If we examine how Laughton and Karloff respond to each other when they *are* briefly on screen together, it's as though they're acting in separate rooms. Laughton's name appears above Karloff's in the credits. Laughton was paid $25,000 while Karloff was paid $6000. The rumor that Laughton actively disliked Karloff appears to emanate from actor Raymond Massey, who worked with both in *The Old Dark House*. This rumor has been disputed by Laughton confidant William Phipps (1922–2018).

If Laughton gave anyone a tough time, it was young British actor Richard Stapley. Initially, Laughton was aloof and unfriendly to Stapley, but in time he was impressed by Stapley's abilities and dedication to his work. Director Pevney found Laughton to be "a great charmer and a great raconteur" (Weaver: 19). Produced under the aegis of Universal-International, *The Strange Door* is a throwback to the original horror cycle spawned by Universal during the 1930s and 1940s. The source for this piece of Grand Guignol was a short story, "The Sire de Maletroit's Door," written by Robert Louis Stevenson in 1878. Historian Tom Weaver has suggested that *Strange Door* screenwriter Jerry Sackheim took the opportunity to interpolate elements from a previous Universal horror film, *The Raven* (Lew Landers, 1935). There are incidental plot similarities such as the hero and heroine nearly being crushed to death by moving walls, and the villain crushed to death instead by this fiendish device. The Karloff character, an unenthusiastic henchman, becomes a reluctant hero and saves the heroine from a fate worse than death, but in doing so he sustains fatal injuries. William Cottrell, an associate of Laughton, appears as Corbeau, which is French for raven.[72] Under the well-planned economy of Joseph Pevney's direction, élan and pace are brought to bear on the material, which however contrived proved not too intractable in delivering an entertaining package.

Director Pevney recalled that the studio thought they were making a horror film, but Laughton had other ideas. He was about to take his stage production of *Don Juan in Hell* on the road and decided he would have fun, and he delivered a wildly camp performance which director Pevney did little to discourage. Laughton in one scene spreads himself on a desk and then simpers for the camera in the fashion of his Dr. Moreau in *Island of Lost Souls* nearly 20 years before. In another scene he parodies his famous eating scene in *The Private Life of Henry VIII*. He is seen slobbering and gorging on food and throwing a chicken bone to Michael Pate. Shooting began on May 15, 1951, on an 18-day schedule, and wrapped on June 5, 1951. The climax where Laughton's character falls through a wooden railing and lands in a stream where his body is caught in the gears of a waterwheel recalls Laughton's equally dramatic death by water in *Devil and the Deep*. Laughton now had a stunt double to spare him the discomfort of simulating drowning.

For Laughton, the film served its purpose of providing ready money and media exposure for the Bible reading and theatrical tours with which he was involved in this period of his career. Critical reaction to *The Strange Door* was one of disappointment given the appearance of two senior actors associated with the horror genre. *Film Bulletin* (November 5, 1951) wrote, "Charles Laughton overplays in his usual forthright fashion, but the old tricks don't work under the unhappy circumstances." The *New York Times* (December 10, 1951) found *The Strange Door* "more ludicrous than chilling." However, the *Monthly Film Bulletin* (December 1951, Vol. 18, No. 215) offered an explanation for Laughton's descent into mugging: "Charles Laughton appears to overact—perhaps to assure us of the Comte's insanity." *Variety* (October 31, 1951) was alone in seeing potential in this minor horror yarn: "There are good elements of suspense and characterization in this celluloid adaptation of a Robert Louis Stevenson Story." It went on to favor Laughton despite his hamming of the role: "As the master fiend, Laughton is well cast. He revels in his lines and leers at his victims almost to the point of overplaying."

The Strange Door was conceived as a low-budget programmer designed to play the top half of a double-bill and when later reissued played the bottom half of a double-bill.[73] A superficial film certainly, but Laughton's barnstorming act is infectious and he has a rare old time chewing the scenery, even at the expense of the other players. As the film is otherwise directed in a professional and stimulating fashion and, arguably, topped with an indulgent (if irresistible) central performance, you might care to overlook its obvious deficiencies. If you are prepared to do so, then you may find yourself being delighted by the sheer fun of its outrages and excesses.

O. Henry's Full House (1952)

Tagline: "12 Great Stars! 5 Great Directors! 5 Great Writers! In One Big Motion Picture"[74]

U.S. (Twentieth Century–Fox)

Credits: Screenplay (a multi-story film): Richard Breen: "The Clarion Call"; Walter Bullock: "The Gift of the Magi"; Ivan Goff: "The Last Leaf"; Ben Roberts: "The Last Leaf"; Lamar Trotti: "The Cop and the Anthem"; Music: Alfred Newman; Vocal Direction: Ken Darby; Orchestrator: Edward B. Powell; Narration by John Steinbeck; Produced by Andre Hakim; Directors: Henry Hathaway: "The Clarion Call"; Howard Hawks: "The Ransom of Red Chief"; Henry King: "The Gift of the Magi"; Henry Koster: "The Cop and the Anthem"; Jean Negulesco: "The Last Leaf"; **Uncredited Technical Credits**: Screenplay: "Ransom of Red Chief": Ben Hecht, Nunnally Johnson, Charles Lederer; Screenplay: "The Last Leaf": Philip Dunne; Photography: Lloyd Ahern Sr.; "The Cop and the Anthem": Lucien Ballard: "The Clarion Call"; Milton R. Krasner: "The Ransom of Red Chief"; Joseph MacDonald: "The Last Leaf," "The Gift of the Magi"; Film Editing: Nick DeMaggio:

(1952) O. Henry's Full House

"The Cop and the Anthem," "The Clarion Call," "The Last Leaf"; Barbara McLean: "The Gift of the Magi"; William B. Murphy: "The Ransom of Red Chief"; Art Direction: Chester Gore, Addison Hehr, Richard Irvine, Lyle R. Wheeler, Joseph C. Wright; Costumes: Edward Stevenson; U.S. release: August 7, 1952; Genre: Multi-Drama; Black and White; Running Time: 117 minutes; Blu-ray Region B, Koch Media (Germany), released August 2012; English subtitle captions for the deaf and hard of hearing are available on this disc.

Cast: "The Cop and the Anthem" Starred: **Charles Laughton** (*Soapy Throckmorton*); Marilyn Monroe (*Streetwalker*); David Wayne (*Horace Truesdale*); "The Clarion Call" Starred: Dale Robertson (*Barney Woods*); Richard Widmark (*Johnny Kernan*); "The Last Leaf" Starred: Anne Baxter (*Joanna Goodwin*); Jean Peters (*Susan Goodwin*); Gregory Ratoff (*Behrman*); "The Ransom of Red Chief" Starred: Fred Allen (*Sam "Slick" Brown*); Oscar Levant (*William Smith*); "The Gift of the Magi" Starred: Jeanne Crain (*Della Young*); Farley Granger (*Jim Young*); Joyce MacKenzie (*Hazel Woods*); Lee Aaker (*J.B. Dorset/Red Chief*); Richard Rober (*Chief of Detectives*); Fred Kelsey (*Mr. Schultz*); Richard Garrick (*Doctor*); **Uncredited Cast**: Richard Allen (*Pete*); Phil Arnold (*Convict*); Irving Bacon (*Ebenezer Dorset*); Carl Betz (*Jimmie Valentine*); Harry Carter (*Cop in Park*); Robert Cherry, Robert Easton, Ann Kunde, Norman Leavitt (*Yokels*); Frank Cusack, Erno Verebes (*Waiters*); Abe Dinovitch (*Barney—Bartender*); Fritz Feld (*Maurice*); James Flavin, Robert Foulk, Tom Greenway, Jack Mather, David McMahon (*Cops*); Kathleen Freeman (*Mrs. Dorset*); Steven Geray (*Boris Radolf*); Everett Glass (*Desk Clerk*); Gloria Gordon (*Ellie May*); A. Cameron Grant, Henry Slate, Herb Vigran (*Poker Players*); Harry Hayden (*A.J. Crump*); Thomas Browne Henry (*Manager*); Bert Hicks (*Sheldon Sidney*); Marjorie Holliday (*Cashier*); Jimmie Horan (*Bookkeeper*); Richard Hylton (*Bill*); Frank Jaquet (*Butcher*); Richard Karlan (*Headwaiter*); Don Kohler (*Secretary*); Nico Lek (*Owner*); Tyler McVey (*O. Henry*); Frank Mills (*Man Being Booked at Police Station*); Alfred Mizner (*Storekeeper*); Ava Norring, Beverly Thompson (*Girls*); William J. O'Brien (*Hotel Clerk*); House Peters (*Dave Bascom*); Stuart Randall (*Detective*); Sig Ruman (*Menkie*); Hal Smith (*Dandy*); Warren Stevens (*Druggist*); Harry Tenbrook (*Bar Customer*); Philip Tonge (*Man with Umbrella*); Phil Tully (*Guard*); William Vedder (*Judge*); Ruth Warren (*Neighbor*); Billy Wayne (*Bystander*); Martha Wentworth (*Mrs. O'Brien*); Will Wright (*Manager*); May Wynn (*Mother*).

Working Titles: *The Full House*; *Bagdad on the Subway*; *O'Henry's Bagdad on the Subway*

Synopsis: Writer John Steinbeck hosts a compendium of five stories written by O. Henry:

"The Cop and the Anthem": Soapy Throckmorton, a gentleman tramp sleeping on a park bench, is woken by a cop. To avoid arrest, he moves along. He is joined by Horace Truesdale, a fellow vagrant. Horace asks Soapy if he has any plans for the winter. Soapy declares he will spend a couple of months in jail as he has done for many years. Horace points out that accommodations are available in a charitable mission, but Soapy is averse to charity. Soapy shows Horace the devious ways he intends to go about being arrested. He launches into action by taking an umbrella from a customer in a store. When the man does not wish to involve the police, Soapy concludes that he's a petty thief. Soapy goes to a restaurant and orders breakfast. When presented with the check, he admits to having no money. The restaurant owner merely ejects him into the street where the loyal Horace is waiting. A cop is bent over, tying his shoelace. Soapy attempts to kick

A cop (Harry Carter), a park and a tramp (Laughton) in "The Cop and the Anthem" episode from *O. Henry's Full House* (1952).

the officer in the pants, but instead slips on a banana peel and falls to the ground. The officer helps Soapy back to his feet and he continues his walk. Soapy stands and admires a dress in the window of a fashion shop. Finding a horse shoe in the road, he shatters the shop window. The crowd chases Horace despite Soapy's cries that *he* is the guilty party. Soapy approaches a young woman, intending to annoy her so a cop nearby will arrest him. But it turns out the woman is a prostitute, and to spare her trouble with the law, he decides to leave. But first he makes her a gift of his acquired umbrella. When the cop asks her what he was up to, she replies, "He called me a lady." Soapy and Horace sit outside a church in desperation, then decide to enter. During the service, Soapy undergoes a moral conversion and decides he must try to better himself and get a job. But a cop arrests him on the street for loitering. He is brought to court where, to his consternation, he is sentenced to 90 days in jail on a charge of vagrancy.

"The Clarion Call": Barney Woods, a New York police detective, calls in at a New York press office after catching an elderly counterfeiter. On his way out, he sees a piece of evidence in an unsolved murder investigation. He recognizes a gold pencil holder as an artifice from his childhood and he tracks down the owner, Johnny Kernan. They were friends in college and Kernan reminds Barney he still owes him a debt of $1000. Though Barney offers Kernan a $300 deposit, he rejects the offer and says only the full amount will wash the slate clean. In the newspaper, Barney sees that a $1000 reward is being offered for the capture of the murderer. Barney later confronts Kernan as he makes his getaway on a train and gives him the full $1000 given as reward money for apprehending the killer.

"The Last Leaf": In snowy Greenwich Village, a young woman, Joanna Goodwin, collapses with pneumonia and is taken in by Behrman, an impoverished painter. A doctor tells her sister Susan that Joanna appears to lack the will to live. Joanna counts the leaves on a vine outside her bedroom, and feels certain that when the last leaf falls away, she will die. That night, all the leaves but one fall away. Susan later learns that Behrman had spent the last few hours before his death out in snow during the night. Susan looks and realizes that the leaf had been painted on the vine by the artist.

"The Ransom of Red Chief": Two novice kidnappers, "Slick" and William, go to the countryside in their car with the intention of kidnapping someone they can ransom. When they kidnap a young boy, J.B., they encounter all sorts of mishaps and problems.

"The Gift of the Magi": Christmas, 1905: Newlyweds Della and Jim Young dream of a perfect Christmas in contrast to their current financial circumstances. Each decides to make sacrifices to give the other Christmas presents.

Selected Dialogue:

THROCKMORTON: "It may interest you to know, my good man, that I and the minutest coin of the realm are total strangers.... I said I was broke!"

THROCKMORTON: "Don't just stand there with your adenoids showing. Go and call a cop."

THROCKMORTON: "Since my means are limited, I can only ask your pardon, perhaps persuade you to accept, as a token of my regard the last uh, valuable left to me from a once formidable estate. My compliments to a charming and delightful young lady."

THROCKMORTON: "I seem to remember that tune from somewhere. No? Well, this might be a country churchyard such as I knew in my youth in the days when life contained such things as mothers and roses, ambition and friends, immaculate thoughts and Little Lord Fauntleroy collars."

Production Commentary: In his autobiography, Charles Chaplin revealed his approach to staging the art of film comedy: "All I needed to make a comedy is a park, a policeman and a pretty girl" (Chaplin: 159). These modest ingredients are all featured in the short story "The Cop and the Anthem," the first of five vignettes comprising *O. Henry's Full House*.

Laughton's appearance in this first episode of a portmanteau picture suggests that he was still considered a bankable draw with the paying public. This was doubtless assisted by his numerous TV appearances and nationwide one-man shows. Laughton receives fifth billing out of a total of 12 star names in the film's credits. He is also given the spotlight in the theatrical trailer. He appears on camera as himself and introduces the film to would-be patrons.

Like Chaplin, Laughton wanted to tackle all aspects of the film process and was meticulous in the devising and staging of his artistry. As the episode plays out, there is more than a little of the Chaplinesque about Laughton's performance in its dealings with poverty, battling against authority and taking a comic pratfall. There is something very winning about the pace and the intent of this vignette. The succeeding four episodes lack a tightness of construction and the sure touch which Laughton brings to his characterization. He brings nobility to the shabby Soapy. Even pitted against younger star names, Laughton holds his own by dint of his acting repertoire, total concentrated skill and sheer determination in the face of multiple private demons.

There is in the film a historical bonus of two acting generations caught together briefly. Laughton has a 90-second encounter with the legendary and tragic Marilyn Monroe. Laughton's Soapy sees a girl on the street and extends her every courtesy in the hope this will enable him to be put in jail for propositioning. In a twist typical of the author O. Henry, he soon finds out she is a streetwalker. At this stage of her career, Monroe was on the cusp of her meteoric film stardom which lends a sense of poignancy to the scene.

The film did good business, earning a respectable $1,000,000 (*Variety*, January 7. 1953). Writing in the *New York Times* (October 26, 1952), Bosley Crowther was dubious of several episodes in the film compendium, but he singled out the first episode and Laughton for praise: "Mr. Laughton ... makes a highly amiable character of the roguish bum who is balked in his desperate endeavors to arrange a winter vacation in jail. It is a neatly contrived little comment, embracing a social irony." *Motion Picture Daily* (August 18, 1952) wrote of Laughton, "His is an effective, if somewhat flamboyant, portrayal...."

Laughton yet again demonstrates his ability to bring to life a downtrodden character on the margins of society and infusing a perilous social predicament with comic wit and humanity. He is here in peak form producing a character study combined with a series of emotional truths. As ever, Laughton manages to make his gargantuan efforts appear simple and direct in performing a rare comic delight.

Abbott and Costello Meet Captain Kidd (1952)

Tagline: "It's One Big Roar from Shore to Shore."[75]

U.S. (Warner Bros./Woodley Productions)

Credits: Writers: Howard Dimsdale, John Grant; Songs by Bob Russell, Lester Lee;

Left to right: Lou Costello, Laughton and Bud Abbott relax in a photo shoot taken while working on *Abbott and Costello Meet Captain Kidd* (1952).

Photography: Stanley Cortez; Color Consultants: Wilton R. Holm, Clifford D. Shank; Music Composed and Conducted by Raoul Kraushaar; Musical Numbers Staged by Val Raset; Choral Arrangements: Norman Luboff; Production Supervisor: Maurie M. Suess; Editor: Edward Mann; Art Director: Daniel Hall; Set Decorator: Al Orenbach; Assistant Director: Robert Aldrich; Special Effects: Lee Zavitz; Dialogue Director: Milt Bronson; Script Supervisor: Don McDougall; Makeup: Abe Haberman; Men's Wardrobe: Albert Deano; Ladies' Wardrobe: Maria Donovan; Sound: Ben Winkler, "Mac" Dalgleish; Produced by Alex Gottlieb; Directed by Charles Lamont; U.S. release: December 27, 1952; U.K. release: August 17, 1953; Genre: Comedy; Super Cine Color; Running Time: 70 minutes; Restored 35mm print at UCLA Archives; DVD from Warner Archive Collection, released June 2011; no English subtitle captions for the deaf and hard of hearing.

Cast: Bud Abbott (*Rocky Stonebridge*); Lou Costello (*Oliver "Puddin' Head" Johnson*); **Charles Laughton** (***Captain Kidd***); Hillary Brooke (*Captain Bonney*); Bill Shirley (*Bruce Martingale*); Leif Erickson (*Morgan*); Fran Warren (*Lady Jane*); **Uncredited Cast**: Lester Dorr, Frank Yaconelli (*Tavern Waiters*), Rex Lease (*Tavern Waiter with Black Eye*); Paul Newlan (*Tavern Owner*); Milicent Patrick (*Tavern Wench*); Suzanne Ridgway (*Pretty Maid in Tavern*); Syd Saylor (*Tavern Waiter Spitting Teeth*); Joe Kirk (*Flirtatious Pirate*); Leonard Mudie (*Captain Bonney's First Mate*); Harry Wilson (*Ugly Pirate*).

Synopsis: Rocky Stonebridge and Oliver "Puddin' Head" Johnson, Americans stranded on the pirate island of Tortuga, work as waiters at an inn which is frequented by pirate Captain Kidd. Kidd and an attractive female pirate, Captain Bonney, are vying for buried treasure. An aristocratic, Lady Jane, entrusts Rocky and Oliver to deliver a love letter to a singer at the inn, Bruce Martingale. The love letter is accidentally switched with Captain Kidd's treasure map, leading to frantic attempts to recover the missing map. Captain Kidd then kidnaps Lady Jane and the two waiters and takes them on a voyage to Skull Island where the treasure is buried. After several narrow escapes, Rocky and Oliver capture Kidd and haul him up by the feet onto the ship's yardarm. Following a romantic kiss with Bonney, Oliver takes over as ship's captain and they all sail away happily.

Selected Dialogue:
   KIDD: "The things I have to do to go down in history!"
   KIDD: "I hope the London papers get this straight. They haven't been too kind to me lately."
   KIDD: "I enjoyed that!"
   KIDD: "Get off my foot!"

Production Commentary: Film critics Leslie Halliwell and Clive Hirschorn describe Laughton's performance in *Abbott and Costello Meet Captain Kidd* to be an embarrassment.[76] If there is embarrassment, it comes from the anodyne script and not from Laughton's performance as Captain Kidd.

Abbott and Costello were hardly strangers in Laughton's professional life. Laughton first encountered the comic duo on Edgar Bergen and Charlie McCarthy's radio show. He later appeared numerous times as a guest on their NBC radio show during the 1940s, the height of their comic fame. In 1952 he also appeared on their television show, and was even happy to make a cameo appearance in a public information film with the boys during the summer of 1952. So much for embarrassment!

The film was made by Woodley, an independent production company founded by Bud Abbott, and released through Warner Bros. It bears the hallmarks of the Universal "Abbott and Costello Meet..." series that began with *Abbott and Costello Meet Frankenstein* (Charles Barton, 1948). This series of cinematic encounters pitted Bud and Lou against an assortment of monsters and hissable villains.

Produced on a standard budget of $702,000, and with a reliable director, Charles Lamont, *Abbott and Costello Meet Captain Kidd* is essentially a costume pantomime tailored to the broad slapstick routines and wisecracking patois associated with stand-up comics Bud Abbott (1897–1974) and Lou Costello (1906–1959).[77] It incorporates a lampoon on the Captain Kidd legend and a burlesque of Laughton's martinet Captain Bligh. The story may be weak and absurd, but it serves to interpolate the all-too-familiar Abbott and Costello gags and six Bob Russell-Lester Lee songs sung by Fran Warren and Bill Shirley.

Producer Alex Gottlieb recalled that he approached Laughton backstage in a Boston theater where he was performing in a play. Gottlieb explained the scenario of the film and Laughton was so intrigued with the idea of performing in "low comedy" that he accepted the offer without reading the script. However, Laughton soon became bewildered by not being given cues for his lines and constant ad-libbing from the comic pair. In addition, rehearsals were hardly used. He became disorientated by the casual improvisation of the comic duo, but co-star Hillary Brooke advised him to relax and enjoy himself. He soon became fascinated by the pair and was particularly taken by Costello. On set Laughton encouraged the comic to teach him how to perform double takes.

Laughton plays Captain Kidd to the hilt and joins in the slapstick to good effect. The action remains fast-paced all the way through and the principals yell, splutter and scurry their way through the picture so attention doesn't flag too much. Filming took place at the Motion Picture Center Studios where the boys' TV series was also produced. *Abbott and Costello Meet Captain Kidd* was the second and final color film in which Bud and Lou appeared (the previous film was *Jack and the Beanstalk*, made by Costello's production company, Exclusive Films); it was Laughton's second color film as well. Photographed in the short-lived Super Cine Color process by renowned cinematographer Stanley Cortez, the film was for many years only available in either black and white or dupe color copies. It was finally restored in 2002 by UCLA archivists following the discovery of a duplicate set of the film's color negatives by film historian Bob Furmanek.

The reviews were mixed, to say the least. *Focus: A Film Review 1952–1953* (July 1953) struck a tone of annoyance and disappointment in its review: "All this would be harmless enough and some of it quite fun were it not for the presence of Mr. Charles Laughton as a comic pirate captain. To see this great actor wasting his time and talent on nonsense of this sort is indeed sad: the fact that he plays his absurd part magnificently only makes it sadder." *Film Bulletin* (November 17, 1952) declared that Laughton "checks in with a performance that rivals Abbott and Costello at their zaniest. He's the 'ham' to end all 'hams.'" *Motion Picture Daily* (November 25, 1952): "It is one of the better films coming from the team lately due largely to the fine spoofing done by Laughton and Hillary Brooke...." *Variety* (November 26, 1952) also saw positive qualities: "Laughton hams delightfully, thoroughly enjoying himself in abandoning long-hair dramatics for low comedy." The *Monthly Film Bulletin* (June 1953, Vol. 20, No. 233) observed, "Charles Laughton is the butt of everyone as the villainous Captain Kidd and generally gets knocked about."

Despite all the critical negativity, the paying public lapped it all up. *Variety* (January 13, 1954) noted it was a top grosser of 1953, earning $2,000,000. *Abbott and Costello Meet Captain Kidd* finds Laughton unimpaired and unbowed by the absence of a film scenario and the substitution of lowbrow comic schtick, accompanied by the cross-talking slapstick of an aging vaudeville duo. This was a rare occasion when he was not intimidated by the prospect of appearing in front of the camera. He was able to relax and enjoy himself in the company of two professional comics with whom he shared a mutual admiration and respect. Granted, some of the gags are introduced in too much detail and in consequence they appear heavy-handed, but *Abbott and Costello Meet Captain Kidd* remains one of the least pretentious things he ever attempted during his film career.

Salome (1953)

Tagline: "Passion and Pageantry Unparalleled in All the Pages of Love and Evil!"[78]

U.S. (Columbia)

Credits: Screenplay: Harry Kleiner; Story: Jesse L. Lasky Jr., Harry Kleiner; Photography: Charles Lang; Technicolor Color Consultant: Francis Cugat; Art Director: John Meehan; Editor: Viola Lawrence; Set Decorator: William Kiernan; Assistant Director: Earl Bellamy; Technical Consultant: Millard Sheets; Men's Costumes: Emile Santiago; Makeup: Clay Campbell; Hair Styles: Helen Hunt; Sound Engineer: Lodge Cunningham; Orchestrations: Arthur Morton; Choral Music: Roger Wagner Chorale; Oriental Dancers: Sujata and Asoka; Dances for Miss Hayworth Created by Valerie Bettis; Gowns: Jean Louis; Musical Director: Morris Stoloff; Musical Score: George Duning; Music for Dances: Daniele Amfitheatrof; Produced by Buddy Adler; Directed by William Dieterle; U.S. release: March 24, 1953; U.K. release: September 7, 1953; Genre: Epic; Technicolor; Running Time: 103 minutes; DVD Region 1 and Region 2, Sony Pictures, released July 2013; English subtitle captions for the deaf and hard of hearing are available on this disc.

Cast: Rita Hayworth (*Princess Salome*); Stewart Granger (*Commander Claudius*); **Charles**

Laughton (*King Herod*); Judith Anderson (*Queen Herodias*); Sir Cedric Hardwicke (*Tiberius Caesar*); Basil Sydney (*Pontius Pilate*); Maurice Schwartz (*Ezra*); Arnold Moss (*Micha*); Alan Badel (*John the Baptist*); **Uncredited Cast**: Ray Beltram, Merrill McCormick, Franz Roehn, Joe Sawaya, Carlo Tricoli, David Wold (*Herod's Council Members*); Bobker Ben Ali, Henry Dar Boggia, Don De Leo, Eddie Fields, Robert Garabedian, John Parrish, Sam Scar (*Politicians*); Frederic Berest, George Keymas (*Sailors*); Barry Brooks, Eduardo Cansino (*Roman Guards*); Bruce Cameron, Tristam Coffin, John Crawford, Tony Urchel (*Guards*); Bud Cokes (*Galilean Soldier*); Carmen D'Antonio (*Salome's Servant*); Karl "Killer" Davis (*Slave Master*); Leslie Denison (*Court Attendant*); David Ahdar, Italia DeNubila, Tina Menard, Charles Soldani, Dimas Sotello, Billy Wilkerson (*Converts*); Henry A. Escalante, Gilberto Marques, Abel Pina, Jerry Pina, Tony Pina, Ramiro Rivas, Richard Rivas, Ruben T. Rivas (*Acrobats*); Chief Leonard George, George Khoury (*Assassins*); Michael Granger (*Captain Quintus*); Tom Hernandez, Jack Low, Bob Rose (*Townsmen*); Paul Hoffman (*Sailmaster*); Eva Hyde (*Herodias' Servant*); Duke Johnson (*Juggler*); Guy Kingsford (*Officer*); David Leonard, Ralph Moody (*Old Scholars*); Freddie Letuli (*Sword Dancer*); Michael Mark (*Old Farmer*); Saul Martell (*Dissenting Scholar*); John Merton (*Baptism Attendee*); Anton Northpole (*Advisor*); Lou Nova (*John's Executioner*); Rex Reason (*Marcellus Fabius*); Maurice Samuels (*Old Scholar*); Joe Schilling (*Advisor*); Mickey Simpson (*Herod's Guard Captain*); William Spaeth (*Fire Eater*); Bert Stevens (*Caesar's Scrivener*); Rick Vallin (*Sailor*); Charles Wagenheim (*Simon*); Trevor Ward (*Blind Man Given Sight*); Robert Warwick (*Courier*); Stanley Waxman (*Patrician*); John Wood (*Sword Dancer*); Carleton Young (*Officer*).

Working Titles: *Dance of the Seven Veils*; *Salome—the Dance of the Seven Veils*

Synopsis: The province of Galilee, in the Holy Land, is ruled by King Herod, a licentious man, and Queen Herodias, his scheming wife, who had divorced Herod's brother to marry him. Both are fearful of John the Baptist, the prophet whose preachments against "the adulteress queen and pagan king" gain vast numbers of listeners. Herodias constantly urges the king to have John the Baptist executed, but he does not dare to kill him in case he proves to be the Messiah. Princess Salome, Herodias' daughter by her first marriage, returns from Rome where she was sent as a child due to Herod's unwanted attentions. She has been banished from Rome as a barbarian and Claudius, a handsome Roman officer, is charged with accompanying her home. She falls in love with Claudius, who is a secret convert to the prophet's new religion and saves John when he is attacked for preaching against Rome. The frightened king arrests John for treason to protect him from the queen's assassins. Herodias, aware that Herod coveted her daughter, asks Salome to offer herself to the king through a dance in exchange for the Prophet's head. Salome is revolted and disillusioned by her mother's suggestion, but when the Prophet's life is threatened once again, she performs the dance in the hope of winning John his release. The scheming Herodias, however, convinces Herod that Salome will be his in exchange for the Prophet's head, which is borne into the banquet hall just as Salome finishes her dance. Horrified, Salome denounces her mother and the king and flees with Claudius to the countryside, where they join crowds on a hillside listening to the teachings of Christ.

King Herod (Laughton) is fixated by the exotic allure of Princess Salome's (Rita Hayworth) terpsichorean talents in *Salome* (1953).

(1953) *Salome*

Selected Dialogue:

HEROD: "The blossom does justice to the bud."

HEROD: "Well, wretch, still dumb? Perhaps the rack will oil the hinges of your tongue."

HEROD: "To be a realist is the beginning of wisdom, and the wise know that nothing matters except to find pleasure."

Production Commentary: *Salome* was produced by Columbia to cash in on the cycle of religious epics spawned by the CinemaScope epic *The Robe* (Twentieth Century–Fox, Henry Koster, 1953) and also as promotion for their current star attraction, Rita Hayworth. In doing this, the studio, by default, reteamed William Dieterle and Cedric Hardwicke again with Laughton.

Alas, *Salome* does not have the budget or the ambition of *The Hunchback of Notre Dame*. Laughton co-stars as a somewhat lethargic and libidinous Herod Antipas. *Salome* is no DeMille epic and it's often burdened with leaden dialogue and a pedestrian pace, but it remains watchable for the obsessive and fanatical intrigues and machinations of power-broking wrought by both Laughton's Herod and Judith Anderson as his wife Herodias. To their detractors, "ham" comprised the former performance, while "mania" explained the latter performance. As a power couple they deserve each other.

Laughton heads a retinue of distinguished British actors including: the venerable Sir Cedric Hardwicke as Emperor Tiberius, Basil Sydney as Pontius Pilate, and a younger generation comprising Stewart Granger (on loan from MGM) as Roman commander Claudius and Alan Badel as John the Baptist. *American Cinematographer* (May 1952) reported that cameraman Winton Hoch, under the supervision of director Dieterle, spent four weeks in Egypt shooting second-unit exteriors and local atmosphere.

The film began shooting in late June 1952. Despite undergoing a substantive promotional campaign, *Salome* opened to hostile and generally negative reviews. Typical was Bosley Crowther (*New York Times*, March 25, 1953), who was unimpressed by the "lush conglomeration of historical pretenses and make-believe, pseudo-religious ostentation and just plain insinuated sex." Of Laughton's performance he lamented, "[T]he pop-eyed entrancement of Charles Laughton as Herod in watching [Rita Hayworth] is a pretty fair indication of what her fans are expected to do. Like Miss Hayworth's, Mr. Laughton's performance is not impressive in earlier phases of the film. Where he used to belch when he was sated, now he merely yawns."

Though the film has major deficiencies, Laughton's performance isn't among them. His handling of dialogue is impeccable and he communicates a self-confident gravitas in the role. Co-star Stewart Granger described Laughton contemptuously as "that scene stealer" (Granger: 272). Laughton took it upon himself to leave the set at regular intervals and read the Bible; whether this was for his own amusement or to infuriate the crew and cast is unknown. This provoked Granger's displeasure. As the male star lead, he was struggling to provide a decent performance from Harry Kleiner's script, derived from a source play via Jesse Lasky Jr., a regular contributor to Cecil B. DeMille's Paramount epics. Granger told Laughton in no uncertain terms that he should refrain from such behavior. Laughton, faced with suffering dire consequences, complied.

According to *Variety* (January 13, 1954), the film earned grosses of $4,750,000 in domestic rentals during 1953. However, it was in fact a modest return for a production that had already cost four million dollars. In the midst of all the excess and ballyhoo associated with Ancient World epics, Laughton's acting is professional. He even manages to scrutinize members of the cast with an equivocal eye that seems to gleam with a mixture of lasciviousness and/or mock irony. One is never quite sure.

Laughton had already been involved in his share of historical blockbusters such as *The Sign of the Cross*, *The Private Life of Henry VIII*, *Mutiny on the Bounty* and *The Hunchback of Notre Dame* and was well aware of the constraints and pitfalls within which commercial filmmakers operated. Realism is shown the door and everything is subordinate to the authenticity of lavish spectacle, the predominance of costume pageantry and the need of didactic melodrama. Fidelity to historical facts is not the name of the game; rather, they must conform to the presumptions of: the duration of the film, the exigencies of dramatic license and audience expectations. Magnitude of form is stressed rather than a faithful rendering of scholarly content based on accredited historical research. Taking liberties with Biblical texts is a given in Hollywood scenarios where stark commercial considerations collide with notions of creating high art. In this context, the film's disregard for historical verisimilitude is neither remarkable nor unique.

Salome was Laughton's third color feature film. His penultimate film, Spartacus, produced seven years later, would be another Ancient World epic and his last appearance in a color production. Although beset with problems of egos, structure and scale, Spartacus proved a weightier contender. In contrast, Salome lacks any clear distinction that would place it above what was an already crowded market of indifferent toga dramas.

Young Bess (1953)

Tagline: "Young Bess—*Yes!*"[79]

U.S. (Metro-Goldwyn-Mayer)

Credits: Screenplay: Jan Lustig, Arthur Wimperis; Based on the Novel by Margaret Irwin; Music: Miklos Rozsa; Photography: Charles Rosher; Technicolor Color Consultant: Henri Jaffa; Color Consultant: Alvord Eiseman; Art Directors: Cedric Gibbons, Urie McCleary; Editor: Ralph E. Winters; Assistant Director: George Rhein; Recording Supervisor: Douglas Shearer; Set Decorators: Edwin B. Willis, Jack D. Moore; Special Effects: A. Arnold Gillespie, Warren Newcombe; Costume Designer: Walter Plunkett; Hair Stylist: Sidney Guilaroff; Makeup Creator: William Tuttle; Produced by Sidney Franklin; Directed by George Sidney; U.S. release: May 29, 1953; U.K. release: August 10, 1953; Genre: Historical Drama; Technicolor; Running Time: 112 minutes; DVD from Warner Archive Collection, released August 2010; no English subtitle captions for the deaf and hard of hearing; Theatrical trailer and film extracts are available to download from Turner Classic Movies.

Cast: Jean Simmons (*Young Bess*); Stewart Granger (*Thomas Seymour*); Deborah Kerr (*Catherine Parr*); **Charles Laughton** (*King Henry VIII*); Kay Walsh (*Mrs. Ashley*); Guy Rolfe (*Ned Seymour*); Cecil Kellaway (*Mr. Parry*); Kathleen Byron (*Ann Seymour*); Leo G. Carroll (*Mr. Mums*); Rex Thompson (*Edward*); Robert Arthur (*Barnaby*); Norma Varden (*Lady Tyrwhitt*); Alan Napier (*Robert Tyrwhitt*); Noreen Corcoran (*Young Bess at Six*); Ivan Triesault (*Danish Envoy*); Elaine Stewart (*Anne Boleyn*); Dawn Addams (*Kate Howard*); Doris Lloyd (*Mother Jack*); Lumsden Hare (*Archbishop Cranmer*); Lester Matthews (*Sir William Paget*); **Uncredited Cast**: David Bair (*Ned's Page*); David Cavendish, Sam Harris, Raymond Lawrence, Norman Rainey, Eric Wilton (*Councilmen*); Dick Cherney, Charles Morton, Arthur Tovey (*Royal Court Members*); Frank Eldredge, John Sheffield, Patrick Whyte (*Officers*); Jean Fenwick, Carol Savage (*Ladies in Waiting*); Al Ferguson (*Guard*); Chester Keane (*Halberdier*); Guy Kingsford (*Lookout*); Fee Malten (*Woman*); Clive Morgan (*Halberdier*); Ernest Newton (*Singer at Banquet*); Jack Raine (*Governor of Tower*); John Rice (*Major Domo*); Leoda Richards (*Royal Subject*); Carl Saxe (*Executioner*); Robert Shafto (*Secretary*); Reginald

Jean Simmons as the young Princess Elizabeth and, in a repeat piece of casting, Laughton as King Henry VIII in *Young Bess* (1953).

Sheffield (*Court Recorder*); Ann Tyrrell (*Mary*); Ian Wolfe (*Stranger*).

Awards: Academy Award Nomination: Best Art Direction (Color): Cedric Gibbons, Urie McCleary; Set Decorators: Edwin B. Willis, Jack D. Moore; Academy Award Nomination: Best Costume Design (Color): Walter Plunkett.

Synopsis: Fifteen-year-old Princess Elizabeth, called Young Bess by her father King Henry VIII, is already a woman, endowed with her father's determination and temper, and the charm of Anne Boleyn, her mother, who was beheaded when Bess was still an infant. At that time, Bess was banished to lonely Hatfield House, and with each new marriage Henry had brought her back to London to be accepted at court only to banish her as each successive stepmother was beheaded. Bess' stay at the palace becomes permanent when she meets and feels an instant affection for Catherine Parr, the newest queen, and she renews her acquaintance with Edward, the Prince of Wales, her half-brother, who was a frail child of eight. At court, Bess finds herself attracted to Lord Admiral Tom Seymour, the king's confidante. With the death of Henry, little Edward ascends the throne. Ned Seymour, Tom's powerseeking brother, persuades the Council to declare him Lord Protector of the Realm, despite Henry's dying wish that the position be given to Tom. Ned orders that Bess return to Hatfield, but Tom defiantly takes her to Queen Catherine at Chelsea. There, Bess is extremely happy until she learns that Tom and Catherine had long been in love. Although broken-hearted, she persuades young Edward to order Catherine to marry Tom. This move infuriates Ned because it puts Tom in a stronger position in the court. To remove Bess as a possible future queen, Ned tries to promote her marriage to a Danish prince. This attempt fails, but it brings Tom to the realization that he loves Bess deeply. Bess returns to Hatfield so as not to disrupt the marriage of Tom and Catherine. Months later, Catherine becomes ill and dies. Tom, now free to go to Bess, is arrested by Ned on a fabricated charge of treason. Bess uses her influence with the young king to free Tom, but Ned, through political intrigue, succeeds in beheading Tom before Edward can act. Shortly thereafter, young Edward dies and Bess becomes queen, and proves herself to be one of the greatest monarchs in English history.

Selected Dialogue:

KING HENRY: "Is this a war or a picnic?"

Production Commentary: So convincing and popular to the cinema-going public was Laughton's portrayal of Tudor monarch Henry VIII in Alexander Korda's groundbreaking *The Private Life of Henry VIII*, that 20 years later Laughton reprised the role in *Young Bess*.

The focus of attention in this handsome romantic historical drama had shifted from the king to his daughter, the young Princess Elizabeth. The film begins with her birth and ends with her ascension to the throne. This intimate drama was produced to coincide with the 1953 coronation of Elizabeth II.

Young Bess is a good example of the old MGM studio machine beginning to wind down. Perfectly competent it most surely is, but beyond good taste, a fine display of lavish costumes, and veteran Charles Rosher's splendid Technicolor photography, it lacks finesse and any sense of intent or purpose beyond restating and reminding anyone who cared the studio's capabilities in such matters. Laughton revisits the role, but finds he no longer has anything to offer beyond a certain faded verisimilitude. There was no longer any creative producer to fill the late Irving Thalberg's shoes and it shows. Nevertheless, as *Variety* (January 13, 1954) noted, *Young Bess* was a top grosser of 1953, earning some $1,850,000. *Variety*'s reviewer (April 29, 1953) wrote of Rex Thompson, who played the young prince Edward, "[A]t times his dialogue is mumbled, also a fault to be found with Laughton's delivery."

Laughton's performance amounts to a cameo as his appearances on screen are confined to the film's first half hour. He successfully shows the king as troubled and subject to mood swings. He first appears on screen five minutes into the film. A proud father, he presents his baby daughter to his court, who exchange hearty laughter and bonhomie. His next scene is with Elizabeth as a child; the gross and pompous King parries with her on the subject of the discharge of royal duty. His final deathbed scene some 25 minutes later finds his kingship challenged by his recalcitrant daughter.

Stewart Granger had by now recovered

from his altercation with Laughton. He later said, "My best film for [MGM] was *Young Bess*—for the costumes, the cast and the story" (McFarlane: 231). As with *Salome*, Laughton is part of an impressive British cast consisting of over 20 names: Laughton, Granger, Jean Simmons (then married to Granger), Deborah Kerr, Kay Walsh, Guy Rolfe, Kathleen Byron, Leo G. Carroll, Norma Varden, Alan Napier, Doris Lloyd, Lumsden Hare, Lester Matthews, David Cavendish, Guy Kingsford, Raymond Lawrence, Clive Morgan, Jack Raine, Reginald Sheffield, John Trueman and Eric Wilton.

Laughton does what he does, very well, but when all is said and done, he was being paid a lot for producing what he had done so brilliantly 20 years before. Unfortunately, times change and Laughton had moved on, even if MGM had not. In consequence, despite the efforts of director George Sidney, fresh from directing *Scaramouche* and associated more with producing Hollywood musicals, there is little in its nearly two hours duration that can be considered either creative, imaginative or innovatory.

Young Bess' costumes and art direction were Oscar-nominated but both lost to *The Robe*.

Hobson's Choice (1954)

Tagline: "Come and enjoy yourselves. For Here is Riotous Comedy and a Hilarious Cast Gleefully portraying—*Hobson's Choice*."[80]

U.K. (London Films/British Lion)

Credits: Screenplay: David Lean, Norman Spencer, Wynyard Browne; Based on the play by Harold Brighouse; Music Composed by Malcolm Arnold; Played by the Royal Philharmonic Orchestra; Music Director: Muir Mathieson; Photography: Jack Hildyard; Art Director: Wilfred Shingleton; Editor: Peter Taylor; Costume Designer: John Armstrong; Costume Supervisor: Julia Squire; Production Manager: John Palmer; Assistant Director: Adrian Pryce-Jones; Camera Operator: Peter Newbrook; Sound Supervisor: John Cox; Sound Recording: Buster Ambler and Red Law; Assistant Art Director: Bill Hutchinson; Makeup: Tony Sforzini, George Partleton; Hairdressing: Gladys Atkinson; Continuity: Margaret Shipway; Associate Producer: Norman Spencer; Produced and Directed by David Lean; U.K. release: Passed by the British Board of Film Censors on January 5, 1954; General release: April 19, 1954; U.S. release: June 14, 1954; Genre: Comedy; Black and White; Running Time: 107 minutes; DVD Region 1, The Criterion Collection, released June 2010; Blu-ray Region B, Studio Canal, released May 2014; English subtitle captions for the deaf and hard of hearing are available on these discs.

Cast: **Charles Laughton** (*Henry Hobson*); John Mills (*William Mossop*); Brenda De Banzie (*Maggie Hobson*); Daphne Anderson (*Alice Hobson*); P. Joseph Tomelty (*Jim Heeler*); Richard Wattis (*Albert Prosser*); Prunella Scales (*Vicky Hobson*); Derek Blomfield (*Freddy Beenstock*); Helen Haye (*Mrs. Hepworth*); Julien Mitchell (*Sam Minns*); Gibb McLaughlin (*Tudsbury*); Philip Stainton (*Denton*); Dorothy Gordon (*Ada Figgins*); Madge Brindley (*Mrs. Figgins*); John Laurie (*Dr. McFarlane*); Raymond Huntley (*Nathaniel Beenstock*); Jack Howarth (*Tubby Wadlow*); Herbert C. Walton (*Printer*); **Uncredited Cast**: Edie Martin (*Old Lady Buying Shoelaces*).

Synopsis: In 1880s Salford, bootmaker Henry Hobson is a successful tradesman who runs a shoe shop. Returning home drunk from a mason's meeting at the local pub, the Moonrakers, Hobson finds two of his three daughters are discussing plans to marry, which threatens his comfortable lifestyle as patriarch of a respectable family. A well-to-do customer, Mrs. Hepworth, demands to know

Laughton indulges himself as bootmaker Henry Hobson in a celebrated scene of rollicking drunkenness in David Lean's expressionistic direction of *Hobson's Choice* (1954).

who made the boots she is wearing. When she is presented to the workman, Will Mossop, she commends him on his expertise. Hobson's eldest daughter, Maggie, decides she will forge a marriage–business partnership with Will. She tells Will she will be courting him at Peel Park the following Sunday afternoon. When Maggie returns home, her sisters Alice and Vicky and her father are neither amused nor pleased by her plans to marry Will. Hobson decides to teach Will a lesson and threatens physical chastisement. Will decides to assert himself and threatens to take Maggie away from the shop if Hobson carries out his threat. When Hobson begins brandishing his belt, the couple leaves and pays a call on Mrs. Hepworth to raise capital to start a business. Mrs. Hepworth agrees to a £100 loan to be paid back in three installments. The pair begins the task of finding business premises, fitting out the shop and distributing hand bills to advertise the opening of the business. Back at Hobson's home, Hobson has an altercation with his two daughters and retires to the comfort and camaraderie of the Moonrakers. After several pints, he insults his drinking pals. He begins to hallucinate and decides to return home, but out in the street he becomes distracted and fascinated by the moonlight. Missing his footing, he plunges into the cellar of a solicitor, Beenstock & Co. The following morning, after climbing out of the cellar, he is served a notice of trespass by Beenstock solicitors. Realizing the seriousness of the situation, Hobson goes to Maggie for help. In return for her assistance, she asks that he give his two younger daughters financial settlements for their marriages. Alice is to marry Albert Prosser, an up-and-coming solicitor, while Vicky is engaged to Freddy Beenstock. He reluctantly agrees. Will proposes that Hobson's business be merged with his own thriving boot business. After initial shock and not a little bluster, Hobson decides they must make the partnership a legal entity. Together Will, Maggie and Hobson march off to a solicitor's office to sort out the legal formalities.

Selected Dialogue:

HOBSON: "Providence has decreed that you should lack a mother's hand at the time when single girls grow bumptious and must have somebody to rule. Well, I'll tell you this. You'll not rule me!"

HOBSON: "There's been a gradual increase of uppishness towards me."

HOBSON: "Female perversity comes from leading an indoor life."

HOBSON: "Thou's got nowt to think of but providing me with my rightful home comforts. What's for puddin'?"

HOBSON: "Fish, that's what I am. Big fish, little pond. It's a stinking little pond, and I'm getting out of it!"

HOBSON: "When ruin and disaster overwhelm a man of my importance, it's reported in t' *Manchester Guardian* for the whole country to read."

HOBSON: "Carpet? Morocco? Young man, do you think this shop is in St. Ann's Square, Manchester?"

Production Commentary: In his diaries, comic actor Kenneth Williams (1926–1988) records having viewed *Hobson's Choice* on television in 1982. He thought how stagy and theatrical the film and everyone in it seemed (Davies: 664).[81] Other critics share similar misgivings about the film and Laughton's larger-than-life performance. David Shipman declared, "[H]is performance was over-exuberant and threw the film off-balance" (Shipman: 341). David Thomson described his acting as "tedious" (Thomson: 425). Leslie Halliwell, though admitting a liking for the film and emphasizing the brilliant playing, memorable sets and photography regretted, "the slight decline of the predictable third act" (Halliwell, 1977: 330). Here is a Laughton film which causes consternation among critics, but the paying public lapped it up and it continues to garner popular acclaim whenever it is revived.

In truth, Laughton's portrayal is just too much in the vein of a Wallace Beery: Hobson as a lovable old soak. What is missing is any sense of the unpredictable, the latent sadism of a Barrett, say, or the unbending fanaticism of a Javert. Patriarchy was never played in so dull and tedious a manner. To this day, *Hobson's Choice* remains instantly recognizable and popular, but Laughton's interpretation, though it certainly has breadth, lacks any real psychological depth. Is his performance rumbustious? Yes. Is it exuberant? Yes. But, to the point of oversaturation. Combined with David Lean's unremittingly expressionistic direction, this exuberance doesn't serve the source material particularly well. In consequence, the audience comes away with the distinct impression of Laughton as a typically over-the-top actor.

Laughton was well aware that critics would pick up on this in their reviews. His spectacular, overstated performance was, however, encouraged by director Lean (too much in awe of Laughton's status), and Lean was remiss in not reining in the flamboyance. The excesses of Laughton's performance are aided and abetted by Malcolm Arnold's chirpy score that carries the film down a path of predictable burlesque and leaves little to the imagination. As a technical exercise, the film is very good, but its form has a tendency to suffocate the intent of the play by misapplying German expressionism in photography and art direction. In this, Lean seems to be recalling the virtuosity of F.W. Murnau's *Der Letzte Mann* aka *The Last Laugh* (UFA, 1924) and, in particular, the outstanding agility of Karl Freund's cinematography. In contrast, Jack Hildyard's camera set-ups and movements often seem calculated to generate exuberance for its own sake. In doing so, the serious theme of the play, confrontation of women in a male-dominated world, is lost as a provincial drama is spun, via Germanic expressionism, into something grotesque and uneven.

There are, however, some memorable moments, such as the opening sequence showing Hobson's shop in the dead of night, in the rain, the sign of a boot creaking in the wind. Inside the deserted shop, the camera delicately glides over several pairs of elegant shoes. A clock strikes one and abruptly the shop door flies open and the huge shadow of Hobson looms. He then burps! This is a deliberate and delightful parody of Lean's celebrated dramatic beginning of *Great Expectations*, set in a cemetery in the dead of winter. As actor Robert Powell suggests, no matter how famous a role any actor becomes associated with, it will originally have been conceived of in relation to other actors, and even offered to them.[82]

In fact, the casting of the *Hobson's Choice* lead was anything but straightforward. It began with actor Wilfred Pickles approaching his agent, Christopher Mann, who also represented director Lean, with the suggestion of appearing in a film of Harold Brighouse's comedy. However, Launder and Gilliat told Mann they were not keen on the casting of Pickles. Mann suggested they approach producer Alexander Korda for his opinion. Korda readily agreed with their reservations. In the meantime, Korda decided to buy the rights to the play. Needless to say, Pickles and Mann were aggrieved and accused Korda of being underhanded in his dealings.

Korda then offered the play to David Lean who, with writer Norman Spencer, decided to take on the project. Lean considered Roger Livesey for the central role, but Spencer argued for Laughton. Lean was hesitant as he had offered Laughton the central role in a proposed filming of H.E. Bates' *The Cruise of the Breadwinner*, but Laughton had rejected it. Korda, who knew Laughton of old, warned Lean, "Charlie will do the most difficult scenes, like the eating scene in *The Private Life of Henry VIII*, but give him something simple to do and he'll take three weeks and cause you endless trouble" (Brownlow: 299). To Lean's surprise, Laughton readily accepted the leading role in *Hobson's Choice* with apparent enthusiasm. Laughton was even more pleased when he learned that he was to appear again on screen opposite Robert Donat, who was to have played Willie Mossop. Donat, like Laughton, was another tortured soul for whom acting was self-doubt manifest; any project was a trial, a catastrophe waiting to happen. The situation had the effect of producing psychosomatic illness in the form of chronic asthma. As a result of Donat's poor health, no one would insure him and he was taken off the picture. His indisposition gave Laughton an excuse to backtrack. Only blackmail threats from Korda to go to the media and reveal Laughton's sexual orientation made the actor reluctantly stay the course. John Mills, by then a Lean veteran (having already appeared in *In Which We Serve*, *This Happy Breed* and *Great Expectations*), was approached and accepted the role of Mossop. Actress Brenda de Banzi played the elder daughter, Maggie Hobson. They are both excellent. Mills' career was in the doldrums and his performance as Mossop put him back on track again.

De Banzi manages to upstage Laughton all the way. Despite her being born in

Manchester, Laughton disapproved of the actress, claiming she was failing to get her part right! Her Maggie is level-headed and formidable whereas Laughton's Hobson is no match and reacts with mere bluster and incomprehension. Laughton hated playing a drunk. For the famous scene of seeing a double reflection of the moon in a puddled street, Laughton called upon an old music hall performer to teach him a drunken walk.

According to Simon Callow, Laughton ended up floundering with the role due to apathy. He had in fact been involved in an amateur production of the play, playing Willie Mossop (see amateur stage appearances). The result is that Laughton's Henry Hobson is akin to his Squire Humphrey Pengallan in *Jamaica Inn*: too overpowering, one-sided and full of regurgitated comic asides. He gives a popular performance that plays to the gallery, and the public loved him for it. In the end, Laughton provides a performance that is calculated to be popular but misses both nuance and ingenuity. It comes across as designed to give a moneymaking star performance. Laughton has not really come to an understanding of his material; he is merely content to follow and meander with it.

Hobson's Choice is a heavily stylized and self-conscious piece of filmmaking of a well-known stage original. It badly needs scaling down to its social realist roots. Writing in the *Monthly Film Bulletin* (March 1954, Vol. 21, No. 242), Penelope Houston was correct to contend, "Charles Laughton's playing, for all its technical finesse, fails to bring Hobson convincingly to life…." Asked towards the end of his life by *Variety* (October 26, 1960) whether he was a superb actor or a magnificent ham, Laughton replied, "I don't think there is a difference. All acting, like painting, is exaggeration of a kind. It's just a difference of degree and whether you get caught at it." This was one role where Laughton needed to give a nuanced interpretation not just slip into broad declamatory effects. As it stands, his playing of Hobson may be overrated, but the part did him professional good; it secured him kudos from cinemagoers and producers. His next film would prove to be something unique, quite different from anything else he had attempted previously in his career.

The Night of the Hunter (1955)

Tagline: "This morning we were married … and now you think I'm going to kiss you, hold you, call you my wife!"[83]

U.S. (United Artists)

Credits: Screenplay: James Agee; From the Novel By Davis Grubb; Music: Walter Schumann; Photography: Stanley Cortez; Art Director: Hilyard Brown; Assistant Director: Milton Carter; Editor: Robert Golden; Production Manager: Ruby Rosenberg; Set Decorator: Al Spencer; Wardrobe: Jerry Bos; Wardrobe Assistant: Evelyn Carruth; Makeup: Don Cash; Hair Stylist: Kay Shea; Sound: Stanford Naughton; Property Man: Joe La Bella; Special Photographic Effects: Jack Rabin, Louis DeWitt; Produced by Paul Gregory; **Directed by Charles Laughton**; U.S. release: July 26, 1955; Genre: Drama/Thriller; Black and White; Running Time: 93 minutes; DVD Region 1 and Blu-ray Region A, The Criterion Collection, released November 2010; Blu-ray Region B, Arrow Academy, released October 2013; English subtitle captions for the deaf and hard of hearing are available on these discs.

Cast: Robert Mitchum (*Preacher Harry Powell*); Shelley Winters (*Willa Harper*); Lillian Gish (*Rachel Cooper*); James Gleason (*Uncle Birdie Steptoe*); Evelyn Varden (*Icey Spoon*); Peter Graves (*Ben Harper*); Don Beddoe (*Walt Spoon*); Billy Chapin (*John Harper*); Sally Jane Bruce (*Pearl Harper*); Gloria Castilo (*Ruby*); **Uncredited Cast**: Corey Allen (*Young Man in Town*); Paul Bryar (*Bart—Hangman*); Cheryl Callaway (*Mary*); Michael Chapin (*Ruby's Boyfriend*); Mary Ellen Clemons (*Clary*); Kathy Garver (*Child*); James Griffith (*District Attorney*); John Hamilton (*Townsman Who Greets Rachel*); Kay Lavelle (*Miz Cunningham*); Gloria Pall (*Burlesque Dancer*).

Synopsis: A psychopathic killer, Harry Powell, a self-styled "reverend," roams the West Virginia countryside during the 1930s. He believes he is tasked to do the Lord's work by murdering rich widows. While in prison on a charge of stealing a car, his cellmate is Ben Harper, a condemned man who killed two bank employees and stole (and secreted $10,000) of stolen money. Unbeknownst to Powell, Harper hid the stolen loot in a rag doll carried by his young daughter Pearl. Both Pearl and her older brother John swear to their father never to divulge where the money is hidden. After Harper is hanged, his widow Willa takes a job at Walt and Icey Spoon's ice cream store. John visits an old friend, Uncle Birdie Steptoe. During conversation, the old man tells John he met a stranger who claimed to have known his late father. John returns home to find his mother, sister and the Spoons being charmed by the Biblical oratory of "Reverend" Powell. He demonstrates the triumph of love over hate using the tattoos of "LOVE" on his right hand and "HATE" on his left hand. Icey is delighted by this dramatic performance and asks Powell to attend the town picnic the following Sunday. At the picnic, Willa confronts Powell asking if her late husband Ben had told him anything about the loot. Powell claims that Ben said he threw the money in the river. Willa receives the answer with relief. Powell later tells John that his mother and he are to be married. John reacts negatively, saying Powell will never be his real father, and then blurts out in the heat of the moment that he will "never tell." Powell realizes the boy knows where the money is hidden, but decides to pick his time and he allows the boy to run off. On their wedding night, Willa is deeply ashamed when Powell proclaims the marriage will not be consummated as it the business of their marriage to tend to the children she already has and not to beget more. To please Powell, Willa leads a revivalist meeting and renounces her sins. Powell reproves John for telling his mother he has been asking him about the money and Willa scolds John for deceit as she believes Powell is innocent. But when Willa leaves the house, Powell locks John in his bedroom and begins to question Pearl severely. On returning, Willa overhears Powell threatening Pearl. Later, in bed, she realizes that Powell knew Ben did not discard the money and that her son does know where the money is hidden. She lies submissively in her bed as Powell cuts her throat with his switchblade. The following morning, Powell tearfully tells the Spoons that Willa has run away. Meanwhile, Uncle Birdie is quietly fishing when he sees the body of Willa trapped in her car at the bottom of the river. Agitated, he returns to his boat and gets drunk, afraid he will be accused of her murder. Back home, John lies to Powell that the money is buried in the cellar. Powell forces the children to go to the cellar with him, but John manages to escape with Pearl. They run to Uncle Birdie, but he is asleep drunk and cannot be roused. John and Pearl clamber aboard a small boat and set off just before Powell can catch them. The children float down the river, still pursued by Powell on horseback. They fall asleep, and are woken later by Rachel Cooper, an elderly farmer who cares for foundling children. Rachel already has charge of Ruby, Mary and Clary, but decides to add John and Pearl to her litter. One evening, Ruby goes to town on the pretext of a sewing lesson; her real reason is to meet young boys. Powell approaches her and inquires about John and Pearl. After he is given the information, he leaves despite Ruby having become fascinated by him. Returning home, Ruby confesses her transgression to

Laughton in charge behind the camera brings his perfectionism to bear on *The Night of the Hunter* (1955). A stylized, mesmerizing, offbeat tale of childhood innocence and trauma, suffused with gothic horror and dramatic suspense.

Rachel. Although Rachel forgives the susceptible adolescent, she is worried about Powell. Next day, Powell pays a visit and claims to be John and Pearl's father, something John denies. Rachel realizes he is up to no good and chases him away with her shotgun. As he runs away, Powell shrieks that he will come back at nighttime. Rachel responds by holding a vigil with her gun at the ready. Powell sits in the front yard and waits for Rachel to become distracted. He manages to slip into the house, but when Powell appears unexpectedly in front of her she fires her gun and wounds him. He runs into the barn. In the company of John, Rachel waits and watches throughout the night. In the morning, state troopers arrive to arrest Powell. As he is taken away, John is overwhelmed by memories of his father's arrest and runs to Powell and hits him with the rag doll which soon bursts and the money pours out. At the trial, John is incapable of looking Powell in the face and thus unable to identify him for Willa's murder. Following the trial, the angry Spoons lead a large mob to lynch Powell, but he is smuggled out of the back door by the police. The crowd is assured by Bart the hangman that it will be a real pleasure to undertake his professional duties. Afterwards, on Christmas Day, Rachel is given gifts by the girls and John timidly presents an apple wrapped in a doily. In return, Rachel gives John a pocket watch. After the happy boy returns upstairs to bed, Rachel warmly declares that children continue to abide and endure.

Production Commentary: When biographer James Boswell asked Dr. Samuel Johnson, "Sir, what is poetry?" Johnson replied, "Why, sir, it is much easier to say what it is not. We all know what light is; but it is not easy to *tell* what it is" (*Life of Samuel Johnson*, 1791, April 12, 1776). In a similar vein, director Charles Laughton's *The Night of the Hunter* is steeped in images that are memorable and striking. And yet at the same time, the hypnotic nature of these images is often complex and difficult to fathom.

It is a source of some irony that Laughton is today remembered for what turned out to be his sole fully-fledged venture behind the camera (notwithstanding his previous foray as director in *The Man on the Eiffel Tower*). His many achievements as an actor tend to be overlooked in favor of this magnificent, distinctive and yet troubling film. Although Laughton does not appear on screen, it is an essential film in the Laughton canon. *The Night of the Hunter* is a distillation of Laughton's lifelong influences and interests. There is, for example, the strong representation of German expressionism in both Stanley Cortez's cinematography and Hilyard Brown's décor. Davis Grubb's gothic novel is full of the moral melodrama of D.W. Griffith. There is also a love of the theater and theatrical staging and use of striking visual and aural effects to function as Brechtian elements integrated into the film…melodrama is suffused with a poetry of stark imagery. Laughton unleashes a maelstrom of divergences that compete for the audience's attention throughout the film.

The narrative involves a toxic mix of impulsiveness and deliberation, pitting the innocence and tenderness of childhood against the corruption and cruelty of adulthood. One faction struggles and rages against the other. A frightening Manichean universe of nightmare gives way finally to a soothing, oneiric vision of redemption.

Composer Walter Schumann had worked with Laughton on the stage production *John Brown's Body*. He provides a fine range of cues that stress distinct contrasts of aural discord, indicative of chaos and mayhem vs. aural harmony indicative of calm and solace. The presentation and use of *mise en scène* contains numerous allusions to the early melodrama of D.W. Griffith and the film makes specific reference to the silent era with use of the camera iris-in and iris-out trope associated with silent film. Both Paul Gregory and Laughton went to the Museum of Modern Art in New York to study surviving Griffith films.

Sparrows (United Artists, William Beaudine, 1926), an acclaimed Mary Pickford suspense drama with a distinct visual gothic style, is also a likely influence on Laughton's film. Pickford plays Molly, the eldest child in a baby farm hidden deep in a swamp. She is compelled to rescue the other children when their cruel master decides one of them must be disposed of. For this film, art director Harry Oliver recreated an alligator-infested swamp. As in *The Night of the Hunter*, the use of studio artifice is obvious and yet appropriate for suggesting a misshapen universe. *Sparrows*' story hovers between a Dickensian depiction of child cruelty against the solidarity and resourcefulness of children as depicted in Grimms' Fairy Tales. Both films share a notable visual style influenced by German expressionism. In *The Night of the Hunter*, one of the set pieces (the children "going down river" à la Mark Twain) involves emphasis on fauna and flora all recreated in the studio environment with use of shadow and light reminiscent of the German director F.W. Murnau, and especially his work on *Sunrise: A Song of Two Humans* (Fox, 1927).

In hindsight, the casting of *The Night of the Hunter* seems a done thing, though at the time it was far from straightforward. Laughton had phoned Robert Mitchum and explained he had a story which he was hoping to make into "a little film." The conversation turned to Laughton's request for Mitchum to take on the leading role: "The character is a bit different. He's a terrible, evil ... shit of a man." "Present," responded Mitchum, eager to be onboard (Server: 264). Rather later in the day, Laurence Olivier let it be known to Gregory and Laughton that he wanted to play the lead. United Artists was not prepared to back the production with Olivier in the film. The part of Rachel Cooper was offered to Elsa Lanchester, but she turned it down. The many hours watching Griffith silents brought the exceptional talent of Lillian Gish to Laughton's attention. The part was offered, and Gish accepted.

For the part of Willa, the filmmakers had Betty Grable in mind! Grable was unsure and kept them waiting until they were forced to look elsewhere. Shelley Winters, a former pupil of Laughton, was offered the part, much to the chagrin of Robert Mitchum.

Set in the rural South during the great Depression of the 1930s, the film denounces falsity of values. This can be viewed as a nuanced critique against the alliance of American patriotism-fascism and religious mass hysteria which during the 1950s was sweeping the country in the guise of McCarthyism. Unfortunately, both form and content of the film proved too radical for its time. Unlike *Hobson's Choice* which had critical kudos lavished on it, *The Night of the Hunter* puzzled and dissatisfied many critics and audiences at the time of its release. The film's presentation of hybrid melodramatic and allegorical forms perplexed Bosley Crowther of the *New York Times* (September 30, 1955). He noted a style of "obvious pretense" and went on to suggest, "The toughness of the grain of the story goes soft and porous towards the end." *Variety* (December 31, 1954) also viewed the film with dismay: "This start for Gregory as producer and Laughton as director is rich in promise but the completed product, bewitching at times, loses sustained drive via too many touches that have a misty effect." More sympathetic was *Monthly Film Bulletin* (January 1956, Vol. 23, No. 264): "The first film directed by Charles Laughton and the last written by the late James Agee, is one of the most daring, eloquent, and personal in style to have come from America in a long time." In addition to critical misunderstanding and public apathy *The Night of the Hunter* suffered from poor distribution. United Artists saw it as too "arty" to promote successfully. In consequence, the film performed poorly on release. Laughton's chance to continue as a film director was stymied.

As a sidebar, in the summer of 1974, Laughton's widow Elsa Lanchester decided to bequeath numerous artifacts relating to the film to the American Film Institute for deposit at the Library of Congress in Washington, D.C. AFI Curator Larry Karr sent two archivists, Robert Gitt and Anthony Slide, to pick up the material. During their time at her home, Lanchester mentioned storing boxes of outtakes from the film. She had decided to send them over to the AFI Film School at the Doheny Mansion in Beverly Hills. The outtakes could be useful for students as teaching material or scholarly research. News reached curator Karr that the outtakes were indeed being used, but not for study purposes. Students were using the picture and magnetic sound trims as "fill leader," constructing work-prints for their own film projects. Horrified, Karr had the film repacked and sent to Washington. When the boxes were opened, an inventory revealed there were more than 80,000 feet of picture and sound trims of varying lengths, all on cores. Before leaving the AFI in November 1975 for Los Angeles, Gitt managed to assemble just the first 20 minutes of footage. The rushes remained stored in an attic at the Kennedy Center in Washington until 1981. Karr then arranged for the material to be sent to Gitt, now working at UCLA Film and Television Archive.

Over the following 20 years, Gitt (with help from UCLA colleagues and work-study students) identified and assembled all the surviving material. In the summer of 2002, a program of two and a half hours of the most interesting selections of the rushes were presented at UCLA's Festival of Preservation. By this time, *The Night of the Hunter* had acquired a reputation as an offbeat cult film. These invaluable documents are illuminating as they give unparalleled access to Laughton's work methods as both director and actor. He spent considerable effort, time and attention on coaching and interacting with the two children. He insisted the camera be left running most of the time so the mood he was trying to create was not interrupted. We can hear and sometimes see Laughton coaxing performances in a firm but agreeable manner from the children and adults in the film. He was less apt to work so closely with the more experienced actors in the cast (Mitchum, Gish, James Gleason and Norma Varden). Though he often interrupted an actor if the performance dissatisfied him, Laughton was accorded respect from cast and crew. As an actor, Laughton would act out all the characters in the film without difficulty and with sensitivity. These surviving rushes also dispel the myth that Laughton disliked both Billy Chapin and Sally Jane Bruce and had trouble directing them. In fact, he established a good rapport with Chapin and was patient, polite and kind as he labored to get the performance he required from Bruce.

This priceless footage demonstrates Laughton's collaborative instincts working at every level. Simon Callow is among many who lavish praise on this gothic hybrid with its visual and aural panache and superb ensemble performances across several generations of actors. I first came across the film over 40 years ago on British television in a series of films intriguingly titled "Images of Childhood."[84] It developed a unique hold on my attention with its depiction of cruel adult terror alongside the naive astonishment indicative of childhood. *The Night of the Hunter* remains both singularly audacious and inspired, yet also a profoundly disturbing and frightening film supportive of a distinctive cinematic style that reveals countless nuances with multiple viewings. Though the narrative does not always run smoothly, didactic and self-conscious elements are inclined to creep in, it is held together by splendid moments of great imagination. Incredibly, Laughton and his collaborators make the film work against all the odds.

Witness for the Prosecution (1957)

Tagline: "The Most Electrifying Entertainment of Our Time!"[85]

U.S. (United Artists/Edward Small/Theme Pictures/Arthur Hornblow)

Credits: Based on the Stage Play by Agatha Christie; Screenplay: Billy Wilder, Harry Kurnitz; Adaptation: Larry Marcus; Photography: Russell Harlan; Assistant Director: Emmett Emerson; Miss Dietrich's Costumes: Edith Head; Costumer: Joseph King; Makeup: Ray Sebastian, Harry Ray, Gustaf Norin; Hairdressers: Helene Parrish, Nellie Manley; Editor: Daniel Mandell; Set Decorator: Howard Bristol; Property Master: Stanley Detlie; Sound: Fred Lau; Song "I May Never Go Home Anymore": Music: Ralph Arthur Roberts; Lyrics: Jack Brooks; Art Director: Alexandre Trauner; Musical Score: Matty Malneck; Music Arranged by Leonid Raab; Music Conducted by Ernest Gold; Production Associate: Doane Harrison; Script Supervisor: John Franco; Production Supervisor: Ben Hersh; Produced by Arthur Hornblow, Jr.; Directed by Billy Wilder; U.S. release: December 17, 1957; Genre: Crime; Black and White; Running Time: 114 minutes; Blu-ray Region A, Kino Lorber, released July 2014; no English subtitle captions for the deaf and hard of hearing; Blu-ray Region B, Masters of Cinema, Eureka Entertainment, released September 2018; English subtitle captions for the deaf and hard of hearing are available on these discs.

Cast: Tyrone Power (*Leonard Vole*); Marlene Dietrich (*Christine Vole*); **Charles Laughton** (*Sir Wilfrid Robarts*); Elsa Lanchester (*Miss Plimsoll*); John Williams (*Brogan-Moore*); Henry Daniell (*Mayhew*); Ian Wolfe (*Carter*); Torin Thatcher (*Mr. Myers*); Norma Varden (*Emily Jane French*); Una O'Connor (*Janet McKenzie*); Francis Compton (*Judge*); Philip Tonge (*Inspector Hearne*); Ruta Lee (*Diana*); **Uncredited Cast**: Patrick Aherne, Frank McClure (*Court Officers*); Walter Bacon (*Bar Patron*); Eddie Baker, Danny Borzage, George Bruggeman, George Calliga, Bess Flowers, Herschel Graham, Stuart Hall, Art Howard, Paul Kruger, Jeanne Lafayette, Wilbur Mack, Paul Power, Waclaw Rekwart, John Roy, Scott Seaton, Lucile Sewall, Cap Somers, Bert Stevens, Arthur Tovey, Glen Walters (*Courtroom Spectators*); Brandon Beach; Bill Erwin, Fred Rapport (*Jurors*); Steve Carruthers, Franklyn Farnum, William H. O'Brien (*Barristers*); Marjorie Eaton (*Miss O'Brien*);

Michael Jeffers, Leoda Richards (*Café Patrons*); Colin Kenny (*Jury Foreman*); Thomas Martin (*Bailiff*); Ottola Nesmith (*Miss Johnson*); J. Pat O'Malley (*Shorts Salesman*); Jack Raine (*Doctor*); Molly Roden (*Miss McHugh*); Jeffrey Sayre (*Clerk at Old Bailey*); Norbert Schiller (*Spotlight Operator in German Cafe*); Ben Wright (*Barrister Reading Charges*).

Awards: Academy Award Nomination: **Best Actor in a Leading Role**: **Charles Laughton**. Academy Award nomination: Best Picture; Academy Award Nomination: Best Director: Billy Wilder; Academy Award Nomination: Best Supporting Actress: Elsa Lanchester; Academy Award Nomination: Best Film Editing: Daniel Mandell; Academy Award Nomination: Best Sound Recording: Samuel Goldwyn Studio Sound Department, Gordon E. Sawyer.

Synopsis: Renowned barrister Sir Wilfrid Robarts, recently discharged from hospital following a heart ailment, decides against medical advice to take on a new criminal case. His client Leonard Vole is charged with the murder of Emily Jane French, a rich widow. Despite rebukes from his nurse Miss Plimsoll, he hears the background of the case. Although Vole is the main beneficiary of the late Mrs. French's will, Sir Wilfrid believes him innocent of the crime. Sir Wilfrid next interviews Vole's German wife Christine, who remains self-possessed under sustained questioning. She is able to provide an alibi, although not an entirely plausible one. Sir Wilfrid is surprised when during the trial, she is called as a witness for the prosecution. Though a wife cannot be compelled to testify against her husband, it seems Christine was still married to a German when she married Vole, who was in the British army of occupation in Germany. On the witness stand, she testifies that Vole had confessed the murder and that her conscience dictated that she provide the whole truth. Sir Wilfrid is contacted by a mysterious woman who, for a fee, hands over love letters from Christine to her lover Max. Christine's secret affair provides such a strong motive for her to have lied that the jury finds Vole not guilty. Sir Wilfrid finds the verdict troubling. After the conclusion of the trial, Christine, alone in the courtroom with Sir Wilfrid, reveals that his suspicions are correct. Vole had told Christine before the trial that a jury would not believe the alibi of a loving wife. Instead, she had given testimony implicating him and then had forged letters from a non-existent lover, and in disguise had played the mysterious woman who provided them to Sir Wilfrid. She further admits she saved Vole knowing him to be guilty because she loves him. Vole overhears his wife's admission and, safe in the knowledge he cannot be tried twice for the same crime, he confirms he did indeed murder Mrs. French. Sir Wilfrid is incensed. Christine receives a nasty surprise when she finds Vole has befriended a younger woman and is intending to go abroad with her. In a fit of jealousy, she picks up the knife used as evidence in the trial and stabs Vole to death. Sir Wilfrid decides to cancel his Bermuda vacation so he can take on Christine's defense in court.

Selected Dialogue:

ROBARTS: "Just roll up your mouth. You talk too much. If I'd known how much you

A consummate double act caught on film for a final time. Elsa Lanchester as Miss Plimsoll and Laughton as Sir Wilfrid Robarts QC in *Witness for the Prosecution* (1957).

talked, I'd never have come out of my coma."

ROBARTS: "Mr. Vole, you must learn to trust me. For no other reason than I'm a mean, ill-tempered old man who hates to lose."

ROBARTS: "If you were a woman, Miss Plimsoll, I would strike you."

Production Commentary: On February 4, 1956, *Motion Picture Herald* announced Edward Small had purchased the rights to film Agatha Christie's play *Witness for the Prosecution*. Arthur Hornblow, Jr., was assigned as producer. From the beginning, famed director Billy Wilder had Laughton penciled in for casting in the central role of the testy barrister. Theirs was a match, if not made in Heaven, then one based on mutual respect. Both director and star shared careers based on toil and perfection. Wilder was intrigued by Laughton's abilities as a star performer, and he allowed him a great deal of leeway in taking on board some of the many suggestions Laughton offered concerning how to play a particular scene. Wilder and his writers made important changes to Christie's play. They gave the leading character of the barrister a heart infirmity, cognac and cigars. They also introduced a new character, Nurse Plimsoll, played marvelously by Elsa Lanchester. The interchange between Laughton and Lanchester is peerless in its comic timing and delivery. Having been married for nearly 30 years, their familiarity and understanding of each other's foibles lends a potency to their many acerbic exchanges and witty repartee. It was to be their final screen encounter.

As a tribute to Marlene Dietrich, Wilder devised a flashback sequence showing her character, a chanteuse in a basement Berlin café, singing, "I May Never Go Home Again." The scene ends with a raucous fistfight. To stage this scene cost $90,000. This change of *mise en scène* is a welcome diversion from the formal judicial procedures of the Old Bailey backdrop. Underneath the acerbic comedy, Wilder explores the human condition. He shows the darker side of human nature with characters who are avaricious, conceited and deceitful. Laughton is outstanding as the pompous lawyer and Wilder casts a wonderful supporting cast for the main three stars to interact with.

Laughton seems to relax and enjoy himself. He was in fact in the company of such old friends as Henry Daniell, who had acted with him in *The Suspect* and *Captain Kidd*; Una O'Connor, who had appeared in *The Barretts of Wimpole Street* and played his old mother in *This Land Is Mine*, and John Williams, who had played a barrister to Laughton's judge in *The Paradine Case*.

Contemporary critics called Laughton's performance as a major asset of the film. Richard Gertner of *Motion Picture Daily* (November 27, 1957) was effusive:

[M]ajor thespian honors go to Laughton as the crotchety old criminal lawyer whom success has made arrogant but who still holds vast respect for the English law. This is easily his juiciest role since Captain Bligh, and he plays it in full knowledge of that fact— whether he is hurling insults at his nurse, dropping his monocle in feigned surprise, or spluttering protests in the courtroom. His is a marvelously entertaining performance in a wholly enjoyable show.

Film Bulletin (November 25, 1957) considered his performance a tour de force and went on to enthuse, "If there was ever any doubt on how droll and devastating [Laughton] could be, his crusty and complex portrait of a brilliant criminal barrister should dispel it forever." *Harrison's Report* (November 30, 1957) stated, "Charles Laughton turns in one of the best performances of his distinguished career...." It went on to note, "[T]he comedy stems from the quarrelsome byplay between him and Elsa Lanchester, his private nurse, who hounds his every movement with warnings about what he can and cannot do. Laughton's remarks as he tries to escape Miss Lanchester's proprietary clutches are hilariously funny."

Laughton enjoyed the divergence from the original source of short story and play. He delighted in the many touches Wilder was able to bring to the script: the humor and banter of the dialogue, and a sense of a last hurrah for an old order on the cusp of extinction in Hollywood itself. Laughton attacks his role with relish and has a field day with various props that appear during the course of the film. These include a stairlift, cigars and a monocle. His performance as a grand inquisitor is suitably magisterial.

Tyrone Power and Dietrich also deliver powerful performances. It proved to be Power's final completed film before his early tragic death of a heart attack on the set of *Solomon and Sheba* in 1958.

Witness for the Prosecution proved a huge box office draw, earning almost $4,000,000. It still stands today as a model of its kind, both as a successful adaptation of a high-profile stage property to the demands of cinematic exposition and as a vivid demonstration of Laughton's capacities and contradictions as an actor. His pacing of barrister Robarts is split between an astute, professional, pragmatic approach to the judicial process based on the adversarial examination of facts in a court of law, and a private disregard for colleagues and clients, with a penchant for indulging in caustic barbs at the foibles of the legal and medical professions, and insulting those who are its representatives. In the end, Robart's self-assurance is revealed to be misplaced. He is shaken by the travails of the trial and the final revelation following the verdict, but remains unbowed at the end. All in all, it's a winning combination. *Witness for the Prosecution* remains a supreme delight for Laughton aficionados.

Under Ten Flags aka Sotto Dieci Bandiere (1960)

Tagline: "The Killer-Ship Atlantis ... She Sailed Under Many Flags—She Fought Under One!"[86]

U.S. (Paramount Pictures)/Italy (Dino De Laurentiis)

Credits: Based on the original diaries of Bernhard Rogge; Screenplay: Vittoriano Petrilli, Duilio Coletti, Ulrich Mohr; Additional Dialogue: William Douglas Home; Military and Historical Advisor: Ulrich Mohr; Photography: Aldo Tonti; Music: Nino Rota; Conducted by Franco Ferrara; Art Director: Mario Garbuglia; Costumes: Piero Gherardi; Editor: Jerry Webb; Dialogue Supervisor: Manuel Del Campo; Associate Producer: Ralph B. Serpe; Production Assistant: Alfredo De Laurentiis; Sound Engineer: Piero Cavazzuti; Sound Editor: Renzo Lucidi; Camera Operator: Riccardo Pallottini; Assistant Directors: Mario Maffei, Davide Carbonari; Makeup: Goffredo Rocchetti, Giuliano Laurenti; Associate Director: Silvio Narizzano; Produced by Dino De Laurentiis; Directed by Duilio Coletti; U.S. release: September 15, 1960; Genre: War; Black and White; Running Time: 92 minutes; DVD Region 2, Miramar (Spain), released February 2009; no English subtitle captions for the deaf and hard of hearing.

Cast: Van Heflin (*Commander Reger*); **Charles Laughton** (***Admiral Russell***); Mylène Demongeot (*Zizi*); John Ericson (*Lt. Krueger*); Cecil Parker (*Col. Howard*); Folco Lulli (*Paco*); Alex Nicol (*Knoche*); Liam Redmond (*Capt. Windsor*); Eleonora Rossi Drago (*Sara Braun*); Ralph Truman (*Adm. Benson*); Gregoire Aslan (*Master of the Abdullah*); Peter Carsten (*Lt. Mohr*); Gianmaria Volontè (*Sam Braun*); Dieter Eppler (*Dr. Hartmann*); Edith Arlene Peters (*Nun*); Corrado Pani, Geronimo Meynier (*German Sailors*); Walter Barnes (*Mr. Andrews*); Moira Orfei (*Clown's Assistant*); Gérard Herter (*German Submarine Captain*); Umberto Spadaro (*Radio Operator*); Philo Hauser (*Clown*).

Synopsis: Commander Reger is skipper of a mystery surface raider, *Atlantis*, a heavily armed German ship which masquerades as a merchantman and flies whatever flag is convenient. He has been wreaking havoc on British shipping. Reger uses the trick of revealing his identity at the final moment, forcing the other ship to surrender without sending an SOS or describing its attacker. Reger always aims to take passengers and crew aboard his ship before sinking theirs. Admiral Russell of the British Security Lanes Command, confident that the raider must be a surface vessel, orders British freighters to describe any vessel approaching them. Krueger, a fanatic Nazi lieutenant on the *Atlantis*, wants to sink all British shipping on sight. Reger overrules him. Disguised as a Japanese ship, the *Atlantis* captures the British *City of Liverpool*. Her captain, Windsor, is taken prisoner. When the *Atlantis* stops the *Abdullah*, its crafty master hoists a surrender flag, then fires on the raider, forcing Reger to fire back and cause injury and death among those aboard. The *Abdullah*'s radio operator is able to give the British Admiralty its position. Among the *Abdullah* survivors are Zizi, a French entertainer; Jewish refugees Sam and Sara Braun, and a nun. Reger tells the *Abdullah* captain that he will be tried for his crime of firing after surrender, by an international court. Both the master of the *Abdullah* and Krueger want the Jewish couple killed, but Reger befriends them. Pregnant Sara gives birth to her baby. The *Atlantis* next outwits and sinks a cruiser sent after her. Knoche, an American who resembles a certain German naval officer, is assigned to steal a chart from the

German's office, which will help Admiral Russell determine where the raider is. Knoche is successful in obtaining the chart. Aboard the *Atlantis*, Zizi loses interest in Krueger when she realizes how pro–Nazi he is. The *Atlantis* transfers its prisoners to a Norwegian ship. Captain Windsor, ill, remains aboard. Although not definitely sure it is the *Atlantis*, Russell orders a cruiser to open fire on the ship which has hoisted its Nazi flag. Reger does not return fire and scuttles his disabled ship so that the British won't know if they have sunk the right vessel. Captain Windsor is killed on the *Atlantis* by British shrapnel. At the British Admiralty, Russell admits he doesn't know if he destroyed the right ship and will keep forces looking for the *Atlantis*. He praises the action taken by Reger.

Selected Dialogue:

RUSSELL: "Russell speaking…. Which Russell? I'll tell you! The one who roasts ignorant operators on a spit and eats them for his dinner! *Admiral* Russell!"

Production Commentary: In his biographical sketch of Laughton, critic David Shipman suggested that Laughton undertook this film merely to show Rome to his new lover (Shipman: 341). Superficial though this appears, it is as good a reason as any to explain Laughton's supporting part. In his final playing of a nautical officer, Laughton's performance as Admiral Russell is one-note: cantankerous and curmudgeonly. It was the sort of one-dimensional part he could do by expending little effort and yet guaranteed to produce the maximum effect of chewing the scenery and going way over the top. One is reminded of the sort of role a Laird Cregar or Sydney Greenstreet were given during the halcyon days of the studio system.

To be fair to Laughton, the fanciful plot is hardly congenial to logical, moderate acting on his part. *Harrison's Reports* (September 3, 1960) was somewhat charitable in its assessment of the film: "A fairly good, suspenseful naval war picture…. Charles Laughton is very believable as the clever British admiral in charge of tracking down the elusive raider." *Film Bulletin* (September 5, 1960) was nearer the mark when it pointed out that Laughton was cast for "mild marquee value." The *Monthly Film Bulletin* (January 1961, Vol. 28, No. 324) gave leeway to the gravitas of an

Laughton appears in the uniform of a naval officer for the last time as the curmudgeonly Admiral Russell in *Under Ten Flags* (1960).

old thespian, "Laughton's bulldog manner crunches a quip or two from an ill-conceived script."

Like many international co-productions, *Under Ten Flags* is overly ambitious and too eager to please the international market. Though perfectly watchable, its story is muddled and the direction is wanting in imposing any real cinematic style. Duilio Coletti had directed a submarine drama in 1954. *La Grande Speranza*, known in translation as *Submarine Attack*, shot aboard a real sub. That film competed for the Golden Bear prize at the 1954 Berlin International Film Festival—and lost to *Hobson's Choice*.

Under Ten Flags finds Laughton merely slumming, and glad to accept the hospitality of his Italian hosts.

Spartacus (1960)

Tagline: "They trained him to kill for their pleasure … but they trained him too well…."[87]

U.S. (Universal-International/Bryna Productions)

Credits: Screenplay: Dalton Trumbo; Based on the Novel by Howard Fast; Photography: Russell Metty; Production Designer: Alexander Golitzen; Art Director: Eric Orbom; Set Decorators: Russell A. Gausman, Julia Heron; Additional

Spartacus (1960)

Scenes Photographed by Clifford Stine; Production Aide: Stan Margulies; Wardrobe: Peruzzi; Miss Simmons' Costumes: Bill Thomas; Costumes: Valles; Editor: Robert Lawrence; Assistants to the Editor: Robert Schulte, Fred Chulack; Score Co-conductor: Joseph Gershenson; Music Editor: Arnold Schwarzwald; Makeup: Bud Westmore; Hair Stylist: Larry Germain; Assistant Director: Marshall Green; Music Composed and Conducted by Alex North; Executive Producer: Kirk Douglas; Produced by Edward Lewis; Directed by Stanley Kubrick; U.S. release: October 6, 1960; Genre: Historical Epic; Technicolor and Super Technirama 70; Running Time: 196 minutes; DVD and Blu-ray all Regions, Universal Studios, released October 2015; English subtitle captions for the deaf and hard of hearing are available on these discs.

Cast: Kirk Douglas (*Spartacus*); Laurence Olivier (*Crassus*); Jean Simmons (*Varinia*); Tony Curtis (*Antonius*); **Charles Laughton (Gracchus)**; Peter Ustinov (*Batiatus*); John Gavin (*Julius Caesar*); Nina Foch (*Helena*); Herbert Lom (*Tigranes*); John Ireland (*Crixus*); John Dall (*Marcus Glabrus*); Charles McGraw (*Marcellus*); Joanna Barnes (*Claudia*); Harold J. Stone (*David*); Woody Strode (*Draba*); Peter Brocco (*Ramon*); Paul Lambert (*Gannicus*); Robert J. Wilke (*Guard Captain*); Nicholas Dennis (*Dionysus*); John Hoyt (*Caius*); Frederic Worlock (*Laelius*); **Uncredited Cast**: Philip Altman, John Barton, David Bond, Polly Burson, Doris Darling, Mary Donovan, Lila Finn, Harold Goodwin, Donna Hall, Don Happy, Edith Happy, Betty Harford, Harry Harvey Jr., Lars Hensen, Shep Houghton, Pete Kellett, Joan McKellen, Eddie Parker, Lorrie Pettit, Chuck Roberson, Frosty Royce, Helen Thurston (*Slaves*); Arthur Batanides, Ted de Corsia, Robert Stevenson (*Legionnaires*); Paul Baxley, Don Bramblett, Rudy Bukich, Al Carmichael, Frank Donahue, Louie Elias, Maurice Elias, Hubie Kerns, Gordon Mitchell, Regis Parton, Victor Paul, Jack Perkins, Wally Rose, Aaron Saxon, Jim Sears, Alex Sharp, Tom Steele, Jerry Summers, Glen Thompson, Charles Wilcox, Billy Williams (*Gladiators*); John Benson, Wayne Burson, Dick Crockett, Carey Loftin, Rod Normond, Robert Osborne, Larry Perron, Harvey Parry, Ronnie Rondell Jr., Peter Virgo, Will J. White (*Guards*); Shari Lee Bernath (*Little Girl*); Norman Bishop, Courtney Brown, Bob Burns, Seamon Glass, Stubby Kruger, Preston Peterson, Eugene Poole, George Robotham (*Pirates*); Bill Blackburn (*Prisoner*); Buff Brady, Brad Brown, Jerry Brown, Joe Canutt, Tap Canutt, Bill Catching, Chuck Courtney, Robert F. Hoy, Valley Keene, Desmond Koch, Irvin "Zabo" Koszewski, Cliff Lyons, Russell Saunders, Charles Schaeffer, Bill Shannon, Buddy Van Horn, Jack Williams (*Soldiers*); Paul E. Burns (*Fimbria*); John Daheim (*Capua Guard*); Tony Dante (*Roman Soldier/Christian Soldier*); Terence de Marney (*Majordomo*); Craig Duncan (*Petitioner*); Johnny Duncan (*Beheaded Man*); Roy Engel (*Roman Businessman*); Richard Farnsworth (*Salt Mine Slave/Gladiator/Slave General*); Logan Field, John Stephenson (*Centurion*); Duke Fishman, Kenner C. Kemp, Paul Kruger (*Roman Senator*); Charlotte Fletcher (*Mother with Child*); Paul Frees (*The Voice of Caius*); Jeanne Gerson (*Woman Selling Chestnuts*); Joe Gold, Chuck Hayward, Manuel Herreros, Sol Gorss, Charles Horvath, Gil Perkins (*Slave Leaders*); Marvin Goux (*Trainer*); James Griffith (*Otho*); Jack Grinnage (*Petitioner*); Brad Harris (*Gladiator/Soldier*); Joe Haworth (*Marius*); Vinton Hayworth (*Metallius*); Wayne Heffley (*Slave Guard*); Hallene Hill (*Beggar Woman*); Basil Howes (*Orderly*); Loren Janes (*Salt Mine Slave/Gladiator/Slave General*); Jil Jarmyn (*Julia*); Anthony Jochim (*Petitioner*); Duke Johnson, Harry C. Johnson (*Jugglers*); Paul Keast (*Roman Businessman*); Aron Kincaid (*Crassus' Standard-Bearer*); Dayton Lummis (*Symmachus*); Otto Malde (*Roman General*); Bob Morgan (*Galeno*); Tracy Olsen (*Girl*); Dayton Osmond (*Boy—Chicken Seller*); Leonard Penn (*Garrison Officer*); Vic Perrin (*Narrator*); Bill Raisch (*Soldier Whose Arm is Hacked Off*); Evelyn Rudie (*Little Girl in Slave Camp*); Scott Seaton (*Roman Senator*); Carol Daniels, Autumn Russell, Kay Stewart, Jo Summers, Lynda Lee Williams (*Slave Girls*); Larry Thor (*Staff Officer*); John Truax (*Prisoner*); Don Turner, Fred Zendar (*Guards*), Lil Valenty (*Old Crone*); Dale Van Sickel (*Trainer*); Louise Vincent (*Slave at Gracchus' House*); Judy Whitney (*Child*); Carleton Young (*Herald*).

Awards: Academy Award: Best Actor in a Supporting Role: Peter Ustinov; Academy Award: Best Color Cinematography: Russell Metty; Academy Award: Best Color Art Direction-Set Direction: Alexander Golitzen, Eric Orbom, Russell A. Gausman, Julia Heron; Academy Award: Best Color Costume Design: Valles; Bill Thomas.

Synopsis: Spartacus, a proud Thracian slave, left to starve to death after disabling a guard by biting his leg, is rescued and bought by Batiatus, wealthy head of the gladiator school at Capua. General Marcus Licinius Crassus, a wealthy and powerful patrician, pays Batiatus to stage a fight-to-the-death between several gladiators, to be selected by the women of the party—one of them being Helena. An Ethiopian, Draba, is matched against Spartacus. Draba refuses to kill his friend and turns instead on the spectators. Crassus finishes him off with a knife in the neck. A slave, Varinia, falls in love with Spartacus. He soon leads a gladiator revolt, frees slaves everywhere and marches to the south

148 (1960) Spartacus

toward freedom. Varinia, sold to Crassus, runs away from Batiatus, by Spartacus. The two vow never to separate. Spartacus' growing might causes a crisis in the Roman Senate. Lentulus Gracchus, a Roman political leader, opposes Crassus for control of the empire. Gracchus' strength as a plebeian lies in controlling the mob which Crassus abhors. While Crassus is away, Gracchus proposes to the Senate that Glabrus, a commander of the Roman Garrison, be sent against Spartacus. Crassus knows this means defeat for Glabrus and orders the youthful commander to silently leave Rome with his troops. Crassus' body slave Antonius (with whom, it is suggested, he seeks a gay affair) escapes to join Spartacus. Spartacus crushes Glabrus' legions and sends the young officer back to Rome to convey the message that Spartacus asks only freedom for himself and his followers. Spartacus has bribed some pirates to carry his army from the mainland. But Roman bribes are greater. On the eve of freedom, the ships are unavailable to Spartacus. Meanwhile, Roman forces have landed on each side of Spartacus to cut him off. Crassus commands a third army attacking from the north. Spartacus and his men put up a strong fight, but are defeated. Six thousand of his soldiers refuse to identify him. All are crucified except Spartacus and Antonius, who has become Spartacus' friend and lieutenant. Crassus, aware who Spartacus is, orders that he and Antonius fight to the death. Knowing that the loser will be crucified, Spartacus slays Antonius. Crassus has captured Varinia and her newborn child and wants her to be his wife. But Gracchus has her kidnapped by Batiatus and gives them both papers to escape, making Varinia a free woman. Then he commits suicide. While escaping, Varinia passes the dying crucified Spartacus, shows him their child, and continues on her journey to freedom.

Selected Dialogue:
GRACCHUS: "Let's mix business with pleasure."
GRACCHUS: "Don't be so stiff-necked. Politics is a practical profession. If a criminal has what you want, you do business with him."

Production Commentary: *Spartacus* was Kirk Douglas' film company Bryna Productions and Universal-International's entry into high-class, big-budget spectacle. Allocated a budget of $5,000,000 and Anthony Mann as director, the epic had a troubled production. Mann was dropped and Stanley Kubrick took over the directorial duties. In the end, it took two years of filming and some $12,000,000 to bring *Spartacus* to the screen.

The film was taken from a novel by staunch Communist Howard Fast. Fast was assigned to adapt his own novel for the screen, but Douglas was nonplussed by his efforts and the script was handed over to Dalton Trumbo. Trumbo, a victim of the Hollywood blacklist, had recently been reduced to working as a screenwriter under a series of pseudonyms. In 1960 he was rehabilitated when he received on screen credit for scripting Otto Preminger's *Exodus*. Douglas also

A candid photo on the set of *Spartacus* (1960) during a break in filming. Left to right: Laughton in casual clothes, chats to a relaxed Jean Simmons, in costume as Varinia. Peter Ustinov, also in costume as Batiatus, looks on listening with intense interest.

decided to give Trumbo full credit for the *Spartacus* screenplay.

The film was almost entirely produced in Hollywood (with the exception of battle scenes shot in Spain). Shooting began in November 1958. Laughton's work schedule dictated that he worked on the film for only three weeks, but for this assignment he was paid a substantial $41,000. In order to assemble a starry cast, Douglas as producer had sent each star a customized version of the script in which their role appeared to offer the most substantial part. Laughton was unhappy, for on arrival he noted that the script had been altered substantially from the version he had been sent. He spent his time sulking as Laurence Olivier appeared to have the upper hand in terms of dialogue and screen time. This antipathy translated itself to their on-screen characters. Their exchanges are brief, acerbic and businesslike. Laughton may have fewer scenes than his younger counterpart, but each is instilled with minute attention to detail that marked Laughton out from his peers. Whereas Olivier portrays the autocratic Roman patrician Crassus as cold, superior and power-obsessed, Laughton's good Roman republican Gracchus is warm, witty, hedonistic and pragmatic in attitude.

Nearly an hour passes before Laughton appears in the film, walking into the Senate accompanied by John Gavin as Julius Caesar. On his feet speaking is Senator Laelius (Frederic Worlock). Laughton's patrician statesman has sharp disquisitions and exchanges with an unctuous slave trader, Batiatus (Peter Ustinov). The pair conduct their business while dining on an epicurean spread of cooked birds. Ustinov volunteered to rewrite the scene and Laughton was happy for him to do so. Their witty banter whilst gorging themselves is a welcome distraction from the bombast and visceral sound and fury of gladiator combat that fills much of the three-hour screening time.

The next scene has Gracchus on the floor of the Senate speaking his mind. He points out that it is just a ploy by Crassus to resign from public life in shame following the defeat of the Roman army by slaves. He will be plotting a comeback as supreme ruler of Rome. Another scene has Laughton on the Senate floor again responding to the conquering army headed by Spartacus. In a Roman steambath, he asks Crassus to head the Roman army to defeat Spartacus. In return, Crassus requests he be made dictator of Rome. The request is denied, but Crassus knows too well the deteriorating situation of the Roman armies will force Gracchus to change his mind.

The final scene before Gracchus' suicide finds him resigned to his fate, but taking care to arrange the lives of others before his own death. Here he again encounters Jean Simmons, with whom he had appeared in *Young Bess*. Alas, the suicide of Gracchus, though filmed, was discarded.

In 1991, Robert A. Harris and James C. Katz undertook a thorough restoration of the film. During a nine-month restoration sponsored by Universal and the American Film Institute, they brought the original color negative back to life as it had undergone fading and notable deterioration over decades. Their researches also yielded several deleted scenes being restored to the film including a "oysters and snails" conversation between Olivier and Tony Curtis. Unfortunately, several cut scenes involving Gracchus have been irretrievably lost. Some of these deleted scenes can be glimpsed in early distributed lobby cards. Harris and Katz later supervised a digital restoration for the film's fifty-fifth anniversary in 2015. Lost these scenes may be, but Laughton's performance as a patrician Roman senator has not diminished in its insolence, contempt and hardheaded sensibility. This epic is an amalgam of old-school acting (Laughton, Olivier) and contemporary acting styles (a riveting powerhouse central performance from Douglas, the inclusion of Woody Strode's black gladiator a suitable inference to civil rights) combined with technical innovations (stereo track, Techicolor and Super Technirama 70). Laughton's name, billed fourth, was of significant marquee value in an impressive cast list. His character served as a pragmatic antagonist to Olivier's power-hungry Crassus. As Laughton vies with Olivier both politically and financially for control of the Senate, the ghosts of Nero in *The Sign of the Cross*, Claudius in the abandoned *I, Claudius* and Herod in *Salome* are all there in his delivery of Gracchus. Laughton more than holds his own among a galaxy of star talent.

This epic yielded a mammoth $14,600,000

at the box office and won four Oscars, although its failure to be nominated for the four main Oscars (Best Picture, Director, Actor and Screenplay) suggests the influence of right-wing groups opposed to the credits of known Communist sympathizers Howard Fast and Dalton Trumbo.

Film Bulletin (October 17, 1960) presented the film with various eye-catching headlines such as "Film of Distinction" and "*Spartacus* Ranks with Great Films of All Time." It went on to enthuse, "Technically top-drawer in every respect. A roadshow blockbuster for every type of audience."[88] Critical reaction at the time was mixed, but in general favorable. The *Monthly Film Bulletin* (January 1961, Vol. 28, No. 324) spotted the dilemma of the traditional theatrical cerebral approach and the modern flamboyant visceral method of delivering lines with poise and purpose: "[T]he film quickly resolves itself into an unequal contest between players trained in the classical tradition (Olivier, Laughton, Ustinov) who can wear togas with dignity and speak the most fustian speeches with style, and those, mainly represented by Kirk Douglas, who would make even the noblest lines of Shakespeare sound like something out of a Western." *Harrison's Reports* (October 8, 1960) quipped, "A thinking man's star-studded spectacle. Packed with sex, swordplay, slavery and sneaky statesmen, [*Spartacus*] should appeal to both class and unsophisticated audiences…. Charles Laughton is a charming, but hard-hitting politico as Gracchus." Stalwart critic C.A. Lejeune of the *Observer* (December 11, 1960) lambasted the film's blatant commercialism, stating that it was "weighed down by cost and glamour of the stars." Lejeune went on to complain about a lack of imagination in its approach: "And never for a moment could I forget that the characters were actors, earning their salary with exemplary skill but not so often with imagination." However, amid the gloom she gleaned a ray of intelligence and relative restraint among the exhibition of violent butchery and torture: "It is significant, perhaps, that the most completely satisfying scene in *Spartacus* … is a mighty tussle of wits between two superb entertainers, Charles Laughton and Peter Ustinov. Toga-ed, drawling, sophisticated, well aware of each other's virtuosity, they represent a pair of slightly obese Roman patricians, discussing in gentlemanly accents how to be absolutely foul." The London *Times* critic (December 6, 1960) also saluted the duo: "There is a considerable tonnage here and, what is more, a wealth of sly and knowledgeable wit—Mr. Ustinov rolling his eye in half-delighted anticipation of disaster. Mr. Laughton exuding a generous self-indulgence, seem thoroughly to relish their splash of style and personality while, at the same time they do something to make Batiatus and Gracchus credible."

As a penultimate film performance, Gracchus, a charming but equally chastening member of the Roman Senate, who knows what he wants and knows how to acquire it, remains attention-grabbing. Despite the disadvantage of script changes and scenes shot and then deleted, Laughton dominates each scene in which he appears with apparent ease. Upon hearing of Laughton's death, Kirk Douglas paid him this tribute: "Laughton was an actor who dared. The modern trend in acting is to underplay and, as a result, many actors come up doing nothing. But when Laughton was on the stage or screen, you knew it" (Weaver: 11).

Asked in 1960 by *Variety* (October 26) whether he was a superb actor or a magnificent ham, Laughton replied, "I don't think there is a difference. All acting, like painting, is exaggeration of a kind. It's just a difference of degree and whether you get caught at it."

In Laughton's next film, and as it turned out his final appearance, he would unite all the bravura display of acting technique (use of inflection, nuance and intuition) he had applied in *Spartacus* and turn it towards another (modern) political arena with equally fetching results.

Advise & Consent (1962)

Tagline: "Are the men and women of Washington really like this?"[89]

US (Columbia/Alpha-Alpina/Otto Preminger)

Credits: Music: Jerry Fielding; Production Designer: Lyle Wheeler; Photography: Sam Leavitt (Panavision); Camera Operators: Saul Midwall, Emil Oster Jr.; Electrical Supervisor: James Almond; Construction Manager: Arnold Pine; Key Grip: Morris Rosen; Makeup: Del Armstrong, Robert Jiras; Hairdressing: Myrl Stoltz; Wardrobe: Joe King, Adele Parmenter, Michael Harte; Property Master: Meyer Gordon; Still Photographers:

Al St. Hilaire, Josh Weiner; Editor: Louis R. Loeffler; Sound: Harold Lewis, William Hamilton; Music Recording: Murray Spivack; Music Editor: Lee Osborne; Sound Effects Editor: Leon Birnbaum; Script Supervisor: Kathleen Fagan; Set Decorator: Eli Bennechie; Furs: Sol Schulman; Diamond Jewelry: Harry Winston; Production Manager: Jack McEdward; Unit Manager: Henry Weinberger; Production Secretary: Florence Nerlinger; Production Assistant: David De Silva; Costume Coordinator: Hope Bryce; Miss Tierney's Clothes Designed by Bill Blass; Technical Advisor: Allen Drury; Titles Designed by Saul Bass; First Assistant Director: L.V. McCardle Jr.; Assistant Directors: Don Kranze, Larry Powell, Charles Bohart; Lyrics for "The Song from *Advise & Consent*" by Ned Washington; Based on the Novel by Allen Drury; Screenplay: Wendell Mayes; Produced and Directed by Otto Preminger; U.S. release: June 6, 1962; Genre: Political Drama; Black and White; Running Time: 139 minutes; DVD Region 1, Warner Home Video, *Henry Fonda: The Signature Collection* box set released September 2006; *TCM Greatest Classic Legends: Henry Fonda* box set, released April 2014; *Controversial Classics* box set, released May 2005; English subtitle captions for the deaf and hard of hearing are available on these discs.

Cast: Henry Fonda (*Robert Leffingwell*); **Charles Laughton** (***Senator Seabright Cooley***); Don Murray (*Senator Brigham Anderson*); Walter Pidgeon (*Senate Majority Leader*); Peter Lawford (*Senator Lafe Smith*); Gene Tierney (*Dolly Harrison*); Franchot Tone (*The President*); Lew Ayres (*The Vice President*); Burgess Meredith (*Herbert Gelman*); Eddie Hodges (*Johnny Leffingwell*); Paul Ford (*Senator Stanley Danta*); George Grizzard (*Senator Fred Van Ackerman*); Inga Swenson (*Ellen Anderson*); Frank Sinatra (*Voice*); Edward Andrews (*Senator Orrin Knox*); Paul McGrath (*Hardiman Fletcher*); Will Geer (*Senate Minority Leader*); Betty White (*Senator Betty Adams*); Tom Helmore (*British Ambassador*); Rene Paul (*French Ambassador*); Paul Stevens (*Louis Newborn*); Russ Brown (*Mike—Night Watchman*); Malcolm Atterbury (*Senator Tom August*); Janet Jane Carty (*Pidge Anderson*); Hilary Eaves (*Lady Maudulayne*); Michele Montau (*Celeste Barre*); J. Edward McKinley (*Senator Powell Hanson*); William Quinn (*Senator Paul Hendershot*); Tiki Santos (*Senator Kanaho*); Raoul De Leon (*Senator Velez*); Chet Stratton (*Reverend Carney Birch*); Larry Tucker (*Manuel*); Bettie Johnson (*Lafe's Girl*); John Granger (*Ray Shaff*); Sid Gould (*Bartender*); Meyer Davis and His Orchestra; Irv Kupcinet, Robert C. Wilson, Alan Emory, Jessie Stearns Buscher, Milton Berliner, Allen W. Cromley, Wayne Tucker (*Journalists*); William Knighton (*President of White House Correspondent's Association*); The Honorable Guy M. Gillette (*Senator Harper*); The Honorable Henry Fountain Ashurst (*Senator McCafferty*); **Uncredited Cast**: Leon Alton, Walter Bacon, Eddie Baker, Brandon Beach, Mario Cimino, Roger Clark, Harry Denny, George DeNormand, George Ford, Bobby Gilbert, Clive Halliday (*Senators*), Leoda Richards, Clark Ross, Dick Ryan, Hal Taggart, Paul Power, Bernard Sell, Virgil Johanson, Joseph LaCava, Al McGranary, Sol Murgi, William Meader (*Senators*); Paul Cristo, Charles Perry, Stephen Soldi (*Senate Gallery Spectators*); Cay Forester (*President's Secretary*); Polly Guggenheim, Helen Hardin (*Washington Socialites*); Henry Jackson (*Drink Refuser*); Kenner G. Kemp (*Reporter in Senate Chamber*); Harold Miller (*Senate Official*); Norman Papson (*Gay Bar Patron*); Walter Reed (*Senate Staff Clerk*); John Roy (*Reporter*); Evelyn Lincoln, Carlisle Runge, Mrs. Carlisle Runge, Louis Scheyven, Mrs. Louis Scheyven (*Washington Party Guests*); Jeffrey Sayre (*Senate Staff Clerk*); Marion Lloyd Stearns White, Harty Wadsworth, Jerry Wadsworth, Byron White (*Washington Party Guests*).

Just off the streetcar and ready to do battle on (and off) the floor of the United States Senate. In his final film, Laughton gives a superb performance as Washington wheeler-dealer, Senator Seabright "Seab" Cooley in Otto Preminger's *Advise & Consent* (1962).

(1962) Advise & Consent

Synopsis: A determined and headstrong President of the United States, realizing he is terminally ill, requests the United States Senate to "advise and consent" the appointment of controversial Robert L. Leffingwell as a new Secretary of State. Southern Senator Seabright Cooley harbors personal hostility against Leffingwell and is determined to block his appointment. To this end, he produces witness Herbert Gelman, who testifies that Leffingwell had displayed Communist tendencies during his formative years. Leffingwell confesses the truth of the accusation to the president but denies the accusation while testifying under oath in front of the Senate subcommittee. When committee chairman Brigham Anderson learns of his perjury, he demands the withdrawal of Leffingwell's nomination. The President refuses, so Anderson decides, in the public interest, to expose the perjury. Before he is able to do so, he is blackmailed by Senator Fred Ackerman, who threatens to reveal a brief homosexual affair in Anderson's early life. Unable to tell his wife because of the stigma, Anderson commits suicide. Following the tragic news, the Senate votes on Leffingwell's nomination. The result is a tie and the decisive vote is to be cast by the vice president. As he ponders his course, news arrives that the president has died. The responsibility of his new presidential office brings about an about-face: He refrains from casting his vote, and instead decides he will name his own Secretary of State.

Selected Dialogue:

COOLEY: "Us old buzzards can see a mouse dying from 10,000 feet up. Us old buzzards have the sharpest eyes in creation. Right now, I'm studying the terrain."

COOLEY: "It's my day for sunning myself, Mr. Majority Leader, like an old bullfrog on a lily pad."

COOLEY: "I don't expect this apology to wash away my sins, but I hope that it will, in some way, re-establish me as a Senator in the eyes of my colleagues rather than as the flannel-mouthed old curmudgeon I seem to have become in my waning years, and so much for that."

COOLEY: "Haven't had so much fun since the cayenne pepper hit the fan."

Production Commentary: *Advise & Consent* was, in its day, a provocative film. Allen Drury's best-selling novel of 1959 delves into the behind-the-scenes intrigue of powerbroking in the Senate. Director Otto Preminger wisely cast a host of seasoned veteran actors who all deliver exceptional performances. Ever controversial, Preminger invited Senators to a preview of the film. Word soon leaked out to the press that many honorable members felt the film was discourteous to the institutes of the Senate and the White House and portrayed them in an unfavorable light. Of particular concern was the inaccurate impression given to people overseas that the American public life was selfish and corrupt.

The film lifts the lid of political life and the endless crises in the Senate. It details the character-slaying and career-maneuvering associated with power politics. Produced at the height of the Cold War, it touches on the notion of the decline of privacy, and with it the emergence of new, threatening expectations of public revelation and expression. In succeeding decades, the demarcation between the public arena and private sphere has dissolved and morphed into the hyper-reality of contemporary digital online platforms.

The film attracted notoriety as being the first mainstream American film to show a gay bar, in Washington, D.C. The blackmailed Senator (Don Murray) visits a fellow Army veteran who admits that he sold evidence of their past gay relationship. Unable to reconcile his duty and his secret, the Senator commits suicide. In keeping with the exposé tone adopted by the film, this sequence is depicted in a lurid and risible manner. However, the use of location shooting inside Washington's Senate Building and Sam Leavitt's high-contrast black-and-white Panavision photography lends credence to a rendering of intense scrutiny and political disarray appropriate to this political melodrama.

In a *Guardian* article, "Advise and Condense" (October 5, 1961), W.J. Weatherby described the problem Preminger had set himself of adapting Allen Drury's Pulitzer Prize–winning book of some 760 pages: "The real test of the film in the end will be how much has had to be oversimplified or glossed over to keep up with the clock." Weatherby went on to record Laughton's dedication and abilities to bridge the gap between reality and illusion caused by the problem of time. Laughton described his preparation for playing South Carolina Senator Seabright "Seab" Cooley as "an Eliza Doolittle job." To nail the accent, he studied with a phonetics expert and also engaged in conversation with Senators from the Southern states. Weatherby reported, "In the only scene I saw him play, he made his point with lighting professional speed and also managed a suggestion of an iceberg of character waiting to be revealed under the surface."

Throughout, Laughton is in exceptional form and is to be congratulated for his efforts in looking and sounding his fictional part in this, his screen swansong. The performance is not only enticing and engaging, but also poignant, given that his terminal cancer was already upon him. He was to die six months after the film's release. His physical weakness was used to suggest Cooley as a lazy feline who was about to pounce on his opponents. Cooley's mental and oratorical skills in speeches on the Senate floor plays to Laughton's strengths in elocution and rhetorical language. As the aging, right-winger, he provides a nuanced insight into the machinations of power and prejudice.

Critics generally cited Laughton's performance as praiseworthy. *Film Bulletin* (May 28, 1962) felt it merited an Oscar nomination. The *Monthly Film Bulletin* (September 1962, Vol. 29, No. 344) spoke for many when it declared, "Charles Laughton gives his best performance in some 20 years as the sly, devious, purring, oratorical, shapelessly obese Senator Cooley." The London *Times* (September 13, 1962) found Laughton's portrait was akin to the features of the infamous Senator Joseph McCarthy. It went on to say that his performance was "at once flamboyant and (comparatively) restrained: here is a cobra with a benign expression and a shock of amiable white hair." Bosley Crowther of the *New York Times* (June 17, 1962) was hostile to Wendell Mayes' script adaptation, which he found to be contrived and facile. Of Laughton's performance, he wrote, "A Senator from South Carolina, whom Charles Laughton plays with such sly twists and such a corn pone accent that you almost see him in a nightrider's hood, brings in a Red-baiting witness, browbeats the appointee and then blackmails a Treasury official into helping him block the president's choice." Crowther's detailing of the reprehensible nature of Laughton's character is undeniable. Yet, it is all credit to Laughton for bringing a disconcerting individual to full life on the screen, warts and all.

Though the film did not receive any Academy Award nominations, Laughton's name was put forward for the best foreign actor category at the sixteenth British Academy Film Awards. (He lost to Burt Lancaster in *Birdman of Alcatraz*.) Despite a running time of 139 minutes and a narrative which tends towards the cumbersome and the inflated, the film delivers exciting and intriguing entertainment. For Laughton it was an apt end to an extensive film career that certainly had its ups and downs. His filmography contains over a dozen magnificent performances unblemished by his self-loathing, which at its worst led him to indulge in the excesses of a ham. Yet, even when not performing at his peak, there is in the corpus of 54 feature films always something to discern and savor. Charles Laughton was a man who was touched by genius and yet at the same time troubled by his own talent. Luckily for us, his constellation of good, bad and indifferent roles captured on film have, in the main, survived. The fact that many of his performances are available to view and examine for their art and entertainment is cause for celebration.

Shorts and Miscellaneous Films (1930–1952)

Pathé Newsreel (1930)

Credits: Pathetone: Sound, Black and White; Running Time: 3 minutes and 20 seconds; U.K. release: August 12, 1930; Available to download from the British Pathé Newsreel website.

Cast: **Charles Laughton** (*Himself*); Brown (*a male theatrical dresser*).

Brief Synopsis: In an "audio interview" backstage, Laughton, the well-known actor, discusses and demonstrates his makeup for the play *On the Spot*.

Screen Snapshots (1935)

Credits: Series 14, Number 11; Columbia; Directors: Ralph Staub, Harriet Parsons; Black and White; Running Time: 10 minutes; U.S. release: July 5, 1935.

Cast: Tala Birell; **Charles Laughton**; Bela Lugosi; Fredric March; Lyle Talbot; Robert Young.

Brief Synopsis: A behind-the-scenes glimpse of star personalities at work and play.

Lest We Forget (1937)

(British Pictorial Productions/Pathé Pictures)

Credits: Director: Anthony Asquith; Scenario and Producer: Major Lloyd, Appeal Secretary, Enham Village Centre; Photography by British Pictorial Productions and Pathé Pictures; War Scene Kindly Given by Associated British Picture Corporation; Black and White; Running Time: 775 feet; U.K. release: 1937; 35mm print held at the British Film Institute, National Film and Television Archive. Unfortunately, this print has no soundtrack.

Cast: Flora Robson (*A Visitor*); Nicholas Hannen (*A Settler*); Derrick de Marney (*A Clerk*); **Charles Laughton** (*Appellant*); Enham Personnel.

Brief Synopsis: The story of Enham Village Center, a charitable trust set up following the First World War, takes a flashback to the battlefields the plight of disabled ex-servicemen who are destitute unable to find employment. Return to the visitor in the workshop where she talks to workmen. Several occupations are shown: basket weaving, a sawmill and various types of carpentry. Charles Laughton presents the appeal to camera and the film ends with the address for sending donations. N.B. Laughton appears on camera wearing a slight moustache; suggesting that he was working on *Rembrandt* at the time *Lest We Forget* was produced.

British Movietone Newsreel (1938)

Credits: British Movietone Newsreel Footage: Sound; Black and White; U.K. release: June 23, 1938; Running Time: 1 minute; Available to download from the British Movietone Newsreel website.

Cast: Noël Coward; Gladys Cooper; **Charles Laughton**; Elsa Lanchester; Leslie Mitchell; Leslie Banks; Dame Marie Tempest; Evelyn Laye; Edith Evans; Owen Nares; Valerie Hobson; Alfred Drayton; Robertson Hare; Sydney Howard; Charles Coburn.

Brief Synopsis: "The Theatrical Garden Party." Newsreel footage of a charity benefit shot on June 23, 1938, in Regent's Park, London. It shows a theatrical garden party in aid of the Actors' Orphanage Fund. Noël Coward with Gladys Cooper is seen fishing for champagne and soliciting aid for the charity fund. Laughton with his wife Elsa Lanchester also appeal for funds. He puts on the accent of a London busker in the style of his latest film, *St. Martin's Lane* aka *Sidewalks of London*. Newsreel commentator Leslie Mitchell chats with star Leslie Banks. Brief shots are seen of actresses Dame Marie Tempest, Evelyn Laye,

Edith Evans with Owen Nares, Valerie Hobson, comedians Alfred Drayton, Robertson Hare and Sydney Howard, and music hall veteran Charles Coburn.

British Paramount Newsreel (1938)

Credits: British Paramount Newsreel Footage: Silent; Black and White; U.K. release: November 14, 1938; Running Time: 55 seconds; Available to download from British Pathé Newsreel website.

Cast: Captain Wilcockson; Tommy Rose; C.W.A. Scott; Sir Alan and Lady Cobham; Amy Johnson; Jim Mollison; Mrs. Phyllis Hussey; Captain Bennett; Mr. and Mrs. Robert Sweeney; Sir A.V. Roe; Lord Louis Mountbatten; Ben Lyon; Bebe Daniels; **Charles Laughton**; Elsa Lanchester; Joseph Kennedy (U.S. Ambassador); Lord Halifax; King George II of Greece.

Brief Synopsis: "Aces at Film Night." A film premiere of *Men with Wings* (Paramount, William A. Wellman, 1938) at the Carlton Cinema, London, attracts royalty and various celebrities. Laughton is briefly seen with Elsa Lanchester in the lobby.

Cavalcade of the Academy Awards (1940)

Credits: Warner Bros., Supervisor: Frank Capra; Commentator: Carey Wilson; Other Contributors: Gordon Hollingshead; Jack Chertok, Ira Genet, Owen Crump, Charles Rosher, DeLeon Anthony; Black and White; Running Time: 18 minutes; Available to download from the Academy of Motion Picture, Arts and Sciences website.

Cast: Shirley Temple; Walt Disney; George Bernard Shaw; James Stewart; **Charles Laughton**; Elsa Lanchester; Jean Hersholt; Hedy Lamarr; Mitchell Leisen; Melvyn Douglas; Helen Gahagan; Irving Pichel; Vivien Leigh; David O. Selznick; May Robson; Olivia de Havilland; Louella Parsons; Hedda Hopper; John Carroll; Jack Warner; Harry Warner; Ann Rutherford; Virginia Bruce; J. Walter Ruben; Douglas Fairbanks Jr.; Elsa Maxwell; Gregory Ratoff; Laurence Olivier; Mickey Rooney; Eddie Mannix; Judy Garland; Norma Shearer; George Raft; Bette Davis; Walter Wanger; Frank Capra; Darryl Zanuck; William Cameron Menzies; Dr. Herbert T. Kalmus; Hal C. Kern; James Newcom; Ernest Haller; Ray Rennahan; Bernard B. Brown; Fred Sersen; Lyle R. Wheeler; Edmund H. Hansen; Hamilton Luske; George Bagnall; Herbert Stothart; Harold Arlen; E.Y. Harburg; Bob Hope; Gordon Hollingshead; Sinclair Lewis; Lewis R. Foster; Victor Fleming; Mervyn LeRoy; Dr. Ernest Martin Hopkins; Fay Bainter; Thomas Mitchell; Hattie McDaniel; Spencer Tracy.

Brief Synopsis: Highlights of the 1939 Academy Awards held at the Cocoanut Grove of the Ambassador Hotel, Los Angeles, on February 29, 1940. Laughton is seen accompanying Elsa Lanchester.

Passport to Destiny (1944)

Tagline: "She scrubbed her way from London to Berlin—To Get a Shot at Hitler!"

U.S. (RKO Radio Pictures)

Credits: Original Screenplay: Val Burton and Muriel Roy Bolton; Photography: Jack Mackenzie; Special Effects by Vernon L. Walker; Art Directors: Albert S. D'Agostino, Jack Okey; Set Decorations: Darrell Silvera, Harley Miller; Dialogue Director: Hal Yates; Makeup: Mel Berns; Music: Roy Webb; Musical Director: C. Bakaleinikoff; Gowns: Edward Stevenson; Recorder: James S. Thomson; Rerecorded by James G. Stewart; Editor: Robert Swink; Assistant Director: Lloyd Richards; Produced by Herman Schlom; Directed by Ray McCarey. Genre: Drama; Black and White; Running Time: 65 minutes. Not commercially available on digital media.

Cast: Elsa Lanchester (*Ella Muggins*); Gordon Oliver (*Captain Franz von Weber*); Lenore Aubert (*Greta Neumann*); Lionel Royce (*Sturmfuehrer Karl Dietrich*); Fritz Feld (*Chief Janitor*); Joseph Vitale (*Lieutenant Bosch*); Gavin Muir (*Herr Joyce/Lord Haw-Haw*); Lloyd Corrigan (*Professor Frederick Walthers*); Anita Bolster (*Agnes*); Lydia Bilbrook (*Millie*); Lumsden Hare (*Freighter Captain Mack*); Hans Schumm (*Miniger, Dietrich's Aide*); **Uncredited Cast**: Harry Allen (*First Bus Conductor*); Robert Bice (*German Troop Leader*); Heinie Conklin, Edmund Glover (*Sailors from Freighter*); Georgie Cooper (*First Scrubwoman*); Alec Craig (*Freighter's Cook*); Eddie Hart (*German Soldier Shadowing Grete and Franz at Airport*); Olaf Hytten (*Mr. Hawkins*); Charles Irwin (*British Reporter*); Guy Kingsford (*Willis—Freighter's Mate*); **Charles Laughton** (*Photo of Sergeant Major Henry Albert Muggins*); Pat McKee (*Sailor*); Fred Nurney (*Weirmacht General*); Otto Reichow (*German Soldier at Beach*); Betty Roadman (*Prison Matron*); John Rogers (*Second Air Raid Warden*); Marshall Romer (*Gestapo Soldier*); Reginald Sheffield (*Mr. Thomas*); Sada Simmons (*Third Scrubwoman*); Wyndham Standing (*Doctor*); Harry Strang (*Impatient German Officer*); Philip Van Zandt (*Dietrich's Secretary*); Dorothy Vernon (*Second Scrubwoman*); Paul Weigel (*Hotel Proprietor*); Pat West (*Conductor*); William Yetter Sr. (*German Patrol Officer*).

Working Titles: *Dangerous Journey*; *Passport to Adventure*

Brief Synopsis: London scrubwoman Ella Muggins reminisces about her late husband, Sergeant Major Albert Muggins, a teller of tall tales. While cleaning the attic, she opens a trunk and finds a magic eye that her husband claimed would protect its bearer from all harm. Ella is skeptical until it "saves her life" during an air raid. Convinced that the "eye" will always protect her, she decides to go to Berlin and assassinate Hitler. Ella stows away aboard a ship, but it is attacked by German bombers. Ella and the crew board a lifeboat and when they land, German soldiers arrest the crew. Ella hides and escapes capture. Posing as a deaf and dumb cleaning woman, she scrubs her way across the continent to Germany. She poses as a refugee from devastated Hamburg and manages to obtain a cleaning job in the Chancellery itself. While there, she overhears a quarrel between Karl Dietrich, a German commandant, and Lord Haw-Haw, who has fallen in disfavor with the Nazis. She learns that Greta Neumann, English-born fiancée of German air ace Franz von Weber, has been imprisoned. She helps Franz free the girl by loaning him the "eye." However, in aiding Franz, Elsa arouses Dietrich's suspicions. He investigates and uncovers Ella's masquerade. Franz and Ella are arrested. While Dietrich is questioning Franz, his fiancée Greta and Ella, there is an RAF air raid. In the commotion, the three manage to escape, steal a plane and fly back to England. Though Ella has failed to kill Hitler, she is acclaimed as a heroine. She rummages through her husband's effects again and finds a box full of glass eyes, souvenirs of a glass blowers convention. She belatedly realizes that her late husband was a habitual liar.

Galileo/Leben des Galilei (1947)

United States

Credits: Directors: Ruth Berlau, Joseph Losey; Based on the Play by Bertolt Brecht; Translation: **Charles Laughton**, Margarete Steffin (uncredited); Music: Hanns Eisler; Production Design: Robert Davison; Art Direction: John Hubley, Caspar Neher; Costumes and Wardrobe: Robert Davison, Helene Weigel; Choreographer: Lotte Goslar; Stage Director: Joseph Losey; Scientific Advisor: Morton Wurtele; 16mm; Black and White; Sound Mix: Mono; Running Time: 30 minutes.

Cast: Peter Brocco (*Old Cardinal*); Stephen Brown (*Street Singer*); Hugo Haas (*Cardinal Barberini, later Pope Urban VIII*); Frances Heflin (*Virginia Galilei*); **Charles Laughton** (*Galileo Galilei*); Eda Reiss Merin (*Mrs. Sarti*); William Phipps (*Andrea Sarti*).

Brief Synopsis: During the seventeenth century in the Venetian Republic, an eminent scientist and scholar, Professor Galilei, learns via a student of the existence of a scientific instrument, the telescope, which is for sale in Amsterdam.

Christmas Seals Public Service Announcement (1952)

U.S. (Metro-Goldwyn-Mayer)

Credits: Black and White; Running Time: 2 minutes.

Cast: Lou Costello; Bud Abbott; **Charles Laughton**.

Brief Synopsis: Studio gateman Lou Costello requests the assistance of his stage partner Bud Abbott, who draws up in a motor car at the studio. The chauffeur is none other than actor Charles Laughton. Together, they appeal to movie audiences to give generously to Christmas Seals to fight tuberculosis.

Unreleased and Re-Edited Films (1937–1959)

I, Claudius (1937)

U.K. (London Films)

Credits: Producer: Alexander Korda; Director: Josef von Sternberg; Photography: Georges Périnal; Music: Arthur Bliss; Writers: Lester Cohen, Curt Siodmak; Based on the novel by Robert Graves; Costume Designer: John Armstrong; Makeup: George Blackler; Set Designer: Vincent Korda; Mosaic Settings: Ferdinand Bellan; Script Supervisor: Eileen Corbett; Genre: Historical Epic; Black and White; Film was never released.

Cast: **Charles Laughton** (*Claudius*); Merle Oberon (*Messalina*); Emlyn Williams (*Caligula*); Flora Robson (*Livia*); Alan Aynesworth (*Asiaticus—Senator*); John Clements (*Valente*); Leonora Corbett (*Caesonia*); Roy Emerton (*Octavius*); Gina Evans (*Vestal Virgin*); Frank Forbes-Robertson (*Lupus, Captain of the Guard*); Basil Gill (*Xenophon—Claudius Doctor*); Morland Graham (*Halotus—Master of Livia's Household*); Everley Gregg (*Domita—Messalina's Mother*); Lyn Harding (*Vespasian*); Allan Jeayles (*Musa—Emperor's Physician*); Robert Newton (*Cassius Chaerea—Captain of Caligula's Guards*); Bruce Winston (*Asiaticus*).

Brief Synopsis: A chronicle of the life of Roman Emperor Claudius (10 BC–54 AD).

Short Commentary: Although the film was aborted and never released, 58 cans of negative, were found stored at Denham Studios and clips were shown by the BBC in 1965 as a documentary, *The Epic That Never Was*; DVD Region 2 available as a supplement on BBC television *I, Claudius* box set.

On Our Merry Way a.k.a. *A Miracle Can Happen* (1948)

Tagline: "Did you Ever See a Miracle Walking?"

United Artists/Benedict Bogeaus

Credits: Screenplay: Laurence Stallings; Adapted from Original Stories by John O'Hara, Arch Oboler, Lou Breslow; Production Manager: Ken Walters; Set Decorators: Fred Widdowson, Eugene Redd; Sound Technician: William Lynch; Women's Wardrobe: Greta; Men's Wardrobe: Jerry Bos; Makeup: Otis Malcolm; Head Hairdresser: Scotty Rackin; Assistant to Directors: Joseph Depew; Photography: Edward Cronjager, John Seitz, Joseph Biroc, Gordon Avil; Production Associate: Arthur M. Landau; Art Director: Ernst Fegte; Supervising Editor: James Smith; Music: Heinz Roemheld; Musical Supervisors: David Chudnow and Skitch Henderson; "Baby Made a Change in Me" by Skitch Henderson and Donald Kahn; Assistant to Producer: Carley Harriman; Produced by Benedict Bogeaus, Burgess Meredith and Fred MacMurray; Directed by Leslie Fenton and King Vidor. U.S. release: February 3, 1948; Genre: Multi-Comedy; Black and White: Running Time: 108 minutes.

Cast: Paulette Goddard (*Martha Pease*); James Stewart (*Slim*); Henry Fonda (*Lank Solksy*); **Charles Laughton** (*The Rev. John B. Dunne*): Fred MacMurray (*Al*); Burgess Meredith (*Oliver M. Pease*); Harry James (*Guest Star*); William Demarest (*Floyd*); Hugh Herbert (*Eli Hobbs*); Eduardo Ciannelli (*Maxim*); Henry Hull (*Dying Man*); Charles D. Brown (*Mr. Sadd*); John Qualen (*Mr. Atwood*); Dorothy Ford (*Lola Maxim*); Frank Moran (*Bookie*); Carl Switzer (*Leopold "Zoot" Wirtz*); Nana Bryant (*Housekeeper*); Betty Caldwell (*Cynthia Robbs*); David Whorf (*Edgar Hobbs aka Sniffles Dugan*); Orley Lindgren (*Boy*).

Brief Synopsis: At the suggestion of his wife, a newspaper reporter inveigles the editor to assign him the day's roving question concerning the theme of the inspiration of children. Through a series of three separate stories, he attempts to answer the topical question: "Has a little child ever changed your life?" Laughton played a minister who was changed by a small child coming to his home to request he tend his sick father. When he reached the destination, the boy had disappeared. The sick father was surprised to see the reverend as he had not asked him to come. After reading the Bible, the father begins to feel better. As the minister prepares to leave, he sees a picture of the little boy who had brought him there. He exchanges words with the father and learns that the boy, the father's son, had passed away many years ago.

Short Commentary: This sequence was deleted from U.S. domestic prints but was retained in a foreign distribution print. In a recut version of 98 minutes, the deleted Laughton sequence was replaced by a new story: Dorothy Lamour and Victor Moore are movie extras who contend with an obnoxious child (Eileen Janssen). Lamour sends up her sarong image in the musical number "Queen of the Hollywood Isles." This comedy sequence was directed by Leslie Fenton.

A Midsummer Night's Dream (1959)

NBC Television

Credits: Director: Peter Hall; Producer: Hubbell Robinson; Associate Producer: Denis O'Dell; Music: Raymond Leppard; Production Designer: Lila De Nobili; Black and White; 90 minutes.

Cast: Georgina Anderson (*Fairy*); Stephanie Bidmead (*Hippolyta*); Michael Blakemore (*Tom Snout*); Zoe Caldwell (*Fairy*); Edward de Souza (*Demetrius*); Roy Dotrice (*Egeus*); Judith Downes (*Fairy*); Donald Eccles (*Robin Staveling*); Albert Finney (*Lysander*); Julian Glover (*Snug*); Robert Hardy (*Oberon*); Ian Holm (*Puck*); **Charles Laughton** (**Nick Bottom**); Donald Layne-Smith (*Philostrate*); Cyril Luckham (*Peter Quince*); Priscilla Morgan (*Hermia*); Anthony Nicholls (*Theseus*); Margaret O'Keefe, Jean Owen, Malcolm Ransom, Michael Scoble (*Fairies*); Vanessa Redgrave (*Helena*); Mary Ure (*Titania*); Peter Woodthorpe (*Francis Flute*).

Brief Synopsis: A television transcription of Shakespeare's fantasy as performed on stage by the Royal Shakespeare Company at Stratford.

Short Commentary: This unique recording of a historic performance was produced for American television, but was never aired. Before the play begins, there are brief shots of Laughton walking on the theater grounds.

Film Projects Announced but Abandoned or Rejected (1932–1962)

Throughout his screen career, Charles Laughton was offered numerous roles. The following list of parts offered but declined is far from definitive. However, the selection demonstrates the demand of producers and public alike for Laughton's acting and directing talents.

The Kiss Before the Mirror—as the lead, Dr. Paul Held, in Ladislas Fodor's stage success, to be produced at Universal and directed by James Whale. In the event, Frank Morgan was cast as Dr. Held (*Hollywood Filmograph*, Vol. 12, No. 45, November 26, 1932).

Alice in Wonderland—as Humpty-Dumpty. In the released film, W.C. Fields (yet again) took on the role (*Film Daily*, July 17, 1933).

Marie Antoinette—as Louis XVI in an MGM production with Norma Shearer in the title role, and Herbert Marshall as Count Axel von Fersen. In the event, MGM produced the film four years later with actor-playwright Robert Morley as Louis XVI (London *Times*, February 10, 1934).

The Scarlet Pimpernel—in the title part. After the outstanding success of Korda's *The Private Life of Henry VIII*, Laughton agreed to appear in another London Film production. Leslie Howard took on the role in the film (London *Times*, February 22, 1934).

Field of the Cloth of Gold—Bolstered by the success of Laughton's portrayal of Henry VIII and Elizabeth Bergner's in *Catherine the Great*, Alexandra Korda wanted to produce another historical film showing the meeting between Henry VIII and Francis I. Laughton was to repeat his role with Maurice Chevalier as Francis I, Flora Robson as Katherine of Aragon, Douglas Fairbanks Jr. as Charles V and Merle Oberon as (again) Anne Boleyn (London *Times*, March 27, 1934).

Life of Diaghilev—It was reported that the film rights to Madame Nijinsky's biography of her husband were acquired and it was probable that Laughton would play the part of Diaghilev (London *Times*, December 11, 1934).

Mr. Tristram Goes West—Laughton in the title role of a ghost, from a story taken from *Punch*. To be directed by Rene Clair and produced for London Film Productions. This was eventually produced under the title *The Ghost Goes West* starring Robert Donat (London *Times*, March 18, 1935).

Cyrano de Bergerac—title role in a production by London Films with Penelope Dudley Ward as Roxanne. The script, to be written in rhyming couplets, would be prepared by Lajos Biro and Arthur Wimperis. Renowned Hollywood cinematographer Lee Garmes was to have been appointed director of photography and Mort Westmore was to create Laughton's makeup for the title role. The film was scheduled to begin shooting at Worton Hall Studios. However, it was postponed awaiting the completion of the new Stage One at Denham Studio (London *Times*, July 30, 1935; *Film Daily*, February 26, 1936).

159

160 Film Projects Announced but Abandoned or Rejected (1932–1962)

Lion of Mayfair—as a Maître d'hôtel for Alexandra Korda's London Film Productions. Script by Robert Sherwood and Lajos Biro (London *Times*, March 24, 1936).

Life of Chinese Gordon—title role (*Variety*, April 15, 1936).

Goodbye, Mr. Chips—title role in an MGM production (London *Times*, July 28, 1936).

International Quartet—by J.B. Priestley, with Laughton, Sir Cedric Hardwicke, Ralph Richardson, Elsa Lanchester (London *Times*, August 10, 1936).

Danton the Terror of France—title role in a Warner Bros. production directed by Max Reinhardt, assisted by Michael Curtiz as associate director. Screenplay by French author Romain Roland; scenarist Sheridan Gibney was given the task of script doctoring. Spencer Tracy was to play Marat and Claude Rains Robespierre. Production was to have begun in early November 1936 (*Film Daily*, August 17, 1936).

David Copperfield—as Micawber. MGM approached Laughton to play the role. He liked the idea and secured permission from Paramount to do the part on loanout. Despite shooting a silent test successfully, Laughton couldn't deliver the lines to his own satisfaction. He persuaded producer David O. Selznick that the part was unsuitable. W.C. Fields was offered the role and made the character his own (Lanchester 1938: 166–67).

The Admirable Crichton—this Mayflower production was to have featured Laughton in the title role, with Elsa Lanchester and Maureen O'Hara. In the United States, the film would have been distributed by Paramount. Laughton was due to commence the film following the finish of *The Hunchback of Notre Dame* in mid–September 1939, but it was shelved due to the outbreak of World War II (London *Times*, March 8, 1939).

Benjamin Franklin—Erich Pommer would be producer of this biography picture for Laughton at RKO (*Film Daily*, February 23, 1940).

Not Quite a Gentleman—based on an original story by Garrett Fort. Also known as *Half a Rogue* (*Film Daily*, May 28, 1940).

Mr. Pinkie—scheduled to star Laughton and Elsa Lanchester. Shelved by RKO (*Film Daily*, October 30, 1940).

Three Rogues—Laughton and Lucille Ball to co-star in the Ferenc Molnar play, to be produced by RKO. Allan Dwan was assigned director with Graham Baker as producer. Also cast were Louis Hayward and Edmond O'Brien (*Film Daily*, June 18, 1941).

For Whom the Bell Tolls—Laughton was considered, along with Akim Tamiroff, for the role of Pablo the surly guerrilla chief. Tamiroff secured the role in the film (*Film Daily*, June 18, 1941).

Lord Timothy Dexter—John P. Marquand's 1929 novel was purchased as a star vehicle for Laughton. Charles Bennett devised a scenario and David Hempstead as producer (*Film Daily*, October 10, 1941).

Dragon Seed—Pearl Buck's popular World War II novel dealing with Chinese peasants fighting Japanese invaders was purchased by MGM, who put Katharine Hepburn in the lead. Laughton was announced for the role of Wu Lien, but was forced to drop out because of conflicting schedules with *The Canterville Ghost*. Laird Cregar and Sydney Greenstreet were penciled in as replacements but were unavailable. The role was eventually assigned to Akim Tamiroff (*Motion Picture Herald*, August 21, 1943).

Georges Simenon novel—A similar film to *The Man on the Eiffel Tower* was slated to be produced in Stockholm, Sweden, by Irving Allen and Franchot Tone's A&T Film Productions. The unnamed film based on an unspecified Simenon novel would again be lensed in Ansco Color, and *Eiffel Tower* stars Laughton, Tone and Burgess Meredith would be cast. This suggests that the producers were hoping to recast Laughton as Inspector Maigret (*Variety*, December 22, 1948).

The Cruise of the Breadwinner—A proposed film, taken from H.E. Bates' acclaimed novella. After completing *The Sound Barrier*, director David Lean offered Laughton a role in it: Gregson, an old skipper of a battered boat patrolling the South Coast during wartime. Laughton rejected the part on the

Film Projects Announced but Abandoned or Rejected (1932–1962)

grounds that press reaction would have been hostile. How could he possibly play a war hero with authenticity, they would say, given that he had spent the war in Hollywood? (Brownlow: 296).

The Bridge on the River Kwai—Laughton was considered for the part of Colonel Nicholson. David Lean thought Laughton was unsuited: "You can't have a fat man among all those half-starved people" (Brownlow: 352).

The Naked and the Dead—as director. Laughton and Paul Gregory spent a year adapting Norman Mailer's novel *The Naked and the Dead* for the screen. It was to have been produced by Gregory and William Goldman for their new company Gregory-Goldman Enterprises. Laughton was to direct and Robert Mitchum star. Shooting was expected to commence before June 1955. Gregory and Laughton scouted locations in the Bahamas for an expected spring start on this, their second film together (after *The Night of the Hunter*). In the event, poor distribution and reviews of *Night of the Hunter* put paid to this project (*Film Bulletin*, December 27, 1954). The film was eventually produced by Gregory and directed by Raoul Walsh in 1958.

Irma La Douce—Billy Wilder wanted Laughton for the part of Moustache in his 1962 production *Irma La Douce*. Following Laughton's death, Lou Jacobi played Moustache (Norman: 195).

Amateur Stage Appearances (1913–1926)

The Private Secretary, by Charles Hawtrey; Produced at the Academy Room, Stonyhurst College, Lancashire; December 1, 1913.

Cast: Richard Irwin (*Mr. Maisland, M.F.H.*); Joseph D'Abadie (*Harry Maisland, his son*); Stanley Unsworth (*Frank Vernon, his nephew*); Howard Feeny (*Charles Vernon, his nephew*); Dermot Macsherry (*Mr. Cattermole*); Philip Bell (*Douglas Cattermole, his nephew*); Leo Gradwell (*Reverend Robert Spalding*); Richard Gurrin (*Herr Storkmar, tutor*); Wilfred Hull (*Mr. Sydney Gibson, tailor of Bond Street*); **Charles Laughton** (***Mr. Stead, lodging-house keeper***); Bernard Payne (*Knox, a writ server*); Bernard Pimm (*John, Maisland's servant*); H. Broadbent (*Gardener*).

Brief Synopsis: In this farcical comedy, a mild young clergyman is caught up in the machinations of two reckless men who are trying to escape the clutches of various creditors.

Stonyhurst College Choir and Orchestral Concert; Performed at the Academy Room, Stonyhurst College, Lancashire; October 7, 1914.

Concert Program: "God Save the King"; Selection from "The Girl from Utah" by Sydney Jones and Paul A. Rubens, performed by the orchestra; Song: "Come Back to Erin" by Claribel solo by O. Feeny; Violin Solo: "Romance et Boléro" by Dancla performed by M. Dawson; Song: "The Admiral's Broom" by F. Bevan, solo by the Reverend E. Sykes; Cornet Solo: "Legend" by O. Morgan performed by Father O'Connor; Song and Chorus: "Jack" by S. Adams, solo by J. Kenny; Quartet: "The Old Folks at Home" by Foster performed by The Mastersingers; Song and Chorus: "It's a Long Way" by H. Williams, duet by J. Cashman and V. French; March: "The Gladiator" by Sousa performed by the orchestra; Chorus: "For his heart is like the sea," Chorus: "It's a long way that leads to Berlin," followed by the National Anthem.

Choir: Trebles: O. Feeny; J. Malone; H. Hoseason; H. Sire; J. Neely; C. Rockliffe; J. Beveridge; F. Bahr; B. Feeny; M. Trappes-Lomax; R. McQueen; W. Biller; B. McAuliffe; J. Burgess; A. Bisgood; E. Leicester; A. Darwood; R. Cafferata. Altos: C. O'Connor; R.L. Smith; F. Leicester; A. Gibbs; W. Jones; S. Hall; S. [sic] Laughton [*Tom Laughton, Charles younger brother*]. Tenors: the Reverend N. Ryan; V. French; the Reverend J. Rowland; F. van der Taelen; J. Casteiello. Basses: Father Cortie; Father Vignaux; J. Cashman; J. Kenny.

Orchestra: 1st Violins: M. Dawson (leader); H. Slattery; A. Hobbs. **2nd Violins:** C. O'Connor (leader); **C. Laughton**; V. French; F. Leicester. Flutes: A. Gibbs; W. Biller. Clarinets; Father Kellet; J. Cashman; C. Greig [*Colin Glennie Clive Greig, later known by his stage name Colin Clive*]; Harmonicon (for Oboe): J. Castiello; Viola: Reverend J. Rowland. Cellos: S. Slattery; P. O'Mara; G. Mitchell. Double Bass: H.J. McArdle; Cornets: W. Cross; C. Cross; Trombone: J. Wilkinson; Drums, etc.: F. van der Taelen, R.L. Smith, G. Gillings; Piano: J. Kenny.

Trelawny of the Wells by Sir Arthur Wing Pinero Produced at the Spa Theater, Scarborough, North Riding of Yorkshire; Producer: Miss Margaret C. Tree; Performed by the Scarborough Players in aid of the National Society for the Prevention of Cruelty to Children; April 28–29, 1922.

Cast: Miss Gwen Stabler (*Rose Trelawny*); Mr. Douglas Barker (*Mr. Arthur Gower*); **Mr. Charles Laughton** (***The Vice Chancellor, Sir William Gower***); Mr. T.W. Stabler (*Mr. James Telfer*); Mr. George Cooper (*Ferdinand Gadd*); Miss Robbins (*Avonia Burn, an Actress*); Dorothy Dymoke (*Imogen*); John B. Sutherland (*O'Dwyer—Prompter of the Pantheon Theatre*); Mr. E.G. Berry (*Augustus Colfage*); Dorothy Wilson (*Clara*).

Brief Synopsis: A star of the theater attempts to give up her stage profession but is unable to fit into conventional society.

Hobson's Choice by Harold Brighouse at the Arcadia Theatre, Scarborough, in aid of the Scarborough District Nursing Association and the League of Help. Producer: T.E. Constant; Performed by the Scarborough Players; Music: Mrs. Malcolm Rowntree and Misses Horsfall, Wain and Wood; Messrs. Collins and Moss; February 7–10, 1923.

Cast: Charles Laughton (*Willie Mossop*); Mrs. Claude Rowntree (*Maggie Hobson*); Dorothy Macaulay (*Alice Hobson*); Kathleen W. Robins (*Vicky Hobson*); Mrs. Maud Partridge (*Mrs. Hepworth*); Miss Dorothy Wilson (*Ada Figgins*); Mr. A. Neville Gray (*Hobson*); Mr. Alfred Oates (*Tubby Wadlow*); Mr. John Whalley-Whaley (*Jim Heeler*); Mr. Charles F. Turnbull (*Fred Beanstock*); Mr. George Cooper (*Albert Prosser*); Mr. Leonard S. Crawshaw (*Dr. MacFarlane*).

Brief Synopsis: Twelve performers enact the domestic strife of a Lancashire bootmaker. The play is set in Salford in 1893.

Four Plays: Becky Sharp, a play adapted from Thackeray's *Vanity Fair* by Olive Conway, *The Spanish Tragedy—"A Grotesque," Overtones* by Alice Gerstenberg, and *The Dear Departed* by Stanley Houghton. January 8–10, 1925, at the Arcadia Theater, Scarborough, in aid of the Scarborough Hospital. All four plays were produced by Charles Laughton and performed by the Scarborough Players.

Becky Sharp

Cast: Miss Dorothy Macaulay (*Becky*); Mr. Morris Kellett (*Rawdon Crawley*); Mrs. May Kellett (*Amelia Osborne*); **Charles Laughton (*Osborne's middle-aged uncle of military bearing*)**.

Brief Synopsis: The denouement and climax of Thackeray's novel concentrating on its picaresque lead, Becky Sharp.

The Spanish Tragedy—"A Grotesque"

Cast: Mrs. Gwen Rowntree (*The wife*); Mr. Sydney H. Carter (*The husband*); **Mr. Charles Laughton (*The lover*)**.

Brief Synopsis: Set in a high tower in Spain. There was, however, no tower on the stage, and there was no dialog. Laughton serenaded a lady with ardor but ultimately found life too dull to surrender his passion, and he returned to his Mandolin.

Overtones

Cast: Miss Dorothy Macaulay (*Margaret*); Mrs. Maud Partridge (*Harriet*); Mrs. Molly Seaton (*Hetty*); Mrs. Ellen N. Teiley (*Maggie*).

Brief Synopsis: A psychological drama exploring the psyche of two women as they appear to each other and their inner selves as they really are.

The Dear Departed

Cast: Mr. Charles Laughton (*Henry Slater*); Mrs. Rowntree (*Amelia Slater*); Mr. Alfred Oates (*Benjamin*); Miss Dorothy Wilson (*Elizabeth Jordan—Amelia's sister*); Mr. Morris Kellett (*Abel Merryweather*); Miss Beryl Seaton (*Victoria Slater*).

Brief Synopsis: A social play depicting elderly people who are abandoned or neglected by their own children.

Special Performance by Students of the Royal Academy of Dramatic Art—two sketches in Mime arranged and rehearsed by T.H. Komisarjevsky, St. James Theatre; March 26, 1926

The Vagabonds

Cast: Lilian Harrison (*A Blind Woman*); Stella Freeman (*Her Daughter*); Cedric Bowden (*An Acrobat*).

Comedia Del'Arte

Cast: Charles Laughton (*The Husband*); Adele Dickson (*The Wife*); Laurier Lister (*The Lover*); Doreen Buss (*The Maid*); Humphrey Morton (*The Father*); Everley Russell-Greig (*The Mother*); Josephine Rowley (*First Servant*); Eileen L'Anson (*Second Servant*); Leonard Brett (*The Strange Man*).

Scenes from L'Amour Médecin, a comedy in prose by Molière with Ballet and interlude. Music: Lully; Rehearsed by Mlle. Alice Marry Gachet.

Cast: Charles Laughton (*Sganarelle*); Norah Stokes (*Lucinde—Daughter of Sganarelle*); Doreen Buss (*Lisette—Servant of Lucinde*); Marguerite Young (*Clitandre, in love with Lucinde*); Margaret Raymond (*Un Notaire*); Somerled Rorie (*Champagne*); Mollie Barnes (*Rasque*).

Brief Synopsis: The scene is Paris in a room of the house of Sganarelle.

Professional Stage Appearances
(1926–1959)

The Government Inspector at the Barnes Theatre; opened April 28, 1926.

Cast: Elliott Seabrooke (*Swistunov*); James Lomas (*Derzhimorda*); Dan F. Roe (*Luka Lukich*); Hanley Drewitt (*Amos Fyodorovich*); Sidney Benson (*Herr Hübner*); Kimber Phillips (*Artemi Philipovich*); Frederick Lord (*Bobchinski*); Alfred Clark (*Anton Antonovitch*); Neil Curtis (*Ivan Kusmich*); Jack Knight (*Dobchinski*); Hilda Sims (*Anna Andreyeyna*); Stella Freeman (*Marya Antonovna*); Jane Ellis (*Avdoya*); **Charles Laughton** (*Osip*); Claude Rains (*Ivan Alexandrovich Khletakov*); John C. Laurence (*Waiter and Merchant*); Brian Watson (*Third Merchant, Gendarme*); May Agate (*The Locksmith's Wife*); Patricia O'Carroll (*The Sergeant's Wife*).

Brief Synopsis: In a small Russian town, corrupt officials react with terror when they learn that a government inspector is to be sent incognito to investigate their dishonesty.

Pillars of Society at the Everyman Theatre; opened June 13, 1926.

Cast: Gilbert Ritchie (*Krap*); Orlando Barnett (*Aune*); Milton Rosmer (*Dr. Rorlund*); Margaret Carter (*Mrs. Rummel*); Drusilla Wills (*Mrs. Postmaster Holt*); Barbara Everest (*Mrs. Bernick*); Josephine Wilson (*Miss Bernick*); Brember Wills (*Hilmar Tonnesen*); Anne Bolt (*Olaf*); Marie Wright (*Mrs. De Lynge*); Gwendolen Evans (*Dina Dorf*); J. Hubert-Leslie (*Vigeland*); **Charles Laughton** (*Rummel*); Sybil Arundel (*Miss Hessel*); Charles Carson (*Consul Bernick*); Michael Hogan (*Johan Tonnesen*).

Brief Synopsis: A successful businessman in a small Norwegian town finds his past catching up with him.

The Cherry Orchard by Anton Chekhov, translated by Constance Garnett; Directed by M. Komisarjevsky at the Barnes Theatre; opened September 28, 1926.

Cast: Douglas Burbidge (*Lopahin*); Stella Freeman (*Dunyasha*); **Charles Laughton** (*Epihodov*); Edith Harley (*A Servant*); Dan F. Roe (*Firs*); Gabrielle Casartelli (*Anya*); Dorothy Dix (*Madame Ranyevskaya*); Lawrence Hanray (*Gayev*); Josephine Wilson (*Varya*); Martita Hunt (*Charlotta*); Oswald Lingard (*Semenov-Pishchik*); W. Earle Grey (*Yasha*); Wilfred Fletcher (*Trofimov*); Leonard Calvert (*A Tramp, Stationmaster*); Gerard Barton (*A Post Office Clerk*); Leslie Paine (*His Son*); Monica Stracey (*A Young Lady*).

Brief Synopsis: After an extended absence, a Russian aristocrat returns to her estate to find it has been heavily mortgaged to pay for her extravagance and will be sold off.

The Three Sisters at the Barnes Theatre; opened October 1926.

Cast: Martita Hunt (*Olga*); Josephine Wilson (*Irina*); Margaret Swallow (*Masha*); Stella Freeman (*A Maid*); Leonard Upton (*Tusenbach*); Dan F. Roe (*Chebutykin*); **Charles Laughton** (*Vassily Solyony*); Douglas Burbidge (*Andrey Prozorov*); Gerard Barton (*An Orderly*); Elsie French (*Anfisa*); Oswald Lingard (*Ferapont*); Douglas Jefferies (*Vershinin*); Alfred Sangster (*Kulygin*); Dorice Fordred (*Natasha Ivanova*); Anthony Ireland (*Alexey Fedotik*); Lionel Redpath (*Vladimir Rode*).

Brief Synopsis: Three sisters are provided with refined education and culture in Moscow. Then their father, an army general, relocates them to a provincial town where their talents are wasted. The sisters hate the provincial life and dream of returning to Moscow.

Liliom at the Duke of York's; opened December 25, 1926.

Cast: Stella Freeman (*Dancer*); Beryl Harrison (*Marie*); Fay Compton (*Julie*); Violet Farebrother (*Mrs. Muskat*); Ivor Novello (*Liliom*); William Kendall (*Berkovicz*); Ben Webster (*First Mounted Policeman*); J. Hamilton Kay (*Detective*); Margaret

Webster (*Mrs. Kalman*); **Charles Laughton** (*Ficsur*); Ernest Hare (*Second Mounted Policeman*); Dan F. Roe (*Young Kalman*); Douglas Jefferies (*Wolf*); Douglas Burbidge (*Athlete Linz*); Alfred Sangster (*Police Surgeon*); Drew MacIntosh, Alfred Hilliard (*Policemen*); Marjorie Mars (*Louise*).

Brief Synopsis: Liliom, a barker at a carousel fair, loves Julie, a young maid. Shortly after they both lose their jobs, Julie becomes pregnant. Without informing Julie, Liliom plans a robbery to provide for his expectant child. Together with a criminal friend, Ficsur, their attempt at robbery proves disastrous. Ficsur escapes and to avoid capture Liliom kills himself.

The Greater Love A Drama in Four Acts by J.B. Fagan at the Prince's Theatre; opened February 23, 1927.

Cast: Sybil Thorndike (*Nadia*); Ada King (*Tatiana Sergevna*); George Bealby (*Count Pestoff*); Lawrence Hanray (*Professor Panshine*); Brember Wills (*Nuhlin*); Lewis T. Casson (*Polusky, Colonel Schultz*); Colin Keith-Johnston (*Vassli Ivanovich*); Henry Hewitt (*Captain Pavel Kaulbach*); **Charles Laughton** (*General Markeloff*); Basil Gill (*Colonel Tzaloff*); Desmond Deanne (*Colonel Almazoff*); Wallace Wood (*Captain Alexieff*); Elliott Seabrooke (*Captain Nazernoff*); John H. Moore (*Officer*).

Brief Synopsis: Colonel Tzaloff searches the Pestoff family home for papers which will incriminate them in a revolutionary plot. His assignment is diverted when he falls in love with Count Pestoff's daughter Nadia.

Angela by Lady Bell; Prince's Theatre; Directed by Lewis T. Casson; opened March 14, 1927.

Cast: Dora Barton (*Honorable Mrs. Carr*); Jessie Bateman (*Lady Hartley*); Sadie Speight (*Mrs. Priestman*); John H. Moore (*Footman*); Lilian Moubrey (*Servant*); Sybil Thorndike (*Angela Guiseley*); **Charles Laughton** (*Sir James Hartley*); Lewis T. Casson (*Valentine Guiseley*); Lawrence Hanray (*Jack Wilding*); Thomas Warner (*Mr. Priestman*); Percy Varley (*Mr. Lambert*); Zilah Carter (*Violet Guiseley*); Winifred Oughton (*Clare Marriner*); Ronald Kerr (*Geoff Marriner*); Wallace Wood (*Mr. Wilson*); Godfrey Baxter (*Clerk*); Brember Wills (*John Quarl*).

Brief Synopsis: A story of big business and the clash between high ideals and economic realities. This was a charity matinee given in aid of the British Hospital for Mothers and Babies.

Naked by Luigi Pirandello; Translated by Arthur Livingstone; Royalty Theatre; Producer: Theodore Komisarjevsky; opened March 18, 1927.

Cast: Nancy Price (*Ersila Drei*); Allan Jeayes (*Ludovico Nota*); Florence Tyrrell (*Onoria*); **Charles Laughton** (*Cantavalle*); George Relph (*Franco Raspigi*); Joan Levett (*Emma*); Elliott Seabrooke (*Consul Grotti*).

Brief Synopsis: A young woman attempts suicide by poison, but she is found before the poison can kill her. First a journalist becomes interested in her life, and then a novelist. When stories begin to circulate, more and more people are drawn in.

The "Medea" of Eurpides Translated by Gilbert Murray; Prince's Theatre; opened April 27, 1927.

Cast: Sybil Thorndyke (*Medea*); Lawrence Anderson (*Jason*); **Charles Laughton** (*Creon*); Lawrence Hanray (*Aegeus*); Lilian Moubrey (*Nurse*); John H. Moore (*Attendant*); Lewis T. Casson (*Messenger*); Ziliah Carter, Margaret Webster, Iris Baker, Ursula Granville, Renee Rubens, Grace Poole. Penelope Spencer (*Chorus*).

Brief Synopsis: Medea, a former princess of the "barbarian" kingdom of Colchis and the wife of Jason, finds her position in Greek society threatened as Jason leaves her for a Greek princess of Corinth. Medea enacts a terrible act of vengeance on Jason.

The Happy Husband A Light Comedy in Three Acts by Harrison Owen; Criterion Theatre; Produced by Basil Dean; opened June 15, 1927.

Cast: Madge Titheradge (*Dot Rendell*); Stella Arbenina (*Consuelo Pratt*); Madge Sealby (*Stella Todhurst*): Ann Trevor (*Sylvia Fullerton*); Lawrence Grossmith (*Bill Rendell*); David Hawthorne (*Arthur Todhurst*); **Charles Laughton** (*Frank K. Pratt*); Eric Cowley ("*Sosso*" *Stephens*); A.E. Matthews (*Harvey Townsend*).

Brief Synopsis: The Lounge Hall of the Todhursts' small country weekend house is the setting for romantic misadventures among the middle-classes. Dot Rendell decides she must teach her pleasant, mildly stupid husband Bill not to take her for granted.

Paul I by Dmitry Merezhkovsky; Adapted by John Alford and J.C. Dale; at the Royal Court Theatre; Produced by Theodore Komisarjevsky; opened October 4, 1927.

Cast: Carl Harbord (*Grand Duke Alexander*); Lydia Sherwood (*Elizabeth*); George Hayes (*Paul I*); Elliott Seabrooke (*Grand Duke Constantin*); Arthur Macrae (*Lieutenant Martin Ropchinsky*); **Charles Laughton** (***General Count Pahlen***); Hugh Barnes (*General Talyzin*); Bramwell Fletcher (*Colonel Prince Yashvil*); Vivian Beynon (*General Bennigsen*); Ian Davison (*Colonel Argamakov*); Dan F. Roe (*Dr. Rodgerson, Colonel Baron Rosen*); Dorothy Green (*Empress Marie*); Dorothy Cheston (*Princess Anna Gagarine*); W.E.C. Jenkins (*Lieutenant Bibikov Kirilov*); G. Vernon (*Cornet Gardanov*); Scott Sunderland (*Prince Platon*); Barry K. Barnes (*Prince Nicolas Zoubov*).

Brief Synopsis: An enactment of the wretched circumstances leading to the assassination of Paul I of Russia in Petersburg in March 1801.

Mr. Prohack by Arnold Bennett and Edward Knoblock; at the Court Theatre; opened November 16, 1927.

Cast: **Charles Laughton** (***Mr. Prohack***); Hilda Sims (*Mrs. Prohack*); Lydia Sherwood (*Susie Prohack*); Carl Harbord (*Charles Prohack*); Juliet Mansel (*Machin*); Scott Sutherland (*Sofly Bishop*); Frederick Cooper (*Ozzie Morley*); Dorothy Cheston (*Lady Massulam*); Dan F. Roe (*Hollins*); Arthur Macrae (*Tailor's Boy*); Elsa Lanchester (*Mini Winstock*); Elliott Seabrooke (*Sir Paul Spinner*).

Brief Synopsis: The fortunes of the Prohack family seem to be on the downward path, but they are unexpectedly bequeathed £20,000 by a man who Mr. Prohack once lent a few hundred pounds. Unfortunately, this legacy does not produce the contentment that Prohack's wife and children had hoped for.

A Man with Red Hair by Benn Levy, from the novel by Hugh Walpole; at the Prince of Wales; opened February 27, 1928.

Cast: Ion Swinley (*David Dunbar*); Keyo Akimoto (*A Servant*); J.H. Roberts (*Charles Percy Harkness*); Gillian Lind (*Heather Tobin*); **Charles Laughton** (***Mr. Crispin***); James Whale (*Herrick Crispin*); George Bealby (*Dr. Tobin*); Kay Chiba (*Another Servant*).

Brief Synopsis: In a lonely house high on the Cornish cliffs, Crispin, a loathsome, perverted sadist, believes that only through the infliction and suffering of pain can mankind rise superior to itself and become god-like.

The Making of an Immortal by George Moore; at the Arts Theatre Club; April 1–2, 1928.

Cast: Malcolm Keen (*Richard Burbage*); Edmund Gwenn (*Anthony Grindle*); Edward Chapman (*Christopher Firk*); D. Hay Petrie (*Jack Ford*); Billy Shine (*Jack Thornley*); Brian Glennie (*Prenny Lister*); Thomas White (*Robert Warner*); George Brian (*Stephen Frion*); Sandford Gorton (*Henry Cuffe*); **Charles Laughton** (***Ben Jonson***); Leslie Faber (*Francis Bacon*); Charles Carson (*William Shakespeare*); Sybil Thorndyke (*Queen Elizabeth*); Clement Hamelin, Leslie Coles, More O'Ferrall (*Javelin Men*); John Laurie, Geoffrey Clark, Cyril Hardingham (*Players*); Barbara Horder (*Maid of Honour*).

Brief Synopsis: The gardens of the Palace at Whitehall, in October 1599. Queen Elizabeth I finds herself enraged with the production of *Richard II* with its tale of a tumbled throne. The queen wishes to know who this mysterious William Shakespeare is who writes such plays. Comic misunderstandings follow, centered around questions of authorship.

Riverside Nights by A.P. Herbert and Nigel Playfair, at the Arts Theatre Club; Music: Alfred Reynolds; opened June 24, 1928.

Cast: Marie Brett-Davies, Joan Carr, Rene de Vaux, Elsa Lanchester, Florence McHugh, Violet Marqausita, D.H. Petrie, Nigel Playfair, Mark Raphael, Scott Russell, Penelope Spencer, Laura Wilson, Geoff Wincott, Fay Yeatman, **Charles Laughton**.

Brief Synopsis: A musical revue.

Alibi by Michael Morton, from the novel *The Murder of Roger Ackroyd?* by Agatha Christie, at the Prince of Wales; opened November 12, 1928.

Cast: Lady Tree (*Mrs. Ackroyd*); Jane Welsh (*Flora Ackroyd*); E. Disney Roebuck (*Parker*); Basil Loder (*Major Blunt*); Iris Nobel (*Ursula Bourne*); H.J. Forbes Robertson (*Geoffrey Raymond*); Gillian Lind (*Carl Sheppard*); **Charles Laughton** (***Inspector Hercule Poirot***); J.H. Roberts (*Dr. Sheppard*); Norman V. Norman (*Sir Roger Ackroyd*); John Darwin (*Inspector Davies*); J. Smith-Wright (*Mr. Hammond*); Constance Anderson (*Margot*).

Brief Synopsis: Belgian sleuth Hercule Poirot discovers the truth behind a mysterious suicide at a country house.

Mr. Pickwick by Charles Dickens; Adapted by Cosmo Hamilton, F.C. Reilly; at the Haymarket Theatre; Produced by Basil Dean; opened December 15, 1928.

Cast: Eliot Makeham (*Sam Weller*); May Chevalier (*Housekeeper*); Gypsy Raine (*Betsy*); Deering Wells (*Augustus Snodgrass*); Harold Scott (*Nathanial Winkle*); Lamont Dickson (*Tracey Tugman*); Oswald Roberts (*Waiter, Mr. Jackson, Sergeant Snubben*); Wallace Douglas (*Mr. Trundle, Gamekeeper's Boy*); Richard Turner (*Bob Sawyer*); Denis Mowbray (*Ben Allen*); Bruce Winston (*Toby Weller, Sergeant Buzfuz*); Ambrose Manning (*Mr. Wardle*); Kathleen Gelder (*Emily Wardle*); Kathleen Kelly (*Isabella Kelly*); Madeleine Carroll (*Arabela Allen*); Susan Richmond (*Rachel Wardle*); Jack Corps (*Fat Boy*); Dorice Fordred (*Mary*); J. Hubert Leslie (*Mr. Perker*); **Charles Laughton** (***Mr. Pickwick***); D.J. Williams (*Cabman, Justice Stareleigh*); George Curzon (*Alfred Jingle*); Mary Clare (*Mrs. Bardell*); Polly Emery (*Mrs. Cluppins*); George Curzon (*Jingle*); Eliot Makeham (*Sam Weller*); Bruce Winston (*Tony Weller*); Anne Esmond (*Mrs. Sanders*); Huntley Gifford (*Butler*); Archibald McLean (*Mr. Dodson*); Richard Coke (*Mr. Fogg*); Walton Palmer (*Mr. Roker*); Arthur Bawtree (*Job Trotter*).

Brief Synopsis: A number of scenes adapted from Dickens' immortal *Pickwick Papers*.

Beauty by Michael Morton, from the French of Jacques Deval; Produced by Felix Edwardes; Strand Theatre; opened July 16, 1929.

Cast: Oswald Skilbeck (*Gustave*); Lady Tree (*Henriette Sopite*); Morton Selten (*Xavier Sopite*); Grace Wilson (*Madame Vadiche*); Gwendolen Floyd (*Madame Toube*); Ena Grossmith (*Berenice Toube*); Isabel Jeans (*Estelle Duparc*); Eric Maturin (*Paul de Severac*); **Charles Laughton** (***Jacques Blaise***); Alec Chentrens (*Bonamy*); W.E.C. Jenkins (*Adolphe*); Dorothy Dunkels (*Rose*); E. Lyall Swete (*Professor Flammet*).

Brief Synopsis: Jacques Blaise, an ungainly and unprepossessing astronomer, falls madly in love with a beautiful woman.

The Silver Tassie A Tragic-Comedy by Sean O'Casey; Directed by Raymond Massey, at the Apollo Theatre; opened October 11, 1929.

Cast: Barry Fitzgerald (*Sylvester Heegan*); Sidney Morgan (*Simon Norton*); Eithne Magee (*Mrs. Heegan*): Beatrix Lehmann (*Susie Monican*); Una O'Connor (*Mrs. Foran*); Ian Hunter (*Teddy Foran*); **Charles Laughton** (*Harry Heegan*); Billy Barnes (*Jessie Taite, 4th Stretcher Bearer*); S.J. Warmington (*Barry Bagnal, 6th Soldier*); Leonard Shepherd (*The Croucher*); **Charles Laughton** (***First Soldier***); Barry Fitzgerald (*3rd Soldier*); Jack Mayne (*4th Soldier*); G. Adrian Byrne (*5th Soldier*); Sinclair Cotter (*The Corporal*); Ivo Dawson (*The Visitor*); Alban Blakelock (*The Staff Wallah*); Emlyn Williams (*The Trumpeter*); Norman Stuart, Oswald Lingard, Charles Schofield (*Stretcher Bearers*); Clive Morton, James Willoughby (*Casualties*); Hastings Lynn (*Surgeon Forby Maxwell*); Audrey O'Flynn (*Sister of the Ward*).

Brief Synopsis: This anti-war play in four acts focuses on soldier Harry Heegan and the effects of war on his hopes for life during and after the war.

French Leave by Reginald Berkeley, at the Vaudeville Theatre; Produced by Eille Norwood; opened January 7, 1930.

Cast: Charles Groves (*Corporal Sykes*); Frederick Burtwell (*Rifleman Jenks*); Madeleine Carroll (*Mademoiselle Juliette*); James Raglan (*Captain Harry Glenister*); **Charles Laughton** (***Brigadier-General Archibald Root, C.B. D.S.O.***); Edward Scott-Gatty (*Lieutenant George Graham*); Emlyn Williams (*Monsieur Jules Marnier*); May Agate (*Madame Denaux*).

Brief Synopsis: In a mess room of a brigade resting out of line "somewhere in France," Dorothy Glenister, wife of Captain Glenister, appears disguised as the daughter of a local family. Complications arise when she is suspected of being a German spy.

On the Spot by Edgar Wallace, at Wyndam's Theatre; opened April 2, 1930.

Cast: Frank Everart (*Shaun O'Donnell*); Agnes Somerset (*A Nurse*); Philip Valentine (*A Priest*); Julian Andrews (*A Doctor*); Roy Emerton (*Captain Harrison*); Douglas Payne (*Patrolman Ryan*); **Charles Laughton** (*Tony Perelli*); Gillian Lind (*Minn Lee*); John Gold (*Kirki*); Emlyn Williams (*Angelo*); Ben Welden (*Con O'Hara*); Gladys Frazin (*Maria Poulikski*); Ben Smith (*Jimmy McGarth*); W. Cronin-Wilson (*Detective-Commissioner John Kelly*); Dennis Wyndham (*Mike Feeney*).

Brief Synopsis: Gangland life in prohibition Chicago. Mobster Tony Perelli employs henchmen to his gang and women for his love life with equal ruthlessness. When they become irksome, he arranges their disposal.

Payment Deferred by Jeffrey Dell, from the novel by C.S. Forester; at the St. James Theatre, opened May 4, 1931.

Cast: Louise Hampton (*Annie Marble*); Elsa Lanchester (*Winnie Marble*); Jeanne de Casalis (*Madam Collins*); Ernest Jay (*Hammond*); Paul Longuet (*Jim Medland*); Quinton McPherson (*A Prospective Tenant*); A.S. Homewood (*Dr. Atkinson*); Edgar K. Bruce and Ernest Haines

(*Furniture Removers*); **Charles Laughton** (*William Marble*).

Brief Synopsis: A bank official murders for financial gain.

Payment Deferred at the Lyceum Theater, New York; Produced by Gilbert Miller; opened September 30, 1931.

Cast: Dorice Fordred (*Madame Collins*); Stanley Harrison (*Harry Gentle*); Elsa Lanchester (*Winnie Marble*); **Charles Laughton** (*William Marble*); Paul Longuet (*Jim Medland*); Cicely Oates (*Annie Marble*); Lionel Pape (*Dr. Atkinson*); Horace Sinclair (*A Prospective Tenant*); Malcolm Soltan (*Bert Bricketts*); S. Victor Stanley (*Hammond*).

The Fatal Alibi by Michael Morton at the Booth Theater, New York; Directed by **Charles Laughton**; opened February 8, 1932.

Cast: Jane Bramley (*Ursula Bourne*); Lawrence H. Cecil (*Inspector Davies*); Andree Corday (*Margo*); Edward Crandall (*Geoffrey Raymond*); Lowell Gilmore (*Captain Ralph Paton*); Kenneth Hunter (*Major Blunt*); Moffat Johnston (*Dr. Sheppard*); **Charles Laughton** (*Hercule Poirot*); Fotheringham Lysons (*Mr. Hammond*); Lionel Pape (*Sir Roger Ackroyd*); Donald Randolph (*Parker*); Effie Shannon (*Mrs. Ackroyd*); Helen Vinson (*Caryl Sheppard*); Jane Wyatt (*Flora*).

Brief Synopsis: An American adaptation of *Alibi*, with Laughton repeating his role of detective Hercule Poirot and directing as well.

The Cherry Orchard by Anton Chekhov, at the Old Vic; produced by Tyrone Guthrie; October 9–28, 1933.

Cast: **Charles Laughton** (*Lopahin*); Barbara Wilcox (*Dunyasha*); Marius Goring (*Yepikhodov*); Athene Seyler (*Lyubov Andreyevna*); Ursula Jeans (*Anya*); Flora Robson (*Varya*); Leon Quartermaine (*Gaev*); Elsa Lanchester (*Governess*); Roger Livesey (*Semenov-Pishchik*); Morland Graham (*Firs*); James Mason (*Yasha*); Dennis Arundell (*Trofimov*); Ernest Hare (*A Vagrant*); John Allen (*The Station Master*); Raymond Johnson (*A Post Office Clerk*).

Brief Synopsis: Following a long absence in Paris, the widow Madame Ranevsky returns to her family estate to find it has been heavily mortgaged to pay for her extravagances and that it is to be auctioned off.

Henry VIII by William Shakespeare, at the Sadler's Wells Theatre; produced by Tyrone Guthrie; opened November 7, 1933.

Cast: Dennis Arundell (*Duke of Norfolk*); Flora Robson (*Queen Katherine*); Athene Seyler (*Old Lady*); Ursula Jeans (*Anne Bullen*); Elsa Lanchester (*A Singer*); **Charles Laughton** (*Henry VIII*); Nicholas Hannen (*Duke of Buckingham*); Roger Livesey (*Lord Chamberlain*); Richard Goolden (*Lord Sands Cranmer*); Marius Goring (*Cardinal Campeius King-at-Arms*); Ernest Hare (*Lord Abergavenny, Duke of Suffolk*); Christopher Hassell (*Sir Thomas Lovell*); Morland Graham (*Griffith*); Robert Farquharson (*Cardinal Wolsey*); James Mason (*Cromwell*); Desmond Walter-Ellis (*Brandon*); Derek Prentice (*A Sergeant-at-Arms*); Philip Thornley (*Surveyor to the Duke of Buckingham*); Christopher Hassell (*Sir Thomas Lovell*); Bernard Grimley (*Sir Henry Guildford, First Usher*); Raymond Johnson (*First Gentleman*); John Allen (*Second Gentleman*); Orford St. John (*Sir Nicholas Vaux*); Cecil Scott-Paton (*Gardiner*); Morland Graham (*Griffith*); Frank Napier (*Earl of Surrey*); Evelyn Allen (*Patience*); Thorley Walters (*A Messenger*); Peter Copley (*Capucius*).

Brief Synopsis: Monarch Henry VIII has a forbidden love with Anne Boleyn. The Dukes (Norfolk and Buckingham) plot to turn the king against Cardinal Wolsey.

Measure for Measure by William Shakespeare; Produced by Tyrone Guthrie; opened December 4, 1933.

Cast: Athene Seyler (*Mistress Overdone*); Flora Robson (*Isabella*); Ursula Jeans (*Mariana*); Elsa Lanchester (*Juliet*); **Charles Laughton** (*Angelo*); Roger Livesey (*Vincentio*); Lawrence Bascomb (*Pompey*); Frank Napier (*Escalus*); Dennis Arundell (*Lucio*); James Mason (*Claudio*); Ernest Hare (*Provost*); Marius Goring (*Friar Peter*); Morland Graham (*Elbow*).

Brief Synopsis: The Duke of Vienna decides to appoint a nobleman, Angelo, to rule the city in his absence. The ensuing events have profound consequences.

The Tempest at the Sadler's Wells Theatre; opened January 8, 1934.

Cast: Patrick Ross (*Master of the Ship*); John Allen (*Boatswain*); Marius Goring (*King of Naples*); Ernest Hare (*Sebastian*); Dennis Arundell (*Antonio*); Clifford Evans (*Ferdinand*); Evan John (*Gonzalo*); Ursula Jeans (*Miranda*); **Charles Laughton** (*Prospero*); Elsa Lanchester (*Ariel*); Roger Livesey (*Caliban*); Desmond Wallace-Ellis (*Adrian*); James Mason (*Francisco*); Lawrence Baskcomb (*Trinculo*); Morland Graham (*Stephano*); Margaret Field-Hyde (*Iris*); Flora Robson (*Ceres*); Evelyn Allen (*Juno*).

Brief Synopsis: A former Duke of Milan, Prospero, lives on an island with his daughter

Miranda. When his enemies are washed ashore, he uses his magic powers to wreak revenge and restore himself to power.

The Importance of Being Earnest by Oscar Wilde, at the Old Vic produced by Tyrone Guthrie; February 5–March 3, 1934.

Cast: Morland Graham (*Lane*); George Curzon (*Algernon Moncrieff*); Roger Livesey (*John Worthing*); Athene Seyler (*Lady Bracknell*); Flora Robson (*Gwendolen Fairfax*); Elsa Lanchester (*Miss Prism*); Ursula Jeans (*Cecily Cardew*); **Charles Laughton** (*The Rev. Canon Chasuble, D.D.*); James Mason (*Merriman*).

Brief Synopsis: Two young men have double identities either to amuse themselves or maintain their social status in one place, while simultaneously enjoying life under another name in a different place.

Love for Love by William Congreve at Sadler's Wells. Produced by Tyrone Guthrie; March 6–31, 1934.

Cast: Barrie Livesey (*Valentine Legend*); James Mason (*Jeremy*); Dennis Arundell (*Scandal*); Marius Goring (*Buckram*); **Charles Laughton** (*Tattle*); Athene Seyler (*Mrs. Frail*); Morland Graham (*Foresight*); Ursula Jeans (*Angelica*); Sam Livesey (*Sir Sampson Legend*); Flora Robson (*Mrs. Foresight*); Elsa Lanchester (*Miss Prue*); Roger Livesey (*Ben Legend*); Alta Hershey (*Jenny*).

Brief Synopsis: Valentine, the dissolute eldest son of Sir Sampson Legend, finds the only way out of his financial difficulties is to sign his right of inheritance over to his younger brother. Seeing this is a way of escaping his many debtors, Valentine accepts the deal but, fearing he will now be spurned by his beloved Angelica, takes drastic action to retain what is rightfully his.

Macbeth by William Shakespeare at the Old Vic produced by Tyrone Guthrie; April 2–28, 1934.

Cast: Ernest Hare (*Duncan, Seward*); Marius Goring (*Malcolm*); Thorley Walters (*Donalbain*); **Charles Laughton** (*Macbeth*); Frank Napier (*Banquo*); Athene Seyler (*First Weird Sister, Gentle Woman*); Phyllis Hatch (*Second Weird Sister*); Elspeth Currie (*Third Weird Sister*); Flora Robson (*Lady Macbeth*); Alan Foss (*Eleanor*); Morland Graham (*Porter*); Roger Livesey (*Macduff*); James Mason (*Lennox*); Evelyn Allen (*Lady Macduff*); Nigel Stock (*Boy, Son to Macduff*); John Allen (*Menteith*); Derek Prentice (*Caithness*); Cecil Scott-Paton (*Messenger*); John Moody (*Seyton*); Peter Copley (*Young Seward*).

Brief Synopsis: Macbeth, a brave and loyal Thane to King Duncan, hears a prophecy that he will become king himself. Abetted by the prophecy and his wife, he is overcome with ambition and greed and kills King Duncan. Afterwards, fear, guilt and paranoia lead him to commit more murders to secure his power. His "overweening ambition" gets the better of him and eventually leads to his downfall and he is overthrown and killed by those he has wronged.

Peter Pan by J.M. Barrie at the Palladium; Directed by Stephen Thomas; opened December 26, 1936.

Cast: Elsa Lanchester (*Peter Pan*); **Charles Laughton** (*Captain Hook*); Peter Murray Hill (*Mr. Darling*); Cecily Byrne (*Mrs. Darling*); Pamela Standish (*Wendy*); Clive Baxter (*John*); Paul Dunger (*Michael*); Wallie Scott (*Nana*); T. Best (*Tootles*); D. Blatcher (*Nibs*); Charles Hawtrey (*Slightly*); Charles Doe (*Smee*); Harold Scott (*Gentleman Starkey*); William Luff (*Cecco*); Hamilton Hunter (*Jukes*); Granville Darling (*Noodler*); Claude Talbot (*First Pirate*); Richard Turner (*Second Pirate*); Sam Henry (*Black Pirate*); Garrett Hollick (*Great Big Little Panther*); Olive Wright (*Tiger Lily*); M. Milne (*Mermaid*); Kathleen Weston (*Baby Mermaid*); Helen Moore (*Liza*); T. Bray (*Ostrich*); David Little, Basil Macrae (*Crocodile*).

Brief Synopsis: Peter Pan takes Wendy and her siblings to Neverland. There Peter is pursued by the pirate Captain Hook, who is himself pursued by the crocodile who once bit off his hand. After many adventures, Wendy, Peter and the Lost Boys escape Hook's clutches.

Galileo by Bertolt Brecht; English Adaptation by **Charles Laughton**; Staged by Joseph Losey; Settings and Costumes: Robert Davison; Choreography: Lotte Goslar; Music: Hanns Eisler; Lyrics Adapted by Albert Brush; Coronet Theatre, Hollywood; July 30, 1947.

Cast: Burton Karsin, Albert Reid, James Adkins (*Singers*); Donald Pietro (*Curtain Boy*); **Charles Laughton** (*Galileo*); Ray Malkin (*Andrea, the Boy*); Eda Reiss Merin (*Mrs. Sarti*); Herbert Anderson (*Ludovico Marsall*); Ken Jones (*Priull*); Kenneth Patterson (*Sagredo*); Frances Heflin (*Virginia*); David Clarke (*Federzoni*); Peter Brocco (*Old Cardinal*); Nick Volpe (*Christopher Clavius*); Mickey Knox (*Little Monk*); Stephen Brown (*Cardinal

Ballarmin); Hugo Haas (*Cardinal Barberini*); William Cottrell (*Cardinal Inquisitor*); William Phipps (*Andrea the Man*); Peter Brocco (*The Informer*); Stephen Brown (*The Ballad Singer*).

Brief Synopsis: In the seventeenth century, scientists battle with the church.

Galileo by Bertolt Brecht; Directed by Joseph Losey at Maxine Elliott's Theater, New York; opened December 7, 1947.

Cast: Wesley Addy (*Old Cardinal*); Captain Sidney Bassier (*Senator I, a Monk*); Leonard Bell (*A Monk*); Harris Brown (*Ballade Singer*); Frank Campanella (*Senator II, a Scholar*); Mary Grace Canfield (*Elderly Lady*); John Carradine (*Inquisitor*); Michael Citro (*Singer, Andrea*); Taylor Graves (*Clavius*); Don Hanmer (*Little Monk*); Pitt Herbert (*Supporting Monk*); Harry Hess (*Lord Chamberlain*); Werner Klemperer (*Infuriated Monk*); Rusty Lane (*Barbarini*); **Charles Laughton** (*Galileo*); Richard Leone (*Singer*); Iris Mann (*Ballade Singer's Daughter*); Dwight Marfield (*Federzoni*); Allen Martin (*Curtain Boy*); Joan McCracken (*Virginia*); Earl Montgomery (*Duke of Florence*); Elizabeth Moore (*Ballade Singer's Wife*); Thomas Palmer (*Philosopher*); Nehemiah Persoff (*Andrea*); Philip Robinson (*Matti*); Larry Rosen (*Prince*); Lawrence Ryle (*Bellarmin*); Hester Sondergaard (*Sarti*); Warren Stevens (*Informer*); Fred Stewart (*Priuli*); John Straub (*Sagredo*); Philip Swander (*Ludovico*); Donald Symington (*Giuseppi*); Albert Tavares (*Singer*).

Brief Synopsis: The scientist and astronomer Galileo Galilei experiments with telescopes and develops evidence for a new model of the solar system. This threatens the established church and results in Galileo's inquisition and his eventual recantation of his scientific findings.

Don Juan in Hell at the New Century Theater, New York; written by George Bernard Shaw; opened November 29, 1951.

Cast: Charles Boyer (*Don Juan*); Cedric Hardwicke (*The Statue*); **Charles Laughton** (*Devil*); Agnes Moorehead (*Doña Ava*).

Don Juan in Hell at the Plymouth Theater, New York; Written by George Bernard Shaw, Directed by **Charles Laughton**; opened April 6, 1952.

Cast: Charles Boyer (*Don Juan*); Cedric Hardwicke (*The Statue*); **Charles Laughton** (*Devil*); Agnes Moorehead (*Doña Ava*).

Brief Synopsis: The third act of Shaw's philosophical comedy *Man and Superman* depicts the spirited conversation between Don Juan, the Devil, Juan's former paramour Doña Ana, and her father the commander, slain by Juan while defending his daughter's honor. Four voices debate war, love, morality and the eternal battle of the sexes with sublime wit and devilish charm.

John Brown's Body at the New Century Theater, New York; Produced by Paul Gregory; Adapted from Stephen Vincent Benet's book by **Charles Laughton**; Directed by **Charles Laughton**; Music and Effects: Walter Schumann; Onstage Choral Director: Richard White; opened February 14, 1953.

Cast: Judith Anderson (*Principal*); Raymond Massey (*Principal*); Tyrone Power (*Principal*); Joe Baker (*Choral Group*); Betty Benson (*Choral Group, Soloist*); Roy D. Berk (*Choral Group*); Paul Bloom (*Choral Group*); Keith Carver (*Choral Group*); Stephen Considine (*Choral Group, Soloist*); Jack B. Bailey (*Choral Group*); Barbara Ford (*Choral Group*); Gillian Grey (*Choral Group*); Homer W. Hall (*Choral Group*); Lester D. Helsdon (*Choral Group*); William Longmire (*Choral Group*); Donna McDaniel (*Choral Group, Dancer*); John McMahon (*Choral Group*); Roger Miller (*Choral Group*); Smith Russell Jr. (*Choral Group*); Alexander Serbaroli (*Choral Group, Dancer*); Lynda Stevens (*Choral Group*); Robert Vaughn (*Choral Group*); Gordon B. Wood (*Choral Group*).

Brief Synopsis: A staged dramatic reading of the epic American poem covering the American Civil War and the radical abolitionist John Brown, who raided Harper's Ferry, Virginia, in the fall of 1859. Brown was captured later that year and hanged.

The Caine Mutiny Court-Martial by Herman Wouk. Directed by **Charles Laughton** at the Plymouth Theater, New York; opened January 20, 1954.

Cast: Henry Fonda (*Lieutenant Greenwald*); John Hodiak (*Lieutenant Stephen Maryk*); Lloyd Nolan (*Lieutenant Commander Philip Francis Queeg*); Russell Hicks (*Captain Blakely*); Herbert Anderson (*Dr. Bird*); Larry Barton (*Member of the Court*); Paul Birch (*Captain Randolph Southard*); Jim Bum Garner [James Garner] (*Member of the Court*); Stephen Chase (*Dr. Forrest Lundeen*); Richard Farmer (*Member of the Court*); Eddie Firestone (*Signalman Third Class Junius Urban*); Robert Gist (*Lieutenant Thomas Keefer*); John Huffman (*Stenographer*); T.H. Jourdan (*Member of the Court*); Charles Nolte (*Lieutenant [Junior Grade] Willis Seward Keith*); Richard Norris (*Member of* *the Court*); Greg Roman (*Orderly*); Patrick Waltz (*Member of the Court*); Ainslie Pryor.

Brief Synopsis: During World War II, a young ensign serving on the *Caine*, a minesweeper, is witness to the erratic behavior of its captain. The captain is relieved of his command when, during a typhoon in the Pacific, he almost causes the ship to capsize. The captain brings a charge of mutiny against the executive officer who took over his command. The trial that follows reduces the charges and the command of the ship passes to other captains.

3 for Tonight at the Plymouth Theater; Produced by Paul Gregory and **Charles Laughton**; opened April 6, 1955.

Cast: Harry Belafonte; Betty Benson; Gower Champion; Marge Champion (*Performers*); Walter Schumann (*Impressions—Recorded Voices*); Hiriam Sherman (*Story Teller*); Robert Brink, Andrew Case, Gina Christen, Diane Doxee, Elaine Drew, Joyce L. Foss, Dorothy Gill, Nancy Harp, Jimmy Harris, Mark Karl, Jerry Madison, Robert Miller, Ned Romero, Jack Steele, Brad Thomas, Robert Trevis, Karen Vonne, Richard Wessler (*Chorus*).

Brief Synopsis: A musical revue.

Major Barbara by George Bernard Shaw; Martin Beck Theater and Morosco Theater, New York; **Produced by Charles Laughton**; opened October 30, 1956.

Cast: Glynis Johns (*Major Barbara*); **Charles Laughton** (***Andrew Undershaft***); Burgess Meredith (*Adolphus Cusins*); Cornelia Otis Skinner (*Lady Brittomart*); Eli Wallach (*Bill Walker*); Colin Keith-Johnston (*Peter Shirley*); Nancy Malone (*Jenny Hill*); John Astin (*Morrison*); Walter Burke (*Snobby Price*); Myra Carter (*Sarah*); Frank Gero (*Footman*); Sally Gracie (*Rummy Mitchens*); Louise Latham (*Maid*); Richard Lupino (*Charles Lomax*); Patricia Ripley (*Mrs. Baines*); Frederic Warriner (*Stephen*).

Brief Synopsis: Idealistic Barbara Undershaft, daughter of Andrew Undershaft, a wealthy armaments manufacturer, rebels against her father and joins the Salvation Army. Wooed by professor-turned-preacher Adolphus Cusins, she begins to grow disillusioned by her adopted cause and to see things from her father's viewpoint.

The Party by Jane Arden at the New Theatre; **Produced by Charles Laughton**; Settings by Reece Pemberton; Costumes Designed by Jocelyn Rickards; Lighting by William Lorraine; opened May 28, 1958.

Cast: Ann Lynn (*Henrietta Brough*); Joyce Redman (*Frances Brough*); John Welsh (*Harold Lingham*); Elsa Lanchester (*Elsie Sharp*); Albert Finney (*Soya Marshall*); **Charles Laughton** (***Richard Brough***).

Brief Synopsis: A Kilburn family is reluctantly reunited when an alcoholic father returns to his long-suffering wife and a daughter who despises him.

A Midsummer Night's Dream by William Shakespeare at the Memorial Theatre at Stratford-upon-Avon; opened June 2, 1959.

Cast: Anthony Nicholls (*Theseus*); Stephanie Bidmead (*Hippolyta*); Donald Layne-Smith (*Philostrate, Master of the Revels*); Roy Dotrice (*Egeus, Father to Hermia*); Priscilla Morgan (*Hermia*); Albert Finney (*Lysander*); Edward De Souza (*Demetrius*); Vanessa Redgrave (*Helena*); Cyril Luckham (*Quince, a Carpenter*); **Charles Laughton** (***Bottom, a Weaver***); Peter Woodthorpe (*Flute, a Bellow Mender*); Donald Eccles (*Starveling, a Tailor*); Michael Blakemore (*Snout, a Tinker*); Julian Glover (*Snug, a Joiner*); Ian Holm (*Puck [Robin Goodfellow]*); Zoe Caldwell (*A Fairy*); Robert Hardy (*Oberon*); Mary Ure (*Titania*); Mavis Edwards, Georgine Anderson, Judith Downes, Margaret O'Keefe, Jean Owen, Malcolm Ranson, Michael Scoble (*Fairies*).

Brief Synopsis: The marriage of Theseus, Duke of Athens, and Hippolyta, the former queen of the Amazons, causes adventures and misadventures among four Athenian lovers and a group of six amateur actors. All are controlled by fairies who inhabit the woodland forest where the wedding celebrations are held.

King Lear by William Shakespeare at the Memorial Theatre at Stratford-upon-Avon; opened June 13, 1959. Directed by Glen Byam Shaw; Scenery and Costumes Designed by Motley; Music Composed by Antony Hopkins; Lighting: Michael Northen; Fights Arranged by Bernard Hepton, assisted by Kenneth Gilbert; Music Advisor: Leslie Bridgewater; Theater Orchestra under the direction of Harold Ingram; Leader: Nicholas Roth.

Cast: Anthony Nicholls (*Earl of Kent*); Cyril Luckham (*Earl of Gloucester*); Robert Hardy (*Edmund*); **Charles Laughton** (***King Lear***); Stephanie Bidmead (*Goneril*); Angela Baddeley

(*Regan*); Zoe Caldwell (*Cordelia*); Julian Glover (*Duke of Albany*); Paul Hardwick (*Duke of Cornwall*); Edward De Souza (*King of France*); Roy Dotrice (*Duke of Burgandy*); Albert Finney (*Edgar*); Michael Blakemore (*Knight to Lear*); Peter Woodthorpe (*Oswald*); Ian Holm (*Fool*); Stephen Thorne (*Curan*); Michael Graham Cox (*First Regan Servant*); Roger Bizley (*Second Regan Servant*); David Buck (*Third Regan Servant*); Donald Eccles (*Gloucester's Tenant*); Kenneth Gilbert (*Doctor*); Roy Spencer (*Herald*); Peter Mason (*Edmund's Captain*); Stanley Wheeler (*Herald's Trumpeter*); Arthur Allaby (*Edgar's Trumpeter*); Don Smith (*Cordelia Messenger*); Richard Rudd (*Regan Soldier*); Dave Thomas (*Edmund Standard Bearer*); Mavis Edwards, Georgine Anderson, Edna Landor, Diana Rigg, Charles Borromel, Christopher Cruise, Jon Dennis, Nicholas Hawtrey, Norman Henry, Dan Meaden, Robert Russell, Malcolm Taylor, Michael Scoble (*Counsellors, Knights, Squires, Servants, Tenants and Soldiers*).

Brief Synopsis: Lear, the aging king of Britain, decides to step down from his throne and divide his kingdom equally among his three daughters. His actions lead to a divided kingdom and personal family tragedy.

Select British and American Radio Broadcasts (1928–1955)

As the following chronological listings demonstrate, Laughton's attention to wireless broadcasting in Britain was fairly limited. However, from the late 1930s his appearances and commitment to commercial radio in the U.S. was immense and a source of some satisfaction in his search to exercise his acting abilities and reach out to mass audiences. Laughton's work in the medium, particularly with legendary radio producer Norman Corwin, proved creative and original. I have therefore given comprehensive entries to the Corwin broadcasts. I do not claim that the following listings are definitive. I have for instance avoided listing compilation programs which use excerpts from previous broadcasts.

British Broadcasts (1928–1940)

A League of Mercy Program: British Broadcasting Corporation London and Daventry; Broadcast: 6:00 p.m., Wednesday, October 3, 1928.

A charity appeal by Lady Tree, assisted by Gracie Fields and **Charles Laughton**.

Macbeth: BBC National; Performed by the Old Vic Company and Produced by Tyrone Guthrie; Music: Herbert Menges; Broadcast: 5:45 p.m., Sunday, April 8, 1934.

Charles Laughton (*Macbeth*); Flora Robson (*Lady Macbeth*); Frank Napier (*Banquo*); Marius Goring (*Malcolm*); Roger Livesey (*Macduff*); Ernest Hare (*Duncan*); Morland Graham (*Porter*); James Mason (*Lennox*); Athene Seyler, Phyllis Hatch (*Witches*); Elspeth Currie (*Witch*); Dennis Arundell (*Narrator*).

A Scottish lord and soldier discovers ambition, fate and superstition conspiring against him with tragic consequences.

In Town Tonight: BBC National; Second Series: October 1934.

Charles Laughton and Elsa Lanchester are interviewed on their return from Hollywood.

Kerbside Cabaret: BBC National; Written and Devised by B. Martin Marks; Broadcast: 7:00 p.m., Friday, January 27, 1939.

Charles Laughton (*Compere*); The Kentucky Minstrels and Harry S. Pepper.

London Buskers' own show (St. Martin's Lane Edition).

Canadian Red Cross: BBC Forces; Broadcast: 10 p.m., Saturday, October 5, 1940.

30 minutes of a program from Hollywood via Canada. Those taking part include **Charles Laughton**, Norma Shearer, Deanna Durbin, Ronald Colman, Merle Oberon and Alec Templeton.

American Broadcasts (1933–1955)

The Movie Parade: "White Woman" November 1933; Program #3; Paramount

Syndication, Air Trailer; Carole Lombard, Charles Bickford, **Charles Laughton**, Kent Taylor.

The Barretts of Wimpole Street: 1934; MGM Syndication, Air Trailer. **Charles Laughton**, Norma Shearer.

Mutiny on the Bounty: 1935; MGM Syndication. Air Trailer. **Charles Laughton**, Clark Gable, Franchot Tone.

The Magic Key: "Celebrating National Broadcasting Company's Tenth Anniversary," November 15, 1936; Network: Radio Corporation of America; Sponsor: RCA Victor Radios; Announcers: Ben Grauer; Bruce Belfrage; Frank Black and the NBC Symphony Orchestra; John B. Kennedy; The Revelers Male Vocal Quartet; Franz Planck; Stanley Black; Helen Traubel; Alexander Korda; **Charles Laughton**.

The Royal Gelatin Hour "Vallee Varieties," May 6, 1937; WEAF Network; Sponsor: Royal Desserts. A special Rudy Vallee variety show direct from London. The capital was about to celebrate the Coronation of George VI on May 12, 1937. Lord Mayor of London; Royal Horse Guards Band; Will Fyffe; **Charles Laughton**; Elsa Lanchester; Binnie Hale; Stanley Holloway; Richard Tauber.

The World Is Yours: "Freedom, the Living Tradition," February 12, 1939; Red Network; Sponsor: National Broadcasting Corporation; Drama from London. **Charles Laughton** recites Lincoln's "Gettysburg Address." Review of other famous speeches of freedom in American history.

The Lux Radio Theater: "Ruggles of Red Gap," July 10, 1939; Columbia Broadcasting System Network; Sponsor: Lux Soap/Unilever; Adaptor: George Wells; Sound Effects: Charlie Forsyth; Musical Director: Louis Silvers; Director: Frank Woodruff; Host: Cecil B. DeMille; Announcer: Melville Ruick; **Charles Laughton** (*Ruggles*); Zasu Pitts; Charlie Ruggles; Eric Snowden; Lelah Tyler; Hal K. Dawson; Verna Felton; Stanley Farrar; Earle Ross.

The Chase and Sanborn Hour: October 8, 1939; Red Network; Sponsor: Chase and Sanborn Coffee; Announcer: Jim Bannon; Host: Don Ameche; Music: Robert Armbruster Orchestra; Nelson Eddy; Edgar Bergen and Charlie McCarthy; Dorothy Lamour; Guests: **Charles Laughton**; Barbara Jo Allen as Vera Vague.

The Gulf Screen Guild Theater: "The Beachcomber," November 12, 1939; CBS Network; Sponsor: Gulf Gasoline; Host: Roger Pryor; Music: Oscar Bradley Orchestra; Jean Hersholt; Elsa Lanchester; **Charles Laughton**; Reginald Owen.

The Pursuit of Happiness: "John Brown's Body," November 26, 1939; CBS Network; Hosted by Burgess Meredith; Mark Warnow Orchestra with Lyn Murray's Chorus; Reporter: Carl Carmer; Director: Norman Corwin; Script: Eric Barnouw; **Charles Laughton**; Elsa Lanchester in Stephen Vincent Benet's "John Brown's Body."

The Texaco Star Theater: "The Great Adventure," December 27, 1939; CBS Network; Sponsor: Texaco Oil; Announcer: Jimmy Wallington; **Charles Laughton**; Elsa Lanchester.

The Chase and Sanborn Program: January 14, 1940; NBC Network; Sponsor: Chase and Sandborn Coffee; Announcer: Ben Alexander; Music: Robert Armbruster Orchestra; Edgar Bergen and Charlie McCarthy; Guests: **Charles Laughton**, Rudy Vallee.

The Lux Radio Theater: "Sidewalks of London," February 12, 1940; CBS Network; Sponsor: Lux Soap; Host: Cecil B. DeMille; Music: Louis Silvers; Announcer: Melville Ruick; **Charles Laughton**; Elsa Lanchester; Alan Marshal; Claud Allister; Eric Snowden; Jack Lewis; Barbara Jean Wong; Ynez Seabury.

The Chase and Sanborn Program: April 21, 1940; NBC Network; Sponsor: Chase and Sanborn Coffee; Announcer: Ben Alexander; Music: Robert Armbruster Orchestra; Edgar Bergen; Charlie McCarthy and Mortimer Snerd; Donald Dickson sings "Join the Navy"; Guest: **Charles Laughton**.

Mercy Red Cross Broadcast: June 22, 1940; NBC and CBS Networks; Announcers: Hugh Brundage; Ken Carpenter; Warren Hull; Dick Joy; Knox Manning; Ken Niles; Thomas Freebairn-Smith; Jimmy Wallington; Don Wilson; Harry von Zell. More than 50 radio and films stars contributed their services to this special Red Cross appeal in this two-hour broadcast. Shirley Temple and Paul Muni appeared in a dramatic sketch in a salute to America. The all-star cast also included: Don Ameche; The Andrews Sisters; Gene Autry and the Texas Rangers; Kenny Baker; Fanny Brice; Bob Burns; George Burns and Gracie Allen; Jimmy Cagney; Bing Crosby; Charles Dant; Rudolf Friml Jr.; John Garfield; Judy Garland; Gloria Jean; Lud Gluskin; Marie Green and Her Merry Men; The Hall Johnson Choir; Wilbur Hatch; Charles Holland; Gordon Jenkins; Jimmy Joy; Kay Kyser; Arthur Lake; Daryl Harpa; Frances Langford; **Charles Laughton**; Lum and Abner (Chet Lauck and Norris Goff); The Merry Macs; Matty Malneck; Mary Martin; Felix Mills; Pat O'Brien; Joe Penner; Charles Previn; Irene Rich; Edward G. Robinson; Mickey Rooney; Walter Schumann; Artie Shaw; Bob Sherwood; Phil Silvers; Ginny Simms; Penny Singleton; Hanley Stafford; Claude Sweeten; Claire Trevor; John Scott Trotter; Orson Welles; Meredith Willson; Victor Young.

Forecast: "Ever After" and "To Tim at Twenty," August 16, 1940; CBS Network; written and directed by Norman Corwin; Music: Wilbur Hatch; A double feature of two short contrasting plays broadcast from New York and Hollywood. From New York, a light comedy, "Ever After" by Keith Fowler: Edna Best (*Snow White*); Richard Whorf (*Prince Charming*); Roy Atwill (*Doc*); Mark Smith (*Grumpy*). From Hollywood, a serious drama, "To Tim at Twenty" by Norman Corwin: **Charles Laughton** (*Gunner Eric Marshall*); Elsa Lanchester (*Miss Ellen Tewkesbury*). It is set an hour before dawn in the RAF barracks on the north east coast of England. Gunner Marshall, who is leaving at dawn on a mission from which there can be no return, is writing a letter to his five-year-old son, who will open it when he turns 20.

Canadian Red Cross: October 5, 1940; Half-hour broadcast of a program from Hollywood via Canada.

The Chase and Sanborn Program: October 6, 1940; NBC Network; Sponsor: Chase and Sanborn Coffee; Variety show; Edgar Bergen and Charlie McCarthy; Donald Dickson Baritone; Guests: **Charles Laughton** in Flag Day and Works of Art; Eddie Bracken in Military School.

Everyman's Theater: "Flying Yorkshireman," November 15, 1940; NBC Network; Producer-Director-Writer: Arch Oboler; Story: Eric Knight; **Charles Laughton**; Elsa Lanchester.

America Calling: "A Salute to the Greek Nation" February 8, 1941; NBC/CBS Networks; Artists include Jack Benny; Connie Boswell; Madeleine Carroll; Ronald Colman; Melvyn Douglas; Clark Gable; Fay Holden; **Charles Laughton**; Bob Hope; Myrna Loy; Mary Martin; Groucho Marx; The Merry Macs; Frank Morgan; Merle Oberon; Reginald Owen; Dick Powell; Tyrone Power; Mickey Rooney; Ann Rutherford; Barbara Stanwyck; Lewis Stone; Robert Taylor; Shirley Temple; Meredith Willson Orchestra; Don Wilson; Max Taylor's Choral Group; Knox Manning.

Rudy Vallee Sealtest Show: April 24, 1941; The Blue Network; Sponsor: Sealtest Dairy Products; Rudy Vallee; John Barrymore; Guest: **Charles Laughton** in "A Whale of a Sea Story."

The Chase and Sanborn Program: May 18, 1941; NBC Network; Sponsor: Chase and Sanborn Coffee; Host: Jim Ameche; Orchestra Leader: Robert Armbruster; Vocalist: Donald Dickson: Announcer: Buddy Twist; Edgar Bergen and Charlie McCarthy; Abbott and Costello in "New House." Guest: **Charles Laughton** in "Hobos."

The Treasury Hour: July 2, 1941; CBS Network; Sponsor: Sustaining; Producers: William Murray and Paul Monroe; Writers: G.H. Johnson and Herman Wouk; Announcer: Larry Elliott, **Charles Laughton**.

The Columbia Workshop: Twenty-six by Corwin. "Job," August 24, 1941; CBS Network; Sponsor: Sustaining; Adaptor-Director: Norman Corwin; Narrator: Ray Collins; Conductor: Leith Stevens; Music: **Charles Laughton**.

The Chase and Sanborn Program: December 21, 1941; NBC Network; Sponsor: Chase and Sanborn Coffee; Music: Ray Noble Orchestra; Announcer: Buddy Twist; Edgar Bergen and Charlie McCarthy; **Charles Laughton**; Abbott and Costello.

Rudy Vallee Sealtest Show: March 19, 1942; Blue Network; Sponsor: Sealtest Kraft Cottage Cheese; Rudy Vallee; The Connecticut Yankees; **Charles Laughton**; John Barrymore; Joan Davis.

The Cavalcade of America: "The Prophet Without Honor" August 31, 1942; NBC Network; Sponsor: DuPont; Announcer: Bud Collyer; Writer: Robert Tallman; Author: Joshua Powers; Producer-Director: Homer Frickett; Music: Donald Voorhees; **Charles Laughton** (Homer Lea).

Radio Reader's Digest: "Back for Christmas," September 20, 1942; CBS Network; Sponsor: Campbell Soup; Host: Conrad Nagel; Announcer: Ernest Chappell; Director: Robert Nolan; Music: Lynn Murray; Roland Young; **Charles Laughton**.

The Texaco Star Theater: "The Fred Allen Radio Show," October 4, 1942; CBS Network; Sponsor: Texaco; Announcer: Arthur Godfrey; Music: Al Goodman Orchestra; Fred Allen; Alan Reed; Minerva Pious; Portland Hoffa; Guests: The Andrews Sisters; **Charles Laughton**.

Command Performance: December 24, 1942; Armed Forces Radio Station to All Networks; Announcer: Ken Carpenter; Master of Ceremonies: Bob Hope; Music: Twentieth Century–Fox Studio Orchestra Conducted by Alfred Newman; One Hour Xmas Special Program: Elmer Davis; The Andrews Sisters; Harriet Hilliard; Red Skelton; Spike Jones and His City Slickers; Ginny Simms; Bing Crosby; Ethel Waters; Sketch: "Charlie McCarthy Meets Santa Claus" with Edgar Bergen and Charlie McCarthy; **Charles Laughton**; Kay Kyser and His Band; Dinah Shore; Fred Allen; Jack Benny; The Charioteers.

The Abbott and Costello Show: December 31, 1942; Sponsor: Camels Cigarettes; NBC Red Network; Announcer: Ken Niles; Orchestra Leader: Freddie Rich; Vocalist: Connie Haines; Bud Abbott and Lou Costello with Guest **Charles Laughton**.

Over Here: January 2, 1943; Blue Network; Additional Material Written by Thelma Ritter; West Coast Production by Don Bernard; Executive Coordinator: William B. Murray; Producer: Henry Haley; Announcer: James Wallington; **Charles Laughton**; Dinah Shore; Joan Davis; Preston Foster; Lanny Ross; Jane Frohman. Scene from the New Theatre Guild Production *The Russian People*. **Charles Laughton** reads a speech given to a meeting of Durham miners by John Winant, governor of New Hampshire and American Ambassador to Britain from 1941 and 1946.

The George Burns and Gracie Allen Show: February 9, 1943; CBS Network; Sponsor: Swan Soap; George Burns and Gracie Allen; Bill Goodwin; Guest: **Charles Laughton**.

The Lady Esther Screen Guild Theater: "Stand By for Action" March 8, 1943; CBS Network; Sponsor: Lady Esther Cosmetics; Music: Wilbur Hatch; Adaptation by Bill Hampton; Announcer: Truman Bradley; **Charles Laughton** (*Admiral Stephen Thomas*); Brian Donlevy (*Lieutenant Commander Roberts*); Chester Morris (*Lieutenant Masterman*).

Suspense: "ABC Murders" May 18, 1943; CBS Network; Sponsor: Roma Wine; Producer William Spier; Director: Ted Bliss; Story: Agatha Christie; Script: Robert Talbot, William Spier; "The Man in Black" Suspense Announcer: Joseph Kearns; **Charles Laughton** (*Alexander Bonaparte Custer*); Elsa Lanchester (*Librarian*); Bramwell Fletcher (*Franklin Clarke*).

The Chase and Sanborn Program: October 3, 1943; NBC Network; Sponsor: Chase and Sanborn Coffee; Host: Jim Ameche; Music; Ray Noble and His Orchestra; Edgar Bergen and Charlie McCarthy; "Overdrawn Checking Account": Mortimer Snerd as Goodwin's assistant; Victor Moore and William Gaxton in "Pawn Shop." **Charles Laughton** in "The Bank Manager."

Suspense: "Wet Saturday" by John Collier; December 16, 1943; CBS Network; Sponsor: Roma Wine; Producer: Charles Vander; Music: Bernard Herrmann; **Charles Laughton**; Hans Conried; Dennis Hoey.

The George Burns and Gracie Allen Show: December 21, 1943; CBS Network; Sponsor:

Swan Soap; Music: Felix Mills Orchestra; George Burns and Gracie Allen; Hans Conried; Guests: Elsa Lanchester; **Charles Laughton**.

Blue Ribbon Town: January 8, 1944; CBS Network; Sponsor: Pabst Blue Ribbon Beer; Announcer: Ken Niles; Music: Robert Armbruster and His Orchestra; Writer-Producer-Director: Dick Mack; Groucho Marx; Fay McKenzie; Leo Gorcey; Bill Days; Guest: **Charles Laughton**.

The Abbott and Costello Show: February 10, 1944; NBC Network; Sponsor: Camel, Prince Albert Pipe Tobacco; Announcer: Ken Niles; Music: Freddie Rich Orchestra; Vocalist: Connie Haines; Bud Abbott; Lou Costello; Guest: **Charles Laughton**; Mel Blanc; Ted R. Gamble of the U.S. Treasury Department.

The Lady Esther Screen Guild Players: "The Tuttles of Tahiti" March 13, 1944; CBS Network; Sponsor: Lady Esther Cosmetics; **Charles Laughton**; Jon Hall; Florence Bates; Charles Bickford; Harry Owens and His Royal Hawaiians

Radio Almanac: March 15, 1944; CBS Network; Sponsor: Mobil Oil; Announcer: John McIntire; Music: Lud Gluskin Orchestra; Mutt Carey: Trumpet; Kit Ory: Trombone; Jimmie Noone: Clarinet; Buster Wilson: Piano; Budd Scott: Guitar; Ed Garland: Bass; Zutty Singleton: Drums; Orson Welles; Agnes Moorehead; Hans Conried; Guest: **Charles Laughton** as Cassius and Orson Welles as Brutus play the tent scene from *Julius Caesar*.

The Lux Radio Theater: "This Land Is Mine," April 24, 1944; CBS Network; Sponsor: Lux Soap; Host: Cecil B. DeMille; Announcer: Don Kennedy; Music: Louis Silvers; **Charles Laughton** (*Albert Lory*); Maureen O'Sullivan (*Louise Martin*); Edgar Barrier (*Major Keller*); Virginia Wallace (*Mother*); Dennis Green (*George*); Ralph Lewis (*Paul*); Cliff Clark (*Sorel*); Douglas Wood (*Mayor*); John McIntire; Charles Beel; Norman Field; Tyler McVey; Howard McNear; Billy Roy.

Columbia Presents Corwin: "American Trilogy—Carl Sandburg," June 6, 1944; CBS Network; Writer-Director: Norman Corwin; Music: Bernard Herrmann; **Charles Laughton**; Hans Conried; Mercedes McCambridge; Lurene Tuttle.

Columbia Presents Corwin: "American Trilogy—Wolfiana," June 13, 1944; CBS Network; Music: Bernard Herrmann; Narrator: **Charles Laughton**.

Columbia Presents Corwin: "American Trilogy—Walt Whitman," June 20, 1944; Writer-Producer-Director-Host: Norman Corwin; Music: Bernard Herrmann; Announcer: Howard Duff; **Charles Laughton**; John Dehner.

Birds Eye Open House: "The Dinah Shore Show," June 29, 1944; NBC Network; Sponsor: Birds Eye; Host: Dinah Shore; Guest: **Charles Laughton**.

Columbia Presents Corwin: "The Moat Farm Murder," July 18, 1944; CBS Network; Sponsor: Sustaining; Writer-Director: Norman Corwin; Music: Bernard Herrmann; **Charles Laughton**; Elsa Lanchester; Raymond Long.

Suspense: "The Man Who Knew How" by Dorothy L. Sayers; August 10, 1944; CBS Network; Sponsor: Roma Wine; Producer-Director: William Spier; Writer: Lucille Fletcher; Music: Lucien Moraweck; **Charles Laughton** (*Mr. Pender*); Hans Conried (*Buckley*).

The Cavalcade of America: "The Laziest Man in the World," November 13, 1944; NBC Network; Commentator: Walter Huston; Announcer: Gayne Whitman; Writer: Eric Binder; Music: Robert Armbruster; **Charles Laughton** (*Benjamin Franklin*); Eleanor Taylor (*Deborah*); Harry Powers; John McIntire; Dix Davis; Ann Stone; Tommy Cook; Frank Graham; Jack Zoller; Jean Vander Pyl; Billy Roy.

Birds Eye Open House: "The Dinah Shore Show" November 16, 1944; NBC Network; Sponsor: Birds Eye; Producer: Glenhall Taylor; Music: Robert Emmett Dolan; Host: Dinah Shore; Guest: **Charles Laughton**.

The Lux Radio Theater: "It Started with Eve," November 20, 1944; CBS Network; Sponsor: Lux Soap; Host: Cecil B. DeMille; Announcer: John M. Kennedy; Music: Louis Silvers; **Charles Laughton** (***Jonathan***

Reynolds); Dick Powell (*J. Reynolds, Jr.*); Susanna Foster (*Ann*); Charles Seel; Norman Field; Noreen Gammill; Arthur Q. Bryan; Doris Singleton; Joe Forte; Eddie Marr.

Suspense: "The Fountain Plays," November 23, 1944; CBS Network; Sponsor: Roma Wines; Story: Dorothy L. Sayers; Producer-Director: William Spier; Announcer: Truman Bradley; Music: Lud Gluskin; **Charles Laughton**; Dennis Hoey.

The Chase and Sanborn Program: December 31, 1944; NBC Network; Sponsor: Chase and Sanborn Coffee; Music: Ray Noble and His Orchestra; Edgar Bergen and Charlie McCarthy; Don Ameche; Bill Forman; Joan Carroll; Guest: **Charles Laughton**.

The Cavalcade of America: "Grandpa and the Statue" March 26, 1945; NBC Network; Sponsor: DuPont; Music: Robert Armbruster; Play: Arthur Miller; Producer-Director: Jack Zoller; Announcer: Gayne Whitman; **Charles Laughton**; Arthur Shields; Dickie Meyers; Tommy Bernard; Bobby Larson; John McIntire; Frank Graham; Conrad Binyon, Joe Pennario; Joel Davis; Anne Stone.

The Lux Radio Theater: "The Suspect" April 9, 1945; CBS Network; Sponsor: Lux Soap; Host: Thomas Mitchell; Announcer: John M. Kennedy Musical Director: Louis Silvers; **Charles Laughton** (*Philip Marshall*); Ella Raines (*Mary*); Rosalind Ivan (*Cora*); Dennis Green (*Gilbert Simmons*); Lester Matthews (*Huxley*); Truda Marson; Norman Field; Anthony Ellis; Eric Snowden; Tommy Cook; Eric Harford; Charles Field; Gloria Gordon; Tom Collins.

The Lux Radio Theater: "The Canterville Ghost" June 18, 1945; CBS Network; Host: Hal Wallis; Music: Louis Silvers; Announcer: John M. Kennedy; Margaret O'Brien; **Charles Laughton;** Tom Drake; Eric Snowden; Robert Cole.

Hedda Hopper's Hollywood: August 6, 1945; CBS Network; Announcer: Wendell Niles; **Charles Laughton** as host substitutes for a vacationing Hedda Hopper.

Columbia Presents Corwin: "L'Affaire Gumpert / The Case of the Gumpert"; August 21, 1945; CBS Network; Writer-Producer-Director: Norman Corwin; Music: Lud Gluskin; **Charles Laughton**; Elsa Lanchester; David Persina.

This Is My Best: "A Passenger to Bali" November 6, 1945; CBS Network; Sponsor: Cresta Blanca Wine; Producer: Orson Welles; **Charles Laughton**.

Request Performance: "The Bridge Game"; November 25, 1945; CBS Network; Sponsor: Campbell's Soup; Director: William N. Robson; Music: Leith Stevens; Ozzie Nelson; Harriet Hilliard; **Charles Laughton**; Elsa Lanchester; Donald Duck.

The Chase and Sanborn Program: December 9, 1945; NBC Network; Sponsor: Chase and Sanborn Coffee; Announcer: Ken Carpenter; Music: Ray Noble Orchestra; Edgar Bergen and Charlie McCarthy; Guest: **Charles Laughton**.

The Lady Esther Screen Guild Theater: "Ruggles of Red Gap"; December 17, 1945; CBS Network; Sponsor: Lady Esther Cosmetics; Announcer: Truman Bradley; **Charles Laughton**; Charlie Ruggles.

Birds Eye Open House: "The Dinah Shore Show"; January 3, 1946; NBC Network; Sponsor: Birds Eye Gaines Dog Food; Writers: Howard Harris, Sid Zelinka; Host: Dinah Shore; Guest: **Charles Laughton**; Arthur Q. Bryan; Barbara Jo Allen; Frank Nelson; Harry von Zell.

The Alan Young Show: "Housing Shortage" March 22, 1946; ABC Network; Sponsor: Bristol Myers; Writers: David R. Schwatz and Norman Fall; Music: Four Chicks and Chuck; George Wyle Orchestra; Announcer: Michael Roy; Alan Young; Jean Gillespie (*Jean*); Jim Backus (*Hubert Updike*); **Charles Laughton**.

The Theater Guild on the Air: "Payment Deferred"; May 12, 1946; The American Broadcasting Company Network; Sponsor: United States Steel; Announcer: William Langer; **Charles Laughton** (*William Marble*); Elsa Lanchester (*Annie Marble*); Susan Douglas; Eddie Marr; Herbert Rawlinson; Bill Johnstone; Gale Gordon; Joseph Kearns; Gayne Whitman.

Academy Award Theater: "Ruggles of Red Gap"; June 8, 1946; CBS Network; Sponsor: House of E.R. Squibb; Adapter: Frank Wilson; Music Composed and Conducted by Leith Stevens; Producer-Director: Dee Engelbach; Announcer: Hugh Brundage; **Charles Laughton**; Charlie Ruggles.

Hollywood Star Time: "The Suspect" July 6, 1946; CBS Network; Sponsor: Frigidaire–General Motors; Adapter: Milton Geiger; Director: Jack Johnstone; Music: Frank De Vol; Announcer: Wendell Niles; **Charles Laughton** (*Philip Marshall*); Rosalind Ivan (*Cora*).

The Cavalcade of America: "General Benjamin Franklin"; September 16, 1946; NBC Network; Sponsor: DuPont; Announcer: Bud Hiestand; Producer-Director: Jack Zoller; Writer: Zachary Metz; Music: Robert Armbruster; **Charles Laughton**; George Zucco; Joseph Kearns; William Johnstone; Raymond Lawrence; Howard Duff; Jay Novello; Kathleen Lockhart; Junius Matthews.

Radio Reader's Digest: "The Archer-Shee Case"; October 3, 1946; Sponsor: Hallmark Cards; Announcer: Tom Shirley; Host: Richard Kollmar; Music: Lyn Murray Orchestra; **Charles Laughton** (*Sir Edward Carson*).

The Chase and Sanborn Program: November 10, 1946; NBC Network; Sponsor: Chase and Sanborn Coffee; Host: Jim Ameche; Music: Ray Noble Orchestra; Edgar Bergen and Charlie McCarthy; Anita Gordon; Pat Patrick; Guest: **Charles Laughton**.

Studio One: "Payment Deferred"; November 25, 1947; CBS Network; Sponsor: Sustaining; Producer-Director-Host: Fletcher Markle; **Charles Laughton** (*Will Marble*); Hester Sondergaard (*Annie Marble*); Bert Tanswell (*Jim Medland*); Ruth Yorke (*Madame Collins*); Hedley Rennie (*Charlie Hammond*); Mary Kimber; Horace Graham; Robert Dryden.

The Theater Guild on the Air: "Old English" by John Galsworthy; November 30, 1947; ABC Network; Sponsor: United States Steel; Host: Roger Pryor; **Charles Laughton** (*Heythorp*); E.G. Marshall (*Charles Ventnor*); Mary Kimber (*Phyllis*); A.J. Herbert (*Joseph Pillin*), George Benson (*Meller*); Betty Sinclair (*Adela Haythorp*); Chester Stratton (*Farney*); Dorothy Hamilton (*Mrs. Larne*); Owen Holder (*Bob Pillin*).

The Kraft Music Hall: "Al Jolson Show"; February 12, 1948; NBC Network; Sponsor: Kraft Foods; Announcer: Ken Carpenter; Music: Lou Bring Orchestra; Al Jolson; Oscar Levant; Guest: **Charles Laughton**.

The Theater Guild on the Air: "Laburnum Grove"; April 25, 1948; ABC Network; Sponsor: United States Steel; **Charles Laughton** (*George Redfern*).

Studio One: "South Riding" April 27, 1948; CBS Network; Sponsor: Sustaining; Host: Fletcher Markle; Music: Norman Lockwood; Announcer: Lee Vines; **Charles Laughton** (*Robert Carne*); Hester Sondergaard (*Sarah Burton*); Everett Sloane (*Alderman Snaith*); Hedley Rennie (*Mr. Huggins*); Alice John (*Mrs. Beddows*), Niomi Campbell; Neal Fitzgerald; Guy Spaul; Horace Graham; Mary Michael; Miriam Woolf; Gregory Morton; Peter Boyne; Pat Ryan; Betty Tilson; Ronnie List; Ivor Francis.

Lux Radio Theater: "The Canterville Ghost," June 18, 1948; CBS Network; Sponsor: Lux Soap; Host: Hal Wallis; **Charles Laughton**; Margaret O'Brien; Tom Drake.

Suspense: "An Honest Man," August 5, 1948; CBS Network; Sponsor: Auto-Light; Script: Robert L. Richards; Producer-Director: Anton M. Leader; Music: Lucien Maraweck; Conductor: Lud Luskin; **Charles Laughton**; Cathy Lewis.

Suspense: "De Mortuis," February 10, 1949; CBS Network; Sponsor: Auto-Lite; Producer-Director: Anton M. Leader; Story John Collier; Adapter: Ken Prossen; Announcer: Paul Frees; **Charles Laughton**; Cathy Lewis; Paul Frees.

Sealtest Variety Theater: February 17, 1949; NBC Network; Sponsor: Sealtest Dairy Products; Music: Henry Russell Orchestra; The Crew Chiefs Quartet; Writers: Howard Harris, Sidney Zelinka; Director: Glenhall Taylor; Announcer: John Laing; Hostess: Dorothy Lamour; Guests: Dean Martin; Jerry Lewis; **Charles Laughton**.

The Theater Guild on the Air: "Payment Deferred," February 27, 1949; ABC Network; Sponsor: United States Steel; **Charles Laughton**; Susan Douglas; Maria Manton; Jessica Tandy.

The Theater Guild on the Air: "Skin Game," May 1, 1949; ABC Network; Sponsor: United States Steel; **Charles Laughton**, Sir Cedric Hardwicke; Martita Hunt.

Sealtest Variety Theater: June 2, 1949; NBC Network; Sponsor: Sealtest Dairy Products; Music: Henry Russell Orchestra; Crew Chiefs Quartet; Writers: Henry Harris, Sidney Zelinka, Ray Allen, Dick McKnight; Director: Glenhall Taylor; Announcer: John Laing; Hostess: Dorothy Lamour; Eddie Bracken; Frank Nelson; Bea Benaderet. Guest: **Charles Laughton**.

Suspense: "Blind Date," September 29, 1949; CBS Network; Sponsor: Auto-Lite; Producer-Editor: Paul Spier; Director: Norman McDonald; **Charles Laughton**; June Havoc.

The Cavalcade of America: "The Incomparable Doctor," January 3, 1950; NBC Network; Sponsor: DuPont; Producer: Roger Pryor; **Charles Laughton**.

The Theater Guild on the Air: "The Druid Circle," February 19, 1950; ABC Network; Sponsor: United States Steel; **Charles Laughton**; Burgess Meredith.

The Screen Guild Theater: "It Started with Eve," April 6, 1950; NBC Network; Sponsor: Camel Cigarettes; **Charles Laughton**; Diana Lynn; Robert Stack.

The Miracle of America: August 20, 1950; CBS Network; Sponsor: The Advertising Council; Producer-Director: Sterling Tracy; **Charles Laughton**.

The Theater Guild on the Air: "Edward, My Son," September 10, 1950; ABC Network; Sponsor: United States Steel; **Charles Laughton**, Rosalind Russell.

Suspense: "Neal Cream, Doctor of Poison," September 17, 1951; CBS Network; Sponsor: Auto Light; **Charles Laughton**.

Medicine USA: "Alcoholism," March 29, 1952; NBC Network; Sponsor: American Medical Association; Narrator: **Charles Laughton**; a drama documentary about alcoholism.

Medicine USA: "Psychiatry in America," April 5, 1952; NBC Network; Sponsor: American Medical Association; Narrator: **Charles Laughton**; a drama documentary about psychiatry.

Medicine USA: "The Span of Life," April 12, 1952; NBC Network; Sponsor: American Medical Association; Narrator: **Charles Laughton**; a drama documentary about geriatrics and longevity.

Medicine USA: "New Concepts in Contagious Diseases," April 19, 1952; NBC Network; Sponsor: American Medical Association; Narrator: **Charles Laughton**. A tape recording is played of a convention of bacteria! The opening speech is given by choryza and the keynote address is given by plague!

Medicine USA: "Exercise, Athletics and Health," April 26, 1952; NBC Network; Sponsor: American Medical Association; Producer: Marshall Hester; Director: Joel O'Brien; Script: Ira Marion; Music: George Lesner; Narrator: **Charles Laughton**.

Medicine USA: "Your Family Doctor," May 2, 1952; NBC Network; Sponsor: American Medical Association; Producer: Marshall Hester; Director: Joel O'Brien; Script: Peter Lyon; Music: George Lesner; Announcer: Arthur Gary; Narrator: **Charles Laughton**; a portrait of the 140,000 family doctors.

The Theater Guild on the Air: "The Bishop Misbehaves," May 25, 1952; NBC Network; Sponsor: United States Steel; Director: Homer Frickett; Announcer: Norman Brokenshire; Commercial Spokesman: George Hicks; Host: Walter Abel; Music: Harold Levey; **Charles Laughton** (*The Bishop*); Vanessa Brown (*Hester*); Josephine Hull (*Lady Emily*); Michael Evans (*Donald*); Stuart Burge; Niles McGuinness; Phillipa Bevins; Peter Forster; Bertram Tanswell; Frederick Rolfe.

Suspense: "Jack Ketch," September 22, 1952; CBS Network; Writer: Anthony Ellis; Director: Elliott Lewis; Music: Lucien Moraweck; **Charles Laughton**; Ben Wright; Joseph Kearns (*Bartleby*); Joan Banks; Raymond Lawrence; Doris Lloyd; Ramsay Hill.

Stagestruck: "Community Theater," February 7, 1954; CBS Network; Sponsor: The League of New York Theaters; Host: Mike Wallace; **Charles Laughton**.

The Lux Radio Theater: "Holy Matrimony," May 10, 1954; CBS Network; Sponsor: Lux Soap; Announcer: Sanford Barnett; **Charles Laughton** (*Priam Farll*); Fay Bainter (*Alice*); Herb Butterfield; Richard Peet; Edward Marr; Ken Carpenter; Alec Harford; William Johnstone; Rudy Schrager; Earl Eby; Sanford Barnett; Charlie Forsyth; Ben Wright; Edgar Barrier; Joseph Kearns.

Suspense: "The Revenge of Captain Bligh," May 17, 1954; CBS Network; Sponsor: Auto-Lite; Writer: Anthony Ellis; Director: Elliott Lewis; Announcer: Larry Thor; Ben Wright; Bill Johnstone; Joseph Kearns; **Charles Laughton**; Charles Davis; Antony Ellis.

Biography in Sound: "Actor and Director Charles Laughton," August 23, 1955; NBC Network; Announcer: Bill Wendell; **Charles Laughton**.

Television Broadcasts (1949–1962)

We, the People (1948–1952)
Season Two, Episode Ten, aired March 8, 1949; NBC.

The Oscar Bradley Orchestra; Lee Vines (*Announcer*); Dan Seymour (*Host*).
Cliff Edwards, **Charles Laughton** (*Guests*).

The Ed Sullivan Show (1948–1971)
Season Two, Episode 35, aired May 8, 1949; CBS.

Ed Sullivan (*Host*).
Charles Laughton, Nellie Lutcher (*Guests*).

The Paul Whiteman's Goodyear Revue (1949–1952)
Season One, Episode One, aired November 20, 1949; ABC.

Paul Whiteman (*Host*).
Eddie Albert; Jurie Keegan; **Charles Laughton**; Allyn McLerie.

The Ed Sullivan Show
Season Three, Episode 16, aired January 1, 1950; CBS.

Ed Sullivan (*Host*).
Joan Barton, **Charles Laughton** (*Guests*).

The Ed Wynn Show (1949–1950)
Season One, Episode 27, aired May 2, 1950; CBS.

Writers: Seaman Jacobs, Hal Kanter, Leo Solomon; Director: Ralph Levy; Musical Director: Lud Gluskin; Bob LeMond (*Announcer*); Ed Winn (*Host*).
Charles Laughton, Gale Robbins, Bill Shirley, Beverly Tyler (*Guests*).

The Kate Smith Evening Hour (1951–1952)
Season One, Episode 13, aired December 12, 1951; NBC.

Kate Smith (*Host*).
Alan Bunce (*Albert Arbuckle*); Peggy Lynch (*Ethel Arbuckle*); **Charles Laughton**, Kay Thompson, The Williams Brothers (*Guests*).

The Colgate Comedy Hour (1950–1955)
Season Two, Episode 32, aired April 6, 1952; NBC.

Bud Abbott, Lou Costello (*Hosts*).
Charles Laughton (*Guest*); Isabel Bigley (*Singer*); Sid Fields; Joe Kirk; Milton Frome; Bobby Barber; Jill Kraft; Helen Donaldson; Anita Anton; Alex Fossell; Three Beaus and a Peep; Johnny Conrad and His Dancers; Al Goodman and His Orchestra.

This Is Charles Laughton
"Twelfth Night" and "Ages of Man"; Season One, Episode One, aired January 13, 1953; Network Unknown.

Director: Paul Gregory; Producer: Sherman Harris; Photography: Jack Mackenzie; Editor: Robert Golden; Sound: Victor Appel
Charles Laughton (*Host*).

The Jackie Gleason Show (1952–1959)
Season One, Special aired May 6, 1953; CBS.

Jackie Gleason (*Host*); Archie Bleyer (*Orchestra Leader*).
Humphrey Bogart; Charles Boyer; Janette Davis; Jimmy Durante; Haleloke; Julius LaRosa; **Charles Laughton**; Peter Lorre; Marion Marlowe; Tony Marvin; The Maguire Sisters; Frank Parker; Lu Ann Simms.

The Ed Sullivan Show
Season Nine, Episode One, aired September 25, 1955; CBS.

Ed Sullivan (*Host*).
The All-American Baseball Team of 1955, Pearl Bailey, Lillian Gish, Peter Graves, Paul Gregory, **Charles Laughton**, Rocky Marciano, Robert

Mitchum, Archie Moore, The Oberkirchen Children's Choir, Lily Pons, Red Skelton (*Guests*).

Christmas Eve with Charles Laughton (1955)
TV Movie aired December 24, 1955; NBC.

Boris Sagal: Director; Producer: Elliott Lewis.
Charles Laughton (*Host*) reads from James Thurber, the Book of Daniel and Dickens' *The Pickwick Papers*.

Producers' Showcase (1954–1957)
"Festival of Music." Season Two, Episode Six, aired January 30, 1956; NBC.

Director: Kirk Browning; Producer: Sol Hurok; Musical Director: George Bassman; Orchestra Conductor: Max Rudolf; Stage Director: Herbert Graf.
Charles Laughton (*Host*).
Jussi Björling (*Rodolfo in* La Boheme *scene*); Jan Peerce (*Canio in* Pagliacci *scene*); Roberta Peters (*Olympia in* Tales of Hoffman *Scene*); Risë Stevens (*Carmen in* Carmen *Scene*); Renata Tebaldi (*Mimi in* La Boheme *Scene*); Leonard Warren (*Tonio in* Pagliacci *Scene*); Marian Anderson; Zinka Milanov; Mildred Miller; Gregor Piatigorsky; Artur Rubinstein; Isaac Stern; Blanche Thebom.

Ford Star Jubilee (1955–1956)
"The Day Lincoln Was Shot." Season One, Episode Six, aired February 1, 1956; CBS.

Writers: Jean Holloway, Terry Sanders, Denis Sanders; Based on the book by Jim Bishop; Director: Delbert Mann; Sets: Robert Tyler Lee, Buck Henshaw; Producer: Harry Ackerman: Executive Producer; Paul Gregory.
Raymond Massey (*Abraham Lincoln*); Lillian Gish (*Mary Todd Lincoln*); Jack Lemmon (*John Wilkes Booth*); Raymond Bailey (*Secretary Stanton*); **Charles Laughton** (*Narrator*); William Phipps (*Axelrod*).

The Jimmy Durante Show (1954–1956)
Season Two, Episode 17, aired March 3, 1956; NBC.

Writers: Benedict Freedman, John Fenton Murray, Elton Packard; Producer: William Harmon; Art Director: Donald P. Desmond; Musical Director: Roy Bargy; Composer: Jackie Barnett.
Jimmy Durante (*Host*); **Charles Laughton**.

Sir Alexander Korda (1893–1956)/Alexander Korda, Knight
TV special aired March 4, 1956; British Broadcasting Corporation.

Director: Alan Sleath; Introduced by Kenneth More.
Told by: **Charles Laughton**; Robert Donat; Flora Robson, Margaretta Scott; Sir Ralph Richardson; Vivien Leigh; Muir Mathieson; Sir Carol Reed; Ann Todd; David Lean; Laurence Olivier.

The Ed Sullivan Show
Season Nine, Episode 51, aired September 9, 1956; CBS.

Charles Laughton (*Guest Host*); Conn and Mann (*Dancers*); Hugh Jarrett, Elvis Presley, Amru Sani, Dorothy Sarnoff, The Vagabonds (*Guests*).

What's My Line? (1950–1967)
Season Eight, Episode 13, aired November 25, 1956; CBS.

John Charles Daly (*Moderator*).
Arlene Francis, Burgess Meredith, Dorothy Kilgallen, Bennett Cerf (*Panelists*); **Charles Laughton** (*Mystery Guest*).

Washington Square (1956–1957)
Season One, Episode Four, aired December 2, 1956; NBC.

Kay Armen; Bil Baird; Ray Bolger; Rusty Draper; Stanley Holloway; **Charles Laughton**; Arnold Stang; Elaine Stritch.

Hungarian Emergency Relief Organization Christmas Day Special
TV special aired December 25, 1956; NBC.

Writer: David Karp; Producer: Fred Coe; Executive Producers: Thomas Loeb, William Nichols; Music: Franz Allers, Lehman Engel, Herbert Greene; Host: John Daly.
Edie Adams; Julie Andrews; Betty Comden; Sammy Davis, Jr.; Dick Dudley; Arlene Francis; Benjamin T. Gilliard; Adolph Green; Heller Halliday; Richard Halliday; E. Roland Harriman; Mihal Hontvary; Suzanna Hontvary; Susan Johnson; Stubby Kaye; **Charles Laughton**; Mary Martin; Garry Moore; Richard Nixon; Jules Styne; Jo Sullivan; Éva Szörényi; Danny Thomas; The Vienna Boys Choir; Robert Weede; István Örményi.

Chelsea at Nine (1957–1960)
Season One, Episode Two, aired October 1, 1957; Granada, Independent Television.

Coby Ruskin (*Director*); David Hutcheson (*Host*).
Charles Laughton (*Guest*); Frank Schuster; Johnny Wayne.

General Electric Theater (1957–1959)
"Mr. Kensington's Finest Hour." Season Six, Episode Four, aired October 27, 1957; CBS.

Director: James Neilson; Story: Lee McGiffin; Teleplay: Halsey Melone; Producer: William Frye;

Photography: Joseph F. Biroc; Editor: Michael R. McAdam; Progress Reporter: Don Herbert.
Ronald Reagan (*Host*).
Charles Laughton (*Edwin Kensington*); Richard Eyer (*Tommy Stevens*); Phyllis Avery (*Carrie Stevens*); Juney Ellis (*Miss Cullen*); David Armstrong (*McGill*); Charles Watts (*Caldwell*); Grandon Rhodes; Ruth Lee; Janet Stewart; Erik Nielsen (*Knucklehead*); David Wayne (*David Vincent*); Donald Wayne (*Donald Vincent*); Henry Willis; Fred Kruger; Jerry Willis.

The George Gobel Show (1954–1960)
Season Four, Episode Five, aired November 18, 1957; NBC.
Director-Producer: Alan Handley.
George Gobel (*Host*).
Jeff Donnell; Eddie Fisher; Zsa Zsa Gabor; Shirley Harmer; Jack Kirkwood; **Charles Laughton**.

The Tennessee Ernie Ford Show (1956–1961)
Season Two, Episode Nine, aired November 28, 1957; NBC.
Tennessee Ernie Ford (*Host*).
Charles Laughton (*Guest*); The Top Twenty (*Singers*).

The Lux Show (1957–1958)
Season One, Episode Ten, aired December 12, 1957; NBC.
Rosemary Clooney (*Host*).
Fred Fricky; Paula Kelly; **Charles Laughton**; The Modernaires.

The Eddie Fisher Show (1957–1958)
Season One, Episode Six, aired December 24, 1957; NBC.
Director: Barry Shear; Writers: Mac Benoff, Skipper Dawes, Martin Ragaway; Producer: Gil Rodin; Eddie Fisher (*Host*).
Cathy Crosby; Elaine Dunn; George Gobel; **Charles Laughton**; The Lennon Sisters.

The Steve Allen Plymouth Show (1956–1960)
Season Three, Episode 18, aired January 26, 1958; NBC.
Writers: Stan Burns, Don Hinkley, Mike Marmer, Frank Peppiatt, Herbert Sargent.
Steve Allen (*Host*).
Martha Raye; Jimmy Dean; Skitch Henderson; **Charles Laughton** (*Guest*); Erin O'Brien; Gene Rayburn (*Announcer*); David Rubinoff (*Violinist*).

Studio 57 (1954–1958)
"Stopover in Bombay." Season Four, Episode 16, aired February 26, 1958; Syndication.
Director: Sidney Lanfield; Story: Gordon Gaskell; Teleplay: Noel Langley; Producer: Henry Berman; Photographer: Mack Stengler: Editor: Lee Huntington; Art Director: Howard E. Johnson; Supervising Editor: Richard G. Wray; Music Supervisor: Stanley Wilson.
Joel Aldrich (*Host*).
Charles Laughton (*Charles Claxton*); Heather Angel (*Ruth Claxton*); Zina Provendie (*Clara Webb*); Max Showalter; Mary Young; Carleton G. Young; Paul Maxwell; Ernest Sarracino; Leonard Strong; Henry Corden; Reginald Lal Singh.

General Electric Theater
"A New York Knight." Season Six, Episode 21, aired March 2, 1958; CBS.
Director: James Neilson; Story: Richard Connell; Teleplay: Jameson Brewer; Producer: William Frye; Photographer: Benjamin H. Kline; Editor: Michael R. McAdam; Art Director: John Meehan; Sound: John C. Grubb; Production Executive: Don Herbert.
Ronald Reagan (*Host*).
Charles Laughton (*Henry Denry*); Gavin Gordon (*Glynn*); Nestor Paiva (*Perino*); Irving Bacon (*Patch*); Anthony Eustrel; Earle Hodgins; Addison Richards; Bartlett Robinson, Ted Wedderspoon, Norma DeHaan, Gil Donaldson, Boyd "Red" Morgan, John Ayres.

The George Gobel Show
Season Five, Episode Five, aired December 2, 1958; NBC.
Directors: Norman Lear, Grey Lockwood; Writers: Dan Beaumont, Phil Green, Tom Koch, Norman Lear, Joseph Quillan, Leo Soloman; Producer: Bill Burch; Music: Frank De Vol.
George Gobel (*Host*).
Phyllis Avery; The Johnny Mann Singers; **Charles Laughton**; Gisele MacKenzie.

The Tennessee Ernie Ford Show
Season Three, Episode Ten, aired December 11, 1958; NBC.
Directors: Selwyn Touber, Bud Yorkin; Writers: Danny Arnold, Norman Lear, Howard Leeds, Norman Paul; Associate Producer: Jim Loakes; Executive Producer: Cliffie Stone; Producer: Selwyn Touber; Art Director: Edward Stephenson; Costume Designer: Ret Turner; Unit Managers: Larry Fielder, Ronald C. Oxford; Associate Directors: Tom Foulkes, Bob Gilmore, Winfield Opie; Audio: Art Brearley; Lighting Technician: John Freschi; Video Operator: Ken Pascoe; Senior Video Operator: Chuck Smith; Musical Director: Harry Geller; Choreographer: Ward Ellis; Consultant: Roland Kibbee; Production Assistant: Jerien McClure; Technical Directors: Lou Onofrio, Joe Strauss.

Tennessee Ernie Ford (*Host*).
Charles Laughton (*Guest*); The Top Twenty (*Singers*).

The Eddie Fisher Show
Season Two, Episode Six, aired December 23, 1958; NBC.
Directors: Bob Finkel, Grey Lockwood.
Eddie Fisher (*Host*).
Charles Laughton; Jerry Lewis; The Marquis Chimps; Lily Pons; The Lynn Murray Singers.

General Electric Theater
"The Last Lesson." Season Seven, Episode 19, aired February 8, 1959; CBS.
Director: Herschel Daughety; Story: Alphonse Daudet; Teleplay: Jerome Ross; Producer: Harry Tugend; Photographer: Lionel Lindon; Editor: Michael R. McAdam; Art Director: Martin Obzina; Sound: Stephen Bass; Progress Reporter: Don Herbert.
Ronald Reagan (*Host*).
Charles Laughton (*Monsieur Hamel*); Patricia Medina (*Marie-Claire*); Barry Gordon (*Etienne*); Eric Feldary (*Captain*); Roy C. Jenson; Rene Kroper; Lucien Plauzoles; Diane Roter (*French School Girl*); Jack Chefe; Janine Grandel; Beppy DeVries; Cyril Delevanti; Max Dommar; Gregg Martell.

The Joseph Cotten Show–On Trial
(1956–1959)
"Eleanor." Season Two, Episode Two, aired July 13, 1959; CBS.
Joseph Cotten (*Host*).
Charles Laughton (*Guest Star*).

The Dinah Shore Chevy Show (1956–1963)
Season Four, Episode 12, aired December 20, 1959; NBC.
Costume Assistant: Carol Onofrio; Announcer: Joel Aldred.
Dinah Shore (*Host*).
Donna Atwood; **Charles Laughton** (*Guest*); Yves Montand.

The Tennessee Ernie Ford Show
Season Four, Episode 14, aired December 31, 1959; NBC.
Producers: Cliffie Stone, Selwyn Touber, Bud Yorkin; Directed by Bud Yorkin, Selwyn Touber; Writers: Danny Arnold, Norman Lear, Howard Leeds, Norman Paul; Musical Director: Harry Geller; Choreographer: Ward Ellis; Associate Producer: Jim Loakes; Consultant: Roland Kibbee; Unit Managers: Ronald C. Oxford, Larry Fielder; Associate Directors: Tom Foulkes, Bob Gilmore, Winfield Opie; Art Director: Edward Stephenson; Costumes: Ret Turner; Vocals: The Top Twenty; Production Assistant: Jerien McClure; Technical Directors: Lou Onofrio, Joe Strauss; Lighting: John Freschi; Audio: Art Brearley; Senior Video: Chuck Smith; Video: Ken Pascoe.
Tennessee Ernie Ford (*Host*).
Charles Laughton (*Guest*); The Top Twenty (*Singers*).

The Ed Sullivan Show
Season Thirteen, Episode 21, aired February 14, 1960: CBS.
Ed Sullivan (*Host*).
Wisa D'Orso, Peter Gennaro (*Dancers*); Dorothy Dandridge, Birgit Nilsson, Jane Weintraub (*Singers*); Harry James, **Charles Laughton** (*Guests*); Frank Schuster, Johnny Wayne (*Comedians*).

What's My Line?
Season Eleven, Episode 23, aired February 21, 1960; CBS.
Director: Franklin Heller (*Director*).
John Charles Daly (*Moderator*), Dorothy Kilgallen, Steve Allen, Arlene Francis, Martin Gabel (*Panelists*); **Charles Laughton** (*Mystery Guest*).

Startime (1959–1961)
"Academy Award Songs." Season One, Episode 24, aired March 15, 1960; NBC.
Director: Greg Garrison; Writer: Mac Benoff; Executive Producer: Hubbell Robinson; Producer: Gil Rodin; Music: Camarata; Art Director: Spencer Davies; Choreographer: Hermes Pan.
Jane Wyman (*Host*); **Charles Laughton** (*Co-Host*). Laughton sang "Sylvia," "The Last Time I Saw Paris" and a duet with Elsa Lanchester—see below.
Buddy Bryan and Becky Varno performed in "The Continental"; Nat "King" Cole sang "Mona Lisa," "In the Cool, Cool, Cool of the Evening," "Lullaby of Broadway" and "The Five Pennies"; The Four Aces sang "Love Is a Many Splendored Thing," "Three Coins in the Fountain" and "The Best of Everything"; Gogi Grant sang "Strange Are the Ways of Love"; Elsa Lanchester sang "Baby, It's Cold Outside" (with host **Charles Laughton**); Tex Ritter sang "High Noon" and "The Hanging Tree"; Kay Starr sang "Zip-a-Dee-Doo-Dah," "The Way You Look Tonight," "You'll Never Know," "Swinging on a Star" (with host Jane Wyman) and "High Hopes."

The Steve Allen Plymouth Show
Season Five, Episode 26, aired April 18, 1960; NBC.
Writers: Stan Burns, Don Hinkley, Mike Marmer, Herbert Sargent; Conductor: Les Brown.
Steve Allen (*Host*).

Martha Raye; Dayton Allen; Tim Conway; Don Knotts (*Nervous Chap*); **Charles Laughton**, Mark Murphy (*Guests*); Tom Poston (*Perennial Amnesiac*).

Playhouse 90 (1956–1961)
"In the Presence of Mine Enemies." Season Four, Episode 17, aired May 18, 1960; CBS.

Directed by Fielder Cook; Writer: Rod Serling; Produced by Peter Kortner; Art Director: William Craig Smith; Music: Sammy Cahn, Alex North.

Charles Laughton (*Rabbi Adam Heller*); Arthur Kennedy (*Paul Heller*); Susan Kohner (*Rachel Heller*); Oskar Homolka (*Josef Chinik*); George Macready (*Captain Richter*); Sam Jaffe (*Carpenter*); Robert Redford (*Lieutenant Lott*); Otto Waldis (*Kohn*); Bernard Kates (*Israel*); Arlene Martel (*Woman with Baby*); Celia Lovsky (*First Woman*); Lisa Golm (*Second Woman*); Raikan Ben-Ari (*First Councilman*); Norbert Schiller (*Second Councilman*); Harold Dryenforth (*The General*); Peter Coe (*The Officer*); Thomas Delange (*The Little Boy*); Richard Gardner (*The Soldier*); Charles Haren (*Second Soldier*); Hannes Lutz (*The Man*); Richard Joy (*Announcer*); **Uncredited Cast**: Al Bain (*Prisoner*); Stanley Dyrector (*Prisoner*).

Wagon Train (1957–1965)
"The Albert Farnsworth Story." Season Four, Episode Three, aired October 12, 1960; NBC.

Directed by Herschel Daugherty; Writer: Gene L. Coon; Produced by Howard Christie; "Wagon Train" Theme: Jerome Moross; Music Score: Richard Shores; Photography: Benjamin H. Kline; Art Director: Howard E. Johnson; Editorial Supervisor: David J. O'Connell; Editor: Marston Fay; Musical Supervisor: Stanley Wilson; Set Decorator: Ralph Sylos; Assistant Director: Edward K. Dodds; Sound: David H. Moriarty; Costume Supervisor: Vincent Dee; Makeup: Jack Barron; Hair Stylist: Florence Bush.

Ward Bond (*Major Seth Adams*); Robert Horton; **Guest Star**: **Charles Laughton** (*Colonel Albert Farnsworth*); Frank McGrath (*Charlie Wooster*); Terry Wilson (*Bill Hawks*); James Fairfax (*Jeremy Oakes*); Terence de Marney (*Mike O'Toole*); Robert Brown (*Tim O'Toole*); Gina Gillespie (*Peggy O'Toole*); Kathleen O'Malley (*Sharry O'Toole*); Orville Sherman (*Freehan*); John Kroger (*Lieutenant*); Jan Arvan (*Indian Chief*); Quentin Sondergaard (*Soldier*); Neyle Morrow (*Cheyenne Indian*).

Checkmate (1960–1962)
"Terror from the East." Season One, Episode 14, aired January 7, 1961; CBS.

Creator: Eric Ambler; Directed by Herschel Daugherty; Writer: Harold Clements; Music: Johnny Williams; Photography: Lionel Lindon; Art Director: John J. Lloyd; Editorial Supervisor: David J. O'Connell; Editor: Tony Martinelli; Musical Supervisor: Stanley Wilson; Sound: William Russell; Assistant Director: Frank Losee; Set Decorators: John McCarthy, Julia Heron; Costume Supervisor: Vincent Dee; Makeup: Leo Lotito Jr.; Hair Stylist: Florence Bush.

Anthony George (*Don Corey*); Doug McClure (*Jed Sills*); Sebastian Cabot (*Dr. Carl Hyatt*); **Guest Star: Charles Laughton** (*Reverend Wister*); Ken Lynch (*Lieutenant Thomas Brand*); Dale Ishimoto (*General Wu*); Victor Sen Yung (*Han*); Pilar Seurat (*Mrs. Chang*); Weaver Levy (*Chang*); Guy Lee (*Chinese Boy*); William Yip (*Ticket Man*); Willard Lee (*Doorman*); Tommy H. Lee (*Walter*); Lisa Lu (*Wei-Ling*).

The Dinah Shore Chevy Show
Season Five, Episode 17, aired January 22, 1961; NBC.

Costume Assistant: Carol Onofino.
Dinah Shore (*Host*).
Charles Laughton (*Guest*); Bob Newhart; Miyoshi Umeki.

This Is Your Life (1955–2003)
"Flora Robson." Episode aired February 13, 1961; BBC.

Producer: T. Leslie Jackson; Director: Michael Goodwin; Writer: Robert Stuart; Researcher: Shirley MacNab.

Host: Eamonn Andrews; Flora Robson; Robert Beatty; Tyrone Guthrie; Ursula Howells; **Charles Laughton**; James Mason; Henry Oscar; Paul Robeson.

The Tennessee Ernie Ford Show
Season Five, Episode 27, aired April 6, 1961; NBC.

Director-Producer: Bud Yorkin.
Tennessee Ernie Ford (*Host*).
Charles Laughton (*Guest*); The Top Twenty (*Singers*).

The Jack Paar Show (1957–1962)
Season Five, Episode 104, aired March 19, 1962; NBC.

Jack Paar (*Host*); Hugh Downs (*Announcer*); Jose Melis (*Bandleader*).

Betty Johnson (*Herself*); Milt Kamen, Alexander King, **Charles Laughton** (*Guests*).

The Jack Paar Show
"Final *Tonight Show* featuring Jack Paar." Season Five, Episode 111, aired March 29, 1962; NBC.

Director: Hal Gurnee; Music Conductor: Jose Melis; Announcer: Hugh Downs; Host: Jack Paar.

Guests: Tallulah Bankhead (on film); Jack Benny (on film); Joey Bishop (on film); George Burns (on film); Billy Graham (on film); Buddy Hackett; Bob Hope (on film); Robert F. Kennedy (on film); Alexander King; **Charles Laughton** (on film); Jack E. Leonard; Robert Merrill; Robert Morley (on film); Havana Auxiliary Bishop Alfredo Mueller; Richard Nixon (on film); Nipsey Russell (on film); Selma Diamond, Sam Levenson, Tom Poston (audience bows).

Select Audio Recordings (1934–1962)

The Private Life of Henry VIII Regal Zonophone (1934)

Lincoln's Gettysburg Address Columbia (1937)

The Oldest Christmas Story (*The Gospel According to St. Luke*)/***The Story of the Three Wise Men*** (*The Gospel According to St. Matthew*) Music by Hanns Eisler; Decca (1944)

Mr. Pickwick's Christmas Decca (1944)

Moby Dick Laughton as Captain Ahab; Music by Victor Young; Decca (1944)

Don Juan in Hell Columbia (1952)

The Night of the Hunter RCA (1955)

Readings from the Bible Decca (1958)

The Storyteller…A Session with Charles Laughton Capitol (1962). Laughton won a 1962 Grammy Award for Best Spoken Word Album.

Appendix 1
The Films Listed By Studios

The following is an alphabetical list of Laughton's film work by studio from his first Hollywood film in 1932 until his final film in 1962. I have omitted his four silent films and three early English-made talkies due to the sporadic and partial nature of their subsequent distribution and exhibition.

Columbia × 2 films: *Salome*; *Advise & Consent*

London Films × 3 films: *The Private Life of Henry VIII*; *Rembrandt*; *Hobson's Choice*

Mayflower Productions × 3 films: *Vessel of Wrath* aka *The Beachcomber*; *St. Martin's Lane* aka *Sidewalks of London*; *Jamaica Inn*

MGM × 8 films: *Payment Deferred*; *The Barretts of Wimpole Street*; *Mutiny on the Bounty*; *Stand By for Action*; *The Man from Down Under*; *The Canterville Ghost*; *The Bribe*; *Young Bess*

Paramount × 8 films: *Devil and the Deep*; *If I Had a Million*; *The Sign of the Cross*; *Island of Lost Souls*; *White Woman*; *Ruggles of Red Gap*; *The Big Clock*; *Under Ten Flags*

RKO Radio Pictures × 7 films: *The Hunchback of Notre Dame*; *They Knew What They Wanted*; *The Tuttles of Tahiti*; *Forever and a Day*; *This Land Is Mine*; *The Man on the Eiffel Tower*; *The Blue Veil*

The Selznick Studio/Vanguard Films × 1 film: *The Paradine Case*

Twentieth Century–Fox × 2 films: *Tales of Manhattan*; *O. Henry's Full House*

Twentieth Century Pictures × 1 film: *Les Misérables*

United Artists × 5 films: *Captain Kidd*; *The Girl from Manhattan*; *Arch of Triumph*; *The Night of the Hunter*; *Witness for the Prosecution*

Universal × 6 films: *The Old Dark House*; *It Started with Eve*; *The Suspect*; *Because of Him*; *The Strange Door*; *Spartacus*

Warner Bros. × 1 film: *Abbott and Costello Meet Captain Kidd*

Appendix II

The Films Listed By Performers

The following list is a selection of leading actors and character players who appeared in films featuring Charles Laughton—albeit not necessarily acting opposite him—during his career as screen actor and director.

Bud Abbott × 1 film: *Abbott and Costello Meet Captain Kidd*
Larry Adler × 1 film: *St. Martin's Lane* aka *Sidewalks of London*
Talullah Bankhead × 1 film: *Devil and the Deep*
Binnie Barnes × 2 films: *The Private Life of Henry VIII*; *The Man from Down Under*
Ethel Barrymore × 1 film: *The Paradine Case*
Florence Bates × 1 film: *The Tuttles of Tahiti*
Jane Baxter × 1 film: *Down River*
Ingrid Bergman × 1 film: *Arch of Triumph*
Curt Bois × 2 films: *The Tuttles of Tahiti*; *Arch of Triumph*
Charles Boyer × 2 films: *Tales of Manhattan*; *Arch of Triumph*
Hillary Brooke × 1 film: *Abbott and Costello Meet Captain Kidd*
Claudette Colbert × 1 film: *The Sign of the Cross*
Constance Collier × 1 film: *The Girl from Manhattan*
Gary Cooper × 2 films: *Devil and the Deep*; *If I Had a Million*
Lou Costello × 1 film: *Abbott and Costello Meet Captain Kidd*
Henry Daniell × 3 films: *The Suspect*; *Captain Kidd*; *Witness for the Prosecution*
Marlene Dietrich × 1 film: *Witness for the Prosecution*
Robert Donat × 1 film: *The Private Life of Henry VIII*
Melvyn Douglas × 1 film: *The Old Dark House*
Deanna Durbin × 2 films: *It Started with Eve*; *Because of Him*
Henry Fonda × 2 films: *Tales of Manhattan*; *Advise & Consent*
Clark Gable × 1 film: *Mutiny on the Bounty*
Dorothy Gish × 1 film: *Wolves* aka *Wanted Men*
Lillian Gish × 1 film: *The Night of the Hunter*
Stewart Granger × 2 films: *Salome*; *Young Bess*
Cary Grant × 1 film: *Devil and the Deep*
Tyrone Guthrie × 2 films: *St. Martin's Lane*; *Vessel of Wrath*
Cedric Hardwicke × 4 films: *Les Misérables*; *The Hunchback of Notre Dame* (1939); *Forever and a Day*; *Salome*
Rex Harrison × 1 *St. Martin's Lane* aka *Sidewalks of London*
Rita Hayworth × 1 film: *Salome*

Appendix II

Boris Karloff × 2 films: *The Old Dark House*; *The Strange Door*
Buster Keaton × 1 film: *Forever and a Day*
Dorothy Lamour × 1 film: *The Girl from Manhattan*
Elsa Lanchester × 11 films: *Blue Bottles*; *Day-Dreams*; *The Tonic*; *Comets*; *The Private Life of Henry VIII*; *Rembrandt*; *Vessel of Wrath* aka *The Beachcomber*; *Tales of Manhattan*; *Forever and a Day*; *The Big Clock*; *Witness for the Prosecution*
Vivien Leigh × 1 film: *St. Martin's Lane* aka *Sidewalks of London*
Carole Lombard × 2 films: *White Woman*; *They Knew What They Wanted*
Fredric March × 3 films: *The Sign of the Cross*; *The Barretts of Wimpole Street*; *Les Misérables*
Raymond Massey × 1 film: *The Old Dark House*
Jessie Matthews × 1 film: *Forever and a Day*
Burgess Meredith × 3 films: *A Miracle Can Happen*; *The Man on the Eiffel Tower*; *Advise & Consent*
Ray Milland × 4 films: *Piccadilly*; *Payment Deferred*; *Forever and a Day*; *The Big Clock*
John Mills × 1 film: *Hobson's Choice*
Robert Mitchum × 1 film: *The Night of the Hunter*
Marilyn Monroe × 1 film: *O. Henry's Full House*
George Montgomery × 1 film: *The Girl from Manhattan*
Robert Newton × 3 films: *I, Claudius* (unreleased); *Vessel of Wrath* aka *The Beachcomber*; *Jamaica Inn*
Merle Oberon × 2 films: *The Private Life of Henry VIII*; *I, Claudius* (unreleased)
Margaret O'Brien × 1 film: *The Canterville Ghost*
Una O'Connor × 3 films: *The Barretts of Wimpole Street*; *This Land Is Mine*; *Witness for the Prosecution*
Maureen O'Hara × 3 films: *Jamaica Inn*; *The Hunchback of Notre Dame*; *This Land Is Mine*
Maureen O'Sullivan × 3 films: *Payment Deferred*; *The Barretts of Wimpole Street*; *The Big Clock*
Gregory Peck × 1 film: *The Paradine Case*
Tyrone Power × 1 film: *Witness for the Prosecution*
Ella Raines × 1 film: *The Suspect*
Donna Reed × 1 film: *The Man from Down Under*
Stanley Ridges × 2 films: *The Suspect*; *Because of Him*
George Sanders × 1 film: *This Land Is Mine*
Randolph Scott × 1 film: *Captain Kidd*
Norma Shearer × 1 film: *The Barretts of Wimpole Street*
Jean Simmons × 2 films: *Young Bess*; *Spartacus*
Walter Slezak × 1 film: *This Land Is Mine*
Gloria Stuart × 1 film: *The Old Dark House*
Robert Taylor × 2 films: *Stand By for Action*; *The Bribe*
Ann Todd × 1 film: *The Paradine Case*
Franchot Tone × 4 films: *Mutiny on the Bounty*; *Because of Him*; *The Man on the Eiffel Tower*; *Advise & Consent*
Harold Warrender × 1 film: *Day-Dreams*
Emlyn Williams × 2 films: *I, Claudius* (unreleased); *Jamaica Inn*
John Williams × 2 films: *The Paradine Case*; *Witness for the Prosecution*
Shelley Winters × 1 film: *The Night of the Hunter*
Anna May Wong × 1 film: *Piccadilly*
Jane Wyman × 1 film: *The Blue Veil*
Robert Young × 1 film: *The Canterville Ghost*

Appendix III
The Films Listed By Cinematographers

In tribute to the essential, yet often unsung, contribution of transforming the notions of a screenplay and the attributes of direction into specific visual images, I salute the directors of photography who worked on films featuring Charles Laughton.

Lloyd Ahern, Sr. × 1 film: *O. Henry's Full House*
Joseph H. August × 1 film: *The Hunchback of Notre Dame*
Werner Brandes × 1 film: *Piccadilly*
Stanley Cortez × 3 films: *The Man on the Eiffel Tower*; *Abbott and Costello Meet Captain Kidd*; *The Night of the Hunter*
William H. Daniels × 1 film: *The Barretts of Wimpole Street*
Robert De Grasse × 1 film: *Forever and a Day*
Arthur Edeson × 2 films: *The Old Dark House* [uncredited]; *Mutiny on the Bounty*
Harry Fischbeck × 2 films: *If I Had a Million*; *White Woman*
Lee Garmes × 2 films: *Forever and a Day*; *The Paradine Case*
Merritt B. Gerstad × 1 film: *Payment Deferred*
Alfred Gilks × 1 film: *Ruggles of Red Gap*
Irving Glassberg × 1 film: *The Strange Door*
Russell Harlan × 1 film: *Witness for the Prosecution*
Jack Hildyard × 1 film: *Hobson's Choice*
Paul Ivano × 1 film: *The Suspect*
David Kesson × 1 film: *Wolves* aka *Wanted Men*
Bernard Knowles × 1 film: *Jamaica Inn*
Jules Kruger × 2 films: *St. Martin's Lane* aka *Sidewalks of London*; *Vessel of Wrath* aka *The Beachcomber*
Charles Lang × 2 films: *Devil and the Deep*; *Salome*
Ernest Laszlo × 1 film: *The Girl from Manhattan*
Sam Leavitt × 1 film: *Advise & Consent*
Rudolph Maté × 1 film: *It Started with Eve*
Russell Metty × 3 films: *Forever and a Day*; *Arch of Triumph*; *Spartacus*
Hal Mohr × 1 film: *Because of Him*
Nicholas Musuraca × 2 films: *The Tuttles of Tahiti*; *Forever and a Day*
Roy F. Overbaugh × 1 film: *Wolves* aka *Wanted Men*
Georges Périnal × 3 films: *The Private Life of Henry VIII*; *Rembrandt*; *I, Claudius* (unreleased)
Robert Planck × 1 film: *The Canterville Ghost*
Franz Planer × 1 film: *The Blue Veil*
Frank Redman × 1 film: *This Land Is Mine*
Charles Rosher × 2 films: *Stand By for Action*; *Young Bess*
Joseph Ruttenberg × 1 film: *The Bribe*
John F. Seitz × 1 film: *The Big Clock*
Archie Stout × 1 film: *Captain Kidd*

Harry Stradling × 2 films: *Jamaica Inn*; *They Knew What They Wanted*
Percy Strong × 1 film: *Down River*
Karl Struss × 2 films: *Island of Lost Souls*; *The Sign of the Cross*
Gregg Toland × 1 film: *Les Misérables*
Aldo Tonti × 1 film: *Under Ten Flags*
Sidney Wagner × 1 film: *The Man from Down Under*
Joseph Walker × 1 film: *Tales of Manhattan*
F[rederick] A[rchibald] "Freddie" Young × 3 films: *Blue Bottles*; *Day-Dreams*; *The Tonic* (uncredited)

Chapter Notes

Preface

1. Laughton was the last of several individuals Bette Davis thanked for their support and belief in her as an actress. The others were actor George Arliss; studio bosses Jack Warner and Hal Wallis and director William Wyler.

2. Laughton's great friend Robert Donat, who also suffered from self-doubt and insecurity in his professional career, hit the nail on the head when discussing the prevailing attitudes of legitimate theatrical actors to the film making process. "There is a certain snobbery among stage actors where filming is concerned; they look upon it as a rather boring, well-paid joke." (Cardullo: 89). In a similar vein, the cerebral actor Michael Redgrave approached film acting from a position of lofty disdain. He recalled that director Alfred Hitchcock detected this early on when directing him in his first screen role in *The Lady Vanishes* (Gainsborough, 1938). "...[Hitchcock] ... sensed that I thought the whole atmosphere of filming, was, to say the least, uncongenial compared to that obtaining in the theatre where every night I was playing in a Chekhov play with John Gielgud, Peggy Ashcroft, Gwen Ffrangcon-Davies, Alec Guinness and a completely remarkable cast ... I well remember him saying 'Actors are cattle!' I can see now he was trying to jolt me out of my unrealistic dislike of working conditions in the studios and what he thought was a romantic reverence for the theatre" (Cardullo: 101). In her 1938 autobiography, *Charles Laughton and I*, Elsa Lanchester rebukes this contemptuous attitude among stage actors. "Most stage-trained actors on the films seem rather to despise the job and long to get back to the stage. They say: 'The theatre is the place, the films are nice to earn money,' and that sort of thing. Charles never did that" (Lanchester: 94).

3. In *Music Hall Parade* (Butchers, Oswald Mitchell, 1939) boy impressionist Hughie Green (1920–1997) in a solo act from his quick and vast repertoire provides impressions of Lionel Barrymore, Nellie Wallace, Jack Buchanan, Claude Dampier, Charles Laughton, Robertson Hare, Vic Oliver and Harry Tate.

In *One in a Million* (Twentieth Century–Fox, Sidney Lanfield, 1936) the vaudevillian team the Ritz Brothers appear on roller skates to perform a musical comedy number, "The Horror Boys of Hollywood" (written by Harry Rome and Lester Lee). Harry Ritz imitates Charles Laughton, in costume as Captain Bligh, Al Ritz dresses as Boris Karloff, in costume as the Frankenstein's Monster. Both shake hands and are joined by Jimmy Ritz who imitates character actor Peter Lorre. Together the Ritz Brothers sing, "We're the Horror Boys of Hollywood ... / We never get kisses / We just get the hisses."

In a Pathé newsreel dated June 20, 1940 comedian Max Wall (1908–1990) performs an impression of Laughton as Captain Bligh in *Mutiny on the Bounty*.

Nightclub entertainer Arthur Blake (1914–1985) specialized in impersonations of well-known personalities. His forty-five-minute stage act consisted of over eighteen caricatures including: Tallulah Bankhead; James Stewart; Beatrice Lillie; Sydney Greenstreet; Peter Lorre; Barbara Stanwyck; Sophie Tucker; Clifton Webb; Gloria Swanson; Margaret O'Brien; Ethel Barrymore; Mrs. Eleanor Roosevelt; Franklin D. Roosevelt; Louella Parsons; Carmen Miranda; Jose Ferrer; Bette Davis and an accurate Charles Laughton. His rendition of Laughton's Captain Bligh is captured during a few brief seconds in the film *Port of New York* (Eagle-Lion Films / Samba Films, László Benedek, 1949).

Peter Ustinov (1921–2004) in a 1990 interview for the Criterion laser disc of *Spartacus* gives a more nuanced imitation of Laughton in his recollections of the film.

Biography

1. Charles Laughton—General Register Office (GRO) Birth Index, Scarborough, volume 9d, page 398, quarter September 1899.

2. Robert Laughton—GRO Birth Index, Belper, vol. 7b, p. 421, q. December 1868; GRO Death Index, Scarborough, vol. 9d, p. 622 q. March 1924 (Birth: December 1869; Death: February 29, 1924).

Eliza Laughton née Conlon—GRO Birth Index, Easington, vol. 10a, p. 395, q. December 1868; GRO Death Index, Scarborough, vol. 1b, p. 979, q. March 1953 (Death: March 14, 1953).

Robert Thomas Laughton—GRO Birth Index, Scarborough, vol. 9d, p. 412, q. June 1903; GRO Death Index, Scarborough, vol. 2, p. 2811, q. March 1984 (Birth: March 19, 1903. Death: March 7, 1983).

Francis Laughton—GRO Birth Index, Scarborough, vol. 9d, p. 398, q. September 1908; GRO Death

Index, Holborn, London, vol. 3c, p. 978 q. March 1964 (Death: February 23, 1964).

3. On the UK 1911 Census gives Laughton as a boarder at St. John's College, Beaumont, Old Windsor, Egham, Berkshire. UK Census, 1911: Class: RG14; Piece: 6693; Schedule Number: 169. Laughton spent three years at Stonyhurst College from January 11, 1912 to July 26, 1915. (Stonyhurst Register, January 11, 1912 to July 26, 1915) His younger brothers also attended Stonyhurst. Tom from October 10, 1911 to May 1919 (Stonyhurst Register, October 11, 1911 to May 1919) and Francis from January 15, 1918 to April 12, 1925 (Stonyhurst Register, January 15, 1915 to July 26, 1925). Notable alumni at Stonyhurst include author Sir Arthur Conan Doyle (1859–1930), and George Archer-Shee (1895–1914) a young naval cadet who was tried at the high court on whether he had stolen a five-shilling postal order. Archer-Shee was successfully defended in court by Sir Edward Carson and acquitted of all charges. The case was the inspiration for the 1946 play *The Winslow Boy* by Terence Rattigan and has been filmed twice. In 1948 directed by Anthony Asquith and starring Robert Donat, Sir Cedric Hardwicke and Margaret Leighton. In 1999 directed by David Mamet and starring Nigel Hawthorne, Jeremy Northam and Rebecca Pidgeon. Perhaps the most flamboyant Stonyhurst alumni was sportsman, playboy and adventurer Frederick Joseph McEvoy (1907–1951). "Freddie," as he was known, was a close friend of actor Errol Flynn. Freddie appeared in small uncredited roles in two Hollywood films. First, alongside Flynn in a burlesque sendup of his lothario image, "That's What You Jolly Well Get," in the wartime studio musical *Thank Your Lucky Stars* (Warner Bros., David Butler, 1943) and as an adjutant in a wartime iteration of *The Desert Song* (Warner Bros., Robert Florey, 1943) based on the Sigmund Romberg, Oscar Hammerstein II, Otto Harbach, Frank Mandel operetta. Priest and poet Gerard Manley Hopkins (1844–1889) taught for a time at Stonyhurst.

4. Among those fellow schoolboys who witnessed Laughton's first performance on a public stage was Colin Glennie Greig (1900–1937). He was a year below Laughton and attended Stonyhurst from September 17, 1912, to sometime after April 15, 1915 (Stonyhurst Register, September 17, 1912 to April 10, 1915). Unlike Laughton, Greig distinguished himself as a school athlete. In the school athletic sports held on Easter Monday, 1915 Greig received the King's Cup for best all-round athlete in Second Division. During the day Greig came in second place in the 100 yards, second in 440 yards, first place in the half mile with a time of two minutes, thirty-two and one fifth seconds and, finally, came third in the long jump. Greig also excelled at cricket. On July 15, 1915, Stonyhurst played a match against Sedbergh School for boys under sixteen. Greig's prowess on the cricket pitch was described in the school magazine, "…the one-handed catch by which Greig dismissed Binnie, just when he was getting dangerously well set, was not only opportune, but was very fine. The batsman drove a well-pitched up ball with great force over cover-point's head. Greig swung out his right arm and held it. 'A perfect piece of cricket on both sides,' was the comment of an experienced spectator" (*Stonyhurst Magazine*, no. 202, October 1915, p. 1376). Upon leaving Stonyhurst Greig, the son of army officer Colonel Colin Philip Greig (1871–1950), enrolled at the Royal Military Academy Sandhurst from 1918 until 1919. While serving as a cadet he suffered a leg injury, and his military career came to an end. He later enrolled at the Royal Academy of Dramatic Art and took the stage name of Colin Clive—using his mother's maiden name. While at RADA he met and later married a fellow student, Evelyn Taylor, on June 26, 1922. *The Stage* (April 1, 1920) reported they were examined for medals and certificates at the St James Theatre on March 30, 1920 by judges Henry Ainley, Lady Tree and Lady Forbes-Robertson. In an extract from *Twelfth Night* Clive played Sir Toby Belch, while Evelyn Taylor had a small part in Maurice Maeterlinck's *Interior*. Evelyn Taylor was the daughter of master seaman and tea planter Aldwell Henry Taylor (1859–1937) and Mary Liyanage Taylor. By all accounts, she was born on an ocean liner sailing from Ceylon to England, her mother was Spanish, and she inherited her beauty. She was educated at an English convent until eighteen. From her teens she developed an interest in the theater. Under the management of Basil Dean and following experience on the West End stage she became very keen to break into films. For her film appearances she used the Spanish stage name of Nita Alvarez in tribute to her Hispanic heritage. Her filmography is comprised of at least six films: Two features were shot in France, *La Petite Chocolatière / The Chocolate Girl* (Films de France / Société des Cinéromans, Rene Hervil, 1927) and *La Maison du Maltais / Karina the Dancer* (Films de France / Société des Cinéromans, Henri Frescourt, 1928). In Britain she appeared in small supporting roles: A typist in *A Woman in Pawn* (Gaumont, Edwin Greenwood, 1927) and a native girl in *Emerald of the East* (BIP, Jean De Kuharski, 1927). Her final films were an early sound comedy short, *The Tale-Teller Phone* (British Sound Film Productions, 1928), and *The Broken Melody* (Paramount, Fred Paul, 1929). The marriage did not last and in 1928 Clive filed for divorce with actor Carl Harbord (1908–1958) cited as co-respondent. However, these proceedings were halted when Evelyn Greig died as the result of the effects of an abortion the following year on April 9, 1929, just as Clive's career was beginning to take off. In June 1929 he appeared at the Queen's Theatre in *Let's Leave It at That*, a light comedy co-authored by Clive and Jeanne de Casalis who also took the principal leads. The two hit it off which was more than the play did with the critics who dismissed it as ill-conceived. They were married at a registry office in Ashford, Kent on June 29, 1929. His English stage career saw two notable performances. In the London production of *Show Boat*, he played Steve Baker, Julie La Verne's white husband. His other performance as Captain Dennis Stanhope in R.C. Sheriff's war play *Journey's End* proved even more successful. The play was later produced as a film in 1930 by British film veteran George Pearson and directed by theater director James Whale. The cast and crew traveled

over to Hollywood to take advantage of the superior sound facilities available in American studios. Both Colin Clive and director James Whale stayed on in Hollywood. Under Whale's direction, Clive starred as Dr. Henry Frankenstein in the seminal horror film *Frankenstein* (1931) and its cult sequel *Bride of Frankenstein* (1935) at Universal studios. He would die of pneumonia brought on by acute alcoholism, aged just thirty-seven, on June 25, 1937. Despite working at the same studio, Universal Pictures, for the same director, James Whale, Laughton and Clive were never cast in the same film, nor did they appear together on the professional stage. However, they did share a concert platform while schoolboys at Stonyhurst College in October 1914 (see Amateur Stage Performances: 323). For further details of Clive's tragic life see Gregory William Mank's biography.

5. A comprehensive description of Charles Laughton's service in the Huntingdonshire Cyclist Battalion can be found on their website at http://huntscycles.co.uk/ (accessed on September 4, 2016).

6. The California Federal Naturalization Records 1887–1991 database, December 21, 1942, registration number: 118785 for Charles Laughton. Accessed via Ancestry.com on September 4, 2016.

7. Probate records show that Robert Laughton's estate of £37145 11s. 10d. was bequeathed to his widow and eldest son Charles. Probate search Gov. UK (accessed September 4, 2016).

8. Physical descriptions of Charles and Elsa Laughton are given on the California Federal Naturalization Records 1887–1991 database, December 21, 1942, registration number 118785 for Charles and registration number 118380 for Elsa. Accessed via Ancestry.com on September 4, 2016.

9. Elsa Lanchester Sullivan—GRO Birth Index, Lewisham, vol. 1d, p. 1194, q. March, 1902; James Sullivan—GRO Birth Index, Wandsworth, vol. 1d, p. 511, q. December, 1867; GRO Death Index, Lewisham, vol. 1d, p. 875, q. March 1945; Edith Lanchester—GRO Birth Index, Steyning, vol. 2b, p. 265, q. September 1871; GRO Death Index, Brighton, vol. 5h, p. 106, q. March 1966; Waldo Sullivan Lanchester—GRO Birth Index, Lambert, vol. 1d, p. 420, q. September 1897; GRO Death Index, Stratford-upon-Avon, vol. 31, p. 0410, q. December 1978.

10. GRO Marriage Index, St. Martin, vol. 1a, p. 986, q. March 1929.

11. Among his television appearances several standout performances included his introduction of pop idol Elvis Presley on *The Ed Sullivan Show*, which aired on September 9, 1956. Host Charles Laughton, broadcasting from New York and standing in for Ed Sullivan who was recovering from an automobile accident, made reference to four gold records the singer had earned and then with, "Away to Hollywood to meet Elvis Presley," cut to a subdued Presley facing the cameras. After a few brief moments of thanks to "Mr. Laughton," Presley then launched into "Don't Be Cruel." This handover from an older generation of performer schooled in rigor and formal acting traditions to the modernity of brash, intuitive, high-energy counterculture with its explicit notions of youth and rebellion, was a significant watershed moment in popular culture. Indeed, it is in the same league as Marlon Brando's motorcycle gang leader, Johnny Strabler in the *The Wild One* (Columbia, László Benedek, 1953). Strabler's existentialist response to the question, "What are you rebelling against, Johnny?" with "Whaddya got?" marked a paradigm shift in cultural mores of the post-war era. In fact, Presley's image of former prisoner Vince Everett in the film *Jailhouse Rock* (MGM, Richard Thorpe, 1957) was modeled on Brando's performance in the film. Laughton also sang a spirited rendition of the country music standard, "Old Rattler" on *The Tennessee Ernie Ford Show*, which aired on December 11, 1958. This amusing duet, alongside singer television host Ernest Jennings Ford (1919–1991)—known professionally as Tennessee Ernie Ford—demonstrates Laughton's ability to step outside his usual familiar roles and subvert his own image of an elder legitimate actor. For sheer eccentricity, however, Laughton's teaming with Elsa Lanchester on an episode of the *Startime* TV series takes some beating. Aired on March 15, 1960, the program was devoted to performances of Academy Award-winning songs. As a duet they gave an idiosyncratic (if spirited) rendering of Frank Loesser's "Baby It's Cold Outside," first featured in the MGM musical *Neptune's Daughter* (Edward Buzzell, 1949).

12. Robert Thomas Laughton arrived in Los Angeles by BOAC plane on September 1, 1962, and Francis Laughton arrived in Los Angeles from Paris by A.F. on September 21, 1962. Accessed via Ancestry.com on September 6, 2016.

13. Find a grave website. Accessed via Ancestry.com on September 6, 2016.

The Films

1. *Bury Times*, January 16, 1930.
2. *The Bioscope*, February 5, 1930 and *The Bioscope*, September 24, 1930.
3. *Oldham Evening Chronicle*, March 9, 1931. Plot details and review provided in *The Bioscope*, May 21, 1930.
4. *Film Weekly*, February 1, 1930, published this quote attributed to Dorothy Gish given during an interview in the U.S. A few weeks later *Film Weekly*, February 22, 1930, published an unequivocal apology to British Dominion Pictures, His Master's Voice and Dorothy Gish for publishing a spurious interview attributed to the actress. She had contacted the magazine by cable, "Shocked and distressed that such a story about me be broadcast in an English paper. No such statement made by me, and cannot understand where it originated, as I have given no interview since return to America. Please make unequivocal denial on my behalf that I gave any such interview."
5. In the Lancashire town of Oldham *Wolves* was shown on a double-bill with a Columbia B musical, *Personality* (Columbia, Victor Heerman, 1930). *Oldham Evening Chronicle*, March 8, 1931.
6. *Oldham Evening Chronicle*, November 7, 1931.
7. *Motion Picture Herald*, August 6, 1932.
8. *What Shocked the Censor: A complete record of*

cuts in motion picture films ordered by the New York State Censors, October 1932.

9. Universal Studio Theater Poster.

10. Tallulah Bankhead had several wisdom teeth removed in succession by the dentist. As a result, she lost ten pounds, all her gowns had to be refitted and she was placed on a milk diet (*Photoplay*, vol. XLII, no. 3, August 1932).

11. As the lone survivor from the original film, Gloria Stuart recorded a commentary for a laserdisc. *The Old Dark House: Collector's Edition* was released in 1996. It has subsequently been re-released on DVD and Blu-ray discs.

12. Born Philip Adolphus Le Couteur in Reading, Berkshire, England on January 15, 1878 (GRO Birth Index, Reading, Berkshire, vol. 2c, p. 358, q. March 1878), son of Philip Le Couteur, a commercial clerk who was born in the Channel Isles. He was the youngest of three siblings. Le Couteur was a pupil of Maxwell Ryder at the West London Theatre and used the stage name of Brember Wills. *The Era*, September 28, 1901, gives an early stage role in *Greed of Gold* playing Mr. Brightaide, Q.C. for the Thomas Morton Powell Company at the Royal Theatre, Castleford, Yorkshire. He made his London stage debut on April 11, 1906 in *Count Hannibal* and spent the next thirty years in the acting profession. In 1908 he became a member of Miss Annie Horniman's repertory company at the Gaiety Theatre in Manchester. He also played engagements at Glasgow and Bristol. His career was interrupted by military service during the First World War. At the outbreak of war, he joined the United Arts Rifles. In 1915 he transferred as a private to the Royal Army Medical Corps and served two years in France with the 58th Division (UK National Archives, World War I Medal Card, WO 372/21/218012). During the war he married Margaret Susan Carter an actress and writer born in 1879 at Clifton, Gloucestershire. She was the daughter of Reuben Thomas Carter a teacher at Clifton College and Amy Chatfield Carter nèe Seager. At the time of her marriage to Brember Wills in 1916, Margaret Carter was a widow. Her late husband, Arthur Richard Wilson, was a professional opera singer who used the stage name of Wilson Pembroke. They were married at Addleston, Surrey on August 29, 1903 (Church of England Marriages and Banns, 1754–1932; London Metropolitan Archives, London England, Ref No: p. 90 / TMS / 011. Accessed by Ancestry.com on August 20, 2017). He died in a nursing home on January 17, 1916. His estate of £987, 11s was willed to his widow (England and Wales National Probate Calendar 1858–1966, 1916, p. 317. Accessed via Ancestry.com on August 20, 2017). A few months after his death his widow, Margaret Wilson, married Philip Le Couteur at Barnet in Middlesex (GRO Marriage Index, Barnet, Middlesex, vol. 31, p. 826, q. April–June 1916). Wills was demobilized from the army in January 1919 and resumed his stage career during March 1919 at the Scala, appearing as Pope Pius XII in *The Hostage*. He later joined the Everyman repertory company in Hampstead appearing in *The Doctor's Dilemma* in 1921. It was at the Everyman that he first acted on stage with Laughton in *Pillars of Society* in June 1926. He later appeared with Laughton again in two plays, *The Greater Love* as Nuhlin at the Princes in February 1927 and *Angela* as John Quarl, also at the Princes, in March 1927. His stage career concluded at the Embassy playing the Lord High Chancellor in *Cinderella*, December 1936. Throughout the 1930s Wills was a regular actor on British radio. Beginning in 1929 he appeared in over thirty radio dramas for the British Broadcasting Corporation. In one broadcast, *Atmospherics*, a railway drama, Ernest Thesiger and Wills were reunited. The former appeared as "an escaped lunatic" and the latter as a railway guard. The play was broadcast June 15 and repeated June 17, 1937. His final broadcast was *A Revival of Peg O' My Heart* on March 10, 1940. Wills also appeared in two plays on the BBC's fledgling television service. First, *Joan Luxton's Theatre Company* transmitted December 21, 1936 and repeated December 30, 1936. Second, *Cinderella* transmitted January 19, 1937. This was written by his wife who also took the part of the ugly sister. Wills and his wife retired in the early 1940s. The pair were active in supporting local amateur theatrical groups. The New Mill Dramatic Club performed the pantomime *Cinderella* during December 1948 and 1949. These productions were staged using Margaret Carter's script and scenery designed by Brember Wills. *The Old Dark House* was the second of only five appearances in front of the camera. His film debut was *Carnival* (British and Dominion Film Corporation, Herbert Wilcox, 1931) in a small uncredited role as a stage manager. His subsequent films were *What Happened to Harkness?* (Warner Bros. First National, Milton Rosmer, 1934) in the title role of Bernard Harkness; *Unfinished Symphony* (Cine-Allianz / Gaumont-British, Anthony Asquith, Willi Forst, 1934) as Secretary; and another unbilled role as Doman in *The Scarlet Pimpernel* (London Film Production, Harold Young, 1934). On January 14, 1949, the *Bucks Herald* announced the will of "Mr. Philip Le Couteur (professionally known as Brember Wills), of Folly Bridge Bungalow, Bulbourne, [Tring in Hertfordshire] who died on December lst [1948] left £803 55s. 4d. gross, £770 14s. 4d. net value [GRO Death Index, Aylesbury, Buckinghamshire, vol. 6a, p. 302, q. December, 1948]. Probate has been granted to his widow Mrs. Margaret S. Le Couteur (professionally known as Margaret Carter), of the same address" (National Probate Index of Wills 1858–1966, Philip Le Couteur, Death Date: December 1, 1948, Hertfordshire, Hertford, Probate: January 3, 1949). Wills widow died on January 13, 1965, in Kensington, London. Her estate was valued at £1827 (National Probate Index of Wills 1858–1966, Margaret S. Le Couteur, Death Date: January 13, 1965, London, England, Probate: March 1, 1965).

13. Spelling appears to have been an optional exercise at Universal Studios. During the opening and closing credits of *The Mummy's Hand* (Christy Cabanne, 1940) actors Cecil Kellaway and Eduardo Ciannelli appear erroneously as Cecil Kelloway and Eduardo Cianelli!

14. *Film Weekly*, November 4, 1932.

15. Success came slowly for Forester and, thanks to Laughton's championing of his third novel on stage and screen, Forester was propelled into the public

eye and thereafter enjoyed a highly successful career. There followed a succession of highly popular historical novels and from 1937 a series of Hornblower novels. *Payment Deferred* was the first of several films based on Forester's novels. Other films based on his books include *Brown on Resolution / Forever England* (Gaumont-British, Walter Forde, 1935); *Eagle Squadron* (Walter Wanger, Arthur Lubin, 1942); *Commandos Strike at Dawn* (Columbia, John Farrow, 1942); *Forever and a Day* (RKO, Edmund Goulding, Cedric Hardwicke, Robert Stevenson, Victor Saville, Rene Clair, Frank Lloyd, Herbert Wilcox, 1943); *Captain Horatio Hornblower* (Warner Bros., Raoul Walsh, 1951); *The African Queen* (Horizon, John Huston, 1951); *Single-Handed / Sailor of the King* (Twentieth Century-Fox, Roy Boulting, 1953); *The Pride and the Passion* (United Artists, Stanley Kramer, 1957); and *Sink the Bismarck!* (Twentieth Century-Fox, Lewis Gilbert, 1960).

16. Paramount Studio Theater Poster.

17. *The New Movie Magazine*, January 1933.

18. For a description of this now missing, believed lost film see Yorke: 79–80.

19. Halliwell, 1978: 110.

20. *Motion Picture Reviews* published by The Women's University Club, Los Angeles Branch of the American Association of University Women, also rated the film in the most vehement of terms as, "a bad influence" for adolescents 12–16, and "harmful" for children 8–12.

21. Halliwell, 1978: 109.

22. Film Classics 1943 Reissue Lobby Card.

23. *Motion Picture Herald*, September 29, 1934.

24. The stage actor Charles Waldron (1874–1946) appeared in two Broadway productions of the Rudolf Beiser play as Edward Moulton-Barrett. The first at the Empire Theatre ran for 370 performances from February 9, 1931, to December 1931. The second at the Martin Beck Theatre ran for just twenty-four performances from February 25, 1935, to March 1935. Both productions starred and were produced by Katharine Cornell. In a film career of over sixty films that spanned several decades beginning with the short *Big Noise Hank* (Nestor Film Company, Milton J. Fahrney, 1911), it is Waldron's final film role as the elderly and infirm General Sternwood in Howard Hawks' acclaimed adaptation of Raymond Chandler's crime novel *The Big Sleep* (Warner Bros. 1946) for which he is best remembered.

25. *Motion Picture Herald*, March 16, 1935.

26. Paramount remade the film again: *Fancy Pants* (George Marshall, 1950), a musical adaptation of the story, starred Bob Hope in the lead.

27. MGM Theatrical Trailer.

28. Diaries of Adela Stephenson (1933–1937). Sister-in-law of Warner Bros. contract player James Stephenson (1889–1941). The film was viewed on October 1, 1936, at the Odeon, Weybridge in Surrey, South East England, UK.

29. According to *The Films of David Niven* the story about Niven's token appearance in *Mutiny on the Bounty* was just a publicity stunt. He was never in the film. See Garrett: 27.

30. In an article, "The Wonderful World of Ed Sullivan," in *TV Radio Mirror* (September 1962) it was revealed Laughton had attempted to turn down the role of Bligh. While explaining to director Frank Lloyd his severe seasickness he began studying Lloyd's face. He suggested that if given the same bushy eyebrows as director Lloyd he would be able to play Bligh with the necessary conviction.

31. *San Francisco Chronicle*, June 20, 1935.

32. Michael Redgrave Archives, 1936 Diary Entry, TH / 31 / 4 / 4–1936.

33. *Les Misérables* (Pathé-Natan, Raymond Bernard, 1934) ran a mammoth 288 minutes and was released in three parts. Harry Baur was cast as Valjean and Charles Vanel was Javert.

34. *Motion Picture Herald*, December 12, 1936.

35. *Variety*, January 4, 1939.

36. Shooting of *I, Claudius* began on February 15, 1937. On March 16, 1937, Merle Oberon suffered a concussion and facial injuries in a car crash. To complete the picture would have required another forty-three days of shooting. Laughton was already contracted to begin his venture as an independent producer of Mayflower Films with German producer Erich Pommer. Therefore, the decision was taken to shut down the production of *I, Claudius* after thirty-five days of shooting.

37. *Film Daily*, February 5, 1940.

38. *Motion Picture Herald*, September 30, 1939.

39. From the early thirties, Stradling (1901–1970) had worked extensively in Europe. Among the directors he worked under were Belgium born director Jacques Feyder (1885–1948) in *Le Grand Jeu* (1934); *La Kermesse Héroïque / Carnival in Flanders* (1935) and the German version *Die Klugen Frauen* (1936); Robert Siodmak in *Symphonie D'Amour* (1936); Abel Gance in *Le Maitre de Forges* (1933); *Poliche* (1934); *La Dame Aux Camélias* (1934); Marcel L'Herbier in *Le Bonheur* (1934) and Alexander Korda in *Rive Gauche* (1931); and *Die Männer um Lucie* (1931). It was Korda who brought him to England in 1936 before returning to Hollywood in 1940. He was nominated fifteen times for the Academy Award for best cinematography and won two Oscars for *The Picture of Dorian Gray* MGM, Albert Lewin, 1945) and *My Fair Lady* (Warner Bros., George Cukor, 1964).

40. The 1930 Production Code in section VIII on Religion paragraph 2 stated, "Ministers of religion in their character as ministers of religion should not be used as comic characters or as villains" (Steinberg: 551).

41. Laughton's sartorial elegance for the film consisted of boots costing twelve pounds a pair; coats and breeches made by a Bond Street expert; shirts of real lace; and waistcoats adorned with genuine Wedgewood buttons (*Motion Picture Herald*, March 4, 1939).

42. The novel was later adapted as a British television miniseries for ITV in 1983 with Jane Seymour as Mary Yellan and Patrick McGoohan as Joss Merlyn. In 2014 the BBC commissioned a three-part series of the novel written by Emma Frost. The leads were Jessica Brown Findlay as Mary Yellan and Sean Harris as Joss Merlyn. Despite decent ratings of over six million, when the three episodes were transmitted

between 21–23 April 2014 there was a storm of protest from viewers over issues with the soundtrack. TV viewers complained of inaudible dialogue, impenetrable accents and mumbling by members of the cast. Many were forced to use subtitles to find out what was being said. The accompanying visuals were deliberately unappealing; they tended to dwell on the dingy, the murky and the dismal. Even in its compromised form, the Laughton film version is technically robust in both sound and picture. Indeed, more so since its splendid 2014 4K digital restoration. In terms of ham actors, Robert Newton had appeared in *The Beachcomber* (London Independent Producers, Muriel Box, 1954), a remake of *The Vessel of Wrath*. It is interesting to speculate that if Newton had not died prematurely in 1956, he may have been considered for the role of Joss Merlyn in a proposed remake of the film. His exaggerated native West Country accent and flamboyant personality, imported from his imperishable role of Long John Silver in *Treasure Island*, is to suggest an especially attention-grabbing performance. As it is, Newton's Jem Trehearne in the Hitchcock film is played as a subdued and conventional romantic lead with no inclination of the hyperbolic inflection of his later performances.

43. RKO Radio Pictures, Inc. Theatrical Trailer.
44. *Film Daily*, October 4, 1940.
45. Salary earnings for Laughton and Lombard, *Film Daily*, August 4, 1941.
46. *Film Daily*, July 17, 1941—advertised under the working title *Almost an Angel*.
47. Accessed via William K. Everson Archive on March 7, 2020.
48. *Showmen's Trade Review*, March 21, 1942.
49. Twentieth Century–Fox Studio Theater Poster.
50. MGM Theatrical Trailer.
51. United Artists Studio Theater Poster.
52. *Motion Picture Herald*, June 19, 1943.
53. MGM Theatrical Trailer.
54. MGM Theatrical Trailer.
55. Universal Studio Theater Poster.
56. Robert Powell (b. 1944) in conversation with actress Jenny Hanley (b.1947) at 5th Renown Festival of Film, St. Albans, March 24, 2019.
57. *Modern Screen*, vol. 31, no. 4, September 1945.
58. *Motion Picture Herald*, February 2, 1946.
59. Selznick International Theater Poster.
60. In an internet chat forum of July 29–30, 2008 archivist Robert Harris, in an answer to a query from a researcher about Hitchcock's "lost film," confirmed that Selznick's prints were originally stored at the University of Texas, Austin. "There was a 'long version' print on the inventories, but that was apparently destroyed by water damage sometime in the 1980s. There is a picture only element of the longer version at the Museum of Modern Art (originally part of the ABC holdings—pre-Disney) and there is apparently protection on this element. The museum scene … is in this element." The researcher replied he had contacted the University of Texas in Austin. They stated these scenes had been sent over to the George Eastman Museum in Rochester. Accessed via hometheaterforum.com on February 16, 2020.
61. United Artists Theatrical Trailer.
62. Paramount Studio Theater Poster.
63. United Artists Studio Theater Poster.
64. MGM Theatrical Trailer.
65. Cinematographer Joseph Ruttenberg was able to call upon a new, fully motorized camera boom with an electronic control that enabled one operator to move a heavy boom in a fraction of a second at a greater speed than ever before. This was invented by John Arnold. (*American Cinematographer*, July 1948).
66. United Artists Studio Theater Poster.
67. The celebrated critic, director and cineaste, François Truffaut, held director Julien Duvivier in high esteem, not only for his film oeuvre, but as a friend. When they first met at the Cannes Festival in 1956, Truffaut had suggested they collaborate on a film project, but Duvivier was unfortunately in the middle of a film shoot. Three years later Duvivier was the senior director sitting on the jury which awarded Truffaut the prize for best direction for Truffaut's debut feature film *Les Quatre Cent Coups / The Four Hundred Blows* at the 1959 Cannes Festival. Truffaut's next feature, *Tirez sur la Pianiste / Shoot the Piano Player* (1960), was based loosely on a 1956 David Goodis thriller, *Down There*. The film is a homage to American cinema and its influences on that generation of cineastes known as "la nouvelle vague," or the French "new wave." The film's title is a reference to Duvivier's *La Tête d'un homme*. In a sequence where Inspector Maigret (Harry Baur) and several suspects visit a night club, the words, "Ne tirez pas sur le pianiste. Il fait ce qu'il / Don't shoot the piano player. He's doing the best he can" are written on the ceiling. Later in his career Duvivier directed the comedy *La Fête á Henriette* (Filmsonor, 1952) which dealt with the frustrations and vagaries of the filmmaking process. Twenty years later Truffaut would produce the drama *La Nuit Américaine / Day for Night* (Les Films de Carrosse / PECF / PIC / Marcel Berbert, 1973) which dealt with the film aesthetic, its fame and the artifice of the systemic processes and procedures of filmmaking. For a fuller consideration of this neglected director, see *Julien Duvivier* by Ben McCann, Manchester University Press, 2017.
68. These words appear prior to the beginning of the film on the DVD 2 disc released by Odeon Film Entertainment on March 12, 2012 in the Hollywood Studio Collection series. This release uses the restored master from the UCLA film and television archive. It has been suggested that sections of Burgess Meredith's personal 16mm print were used in this restoration.
69. *Motion Picture Herald*, October 27, 1951.
70. Production costs are taken from *The RKO Story*.
71. Universal-International Theatrical Trailer.
72. William Cottrell (1918–2001) had been his acting student and appeared in the 1947 play *Galileo* as a menacing Cardinal Inquisitor. Cottrell made a previous film appearance opposite Laughton in the small part of Moers in *The Man on the Eiffel Tower*.
73. From December 1951 through 1952 cinemas in England screened *The Strange Door* as a double feature with the Dick Powell comedy *You Never Can*

Tell / You Never Know (Universal-International, Lou Breslow, 1951). However, in Wicklow, Ireland (March 22, 1952) it was support to the main feature *Encore* (Two Cities, Pat Jackson, 1951), a portmanteau film based on short stories by Somerset Maugham. When the film was reissued in the mid-1950s, it turned up supporting *Abbott and Costello Meet the Invisible Man* (Universal-International, Charles Lamont, 1951) and *The Mob* shown under its UK title *Remember That Face* (Columbia, Robert Parrish, 1951).

74. Twentieth Century-Fox Theatrical Trailer.
75. Warner Bros. Theater Poster.
76. Halliwell: 1977; Hirschorn: 1980.
77. Of the ten films featuring the comics names in the title, Charles Lamont directed seven. Lamont had first directed *Abbott and Costello in the Foreign Legion* and *Abbott and Costello Meet the Invisible Man* (then the independent *Abbott and Costello Meet Captain Kidd*) followed by: *Abbott and Costello Go to Mars*; *Abbott and Costello Meet Dr Jekyll and Mr Hyde*; *Abbott and Costello Meet the Keystone Kops*; and finally, *Abbott and Costello Meet the Mummy*. All six films were produced for Universal-International from 1950–1955. An earlier film, *Abbott and Costello in Hollywood*, produced in 1945 at MGM (directed by S. Sylvan Simon), is not considered part of the series.
78. Columbia Theater Poster.
79. *Film Bulletin*, May 18, 1953.
80. United Artists Theatrical Trailer.
81. The film aired on BBC 2, November 11, 1982. Twenty-four years earlier on February 14, 1958, Kenneth Williams had met Laughton backstage. He came to see the London revue, *Share My Lettuce*, at the Garrick Theatre. Its huge success had given Williams a real taste of theatrical stardom. Williams noted that Laughton looked tired, though he was complimentary about the show and promised to bring his wife, Elsa Lanchester, along to see it. Laughton also spoke about his deep affection for his home in California (Davis: 140–141).
82. Robert Powell (b. 1944) in conversation with actress Jenny Hanley (b. 1947) at 5th Renown Festival of Film, St. Albans, March 24, 2019. Powell is associated in the public mind with the 1977 British-Italian mini-series *Jesus of Nazareth*.
83. United Artists Theater Poster.
84. "Images of Childhood" was the banner title of a six-week BBC TV series that "features films showing the adult world through the eyes of children." Given a prime slot of 9p.m., the films were broadcast on BBC 2 from April 22, 1975, to May 27, 1975. The six films were, *Sundays and Cybele* (France, Serge Bourguignon, 1962); *The Miracle Worker* (United Artists, Arthur Penn, 1962); *Hugo and Josefin* (Sweden, Kjell Grede, 1967); *Intruder in the Dust* (M-G-M, Clarence Brown, 1949); *The Night of the Hunter* (United Artists, Charles Laughton, 1955); and *The Childhood of Maxim Gorki* (Russia, Mark Donskoi, 1938). Putting such a thoughtful and provocative season of films on public service television would be all but improbable and nigh impossible today.

85. United Artists Theater Poster.
86. Paramount studio theater poster.
87. Universal-International studio theater poster.
88. *Film Bulletin* (October 17, 1960) described the epic: "A blockbuster in every aspect, *Spartacus* goes far beyond the accepted definition of that word." The origin of the term blockbuster refers to large, powerful bombs used in aerial bombardment of cities during World War II. The first mention of the word in the context of film entertainment is a citation in *Variety* (May 19, 1943) advising film exhibitors of "Post-war era when Flying Fortresses carries a film peddler instead of a blockbuster." In a *Motion Picture Daily* (September 15, 1943) review of MGM's wartime star musical *Thousands Cheer*, Virginia O'Brien's "deadpan singing of songs … a favorite entertainment of the servicemen in camps she's visited from border to border, is as surefire as a blockbuster." In a review of *The Canterville Ghost* in the *Exhibitor* (May 31, 1944) the plot synopsis mentions, "…a delayed-action blockbuster comes down by parachute near the castle." In the *Independent* (November 25, 1944) a promotion tagline for *Thirty Seconds over Tokyo* appears as, "A Dramatic Blockbuster that Hits the Target Squarely." It was during the post-war period that the nomenclature of blockbuster was taken up by Hollywood to designate films that are large in scope and scale (both thematically and visually). The Ancient World Epic had held sway during the silent and sound era of super productions, but with the release of the CinemaScope epic *The Robe* in 1953 there began the ascent of the blockbuster with its ability to blow or smash away the box office with its high production costs, reach and production budget, all-star casts, exotic location shooting, and action spectacle aided with high concept special effects. With the decline of the traditional, vertically integrated studio system from the late 1940s, the rise of the blockbuster was a business model based on the notion of independent production. Independent producers hired rented studio space and personnel on a project-by-project basis. In the *Film Weekly 1960–1961 Year Book*, Arthur B. Krim, President of United Artists, was able to declare, "Never before in our history have we had so many films of blockbuster potential completed, in work and preparation." The Ancient World blockbuster epics as a cycle lasted under a decade until the commercial disasters of *Cleopatra* (Twentieth Century-Fox, Joseph L. Mankiewicz, 1963) and *The Fall of the Roman Empire* (Paramount, Anthony Mann, 1964). The modern high concept blockbuster began with the release of *Jaws* in the summer of 1975 followed by *Star Wars* in 1977.

89. United Artists Theater Poster.

Bibliography

Aaker, Everett. *The Films of George Raft*, Jefferson, NC: McFarland, 2013.

Barr, Charles. *English Hitchcock*, Moffat: Cameron & Hollis, 1999.

Barrow, Kenneth. *Mr. Chips: The Life of Robert Donat*, London: Methuen, 1985.

Baxter, John. *The Cinema of Josef von Sternberg*, London: Zwemmer, 1971.

Bentley, Eric. *The Brecht Memoir*, Manchester: Carcanet, 1989.

Bergan, Ronald. *The United Artists Story*, London: Octopus, 1986.

Birchard, Robert S. *Cecil B. De Mille's Hollywood*, Lexington: University Press of Kentucky, 2004.

Bogdanovich, Peter. *Who the Hell's in It?: Conversations with Legendary Film Stars*, London: Faber & Faber, 2004.

Bojarski, Richard, Kenneth Beale. *The Films of Boris Karloff*, Secaucus, NJ: Citadel Press, 1974.

Boswell, James. *The Life of Samuel Johnson*, London: Penguin, 2008.

Brecht, Bertolt. "On Life of Galileo (1947–8) from Constructing a Role: Laughton's Galileo," *Brecht on Performance*, London and New York: Bloomsbury, 2014.

Brownlow, Kevin. *David Lean: A Biography*, London: Faber & Faber, 1997.

Callow, Simon. *Charles Laughton: A Difficult Actor*, London: Methuen, 1987.

Cannell, J.C. *In Town To-Night: The Story of the Popular BBC Feature Told from Within*. London: George Harrap, 1935.

Cardullo, Bert, Harry Geduld, Ronald Gottesman, Leigh Woods (eds.). *Playing to the Camera: Film Actors Discuss Their Craft*, New Haven and London: Yale University Press, 1998.

Chaplin, Charles. *Charles Chaplin: My Autobiography*, Harmondsworth: Penguin, 1974.

Chibnall, Steve. *J. Lee Thompson: British Film Makers*, Manchester and New York: Manchester University Press, 2000.

Chibnall, Steve. *Quota Quickies: The Birth of the British 'B' Film*, London: British Film Institute, 2007.

Chierichetti, David. *Mitchell Leisen: Hollywood Director*, Los Angeles: Photoventures Press, 1995.

Curtis, James. *James Whale: A New World of Gods and Monsters*, London: Faber & Faber, 1998.

Davies, Russell. *The Kenneth Williams Diaries*, London: HarperCollins, 1993.

Drazin, Charles. *The Finest Years: British Cinema of the 1940s*, London: Andre Deutsch, 1998.

Eames, John Douglas. *The M-G-M Story: The Complete History of Fifty Roaring Years*, London: Sundial, 1976.

Eames, John Douglas. *The Paramount Story*, London: Octopus, 1985.

Friedrich, Otto. *City of Nets: A Portrait of Hollywood in the 1940's*, London: Headline, 1987.

Garrett, Gerard. *The Films of David Niven*, London: LSP, 1975.

Gifford, Denis. *The British Film Catalogue 1895–1970: A Guide to Entertainment Films*, Newton Abbot: David & Charles, 1973.

Gish, Lillian, and Ann Pichot. *The Movies Mr. Griffith and Me*, London: W.H. Allen, 1969.

Granger, Stewart. *Sparks Fly Upward*, London: Granada, 1981.

Halliwell, Leslie. *The Filmgoer's Book of Quotes*, St Albans: Hart-Davis, MacGibbon, 1973.

Halliwell, Leslie. *Halliwell's Film Guide*, London: Granada, 1977.

Halliwell, Leslie. *Mountain of Dreams: The Golden Years of Paramount Pictures*, London: Hart-Davis, MacGibbon, 1978.

Herbert, Ian (ed.) *Who Was Who in the Theatre 1912–1976*, Detroit and London: Cengage Gale, 1978.

Higham, Charles. *Charles Laughton: An Intimate Biography*, New York: Doubleday, 1976.

Higham, Charles. *Hollywood Cameramen (Cinema One)*, London: Thames and Hudson, 1970.

Hirschhorn, Clive. *The Columbia Story*, London: Octopus, 1989.

Hirschhorn, Clive. *The Universal Story*, London: Octopus, 1983.

Hirschhorn, Clive. *The Warner Bros. Story*, London: Octopus, 1980.

Hoey, Michael A. *Sherlock Holmes & the Fabulous Faces: The Universal Pictures Repertory Company*, Albany, NY: BearManor Media, 2011.

Jacobs, Jack, and Myron Braum. *The Films of Norma Shearer*, New York: London: A.S. Barnes, 1976.

Jewell, Richard B., and Vernon Harbin. *The RKO Story*, London: Octopus, 1982.

Jones, Ken, and Arthur F. McClure, & Alfred E. Twomey. *Character People*, New York: A. S. Barnes, 1976.

Kael, Pauline. *5001 Nights at the Movies*, London: Zenith, 1984.

Kanin, Garson. *Hollywood: Stars and Starlets, Tycoons and Flesh-Peddlers, Movie-makers and Moneymakers, Frauds and Geniuses, Hopefuls and Has-Beens, Great Lovers and Sex Symbols*, London: Hart-Davis, MacGibbon, 1975.

Knowlden, Marilyn. *Little Girl in Big Pictures: Autobiography of Marilyn Knowlden*, Albany, NY: BearManor Media, 2011.

Korda, Michael. *Charmed Lives: A Family Romance*, London: Allen Lane, 1980.

Lambert, Gavin. *Norma Shearer: A Life*, London: Hodder and Stoughton, 1990.

Lanchester, Elsa. *Charles Laughton and I*, London: Faber & Faber, 1938.

Lanchester, Elsa. *Elsa Lanchester Herself*, London: Michael Joseph, 1983.

Lejeune, C.A. *Chestnuts in Her Lap: 1936–1946*, London: Phoenix House, 1947.

Levy, Bill. *Lest we Forget: The John Ford Stock Company*, Albany, NY: BearManor Media, 2013.

Maltin, Leonard (ed.) *Leonard Maltin's Classic Movie Guide* (2nd ed.), London: Plume, 2010.

Mank, Gregory William. *"One Man Crazy!" The Life and Death of Colin Clive*, Baltimore: Midnight Marquee Press, 2018.

McFarlane, Brian (ed.) *The Encyclopedia of British Film* (4th ed.), Manchester: Manchester University Press, 2013.

Mérigeau, Pascal. *Jean Renoir: A Biography*, Philadelphia: Running Press, 2016.

Milland, Ray. *Wide-Eyed in Babylon*, Falmouth: Coronet, 1977.

Mulholland, Jim. *The Abbott and Costello Book*, New York: Popular Library, 1975.

Norman, Barry. *Barry Norman's Film Greats*, London: W.H. Smith, 1986.

O'Hara, Maureen, and John Nicoletti. *'Tis Herself: A Memoir*, London: Simon & Schuster, 2004.

Parkinson, David. *Mornings in the Dark: The Graham Greene Film Reader*, Manchester: Carcanet, 1993.

Powell, Michael. *A Life in Movies: An Autobiography*, London: Heinemann, 1986.

Quinlan, David. *British Sound Films: The Studio Years 1928–1959*, London: B.T. Batsford, 1984.

Quirk, Lawrence J. *The Films of Fredric March*, New York: Citadel Press, 1971.

Richards, Jeffrey. *Hollywood's Ancient Worlds*, London: Continuum, 2008.

Sanders, George. *Memoirs of a Professional Cad*, Milton Keynes: Dean Street Press, 2015.

Server, Lee. *Robert Mitchum: "Baby, I Don't Care,"* London: Faber & Faber, 2001.

Shipman, David. *The Great Movie Stars: The Golden Years*, London: Angus Robertson (4th ed., 1979).

Silver, Alain, and Elizabeth Ward. *Film Noir*, London: Secker and Warburg, 1980.

Singer, Kurt. *The Charles Laughton Story*, London: Robert Hale, 1954.

Slide, Anthony. *Fifty Classic British Films, 1932–1982*, New York: Dover, 1985.

Spoto, Donald. *The Dark Side of Genius: The Life of Alfred Hitchcock*, London: Plexus, 1983.

Steinberg, Cobbett. *Reel Facts: The Movie Book of Records*, Harmondsworth: Penguin, 1981.

Taylor, Deems. *A Pictorial History of the Movies*, New York: Simon & Schuster, 1943.

Thomas, Tony. *The Films of the Forties*, Secaucus, New Jersey: Citadel Press, 1975.

Thomson, David. *"Have You Seen?" A Personal Introduction to 1,000 Films*, London: Allen Lane, 2008.

Truffaut, François. *Hitchcock*, London: Paladin, 1986.

Twomey, Alfred E., and Arthur F. McClure. *The Versatiles: Supporting Character Players in the Cinema 1930–1955*, New York: A.S. Barnes, 1969.

Vasey, Ruth. *The World According to Hollywood 1918–1939*, Exeter: University of Exeter Press, 1997.

Weaver, Tom, David Schecter, Robert J. Kiss, and Steve Kronenberg. *Universal Terrors, 1951–1955: Eight Classic Horror and Science Fiction Films*, Jefferson, NC: McFarland, 2014.

Wykes, Alan. *H.G. Wells in the Cinema*, London: Jupiter, 1977.

Yorke, Peter. *William Haggar Fairground Film Maker*, Bedlinog: Accent, 2007.

Directories, Journals, Periodicals and Trade Papers

American Cinematographer issues of 1928–1959
Bioscope issues of 1928–1932
Boxoffice issue of 1948
Era issues of 1901–1934
Exhibitor issues of 1943–1945
Exhibitors Herald issue of 1927
Film Bulletin issues of 1954–1960
Film Daily issues of 1936–1948
Film Daily Year Books issues of 1932–1951
Film Weekly issues of 1928–1939
Focus: A Film Review issues of 1948–1951
Focus on Film issues of 1974–1979
Harrison's Reports issues of 1932–1962
Hollywood issues of 1942–1943
Hollywood Filmograph issues of 1932–1939
Independent Exhibitor's Film Bulletin issues of 1934–1962
International Photographer issues of 1932–1939
Kinematograph Weekly issues of 1928–1962
Kinematograph Year Books issues of 1930–1962
Modern Screen issues of 1934–1950
Monthly Film Bulletin issues of 1934–1962
Motion Picture Daily issues of 1933–1960
Motion Picture Herald issues of 1932–1951
Showmen's Trade Review issues of 1941–1948
The Stage issues of 1920–1996
Stonyhurst Magazine issues of 1913–2005
TV Radio Mirror issue of 1962
Variety issues of 1928–1960
World Film News issue of 1938

Newspapers

Abroath Herald & Advertiser for the Montrose Burghs (1937)
Bucks Herald (1948–1949)
Bury Times (1930)
Daily Mail (1935)

Emporia Gazette (1932)
Hull Daily Mail (1915–1935)
Manchester Guardian (1926–1962)
Middlesex Advertiser and County Gazette (1936)
Nelson Leader (1939)
Oldham Evening Chronicle (1930–1931)
Scarborough Evening News (1919–1964)
Scarborough Mercury (1921–1924)
Sunderland Daily Echo and Shipping Gazette (1947–1948)
Sydney Morning Herald (1943)
Times [London] (1928–1964)
Times [New York] (1930–1962)

Websites

Academy of Motion Picture Arts and Sciences. https://www.oscars.org/
American Film Institute Catalog of Feature Films: The First 100 Years 1893–1993. www.afi.com
Ancestry.com Website. www.ancestry.com
BBC radio and TV *Radio Times* Archive 1923–2009. https://genome.ch.bbc.co.uk/
British Board of Film Classification. www.bbfc.co.uk
British Film Institute. www.bfi.org.uk
British Movietone Newreel Archives. www.aparchive.com
British Pathé Newsreel Archives. www.britishpathe.com
Digital Deli Online. www.digitaldeliftp.com
DVD Beaver DVD and Blu-ray Reviews. www.dvdbeaver.com
Find a Grave. www.findagrave.com
Find a Will. https://probatesearch.service.gov.uk/#wills
Findmypast. www.findmypast.co.uk
Internet Movie Database. www.imdb.com
Movie Title Stills Collection. http://annyas.com/screenshots/
William K. Everson Collection. www.nyu.ed/projects/wke/

Index

Numbers in ***bold italics*** indicate pages with illustrations

Abbott, Bud ***128***, 129, 156, 176, 177, 182, 190
Abbott and Costello Go to Mars 201
Abbott and Costello in Hollywood 201
Abbott and Costello in the Foreign Legion 201
Abbott and Costello Meet Captain Kidd 7, ***128***, 129, 130, 189, 190, 192, 201
Abbott and Costello Meet Dr. Jekyll and Mr Hyde 201
Abbott and Costello Meet Frankenstein 129
Abbott and Costello Meet the Invisible Man 201
Abbott and Costello Meet the Keystone Kops 201
Abbott and Costello Meet the Mummy 201
The Abbott and Costello Show (radio) 176, 177
Adler, Larry 59, 190
The Admirable Crichton (film) 160
Advise & Consent (film) 7, 150, ***151***, 152, 153, 189, 190, 191, 192
Advise and Consent (novel) 151, 152
The African Queen (film) 199
The African Queen (novel) 58
Ahern, Lloyd, Sr. 125, 192
Aldrich, Robert 106, 108, 129
Alias Nick Beal (film aka *The Contact Man*) 113
Alibi (play) 166
Alice in Wonderland (1933 film) 159
Aloma of the South Seas (1941 film) 77
America Calling: A Salute to the Greek Nation (radio) 175
Angela (play) 165, 198
Arch of Triumph (film) 7, 106, ***107***, 108, 109, 189, 190, 192
Arch of Triumph (tv) 109
Archer-Shee, George 196

Arnold, Malcolm 135, 137
Arsenic and Old Lace (play) 87
Arthur (1981 film) 75
Atlantic 13
Atmospherics (radio) 198
August, Joseph H. 65, 192

The Baby and the Battleship 81
"Baby It's Cold Outside" 197
The Bachelor Father 24
Ball of Fire 74
Bankhead, Tallulah ***16***, 17, 18, 20, 187, 195, 198
Banton, Travis 16, 34, 36, 43, 99, 102, 105
Barnes, Binnie 37, 39, ***89***, 90, 190
Barrett, Wilson 27, 29
The Barretts of Wimpole Street (1934 film aka *Forbidden Alliance*) **40**, 41, 42, 144, 174, 189, 191, 192
The Barretts of Wimpole Street (1957 film) 42
Barrymore, Ethel 102, 105, 190, 195
Bartholomew, Freddie 2
Bates, Florence ***75***, 177, 190
The Battleship Potemkin 10
Baxter, Jane 15, 190
The Beachcomber (1954 film) 59, 200
The Beachcomber (radio) 174
Beauty (play) 167
Because of Him 99, ***100***, 101, 102, 189, 190, 191, 192
Beery, Wallace 90, 136
The Bells of St. Mary's 114
Benjamin Franklin (film) 160
Bergen, Edgar 129, 174, 175, 176, 178, 179
The Betsy 75
The Big Clock ***109***, ***110***, 111, 112, 113, 189, 191, 192
Big Noise Hank 199
The Big Sleep (1946 film) 199
Biography in Sound: "Actor and Director Charles Laughton" (radio) 181

Birdman of Alcatraz 153
Birds Eye Open House (radio aka *The Dinah Shore Show*) 177, 178
Blake, Arthur 2, 195
Blue Bottles 9, 10, 191, 193
Blue Ribbon Town (radio) 177, 178
The Blue Veil ***121***, 122, 123, 189, 191, 192
Body and Soul (1947 film) 108
Bogart, Humphrey 58, 117, 182
Bogeaus, Benedict 96, 97, 98, 113, 114, 157
Bois, Curt 66, 75, 106, 190
Boleslawski, Richard 33, 41, 49, 52
Le Bonheur (1934 film) 199
Boyer, Charles 78, 79, 106, ***107***, 108, 170, 182, 190
Brandes, Werner 12, 192
Brecht, Bertolt 7, 89, 98, 102, 105, 140, 156, 169, 170, 203
Brennan, Walter ***80***, 117
The Bribe 114, ***115***, ***116***, 117, 118, 189, 191, 192
Bride of Frankenstein 5, 197
The Bridge of San Luis Rey (1944 film) 98
The Bridge on the River Kwai 161
British Movietone Newsreel 154
British Paramount Newsreel 155
Britton, Barbara 96, 98
The Broken Melody (1929 film) 196
Brooke, Hillary 129, 130, 190
Brooks, Hazel 106, ***107***
Brown on Resolution (film aka *Forever England*) 199
Buccaneer Bunny 2
Bunny, Bugs 2, 30
Burke, Kathleen 31, 33

The Caine Mutiny Court-Martial (play) 170, 171
Callow, Simon 1, 53, 77, 81, 88, 95, 98, 99, 116, 119, 138, 142, 203
Canadian Red Cross (radio) 173, 175

207

208 Index

The Canterville Ghost (film) **92**, 93, 94, 98, 160, 189, 191, 192, 201
The Canterville Ghost (radio) 178, 179
Captain Horatio Hornblower 199
Captain Kidd 74, 96, **97**, 98, 99, 144, 189, 191, 192
Captains Courageous 2
Un Carnet de Bal 79
Carnival (1931 film) 198
Carradine, John 27, 50, 96, 98, 170
Carter, Harry **126**
Carter, Margaret Susan 198
The Cat and Canary (1927 film) 21
Cat People (1942 film) 88
Caught (1949 film) 108
Cavalcade (play) 84
The Cavalcade of America: "General Benjamin Franklin" (radio) 179
The Cavalcade of America: "Grandpa and the Statue" (radio) 178
The Cavalcade of America: "The Incomparable Doctor" (radio) 180
The Cavalcade of America: "The Laziest Man in Town" (radio) 177
The Cavalcade of America: "The Prophet Without Honor" (radio) 176
Cavalcade of the Academy Awards 155
Chaplin, Charles 10, 127, 128, 203
Chase, Charley 45
The Chase and Sanborn Hour (radio) 174
The Chase and Sanborn Program (radio) 174, 175, 176, 178, 179
Checkmate: "Terror from the East" (tv) 186
Chelsea at Nine (tv) 183
The Cherry Orchard (play) 164, 168
The Childhood of Maxim Gorki 201
Christie, Agatha 142, 144, 166, 176
Christmas Eve with Charles Laughton (tv) 183
Christmas Holiday 96
Christmas Seals Public Service Announcement 156
Cinderella (play) 198
Cinderella (tv) 198
Citizen Kane 74
Cleopatra (1934 film) 58
Cleopatra (1963 film) 201
Climbing the Matterhorn 120
Clive, Colin 21, 162, 196, 197, 204
Cobra Woman 77

Colbert, Claudette **27**, 30, 190
The Colgate Comedy Hour (tv) 182
Collier, Constance 113, 114, 190
Columbia Presents Corwin: "L'Affaire Gumpert/The Case of the Gumpert" (radio) 178
Columbia Presents Corwin: "American Trilogy–Carl Sandburg" (radio) 177
Columbia Presents Corwin: "American Trilogy–Walt Whitman" (radio) 177
Columbia Presents Corwin: "American Trilogy–Wolfiana" (radio) 177
Columbia Presents Corwin: "The Moat Farm Murder" (radio) 177
The Columbia Workshop: "Twenty-Six by Corwin–Job" (radio) 175
Comets 13, 14, 191
Command Performance (radio) 176
Commandos Strike at Dawn 199
Conan Doyle, Sir Arthur 196
Conrad, Joseph 36
The Constant Nymph (1928 film) 10
Cooper, Gary **16**, 17, 18, 25, 45, 190
Cormack, Bartlett 57, 58, 60
Cortez, Stanley 118, 120, 121, 129, 130, 138, 140, 192
Corwin, Norman 6, 82, 121, 123, 173, 174, 175, 177, 178
Costello, Lou **128**, 129, 156, 176, 177, 182, 190
Cottrell, William 118, 124, 125, 170, 200
Count Hannibal (play) 198
Cregar, Laird 146, 160
Crowther, Bosley 70, 75, 81, 84, 88, 105, 109, 113, 128, 132, 141, 153
The Cruise of the Breadwinner (film) 160
Cry Wolf 16
Cyrano de Bergerac (character in film) 101
Cyrano de Bergerac (film) 159, 160

La Dame Aux Camélias (1934 film) 199
Dangerous Paradise 36
Daniell, Henry 94, 96, 142, 144, 190
Daniels, William H. 40, 192
"Danny Boy" 100, 101
Danton the Terror of France (film) 160
Dark Waters 98

David Copperfield (1935 film) 159
Davidson, Max 45
Davis, Bette 1, 155, 195
Day-Dreams 10, 11, 191, 193
Dead Men Don't Wear Plaid 117, 118
de Casalis, Jeanne 13, 62, 167, 196
Dee, Frances 25, **31**
De Grasse, Robert 82, 192
De Mille, Cecil B. 27, 29, 30, 58, 112, 132, 174, 177, 203
The Desert Song (1943 film) 196
Devil and the Deep **16**, 17, 18, 19, 20, 125, 189, 190, 192
Dietrich, Marlene 142, 144, 190
The Dinah Shore Chevy Show (tv) 185, 186
Disney, Walt 2, 59, 72, 155
Disraeli (1929 film) 39
Dr. No (film) 112
The Doctor's Dilemma (play) 198
Don Juan in Hell (play) 123, 125, 170
Don Juan in Hell (recording) 188
Donat, John **85**, 87
Donat, Robert 37, 39, 87, 137, 159, 183, 190, 195, 196, 203
Donlevy, Brian **80**, 176
"Don't Be Cruel" 197
Don't Change Your Husband 29
Douglas, Melvyn **19**, 20, 155, 175, 190
Down River 15, 16, 190, 193
Dracula (1931 film) 21, 22, 32, 189, 190
Dragon Seed (film) 160
Drake, Peggy 75, 77
Drury, Allen 151, 152
Duel in the Sun (film) 104
du Maurier, Daphne 62, 63, 65
Duncan, Isadora 5
Durbin, Deanna 73, 74, 75, 96, **100**, 101, 173, 190
Duvivier, Julien 77, 79, 120, 200

Eagle Squadron 199
Easter Parade 117
The Ed Sullivan Show (tv) 182, 183, 185, 197
The Ed Wynn Show (tv) 182
The Eddie Fisher Show (tv) 184, 185
Edeson, Arthur 19, 46, 192
Emerald of the East 196
En Rade 11
Encore 201
Evans, Rex 13, 54, 89
Everson, William K. 22, 74, 75, 200, 205
Everyman's Theater: "Flying Yorkshireman" (radio) 175
Exodus 148

The Fall of the Roman Empire 201
Fancy Pants 199

Index

Farrow, John 109, 110, 112, 113, 199
The Fatal Alibi (play) 168
La Fête á Henriette 200
Feyder, Jacques 199
Field of the Cloth of Gold (film) 159
Fields, Gracie 90, 173
Fields, W.C. 25, 26, 78, 79, 159
First Love 74
Fischbeck, Harry 25, 34, 192
Flames of Passion (1922 film) 39,
Flesh and Fantasy 79
Flynn, Errol 196
Fonda, Henry 78, 151, 157, 170, 190
For Whom the Bells Toll (film) 160
Force of Evil 108
Ford Star Jubilee: "The Day Lincoln was Shot" (tv) 183
Forecast: "Ever After" and "To Tim at Twenty" (radio) 175
Forester, C.S. 58, 82, 167
Forever and a Day 16, **82**, 83, 84, 189, 190, 191, 192, 199
Four Faces West 108
Four Frightened People 58
Frankenstein (1931 film) 20, 21, 22, 32, 34, 197
Franklin, Sidney 40, 41, 42, 133
French Leave (play) 167
Frinton, Freddie 84
The Front Page (1931 film) 58
The Front Page (play) 58
A Funny Thing Happened on the Way to the Forum (play) 30

Gable, Clark 46, 47, 49, 174, 175, 190
Galileo (1947 film aka *Leben des Galilei*) 156
Galileo (play aka *Life of Galileo*) 7, 98, 102, 105, 169, 170, 200
Garmes, Lee 11, 82, 102, 105, 160, 192
General Electric Theater: "The Last Lesson" (tv) 185
General Electric Theater: "Mr. Kensington's Finest Hour" (tv) 183, 184
General Electric Theater: "A New York Knight" (tv) 184
The George Burns and Gracie Allen Show (radio) 176, 177
The George Gobel Show (tv) 184
Gerstad, Merritt B. 22, 192
Gilda 117
Gilks, Alfred 43, 192
The Girl from Manhattan 113, 114, 189, 190, 191, 192
Gish, Dorothy 14, 190, 197
Gish, Lillian 138, 141, 182, 183, 190
Gitt, Robert ix, 141

Glassberg, Irving 123, 192
Godfrey, Peter 15, 66, 82
Going My Way 114
Goldfinger (film) 112
Gone with the Wind (film) 61, 69
The Good Companions (1932 film) 39
Goodbye, Mr. Chips (film) 160
The Government Inspector (play) 5, 164
Le Grand Jeu (1934 film) 199
La Grande Speranza (film aka *Submarine Attack*) 146
Granger, Stewart 130, 132, 133, 134, 135, 190
Grant, Cary **16**, 17, 18, 190
Great Expectations (1946 film) 137
The Greater Love (play) 165, 198
Greed of Gold (play) 198
Green, Hughie 2, 195
Greene, Graham 6, 42, 56, 64, 65, 204
Greenstreet, Sydney 112, 146, 160, 195
Gregory, Paul 7, 138, 140, 161, 170, 171, 182, 183
Griffith, D.W. 2, 140
Guthrie, Tyrone 57, 58, 59, 168, 169, 173, 186

Haggar, William 29
Halliwell, Leslie 53, 129, 136
Hangman Also Die! 88
Hanley, Jenny 200, 201
The Happy Husband (play) 165
Harbord, Carl 166, 196
Hardwicke, Sir Cedric 41, 42, 49, 65, **66**, 69, 82, 84, 131, 132, 160, 170, 180, 190, 196, 199
Harlan, Russell 142, 192
Harris, Robert 200
Harrison, Rex 59, 61, 190
Hawks, Howard 74, 87, 117, 125, 199
Hayworth, Rita 78, 117, 130, **131**, 132, 190
Henry VIII (play) 168
Hepburn, Katharine 2, 58, 160
"He's a Cute Brute" 36
Higham, Charles 93, 96, 203
Hildyard, Jack 135, 137, 192
Hitchcock, Alfred 62, 65, 95, 102, 103, 104, 195, 204
Hobson's Choice (1954 film) 99, **135**, 136, 137, 138, 141, 146, 189, 191, 192
Hobson's Choice (play) 138, 163
Hopkins, Gerard Manley 196
Hornblow, Arthur, Jr. 43, 45, 142, 144
Horniman, Annie 198
"The Horror Boys of Hollywood" 195

A House Divided 72
Housman, Arthur 84
Houston, Penelope 138
The Hucksters 112
Hugo, Victor 52, 53, 68
Hugo and Josefin 201
The Hunchback of Notre Dame (1923 film) 68
The Hunchback of Notre Dame (1939 film) 16, 65, **66**, 67, 68, 69, 89, 132, 160, 189, 190, 191, 192
Hungarian Emergency Relief Organization Christmas Day Special (tv) 183
Hunter, Ian **82**, 84, 167
Huxley, Aldous **31**

I, Claudius (film) 58, 149, 157, 191, 192, 199
"I May Never Go Home Again" 142, 144
I'd Rather Be Rich 74
If I Had a Million 11, 24, 25, 26, 189, 190, 192
The Importance of Being Earnest (play) 169
In Town Tonight (radio) 173
In Which We Serve 137
Infatuation (1930 film) 13
International Quartet (film) 160
Intruder in the Dust (film) 201
Irma La Douce 7, 161
The Island of Dr. Moreau (novel) 32
Island of Lost Men 37
Island of Lost Souls 30, **31**, 32, 33, 34, 49, 125, 189, 193
It Started with Eve (film) **72**, 73, 74, 75, 101, 189, 190, 192
It Started with Eve (radio) 177, 178, 180
Ivano, Paul 94, 192

Jack and the Beanstalk (1952 film) 130
The Jack Paar Show (tv) 186, 187
The Jackie Gleason Show (tv) 182
Jailhouse Rock 197
Jamaica Inn (film) 58, **62**, 61, 62, 63, 64, 65, 71, 105, 138, 186, 191, 192, 193
Jamaica Inn (novel) 63, 65
James, Jimmy 84
Jaws 201
Jesus of Nazareth (tv) 95, 201
The Jimmy Durante Show (tv) 183
Joan Luxton's Theatre Company (tv) 198
John Brown's Body (play) 140, 170
John Brown's Body (radio) 174
The Joseph Cotten Show—On Trial: "Eleanor" (tv) 185
Journey's End (play) 196

210 Index

"The Judgment of Paris" (painting) 86

Kanin, Garson **69**, 70, 71, 72, 75, 204
Karloff, Boris 19, 21, 22, 32, 33, 124, 125, 191, 195, 203
The Kate Smith Evening Hour (tv) 182
Keaton, Buster 82, 84, 191
Kerbside Cabaret (radio) 173
La Kermesse Héroïque (film aka *Carnival in Flanders*) 199
Kesson, David 14, 192
The Killers (1946 film) 116
King Lear (play) 101, 171, 172
The Kiss Before the Mirror 159
A Kiss for Cinderella (film) 10
A Kiss for Cinderella (play) 10
Die Klugen Frauen 199
Knowlden, Marilyn 53, 204
Knowles, Bernard 62, 192
Kongo 37
Korda, Alexander 37, 39, 53, 54, 55, 56, 58, 61, 134, 137, 157, 174, 183, 199
Korda, Vincent 37, 53, 157
Koster, Henry 73, 74, 75, 101, 125, 132
The Kraft Music Hall: "Al Jolson Show" (radio) 179
Kramer, Stanley 108, 199
Kruger, Jules 57, 59, 192

The Lady Esther Screen Guild Theater: "Ruggles of Red Gap" (radio) 178
The Lady Esther Screen Guild Theater: "Stand By for Action" (radio) 176
The Lady Esther Screen Guild Theater: "The Tuttles of Tahiti" (radio) 177
A Lady to Love 71
Lamour, Dorothy 77, 113, 114, 158, 174, 179, 180, 191
Lanchester, Edith "Biddy" 5
Lanchester, Elsa Sullivan 5, 6, 8, 9, 10, 11, 13, 17, 20, 24, 37, 39, 52, 54, 55, **57**, 58, 59, 61, 72, 78, 79, 82, 110, 112, 141, 142, **143**, 144, 154, 155, 160, 166, 167, 168, 169, 171, 173, 174, 175, 176, 177, 178, 185, 191, 195, 197, 201, 204
Lanchester, Waldo Sullivan 5, 197
Lang, Charles 16, 130, 192
Lang, Fritz 87, 88, 96
Last of the Pagans 49
Laszlo, Ernest 113, 192
Laughton, Eliza (née Conlon) 4, 195
Laughton, Francis "Frank" 4, 195, 196, 197

Laughton, Robert 4, 195, 197
Laughton, Robert Thomas "Tom" 4, 162, 197
Laurel and Hardy 45
A League of Mercy Program (radio) 173
Lean, David 14, 135, 136, 137, 160, 161, 183, 203
Leavitt, Sam 150, 152, 192
Leigh, Vivien 59, 61, 155, 183, 191
Lejeune, Caroline Alice 42, 56, 77, 79, 81, 84, 91, 99, 150, 204
Leonard, Robert Z. 24, 80, 89, 91, 114, 118
Lest We Forget (1937 short film) 154
Let's Leave It at That (play) 196
Der Letzte Mann (film aka *The Last Laugh*) 137
Life of Chinese Gordon (film) 160
Life of Diaghilev (film) 159
The Life of Samuel Johnson 140, 203
Liliom (play) 164, 165
Lincoln's Gettysburg Address (radio) 174
Lincoln's Gettysburg Address (recording) 188
Lincoln's Gettysburg Address (speech in film) 44, 45, 46
Lion of Mayfair (film) 160
Little Women (1949 film) 117
Lombard, Carole 34, **35**, 36, 37, 61, **69**, 70, 71, 174, 191
Lord Timothy Dexter (film) 160
The Lost Weekend 112
Love for Love (play) 169
Lubitsch, Ernst 24, 26
Lugosi, Bela 31, 32, 33, 154
Lust for Life (1956 film) 55
The Lux Radio Theater: "The Canterville Ghost" 178, 179
The Lux Radio Theater: "Holy Matrimony" 181
The Lux Radio Theater: "It Started with Eve" 177, 178
The Lux Radio Theater: "Ruggles of Redgap" 174
The Lux Radio Theater: "Sidewalks of London" 174
The Lux Radio Theater: "The Suspect" 178
The Lux Radio Theater: "This Land Is Mine" 177
The Lux Show (tv) 184

Macbeth (play) 169
Macbeth (radio) 173
La Maison du Maltais (film aka *Karina the Dancer*) 196
Le Maitre de Forges 199
Major Barbara (play) 171
The Making of an Immortal (play) 166

Malden, Karl 70, 72
Male and Female 29
The Man from Down Under 13, **89**, 90, 91, 92, 189, 190, 191, 193
The Man from Monte Carlo 120
Man Hunt (1941 film) 88
The Man on the Eiffel Tower **118**, 119, 120, 121, 140, 160, 189, 191, 192, 200
A Man with Red Hair (play) 20, 33, 166
Die Männer um Lucie 199
March, Fredric 26, **27**, 40, 49, 154, 191, 204
Marie Antoinette (film) 159
Mason, James 53, 168, 169, 173, 186
Massey, Raymond 19, 20, 124, 167, 170, 183, 191
Maté, Rudolph 72, 192
Matthews, Jessie **82**, 191
Mayer, Louis B. 74
McCarey, Leo 43, 44, 43, 114
McCarthy, Charlie 129, 174, 175, 176, 178, 179
McEvoy, Frederick Joseph "Freddie" 196
McLeod, Norman Z. 93
Measure for Measure (play) 168
The "Medea" of Eurpides (play) 165
Medicine USA: "Alcoholism" (radio) 180
Medicine USA: "Exercise, Athletics and Health" (radio) 180
Medicine USA: "New Concepts in Contagious Diseases" (radio) 180
Medicine USA: "Psychiatry in America" (radio) 180
Medicine USA: "The Span of Life" (radio) 180
Medicine USA: "Your Family Doctor" (radio) 180
Men with Wings 155
Mercy Red Cross Broadcast (radio) 174, 175
Meredith, Burgess 118, 119, 121, 151, 157, 160, 171, 174, 180, 183, 191, 200
Metty, Russell 82, 106, 108, 146, 147, 192
A Midsummer Night's Dream (play) 171
A Midsummer Night's Dream (tv) 158
Milland, Ray 12, 13, 22, 24, 82, **110**, 111, 113, 191
Mills, John 135, 137, 191
Minnelli, Vincente 55, 116
A Miracle Can Happen (film aka *On Our Merry Way*) 157, 191
The Miracle Worker 201

Index

Les Misérables (1934 film) 199
Les Misérables (1935 film) 49, **50**, 51, 52, 53, 68, 95, 189, 190, 191, 193
Miss Bracegirdle Does Her Duty 11
Mr. Pickwick (play) 166, 167
Mr. Pickwick's Christmas (recording) 188
Mr. Pinkie (film) 160
Mr. Prohack (play) 5, 166
Mr. Tristram Goes West (film) 159
Mitchell, Thomas 65, 78, 79, 155, 178
Mitchum, Robert 138, 141, 161, 191, 204
The Mob (film aka *Remember That Face*) 201
Moby Dick (recording) 188
Mohr, Hal 99, 192
Monroe, Marilyn 126, 128, 191
Montagu, Ivor 9, 10, 11
Montgomery, George 113, 114, 191
Montgomery, Robert 49
The Moon and Sixpence (film) 77
Morgan, Frank 93, 159, 175
The Most Happy Fella (play) 72
Mother Goose Goes Hollywood 2
The Mummy's Hand 198
Music Hall Parade 195
Musuraca, Nicholas 75, 82, 192
Mutiny on the Bounty (1935 film) **46**, 47, 48, 49, 52, 76, 81, 98, 99, 132, 189, 190, 191, 192, 195, 199
Mutiny on the Bounty (radio) 174
My Fair Lady (film) 199

Naked (play) 165
The Naked and the Dead (film) 161
Nell Gwyn (1926 film) 14
Neptune's Daughter 197
Newton, Robert 57, 58, 62, 104, 157, 191, 200
Nice Girl? 101
Nichols, Dudley 84, 85, 87, 88
The Night of the Hunter (film) 2, 7, 121, 138, **139**, 140, 141, 142, 161, 189, 190, 191, 192, 201
The Night of the Hunter (recording) 188
"The Night Watch" (painting) 54
No Minor Vices 108
No Way Out (1987 film) 112
Norton, Jack 43, 84
Not Quite a Gentleman (film) 160
Notorious 104
La Nuit Américaine (film aka *Day for Night*) 200

O. Henry's Full House 125, **126**, 127, 128, 189, 191, 192
Oberon, Merle **37**, 82, 157, 159, 173, 175, 191, 199

Oboler, Arch 157, 175
O'Brien, Margaret 92, 93, 94, 178, 179, 191, 195
O'Connor, Una 40, 82, 85, 87, 92, 142, 144, 167, 191
O'Hara, Maureen 1, 62, 64, 65, **66**, **85**, 87, 160, 191
The Old Dark House (1932 film) **19**, 20, 21, 22, 124, 189, 190, 191, 192, 198
"Old Rattler" 197
Old Wives for New 29
The Oldest Christmas Story (recording) 188
Olivier, Laurence 20, 75, 104, 141, 147, 149, 155, 183
On Our Merry Way (film aka *A Miracle Can Happen*) 157
On the Spot (play) 23, 24, 154, 167
On the Waterfront 72
One Hundred Men and a Girl 74
One in a Million 195
One of the Best 10
Operation Petticoat 81
Operator 13 41
O'Sullivan, Maureen 22, 24, 40, 110, 111, 177, 191
The Other Love 108
Our Daily Bread 53
Over Here (radio) 176
Overbaugh, Roy F. 14, 192
Owen, Reginald 82, 92, 96, 98, 174, 191
Ozu, Yasujirô 26

The Paradine Case 102, **103**, 104, 105, 106, 109, 112, 144, 189, 190, 191, 192
The Party (play) 171
Passport to Destiny 155, 156
Pasternak, Joe 73, 74, 101
Pathé Newsreel 154
Paul I (play) 165, 166
The Paul Whiteman's Goodyear Revue (tv) 182
Payment Deferred (film) 6, 22, **23**, 24, 41, 71, 95, 189, 191, 192, 199
Payment Deferred (play) 167, 168
Payment Deferred (radio) 178, 179, 180
Peck, Gregory 102, 105, 191
Pedelty, Donovan 21
Périnal, Georges 37, 53, 157, 192
Personality 197
Peter Pan (play) 169
Peterson, Dorothy 22, **23**, 24
La Petite Chocolatiér (1927 film aka *The Chocolate Girl*) 196
Piccadilly 12, 13
Pickford, Mary 140
Pickles, Wilfred 137
The Picture of Dorian Gray (1945 film) 199

Pillars of Society (play) 164
Pinocchio (1940 film) 74
Planck, Robert 92, 192
Planer, Franz 121, 192
Playhouse 90: "In the Presence of Mine Enemies" (tv) 186
Poliche 199
Pommer, Erich 57, 58, 59, 61, 62, 63, 70, 71, 160, 199
Port of New York 195
Powell, Robert 95, 137, 200, 201
Power, Tyrone 142, 145, 170, 175, 191
Preminger, Otto 7, 148, 150, 151, 152
Presley, Elvis 183, 197
Price, Vincent 115, **116**, 117
The Pride and the Passion 199
The Private Life of Henry VIII (film) 12, **37**, 38, 39, 40, 55, 56, 125, 132, 134, 137, 159, 189, 190, 191, 192
The Private Life of Henry VIII (recording) 188
The Private Lives of Elizabeth and Essex 1
The Private Secretary (play) 4, 162
Producers' Showcase: "Festival of Music" (tv) 183

Les Quatre Cent Coups (film aka *The Four Hundred Blows*) 200

The Racket (play) 58
Radio Almanac 177
Radio Reader's Digest: "The Archer-Shee Case" 179
Radio Reader's Digest: "Back for Christmas" 176
Raines, Ella 94, **95**, 178, 191
Rains, Claude 69, 82, 104, 160, 164
Ramrod 108
Rasputin and the Empress 33
The Raven (1935 film) 125
Readings from the Bible (recording) 188
Red Dust 37
Redgrave, Michael 52, 195, 199
Redman, Frank 85, 192
Reed, Donna 89, 191
Rembrandt 13, **53**, 54, 55, 56, 57, 71, 154, 189, 191, 192
Renoir, Jean 84, 85, 86, 87, 88, 89, 204
Renoir, Pierre-Auguste 86
Ridges, Stanley 94, 96, 100, 191
The Ritz Brothers 2, 195
Rive Gauche 199
Riverside Nights (revue) 166
The Robe (film) 132, 135, 201
Robeson, Paul 78, 79, 186
Robinson, Edward G. 71, 78, 79, 175

212 Index

Roman Legion-Hare 30
Rosher, Charles 80, 133, 134, 155, 192
Rózsa, Miklós 99, 101, 114, 116, 133
Ruggles of Red Gap (1918 film) 44
Ruggles of Red Gap (1923 film) 44
Ruggles of Red Gap (1935 film) 42, *43*, 44, 45, 46, 52, 189, 192
Ruggles of Red Gap (radio) 174, 178, 179
Ruttenberg, Joseph 114, 116, 117, 192, 200

St. Martin's Lane (film aka *Sidewalks of London*) 59, **60**, 61, 62, 154, 189, 190, 191, 192
Salome (1923 film) 11
Salome (1953 film) 130, *131*, 132, 133, 135, 149, 189, 190, 192
Sam, Yosemite 2
Sanders, George 6, 78, 85, 89
Saville, Victor 39, 82, 84, 199
Scaramouche (1952 film) 135
The Scarlet Empress 58
The Scarlet Pimpernel (1934 film) 159, 198
Scarlet Street 96
The Scarlet Woman: An Ecclesiastical Melodrama 10
Scott, Randolph 32, 96, 98, 191
Screen Snapshots 154
Sealtest Variety Theater (radio) 175, 176, 179, 180
The Secret Hour 71
Seitz, John F. 110, 157, 192
Selznick, David O. 102, 103, 104, 105, 106, 112, 155, 159, 189, 200
The Sentimental Bloke (film) 91
Seven Sinners (1940 film) 37
Shakes versus Shav (puppet play) 5
Shanghai Express 36
Share My Lettuce (revue) 201
Shaw, George Bernard 5, 155, 170, 171
Shearer, Norma **40**, 41, 42, 155, 159, 173, 174, 191, 203, 204
Sherwood, Robert 75, 160
Shipman, David 99, 136, 146, 204
Show Boat (play) 196
Shute, Nerina 13
Sidewalks of London (radio) 174
The Sign of the Cross (1904 film) 29
The Sign of the Cross (1914 film) 29
The Sign of the Cross (1932 film) 26, **27**, 28, 29, 30, 132, 149, 189, 190, 191, 193
The Silver Tassie (play) 167
Simenon, Georges 118, 120, 121, 160

Simmons, Jean *133*, 135, 147, **148**, 149, 191
Single-Handed (film aka *Sailor of the King*) 199
Sink the Bismark! 199
Siodmak, Robert 77, **94**, 96, 116, 199
Sir Alexander Korda (1893-1956) (tv aka *Alexander Korda, Knight*) 183
"Situation Wanted" 114, 115
16 Fathoms Deep 120
Skipworth, Alison 25, **31**
"Sleeping Beauty Waltz" 74
Slezak, Walter 85, 87, 191
Slide, Anthony 38, 39, 141, 204
Snow White and the Seven Dwarfs 74
So Ends Our Night 108, 109
So This Is New York 108
Song of the Islands 77
"The Songs of a Sentimental Bloke" (poem) 91
South of Pago Pago 77
Sparrows (1926 film) 140, 141
Spartacus 7, 133, 146, 147, **148**, 149, 150, 189, 191, 192, 195, 201
Spring Parade 74
Stagecoach (1939 film) 68
Stand By for Action (film aka *Cargo of Innocents*) 79, **80**, 81, 82, 91, 189, 191, 192
Stand By for Action (radio) 176
Star Wars 201
Startime: "Academy Award Songs" (tv) 185
Stephenson, Adela Riddlesdale 48, 199
Stephenson, James 199
The Steve Allen Plymouth Show (tv) 184
Stewart, James 93, 155, 157, 195
Stonyhurst College Choir and Orchestral Concert 162
The Storyteller... A Session with Charles Laughton (recording) 188
Stout, Archie 96, 192
Stradling, Harry 62, 63, 70, 71, 193
The Strange Door 7, **123**, 124, 125, 189, 191, 192, 200, 201
A Streetcar Named Desire (film) 72
Strong, Percy 15, 193
Struss, Karl 27, 28, 30, 193
Stuart, Gloria 19, 20, 191, 198
Studio 57: "Stopover in Bombay" (tv) 184
Studio One: "Payment Deferred" (radio) 179
Studio One: "South Riding" (radio) 179
Sullivan, James "Shamus" 5, 197

Sundays and Cybele 201
Sunrise: A Song of Two Humans 141
The Suspect (1945 film) **94**, **95**, 96, 144, 189, 190, 191, 192
The Suspect (radio) 178, 179
Suspense: "ABC Murders" (radio) 176
Suspense: "Blind Date" (radio) 180
Suspense: "De Mortuis" (radio) 179
Suspense: "The Fountain Plays" (radio) 178
Suspense: "An Honest Man" (radio) 179
Suspense: "Jack Ketch" (radio) 180
Suspense: "The Man Who Knew How" (radio) 177
Suspense: "Neal Cream, Doctor of Poison" (radio) 180
Suspense: "The Revenge of Captain Bligh" (radio) 181
Suspense: "Wet Saturday" (radio) 176
Swamp Water 87
Symphonie D'Amour 199

Take Me Out to the Ball Game 117
The Tale-Teller Phone 196
Tales of Manhattan 77, **78**, 79, 189, 190, 191, 193
Tarzan Triumphs 88
Taylor, Evelyn 196
Taylor, Robert **80**, **115**, 116, 117, 175, 191
Tchaikovsky, Pyotr Ilyich 74
The Tempest (play) 168, 169
The Tennessee Ernie Ford Show (tv) 184, 185, 186, 197
La Tête d'un homme (film aka *A Man's Head*) 120, 200
La Tête d'un homme (novel aka *A Battle of Nerves*) 120
Thalberg, Irving 6, 24, 41, 42, 48, 49, 58, 74, 98, 134
"That's What You Jolly Well Get" 196
The Theater Guild on the Air: "The Bishop Misbehaves" 180
The Theater Guild on the Air: "The Druid Circle" 180
The Theater Guild on the Air: "Edward, My Son" 180
The Theater Guild on the Air: "Laburnum Grove" 179
The Theater Guild on the Air: "Old English" 179
The Theater Guild on the Air: "Payment Deferred" 178, 180
The Theater Guild on the Air: "Skin Game" 180

Thesiger, Ernest 19, 20, 198
They Knew What They Wanted **69**, 70, 71, 72, 189, 191, 193
Thirty Seconds over Tokyo 201
This Day and Age 58
This Happy Breed 137
This Is Charles Laughton (tv) 182
This Land Is Mine (film) 84, **85**, 86, 87, 88, 89, 144, 189, 191, 192
This Land Is Mine (radio) 177
Thomson, David 92, 136, 204
Thousands Cheer 201
3 for Tonight (revue) 171
Three Rogues (film) 160
The Three Sisters (play) 164
Three Smart Girls 74
Three Smart Girls Grow Up 74
Thunder Below 36
Tirez sur le Pianiste (film aka *Shoot the Piano Player*) 200
To Have and Have Not (film) 117
Todd, Ann 102, **103**, 105, 106, 183, 191
Tokyo no Onna (film aka *Woman of Tokyo*) 26
Toland, Gregg 49, 50, 53, 193
Tone, Franchot 46, 47, 49, 100, 101, 118, 119, 120, 121, 151, 160, 174, 191
The Tonic 11, 12
Tonti, Aldo 145, 193
Torrid Zone 37
La Tour 11
Tracy, Spencer 2, 155, 160
Treasure Island (1950 film) 59, 200
Tree, Lady 37, 166, 167, 173, 196
Trelawny of the Wells (play) 162
The Trial of Mary Dugan (1929 film) 39
Truffaut, François 64, 106, 200, 204
The Tuttles of Tahiti (film) 7, **75**, 76, 77, 189, 190, 192

The Tuttles of Tahiti (radio) 177
The Two Mrs. Carrolls 16

Under Capricorn 106
Under Ten Flags (film aka *Sotto Dieci Bandiere*) 145, **146**, 189, 193
Undercurrent 116
Unfinished Symphony 198
Up Pompeii! (tv) 30
Ustinov, Peter 2, 81, 147, **148**, 149, 150, 195

Vallee, Rudy 174, 175, 176
Vance, Vivian **121**, 122
Varieté 13
Vessel of Wrath (1938 film aka *The Beachcomber*) **57**, 58, 59, 76, 86, 117, 189, 191, 192, 200
Le Voile Bleu 123
von Sternberg, Josef 18, 36, 58, 157, 203
von Stroheim, Erich 87, 108, 109

Wagner, Sidney 89, 193
Wagon Train: "The Albert Farnsworth Story" (tv) 186
Waldron, Charles 199
Walker, Joseph 77, 193
Wall, Max 2, 195
Warrender, Harold 10, 191
Washington Square (tv) 183
We, the People (tv) 182
Welles, Orson 74, 81, 175, 177, 178
Wells, Frank 9, 10
Wells, H.G. 6, 9, 10, 11, 30, 32, 33, 34, 204
Whale, James 5, 17, 19, 20, 21, 22, 33, 159, 166, 196, 197, 203
What Happened to Harkness? 198
What's My Line? (tv) 183, 185
Whelan, Tim 59, **60**, 61, 62
"When I Sing" 73, 74
When Tomorrow Comes 68

White Woman (film) 34, **35**, 36, 37, 189, 191, 192
White Woman (radio) 173, 174
White Zombie 22
Why Change Your Wife 29
Wilcox, Herbert 14, 39, 82, 198, 199
The Wild One 197
Wilde, Oscar 5, 92, 93, 169
Willard 5
Williams, Emlyn 62, 157, 167, 191
Williams, John 102, 142, 144, 191
Williams, Kenneth 20, 136, 201, 203
Wills, Brember 19, 20, 164, 165, 198
Winters, Shelley 138, 141, 191
Witness for the Prosecution (film) 7, 13, 74, 142, **143**, 144, 145, 189, 190, 191, 192
Witness for the Prosecution (play) 142, 144
Wolves (film aka *Wanted Men*) 14, 15, 190, 192, 197
A Woman in Pawn 196
The Woman in White (1948 film) 16
Wong, Anna May 12, 37, 191
Wyman, Jane **121**, 122, 185, 191

"Yes, My Dear" 36
You Never Can Tell (film aka *You Never Know*) 200, 201
You Only Live Twice (film) 112
Young, Frederick Archibald "Freddie" 9, 10, 193
Young, Robert 92, 93, 94, 154, 191
Young Bess 13, **133**, 134, 135, 149, 189, 190, 191, 192

Zanuck, Darryl F. 87, 155
Zucco, George 65, 69, 179

www.ingramcontent.com/pod-product-compliance
Lightning Source LLC
Chambersburg PA
CBHW080804300426
44114CB00020B/2824